MUNICIPALITIES AND MULTICULTURALISM: THE POLITICS OF IMMIGRATION IN TORONTO AND VANCOUVER

D1524391

The Canadian model of diversity management is considered a success in the international community, yet the methods by which these policies are adopted by local governments have seldom been studied. *Municipalities and Multiculturalism* explores the role of the municipality in integrating immigrants and managing the ethnocultural relations of the city.

Throughout the book, Kristin R. Good uses original interviews with over 100 local leaders of eight municipalities in the city-regions of Toronto and Vancouver, two of Canada's most diverse urban and suburban areas. Grounded by Canada's official multiculturalism policies, the study develops a typology of responsiveness to immigrants and ethnocultural minorities and offers an explanation for policy variations among municipalities.

Municipalities and Multiculturalism is an important examination of the differing diversity management methods in Canadian cities and ultimately contributes to debates concerning the roles that municipal governments should play within Canada's political system.

(Studies in Comparative Political Economy and Public Policy)

KRISTIN R. GOOD is an assistant professor in the Department of Political Science at Dalhousie University.

Studies in Comparative Political Economy and Public Policy

Editors: MICHAEL HOWLETT, DAVID LAYCOCK, STEPHEN MCBRIDE, Simon Fraser University

Studies in Comparative Political Economy and Public Policy is designed to showcase innovative approaches to political economy and public policy from a comparative perspective. While originating in Canada, the series will provide attractive offerings to a wide international audience, featuring studies with local, subnational, cross-national, and international empirical bases and theoretical frameworks.

Editorial Advisory Board

JEFFREY AYRES, St Michael's College, Vermont
NEIL BRADFORD, University of Western Ontario
JANINE BRODIE, University of Alberta
WILLIAM CARROLL, University of Victoria
WILLIAM COLEMAN, McMaster University
RODNEY HADDOW, University of Toronto
JANE JENSON, Université de Montréal
LAURA MACDONALD, Carleton University
RIANE MAHON, Carleton University
MICHAEL MINTROM, University of Auckland
GRACE SKOGSTAD, University of Toronto
LEAH VOSKO, York University
LINDA WHITE, University of Toronto
KENT WEAVER, Brookings Institution
ROBERT YOUNG, University of Western Ontario

For a list of books published in the series, see page 365.

KRISTIN R. GOOD

Municipalities and Multiculturalism

The Politics of Immigration in Toronto and Vancouver

UNIVERSITY OF TORONTO PRESS
Toronto Buffalo London

© University of Toronto Press Incorporated 2009
Toronto Buffalo London
www.utppublishing.com
Printed in Canada

ISBN 978-1-4426-4017-7 (cloth)
ISBN 978-1-4426-0993-8 (paper)

Printed on acid-free, 100% post-consumer recycled paper with vegetable-based inks.

Library and Archives Canada Cataloguing in Publication

Good, Kristin R., 1974–
Municipalities and multiculturalism : the politics of immigration in
Toronto and Vancouver / Kristin R. Good.

(Studies in comparative political economy and public policy)
Includes bibliographical references and index.
ISBN 978-1-4426-4017-7 (bound). – ISBN 978-1-4426-0993-8 (pbk.)

1. Municipal government – Canada. 2. Multiculturalism – Canada. 3. Toronto
(Ont.) – Politics and government. 4. Vancouver (B.C.) – Politics and government.
5. Multiculturalism – Ontario – Toronto. 6. Multiculturalism – British Columbia –
Vancouver. I. Title. II. Series: Studies in comparative political economy and public
policy

JV7295.T6G66 2009   320.8′50971   C2009-903840-4

This book has been published with the help of a grant from the Canadian Federation
for the Humanities and Social Sciences, through the Aid to Scholarly Publications
Program, using funds provided by the Social Sciences and Humanities Research
Council of Canada.

University of Toronto Press acknowledges the financial assistance to its publishing
program of the Canada Council for the Arts and the Ontario Arts Council.

University of Toronto Press acknowledges the financial support for its publishing
activities of the Government of Canada through the Book Publishing Industry
Development Program (BPIDP).

To Chris and Lenore Good

Contents

List of Tables

Abbreviations

ACEP	Asian-Canadian Entrepreneurs and Professionals
AMSSA	Affiliation of Multicultural Societies and Service Agencies of B.C.
BBOT	Brampton Board of Trade
BRRAC	Brampton Race Relations Action Committee
CAF	Canadian Arab Federation
CAO	chief administrative officer
CASSA	Council of Agencies Serving South Asians
CCER	Coordinating Committee on Ethnic Relations
CERIS	Joint Centre of Excellence in Research on Immigration and Settlement
COCC	Coalition of Concerned Canadians
COPE	Coalition of Progressive Electors
C4LD	Citizens for Local Democracy
C5	Charter Five
DMU	Diversity Management and Community Engagement Unit
EEO	Equal Employment Opportunity
FCCM	Federation of Chinese Canadians in Markham
GTA	Greater Toronto Area
GTT	gas tax transfer
GVRD	Greater Vancouver Regional District
ICNSS	Intercultural Neighbourhood Social Services
IOM	International Organization for Migration
ISAP	Immigrant Settlement and Adaptation Program
ISS	Immigrant Services Society
MACA	Markham African Caribbean Association

MBT	Markham Board of Trade *or* Mississauga Board of Trade
MFFC	Markham Federation of Filipino Canadians
MIAG	Multicultural Inter-Agency Group of Peel
MOSAIC	Multilingual Orientation Service Association for Immigrant Communities
MRRC	Markham Race Relations Committee
NPA	Non-Partisan Association
OCASI	Ontario Council of Agencies Serving Immigrants
PICS	Progressive Intercultural Community Services Society
PMC	Peel Multicultural Council
RCMP	Royal Canadian Mounted Police
RIAC	Richmond Intercultural Advisory Committee
RIIM	Research on Immigration and Integration in the Metropolis
SDISS	Surrey-Delta Immigrant Services Society
S.U.C.C.E.S.S.	United Chinese Community Enrichment Services Society
TCSA	Toronto City Summit Alliance
TRIEC	Toronto Region Immigrant Employment Council
VM	visible minority

Preface

Immigrants to Canada concentrate overwhelmingly in urban and sub-urban communities in only a handful of city-regions. Therefore, in many ways, it is surprising that this is the first book-length study of the ways in which municipal governments in these highly dynamic places have adapted their services and governance structures to ethnocultural/ethnoracial diversity. This book is about how local communities and municipalities have responded to dramatic changes in the ethnoracial composition of their populations. It investigates the responses of both urban and suburban municipalities and communities in English-speaking Canada's most numerically significant city-regions – Toronto, Mississauga, Brampton, and Markham in the Greater Toronto Area, and Vancouver, Richmond, Surrey, and Coquitlam in Greater Vancouver. It charts the development of what federal and provincial policy makers call 'multiculturalism policies' at the municipal level. However, though the book is primarily about managing ethnic relations and accommodating ethnoracial diversity in local, municipal policy, its subtext is more radical. The story of municipalities' role in supporting a vibrant and socially sustainable multicultural citizenship in Canada is one piece of a more fundamental story about the emerging importance of municipal governments in the Canadian intergovernmental system. The role of municipalities in managing international migration is one manifestation of the 'rescaling' (i.e., the simultaneous globalization and decentralization) of political authority to large urban centres in Canada.

This book has two primary goals. The first is to document and categorize the array of municipal responses to immigrant and ethnocultural minorities in English-speaking Canada's two most important immigrant destinations – Toronto and Vancouver. The book's second

goal is explanatory: it develops an explanation of why and how municipalities vary in their policy responses to large-scale immigration and
the associated demographic changes in their populations. Though local
leaders do possess degrees of choice in their responses, this book identifies a number of structural factors that shape municipal possibilities. By
identifying the causes of municipalities' responsiveness to immigrants
and ethnocultural minorities, the book lays part of the foundation for
building robust multicultural democracies at the local level. Isolating
structures also illuminates what I hope will be a central message of this
book – the importance of room for degrees of political agency at the local level. Local politics and leadership matter.

The book draws from a variety of sources of data. However, interviews with approximately one hundred local leaders in the Greater
Toronto Area and Greater Vancouver offered the richest data and for
me were the highlight of the research process. Most of the interviews
were conducted in 2004. They were generally one hour long, but many
interviewees generously spent more than an hour with me, and they often offered to put me in contact with other leaders in their community.
Furthermore, the extent to which local leaders knew one another within
and across sectors and could refer me to their colleagues was one clue
as to the nature of local governance in particular cities. I am greatly
indebted to my interviewees, who are listed in this book's appendix.

My findings categorize municipalities into three groups – responsive, somewhat responsive, and unresponsive. I hope that individual
leaders in the 'somewhat responsive' and 'unresponsive' municipalities will not take these categorizations personally. My conclusions are
not meant to cast blame upon individual leaders (political leaders, civil
servants, or leaders in civil society) or to attribute motives to particular municipal approaches. Some will read this and do so. However, a
careful reading of this work will reveal that it attributes municipalities'
overall level of responsiveness largely to the intersection of structural
factors – including the demographic context, resources in civil society,
the political economy of cities, and the intergovernmental system. City
leaders are limited by their institutional, economic, and social contexts.

In this work, 'municipal responsiveness' refers to my assessment of
the actions of the municipal corporation *as a whole* and builds upon
the established literature on institutional responsiveness to ethnocultural minorities. Furthermore, it includes the judgments of leaders in
the settlement sector and other multiculturalism-related sectors as part
of its measurement. It is also worth making clear that my measurement

of municipal responsiveness begins from the norms of Canada's 'multi-cultural' citizenship regime – that is, from a series of norms and a policy 'infrastructure' that have been contested in Canada to varying degrees over the years, especially in the 1990s. The model has also been subject to vigorous debate internationally. However, the literature suggests that though 'multiculturalism policies' are contested, most countries in the Western world have adopted such policies to various degrees (Banting, Johnston, et al. 2006).

The multicultural model of citizenship is widely misunderstood; in my view, this explains a great deal of the lack of consensus on its desirability as government policy. Its premise is that recognizing and accommodating diversity contributes to the development of a common, integrated sense of belonging to and participation in common political, social, and economic communities. In light of instances of domestic and especially international backlash against the 'multicultural' model of citizenship pioneered by Canada in 1971, it is interesting that community leaders in all the municipalities discussed in this book consider the 'multicultural' approach to local citizenship to be 'responsive' to immigrants and ethnocultural minorities. To immigrants and ethnocultural minorities' leaders on the ground, municipal multiculturalism policies matter. Though their preferences in this respect could be influenced by national policies and programs, the fact that practitioners on the ground in Canadian cities acknowledge the value of the multicultural approach is significant. It suggests that they work towards successful immigrant settlement, interethnic equity, and social harmony.

This book illustrates the important and largely unacknowledged work that many municipal officials, civil-society leaders, and civil servants on the ground in municipal departments and agencies are doing to integrate immigrants. The work is difficult and requires creative leadership, as local resources are often scarce.

The research and writing of this book took many years. It began as a PhD dissertation at the University of Toronto's Department of Political Science, which I defended while teaching my first year at Dalhousie University in 2005. I then revised it into a book manuscript while continuing to teach at Dalhousie. I would like to thank my many colleagues, mentors and students for their intellectual engagement with my work at the University of Toronto and Dalhousie University. I am also grateful for the financial support I received from the University of Toronto and the Ontario government through the Ontario Graduate Scholarship program while conducting this research.

I cannot imagine a better mentor than Richard Stren, my PhD supervisor. Richard's intellectual rigour is inspiring, as is his passion for the study of urban politics. His mentorship was multifaceted; it included not only providing invaluable feedback on my work and teaching me about the research process, but also introducing me to the profession of political science in a broader sense. His support and example helped me succeed in making the transition from student to academic. I would also like to thank my committee members Joseph (Joe) Carens, Christopher (Chris) Leo, and Richard Simeon for their work on my committee and, more generally, for their support of my work and career. I would like to thank Joe Carens for introducing me to new approaches to thinking about 'Problems of Political Community' (the title of a class he taught during my PhD program) – approaches that involved probing the importance of context to our normative understanding of diversity policies and rights. This sensitivity to context informs my empirical research greatly. I am deeply grateful to Chris Leo, who so generously agreed to serve on my committee from the University of Winnipeg. I admire the balance he strikes between theoretically driven and empirically rich research. This is a balance I have tried to strike in this book. Richard Simeon was enthusiastic about my project from the beginning (in the Canadian core class), and his helpful suggestions and probing questions throughout my coursework and the thesis-writing phase were invaluable. I would also like to thank Randall Hansen, my 'internal external' examiner, and Caroline Andrew, my external examiner, for their questions and comments on my work. Caroline Andrew's report on my dissertation was enormously helpful as I developed the thesis into a book. A number of other professors in the department also had a major impact on my intellectual development as I 'grew' the research project that led to this book; they include Neil Nevitte and Joseph (Joe) Wong. Their core comparative class was instrumental in sharpening my appreciation of the importance of comparison and of theory-driven research. Susan Solomon and Jeffrey Kopstein's research-design class gave me the opportunity to develop my thesis proposal with their support and the assistance of my colleagues. I would also like to thank Patricia Petersen, who has since retired from her position as Director of the Urban Studies program at Innis College, for reading several drafts of my work in its earliest stages. As I developed my ideas, I especially enjoyed our conversations about urban politics over ginger tea and Thai food. Also, Lionel Feldman was an important mentor and friend during the dissertation and book-writing process. He read and pro-

vided invaluable comments on my entire thesis; he also provided me
with e-mail updates and analyses of key events in urban politics on
a regular basis. Peter Burns read my work and advised me at crucial
times while I was writing my dissertation. He has since become one of
my most highly valued colleagues.

The University of Toronto is a great place to pursue doctoral studies
not only because of the excellence of the faculty but also because of the
high quality of the students. The central research question of this book
can be traced back to the Canadian Politics core class in 2000, which was
taught by Richard Simeon and Graham White during the first year of
my PhD program. I would like to thank all of my friends and colleagues
in that class, including Sophie Bourgault, Marc Hanvelt, Patti Lenard,
Mary Liston, Celine Mulhern, Martin Papillon, Scott Starring, Luc Tur-
geon, and Heather Murray. I benefited greatly from the exchange of
ideas both in class and after class at our regular pub sessions. I would
especially like to thank Heather Murray, my fellow 'urbanist,' for her
intellectual engagement throughout the PhD program. She has become
one of my dearest friends. I would also like to specifically acknowledge
Reuven Shlozberg for his friendship and feedback on my work. I am
grateful to many other colleagues in the University of Toronto's doctoral program, where I developed the central ideas of this book.

Shortly after defending my dissertation I was asked to become a
member of the Ethnicity and Democratic Governance (EDG) research
team, a SSHRC-funded MCRI led by Bruce Berman at Queen's University. I would like to thank Bruce for inviting me to join the group, as
well as Richard Simeon and Joe Carens (who are among the leaders of
the group) for initiating discussions that led to my invitation. I am honoured to be among this highly distinguished group of scholars. I have
benefited greatly from my participation with this team. EDG events
provided a venue for me to sharpen my ideas as I transformed my dissertation into this book.

Since beginning the research for this book, I have presented my
findings regularly at CPSA annual meetings (Local and Urban Politics
Section), at Urban Affairs Association meetings, and at APSA (Urban
Section) meetings. I would like to thank my colleagues in these associations for their intellectual engagement with my work. I am honoured
by the recognition that my research has received from these associations
throughout the various stages of researching and writing this book.

I would also like to thank all of the faculty members and staff at Dalhousie's Department of Political Science for welcoming me into the de-

partment and for providing a supportive environment for writing this book. I love working at Dalhousie and am fortunate to have such supportive and intellectually interesting colleagues as well as to teach such bright, engaging students.

I would like to thank Virgil Duff, Daniel Quinlan, Wayne Herrington, and Jenna Germaine as well as all other staff of the University of Toronto Press who contributed to this project for their support, guidance, and enthusiasm about the book throughout the publication process. In addition, I am very grateful to Matthew Kudelka, my copy editor, for his able and thorough work on the manuscript. I also appreciate Philippa Campsie's editorial work on earlier drafts of the manuscript. I am especially indebted to the manuscript's two anonymous reviewers, whose detailed feedback on my work led to significant improvements in the finished product.

I am indebted to many friends and am grateful to all of them. I would particularly like to acknowledge my long-time friend Nicole Ridgedale and her husband Daryl Rebeck for their support while I was conducting my fieldwork. They very generously opened their home to me for almost two months while I was completing my field research in Vancouver.

Finally, I would like to thank my family. My husband Erick Garand offered many forms of support in the final stages of this book. Everything in life is easier and my successes sweeter since I met him. My sister Karen Laser's friendship and ability to provide perspective on my life was crucial throughout the writing process. Finally, words cannot express how much I appreciate my parents' encouragement, love, and financial support throughout my twelve years of education as I have made the transition to professional life. This book is the culmination of my academic efforts to date and, for that reason, I have dedicated it to Chris and Lenore Good.

MUNICIPALITIES AND MULTICULTURALISM:
THE POLITICS OF IMMIGRATION IN TORONTO
AND VANCOUVER

1 The Municipal Role in 'Managing' Multiculturalism

Globalization is transforming the states, societies, economies, and cultures of the world. International migration is implicated in these global transformative processes. The UN Population Division estimates that there were almost 200 million international migrants in 2005 – a figure that has doubled since 1980 (GCIM 2005, 1). Migrants present both challenges and opportunities to host societies, which must 'manage' changes in the ethnocultural mix of their populations. How effectively this is done has implications for the social and economic well-being of host societies and migrants alike. It follows that managing the processes and consequences of international migration is a key challenge for contemporary global public policy.

As the pace and scale of migration have increased, migrants have become more ethnically and culturally diverse (ibid., 42). Citizens and public officials in many countries are debating the merits and limits of accommodating ethnocultural and religious differences. In some countries, people feel pessimistic about their state's ability to deal with the consequences of ethnic diversity. Highly publicized international examples of failures in immigrant integration, breakdowns in intercultural understanding, and backlashes abound. For instance, observers have cited poverty, years of discrimination in employment, and the lack of cultural accommodation as factors that led to rioting by France's predominantly Muslim North African immigrants in 2005 (Hurst 2005).

In his empirical study of social capital, social solidarity, and social trust in the United States, Harvard political scientist Robert Putnam (2007) found that increases in immigration-induced ethnic diversity reduce positive community attributes. More generally, Will Kymlicka (2008) has observed that internationally, a country's ethnic diversity has been associated with a variety of negative tendencies – for instance, a country's tendency to be less peaceful and less democratic and to have lower rates of economic growth and redistribution (2008, 1). Furthermore, we are seeing the retrenchment of government policies designed to accommodate ethnocultural differences and to facilitate the integration of ethnocultural minorities into social, economic, and political institutions as well as a breakdown in the societal consensus as it relates to the accommodation of ethnocultural differences. Moreover, decisions about how to respond to migration are being made in the context of the global ascendancy of neoliberal ideology, which emphasizes global competitiveness and which calls for a more limited role for the state in society. It is in this context that international debates have arisen regarding the state's role in managing ethnocultural diversity and immigration.

Canada is a settler society, one for which managing international migration has always been especially important. According to the 2006 census, 19.8 per cent of Canada's population is foreign-born, a figure second only to that of Australia (22.2 per cent) and much higher than that of the United States (12.5 percent) (Statistics Canada 2007c, 8). In terms, as well, of absolute numbers of immigrants, Canada is a significant host society: with 6.1 million migrants in 2005, it is among the top seven hosts of international migrants (IOM website).

Canada has been an international leader in developing policies and practices to manage ethnocultural diversity and integrate immigrants (Kymlicka 1998). In fact, the term 'multiculturalism,' an internationally recognized and often applauded model of ethnocultural relations and immigrant integration, originated in Canadian (federal) policy discourse (Inglis 1996; Abu-Laban and Gabriel 2002, 121; Kymlicka 2003; Karim 2008, 7).[1] The model has been emulated in other countries, including Australia and Sweden, which have developed their own explicit national multiculturalism policies (Abu-Laban 2008, 1). The Canadian model of diversity management is, as Will Kymlicka observes, 'often invoked as a "counter narrative" to the "master narrative" of ethnic heterogeneity's pernicious effects ... The Canadian experience suggests that the effects of ethnic diversity and identity politics are not predetermined, and that an explicitly multicultural form of democratic citizenship is viable' (Kymlicka 2008, 1).

This book explores largely uncharted terrain within Canada's model of ethnocultural relations – that is, the role of municipalities in a multicultural citizenship. It discusses whether and how local leaders in

Canada's immigrant-magnet city-regions have adapted municipal governance structures in response to dramatic shifts in the ethnocultural composition of their populations. In other words, it documents and explains the processes underlying municipalities' role in the development of Canada's multiculturalism policy.

The present work is the first comparative study of how and why local leaders in the two most prominent immigrant-receiving city-regions in English-speaking Canada have adapted municipal governance structures and municipal services to accommodate immigrants and ethnocultural minorities. Its central goal is to unearth the factors that lead a municipality to adopt and implement effective, locally tailored multiculturalism policies. At the same time, it sheds light on the limits to local governments' ability to respond effectively to dramatic social change, thus opening a debate on how to overcome those limits.

At another level, the book tells a more general story about (a) the emerging significance of municipal government in Canada's largest city-regions, and (b) the links between patterns of immigrant settlement and debates over the role of municipalities in local communities and in the intergovernmental system. Federal and (where it exists) provincial legislation endorsing multiculturalism in Canada is very general and does not provide clear guidance to local public officials; moreover, there is a lack of societal consensus concerning the proper role of government in managing ethnocultural diversity. In some ways, then, it is not surprising that local approaches to accommodating diversity vary widely (Wallace and Frisken 2000, 1). However, from an institutional perspective, the variation in approaches to diversity management defies the dominant image of Canadian municipalities as mere 'creatures of the provinces' and therefore mere implementers of provincial policy. Instead, municipal governments appear to be important democratic governments in their own right. The variations in multicultural policy making in Canadian cities are evidence that local choices, policies, and politics matter. Municipalities are important vehicles of the democratic will of local communities as well as important sites of multicultural democratic citizenship.

A central message of this book is that metropolitan areas are the places where multiculturalism is experienced. If Canada's model is to continue to be effective, it must be tailored to the particularities of local communities. Municipalities have an important role to play in designing and implementing Canada's model of official multiculturalism in a way that responds to place-based differences. Practitioners in other countries that look to the Canadian case for best practices might learn from the general lesson of this book: that context matters, and so does place. This lesson applies to the country level as well as to the subunit level within countries.

The Canadian Model of Official Multiculturalism

What does it mean for a country to adopt multiculturalism as official policy? And to what extent does this model remain viable? At the most general level, Canada's commitment to official multiculturalism establishes a *normative framework* that prescribes a *proactive public role* in facilitating positive ethnocultural relations and interethnic equity. It represents a rejection of past assimilationist approaches whereby immigrants were expected to integrate into the dominant culture and become culturally indistinguishable from long-standing citizens. In the past, immigrants who were not perceived as capable of assimilating were not permitted entry into Canada (Kymlicka 2008, 2).

Canada's multicultural model of citizenship has evolved since the federal government first adopted official multiculturalism in 1971 (Ley 2007). At that time, members of communities other than the historical 'Charter groups' – English and French – mobilized in reaction to the policy of *biculturalism*, expressed in the mandate of the Commission of Bilingualism and Biculturalism appointed by Prime Minister Lester Pearson (1963–68), which reported during Prime Minister Pierre Elliott Trudeau's (1968–79 and 1980–84) first term. A volume on the cultural contribution of 'other ethnic groups' was added to the commission's report, and Trudeau replaced the concept of biculturalism with that of multiculturalism. Many scholars who were sympathetic to Quebec's aspirations to have its distinctiveness affirmed described the original policy as 'born in sin' (McRoberts 1997), as it was meant to absorb Quebec's distinctiveness as a 'national minority' into a pan-Canadian conception of multiculturalism.

This book follows an internationally accepted approach to conceptualizing diversity by distinguishing between polyethnic, immigrant diversity and national minorities – a distinction first made by Canadian political theorist Will Kymlicka (1995). National minorities are long-standing historical communities that are often territorially based, such as the Québécois and Aboriginal nations in Canada. In this book, official multiculturalism refers to responses to polyethnic diversity that result from immigration (and not to Canada's historic multinational diversity). Whereas national minorities tend to demand more autonomy from Canadian institutions, immigrants tend to demand more inclusion in social, economic, and political institutions. Official multiculturalism implies that recognition and accommodation are means towards the fair inclusion and ultimate integration of immigrants in these institutions. The policy recognizes the impossibility of institutional 'neutrality' with respect to culture and makes accommodations to address cultural disadvantages. In this way, it treats immigrant integration as a two-way process rather than as the immigrant's sole responsibility.

Audrey Kobayashi characterizes the development of official multiculturalism in Canada as comprising three stages: *demographic, symbolic*, and *structural*. From a policy perspective, these stages reflect a shift from a basic recognition of demographic change, to a policy of support for ethnic festivals and celebrations of cultural distinctiveness, to a policy that focuses on addressing systemic barriers to the incorporation of immigrants and ethnoracial minorities into Canadian institutions (Kobayashi 1993; in Ley 2007, 9–10).

Canada's commitment to official multiculturalism is embedded in a range of public institutions and agencies; it is more than a single policy or program (Bloemraad 2006, ch. 3; Kymlicka 2008, 5). It is entrenched in the Constitution, and it is implemented through a variety of policies and programs, including anti-racism programs, employment equity initiatives, and immigrant settlement policies. In practice, it is also, as Kymlicka puts it, 'a response to the pressures that Canada exerts on immigrants to integrate into common institutions' (Kymlicka 1998, 40). Canada's normative commitment to official multiculturalism is a citizenship 'regime' or model – a bundle of norms, policies, and practices – and as such it implies a joint public–private responsibility for the equitable inclusion of all ethnic, religious, and cultural groups within Canadian political, economic, and social systems. The model involves the ongoing 'renegotiation' of the terms of immigrant and ethnocultural-minority integration into Canadian institutions (Kymlicka 1998).

The Changing 'Racial'[2] Composition of Canada

Policies during the 'symbolic' era of multiculturalism recognized the historical and ongoing cultural contributions of groups other than the British and French to the development of Canada. More recent policies have evolved to address profound changes in the ethnocultural composition of Canadian society resulting from new immigration patterns.

Changes in Canada's immigrant selection policies and practices, which were racially biased until 1967, when the 'point system' of immigrant selection was adopted (Abu-Laban and Gabriel 2002, 43), have led to demographic shifts. The shift in immigrant source countries has indeed been dramatic. Before 1961, Europe was the source of 90 per cent of Canada's immigrants and only 3 per cent of Canada's immigrants came from Asia (Statistics Canada 2003, 6). By the 1990s, the leading source of immigrants to Canada was China, followed by India, the Philippines, Hong Kong, Sri Lanka, Pakistan, and Taiwan (ibid., 7). According to figures collected for the 2006 Census, 83.9 per cent of immigrants to Canada between 2001 and 2006 were non-European (Statistics Canada 2008a, 12).

Because of these changes, Canada experienced a threefold increase in its visible-minority population between 1981 and 2001 (Statistics Canada 2003, 10). In addition, there has been an upward trend in the proportion of immigrants who are visible minorities, with 52, 68, and 73 per cent of immigrants to Canada in the 1970s, 1980s, and 1990s, respectively, identifying themselves as such (ibid.). Three-quarters of the immigrants who arrived in Canada between 2001 and 2006 were visible minorities (Statistics Canada 2008b, 2). Furthermore, Statistics Canada forecasts an intensification of the link between the 'racial' diversification of Canada and immigration. In the 2006 Census, 16.2 per cent of the Canadian population reported belonging to a visible minority (Statistics Canada 2008a, 5). The visible-minority population increased by 27.2 per cent between the 2001 and 2006 censuses – a rate five times faster than the growth rate of the total population (ibid.). StatsCan predicts that by 2017, if current immigration trends continue, between 19 and 23 per cent of Canadian residents will belong to a visible-minority group. The report concludes that immigration is 'unquestionably' the most important factor in the increase in Canada's visible-minority population (Statistics Canada 2005, 6). From a policy perspective, the viability of the multiculturalism model will be strongly tied to its ability to 'manage' the ethnocultural diversity arising from immigrant selection practices.

The Successes of the Canadian Model

Though more research is needed to understand the important causal relationships between public policies and immigrant integration, the available empirical research on multiculturalism's effect in achieving ethnic and immigrant integration suggests that the approach has been fairly successful. For instance, Kymlicka (1998) notes that since official multiculturalism was first adopted in 1971, Canada has seen an increase in rates of immigrant naturalization, intermarriage, political participation, and official-language proficiency. More recent comparative research on immigrant integration and 'political incorporation' in Canada and the United States has supported the conclusion that Canada's multicultural model is contributing to integration (Bloemraad 2006). These studies suggest that the multicultural model of immigrant and ethnocultural-minority incorporation works.

What explains the success of the Canadian model? Kymlicka (2008) argues that *timing* and *geography* are central to understanding Canada's exceptionality in the international community in embracing multiculturalism. Kymlicka finds it significant that the policy was adopted *before* the racial diversification of Canada and *before* people from non-Christian religions and from potentially illiberal cultures dominated the country's pool of immigrants: 'If multiculturalism in Canada had initially been demanded by groups who were perceived as having strong religious/cultural commitments to illiberal practices – say by Somalis or Saudis rather than Ukrainians and Italians – and if their demand for multiculturalism had been perceived as a demand that such practices be tolerated and accommodated, then multiculturalism would probably not have arisen' (ibid., 5). He notes that a backlash developed in the early 1990s in Canada after ethnoracial minorities became the central players in multiculturalism policy debates. When Canada's national policy of official multiculturalism was first adopted, just over 50 per cent of immigrants were visible minorities; this figure is now 75 per cent.

In terms of geography, Kymlicka notes that Canadians have embraced multiculturalism because 'we face no threat of large-scale influx of unwanted migrants from neighbouring poor countries, whether illegal immigrants or asylum seekers' (ibid., 7). In other words, Canada's geography reduces Canadians' fear of being 'swamped' by a single ethnic group. Canada's control over its border means that it does not have to deal with debates about illegal migrants to the same degree as many other immigrant-receiving countries. These factors have averted a backlash against immigration in Canada (ibid.).

Geography also matters *within* Canada in local debates over multiculturalism in Canadian cities. Though at the countrywide level Canadians do not have to fear being swamped by a single ethnic group, since immigrants tend to concentrate and cluster in a few cities, local communities do face the threat of immigrant concentration. The cases discussed in this book suggest that the backlash that arose in the 1990s in Canada may have been caused by the ways in which geography, ethnic concentration, and cultural differences combined and intersected in Canadian urban and suburban communities.

One of the most remarkable aspects of Canada's official multiculturalism has been its adaptability: as ethnic-relations challenges take new forms, the model evolves. However, Canada's overall success in integrating immigrants and ethnocultural minorities does not mean it can afford to relax its ongoing efforts to manage its ethnocultural diversity – new challenges are always looming.

Kymlicka (1998) aptly describes multiculturalism as 'a policy in continuous evolution, involving an ongoing renegotiation of the terms of integration in Canada,' whereby elected officials define its legislative framework 'within which more specific issues of multiculturalism are settled on a day-to-day basis' (1998, 104). As we will discover, since the ethnocultural diversity engendered by immigration is largely an urban phenomenon, many of these challenges are place-specific. Local leaders, including municipal elected officials, civil-society leaders, and public employees (such as police officers, teachers, librarians, and recreational program leaders, who interact daily and often face to face with immigrants and ethnocultural minorities) are central to identifying and managing ethnic-relations challenges 'on the ground' in Canadian cities. Public employees in particular function as 'street-level bureaucrats' (Lipsky 1976) who 'represent' government to the immigrants with whom they come into contact (Frisken and Wallace 2000, 14). Canada's largest urban centres are at the forefront of multiculturalism policy making in response to social change.

The Urban Reality of Multiculturalism in Canada

Policy makers and academics have only recently begun to address the urban impacts of multiculturalism in Canada. If multiculturalism policies are to continue to be effective, they must address the geographic *and* jurisdictional dimensions of multiculturalism – that is, the place-specific challenges associated with immigration and ethnocultural diversity as well as the issue of multilevel governance. In particular, the academic community and practitioners must address the role of municipalities in multiculturalism policy.

The social, economic, and political impacts of immigration and changing ethnoracial demographics described above are most immediate in Canada's urban centres. Canada's three largest city-regions – Toronto, Vancouver, and Montreal – are magnets for immigrants. In 2006 close to 63 per cent of immigrants – that is, foreign-born individuals – lived in one of those three Census Metropolitan Areas (CMAs)[3] (Statistics Canada 2007c, 18). Whereas immigrants constituted about 19.8 per cent of Canada's population in 2006, they accounted for 45.7 per cent of Toronto's population and 39.6 per cent of Vancouver's that year (Statistics Canada 2007b). In fact, in 2002 close to 50 per cent of Canada's approximately 230,000 immigrants settled in the Toronto CMA alone (CIC 2002). In 2006, 95.9 per cent of Canada's visible minorities lived in a CMA (Statistics Canada 2008a, 5). Canada's largest cities have become highly racially diverse in a relatively short time.

StatsCan (2005) predicts that Canada's visible minorities (most of whom are foreign-born) are likely to continue to locate in urban centres and that in 2017 close to three-quarters of Canada's visible minorities will be living in Toronto, Vancouver, or Montreal. According to StatsCan's projections, by that year the Toronto CMA will be home to 45 per cent of Canada's visible minorities and the Vancouver CMA to 18 per cent (2005, 7). Visible minorities will be the 'visible majority' in both CMAs (ibid.). Under three of the five scenarios StatsCan used for its projections, Chinese residents will form more than half of the visible-minority population of the entire Vancouver CMA (ibid.).

The dramatic demographic shift in the national and ethnic make-up of Canada's largest city-regions is not only an urban phenomenon, but also increasingly a *suburban* one. Despite the widespread perception that immigrants only move to suburbs after establishing themselves, many immigrants settle directly in suburbs (Lo et al. 2007). In several suburban municipalities in both the Greater Toronto Area (GTA) and Greater Vancouver,[4] more than 50 per cent of the residents are foreign-born; also, more than 50 per cent of some suburban populations in these city-regions are in the 'visible minority' category (Statistics Canada 2007b). In fact, the three municipalities in Canada with the highest proportion of visible minorities and immigrants in their populations are suburbs of Vancouver or Toronto – Richmond, Markham, and Brampton.

Despite these clear trends in the spatial distribution of Canada's immigrants, the ways in which immigration has affected municipal governance have received little attention. The limited but growing literature on this subject documents considerable variation in the extent to which municipal governments respond to immigration by adapting their services and governance structures to incorporate immigrants' preferences and increase immigrants' access to services (Tate and Quesnel 1995; Wallace and Frisken 2000; Edgington and Hutton 2002; Good 2004, 2005, 2006; Graham, Philips, and Maslove 2006; Poirier 2006). Only some municipalities are following Canada's national model of citizenship and immigrant integration – official multiculturalism.

A number of urban scholars have linked diversity to a city's ability to innovate and, ultimately, to its economic performance. For example, the well-known American urban 'guru' Richard Florida has found a statistical correlation between a city's economic performance and its ability to attract the diverse members of the 'creative class' (Florida 2002). However, despite the important economic opportunities associated with immigration to cities, others caution that the population density that characterizes urban places, coupled with rapid social change, can be a source of social stress (Polèse and Stren 2000, 8). Harnessing the benefits of immigration and avoiding social disintegration will require what Mario Polèse and Richard Stren call 'socially sustainable growth' – that is, growth 'that is compatible with the harmonious evolution of civil society, fostering an environment conducive to the compatible cohabitation of culturally and socially diverse groups while at the same time encouraging social integration, with improvements in the quality of life for all segments of the population' (Polèse and Stren 2000, 16).

According to Canada's model of official multiculturalism, this type of growth entails adapting local services and governance structures to facilitate access by immigrants and ethnocultural minorities to services and their participation in local decision making. The rapidity and concentrated nature of changes in the ethnocultural composition of Canadian cities creates the potential for ethnic conflict and segregation if immigrants are not properly accommodated and managed. Fostering socially sustainable cities involves building on Canada's strengths in diversity management at the federal level and appropriately tailored responses at the community level. As we will discover, municipalities as locally based democratic institutions can do much to ensure the harmonious development of civil society in highly diverse immigrant-magnet communities. In other words, their role is crucial to the development of socially sustainable cities.

How are Canada's immigrant-magnet municipalities coping with large-scale social change? Which municipal governments in Canada's most important immigrant-receiving city-regions are behaving as local ambassadors of Canada's national model of immigrant integration and ethnocultural relations (official multiculturalism), to what extent, and why? Given municipal governments' subordinate status in Canadian federalism, how do they cope with dramatic social change?

This book explores how local leaders in some of Canada's most diverse municipalities in the GTA and in Greater Vancouver have adapted (or, alternatively, failed to adapt) municipal governance structures and services in response to shifts in the ethnocultural demographics of their populations. It compares Toronto, Mississauga, Brampton, and Markham in the GTA, and Vancouver, Richmond, Surrey, and Coquitlam in Greater Vancouver.

The two main goals of this book are to document municipal initiatives and innovations in multiculturalism policy and to uncover factors that prompt a municipality to adopt and implement effective, locally tailored multiculturalism policies. A broader theme is the place of municipalities in Canadian federalism. It is municipal governments that are closest to one of the most important public-policy issues of our time. So the question becomes this: Do they have the institutional footing necessary to meet the challenges of multiculturalism?

Few Canadian urban scholars have developed home-grown theories of urban policy making (Graham, Philips, and Maslove 1998, 19). Thus, chapter 2 lays the theoretical foundations for exploring the role of municipalities in managing and responding to ethnocultural diversity by drawing from important theories of urban politics that were developed in the United States. As Warren Magnusson argues, 'local governments are not just national governments writ small' (Magnusson 1985, 51). At the municipal level, one of the most important questions is how municipal governments develop the capacity to manage social change within a highly constrained institutional environment. Following Clarence Stone's seminal *Regime Politics* (1989), urban regime theorists argue that the capacity to achieve local policy goals develops when local leaders build coalitions across the public and private sectors, thereby helping participants pool their resources to develop and implement local policy agendas. Chapter 2 builds a theoretical framework that incorporates institutional factors, global economic forces, and theories of demographic change into an urban regime analysis of multiculturalism policy making in Canadian municipalities.

Chapter 3 documents how municipalities have responded to dramatic changes in the ethnic composition of their populations. It also introduces a typology to characterize the ways in which municipalities vary in their multiculturalism-related policy activities. The extent to which municipalities are important policy makers for the multiculturalism file becomes clear in this chapter.

Chapters 4 and 5 describe the politics and local contexts of the eight municipalities in the GTA (Toronto, Mississauga, Brampton, Markham) and Greater Vancouver (Vancouver, Richmond, Surrey, Coquitlam) respectively. They offer a framework for examining elements of the local contexts that may affect how and whether cities develop productive urban governance arrangements. The chapters are organized by province to highlight intraprovincial variation and, it follows, the importance of local factors and agency among supposed 'creatures of the provinces.'

Chapter 6 compares the eight cases, filtering the findings through the hypothesis that the *ethnoracial configuration of municipal societies* explains the differences in their politics, policy-making processes, and governance arrangements, as well as in their efforts to craft multiculturalism policy. The chapter argues that when combined, urban regime theory and a Canadian-made social diversity perspective offer a powerful explanation for the local politics of multiculturalism. The factors to which urban regime theory draws one's attention – factors that include local resources, as well as the systemic bias towards business participation in local coalitions and therefore also towards a growth agenda – intersect with ethnic configurations in powerful ways to influence the development of multiculturalism policy in the GTA and Greater Vancouver.

Chapter 7 broadens the analytical lens from the micropolitics of municipalities to the impact of the intergovernmental context on municipal responsiveness. It examines how, in the mid-1990s, changes in the intergovernmental system influenced how immigration and ethnocultural diversity were governed at the local level. The chapter shows how global economic forces – including economic rescaling and immigration – and the rise of neoliberalism had an uneven impact on the Canadian intergovernmental system.

Chapter 8 summarizes the study's findings and offers a comparative framework for examining the urban governance of multiculturalism both within Canada and cross-nationally. It demonstrates how urban regime theory contains the building blocks for a powerful theory of the local governance of multiculturalism. By creating a dialogue between urban regime theory on the one hand and a social diversity perspective and structural perspectives on the other, the framework incorporates elements of the three central categories of comparative political analysis – structure, culture, and rationality (Lichbach and Zuckerman

1997) – into regime analysis. Furthermore, though urban regime theory, the central theoretical underpinning of this book, is primarily an empirical theory meant to explain how and why local policy capacity develops, its adherents – including Clarence Stone (2005), the pioneer of the approach – are motivated by a normative concern to understand the barriers to a more progressive local politics. The analytical question to which regime theory draws one's attention is this: Which participants – and ultimately, what resources – must coalesce around a policy problem in order for an effective solution to emerge and be implemented? In comparing instances of success and failure in the development of multiculturalism policy, this book identifies the factors associated with the realization of progressive and multiculturalism-friendly local governance. Therefore, the chapter concludes with a discussion of the implication of the book's findings for policy makers.

2 Linking Urban Regime Theory, Social Diversity, and Local Multiculturalism Policies

The traditional assumption [in Canada] has been that the primary role of the municipal level is to provide services – to ensure that clean water flows from the tap, that the garbage gets picked up, and that kids can find enough ice time at the local arena. However, *municipalities are increasingly understood to be not just service providers but democratic governments*. This reconceptualization highlights the imperative of operating in a democratic, accountable, and transparent manner and brings with it expectations that governments engage citizens and communities in meaningful ways in the policy process. It also *presumes that urban governments possess sufficient policy capacity and have access to appropriate policy tools to undertake strategic leadership*. That such leadership may necessitate collaboration in a governance model ... in no way obviates its importance. With a focus on governing rather than mere service provision comes a concern for equity: that urban governments are *representative* of and *responsive* to the needs of the diversity of communities. The implication for urban research is that the analytical methods employed are *sensitive to group differences* and can accommodate, for instance, a good understanding of *ethno-cultural communities* and gender-based analysis.

Andrew, Graham, and Phillips 2002, 12; emphasis added

As these observations by Canadian urban scholars Caroline Andrew, Katherine Graham, and Susan Phillips attest, the traditional conception of the role of Canadian municipalities is very limited. However, as the authors also highlight, the view that local governments are mere service providers in relatively unimportant areas, or administrative extensions of provincial governments, is giving way to broader notions about the importance of local democracy. And as they also note, with municipal 'democratization' come greater expectations on the part of citizens. The question therefore becomes: Are local governments up to the leadership challenge? Do local leaders have the capacity to respond to urban challenges effectively and in an open and accountable way? How does policy capacity develop at the local level in the context of limited resources and limited institutional autonomy? This chapter establishes the theoretical foundation for exploring these questions by examining Canadian municipalities' 'responsiveness' to social diversity.

As in Canada, the literature on local politics in the United States emphasizes the constraints on municipal autonomy. For instance, Paul Peterson's seminal *City Limits* (1981) argues that, owing to their tight resource and jurisdictional constraints, as well as the political economy of cities, city officials tend to focus on a single policy goal – economic development. Thus, in the Canadian and American urban politics literatures, a central question is *how* municipalities can develop the capacity to achieve local agendas beyond these limits.

Urban regime theory – an approach that American urban scholar Clarence Stone pioneered in *Regime Politics* (1989) – argues that policy capacity develops at the local level when local leaders build public–private coalitions to pool resources across sectors. In this way, through proactive leadership that creates informal governance arrangements, local leaders overcome the formal limitations of local institutions. Since Canadian and American urban politics research is converging on the fundamental question of local capacity, a theoretical dialogue between urban researchers in Canada and those in the United States has become increasingly valuable.

This chapter provides an overview of the central ideas in the literature on urban regime theory, drawing especially on the work of Clarence Stone. It also lays the foundation for a comparative framework capable of explaining how demographic shifts in the ethnocultural composition of urban and suburban societies shape local governance. To this end, the chapter introduces the 'social diversity perspective' put forward by Rodney Hero, who suggests that institutions, politics, and policy outputs are structured by their social contexts – in particular, by the ethnoracial configuration of political societies. It also discusses the importance of placing urban regime analyses in their intergovernmental and global contexts. The chapter concludes by presenting the study's research design and methodology.

Urban Regime Theory: Key Concepts and Ideas

Urban regime theory has dominated urban politics literature since the publication of Clarence Stone's seminal *Regime Politics* in 1989. That theory helps explain how policy capacity develops at the local level, given the tight resource constraints within which local governments operate. According to urban regime theorists, policy capacity develops through coalitions in which local leaders in the public and private sectors pool their resources to achieve local policy goals.

Though Stephen Elkin (1987) and Norman Fainstein and Susan Fainstein (1986) have also contributed to this theory, Clarence Stone's study of Atlanta has been the most influential work and is generally the starting point for any regime analysis (see Mossberger and Stoker 2001; Horan 2002). However, the popularity of the urban regime concept has led to what Giovani Sartori (1991) calls 'conceptual stretching' – a problem that arises when a term is applied so broadly that it begins to lose its meaning and its function as an organizational device and theoretical building block (Stoker and Mossberger 1994; Mossberger and Stoker 2001). It is therefore worth reviewing the concept's core elements by returning to Stone's original study of Atlanta – *Regime Politics*.

Definition

Stone defines an *urban regime* as the 'informal arrangements by which public bodies and private interests function together in order to be able to make and carry out governing decisions' (1989, 6). Urban regimes have three related components – a capacity, a set of actors, and a relationship (ibid., 179). Informal arrangements vary from city to city; that said, all urban regimes are driven by two needs: 'institutional scope (that is, the need to encompass a wide enough scope of institutions to mobilize the resources required to make and implement governing decisions) and ... cooperation (that is, the need to promote enough cooperation and coordination for the diverse participants to reach decisions and sustain action in support of those decisions)' (ibid., 6).

These needs arise from a city's resource and institutional constraints, as well as from the fragmentation of power in urban systems. A regime is more than a temporary partnership. To constitute a 'regime,' an urban coalition must be relatively long-lasting and stable (Mossberger and Stoker 2001). Essentially, to say that a 'regime' exists is to say that an ongoing cooperative arrangement between public officials and civil-society elites has developed to achieve particular policy goals.

Power as 'Social Production' vs. 'Control'

At the foundation of urban regime theory is a novel conception of power that emphasizes the capacity to achieve policy goals rather than the control of one set of actors by another. In this way, urban regime theory builds on and moves beyond what had become a somewhat stale debate between elitists and pluralists. In the former tradition, sociologist Floyd Hunter's study, *Community Power Structure* (1953), documented close but informal links between Atlanta's governmental and economic sectors and suggested that this alliance exerted *control* over policy making. Alan Harding (1995) has summarized the contribution of this work to the field of American urban politics, noting that because of its empirical and methodological rigour, Hunter's study was viewed as 'scientific evidence that local representative democracy in the US was just a smokescreen for dominant economic interests' (1995, 39).

Almost a decade later, in his study of New Haven, *Who Governs?* (1961), Robert Dahl pointed out that control over local decision making was not as concentrated as Hunter had suggested. He found that local decisions in New Haven were made in the context of a 'stratified' form of pluralism, whereby a small group of local leaders had a direct effect on decision making, but indirect influence on public policy making was more diffuse (Judge 1995). Pluralists emphasize the importance of elections to power, stressing the potential of all voters to influence local decision making (Stone 2008, 79). Because of these very different perspectives, a vigorous debate ensued between 'elitists' and 'pluralists.'

Stone's empirical study of Atlanta and his contribution to the development of the urban regime concept broke the impasse in the 'community power' debate by validating the elitist contention that a tight link between Atlanta's mayor and business elite existed, while also showing that group politics, the electoral process, and local entrepreneurship mattered, as Dahl had found in New Haven. In addition, urban regime theory explained why governing coalitions and thus also policy processes and outcomes varied across cases. In Stone's model, neither the preferences of 'elites' nor the preferences of groups can be assumed, since policy preferences vary with the nature of the governing coalition as well as with opportunities for cooperation. Unlike elitist and pluralist perspectives, urban regime theorists do not view preferences as autonomous. For regime theorists, local decision making does not simply involve aggregating individuals' and groups' policy preferences. Rather, urban regime relationships shape actors' behaviours and policy preferences; they 'are not neutral mechanisms through which policy is made' (Stone 1989, 6).

Stone refers to his innovation as the development of a 'social production model' of power: 'The power struggle [in cities] concerns, not control and resistance, but gaining and fusing the capacity to act – power to, not power over' (ibid., 229). In Canadian and American cities, the most fundamental questions concern capacity.

The Bias towards Growth Agendas

In focusing on questions of policy capacity, urban regime theorists acknowledge that power is unequally distributed in urban societies. Thus they have not completely abandoned the question of the relative influence of different actors in urban systems. According to Stone (1989), the business community disproportionately influences municipal affairs, because it possesses an unequal share of the material resources in local societies. Thus, urban regime theory can explain the consensus among urban scholars that local agendas tend to give priority to economic development or 'growth' (Logan and Molotch 1987; Imbroscio 1997).

Urban regime theory in this way accounts for the empirical pervasiveness of what John Logan and Harvey Molotch (1987) refer to as 'growth machines' – coalitions of local leaders who support policies that encourage growth above all else. Like urban regime theorists, growth machine theorists argue that the question of who controls the local agenda is not the only one that must be asked in order to understand community power. However, unlike urban regime theorists, who focus on the fundamental question of *capacity* to govern, Logan and Molotch are concerned with the *purpose* of governing. For them, the central question is this: What takes priority on the local agenda? The answer: growth. Like Clarence Stone and other urban regime theorists, they offer a way out of the impasse between elitism and pluralism. Growth machine theory validates the contention that a small elite group's interests are unduly influential – as Hunter found in Atlanta in the 1950s. To the pluralists, the theory posits that regardless of whether a diversity of local leaders are influential in different policy areas, in the end, economic development trumps other local agendas (Molotch and Logan 1987).

Within the coalition of local leaders that dominates at the local level, a new class that Molotch and Logan call the 'rentiers' (landowners or 'immobile capital') dominates. According to growth machine theorists, cities compete with one another for businesses and residents, and the members of the growth coalition are city boosters who promote competition. Their theory explains why various sectors in a city support the objective of growth. For instance, politicians support growth because they rely on campaign contributions from the development industry. The local media serve as 'statesmen of growth,' because the profitability of their outlets depends on growth. Even labour leaders support growth, because it brings jobs to a city. Indeed, many residents have a stake in the growth of their community – a stake that leads them to support development at any cost, that is, 'value-free development.' Rentiers actively try to reinforce a growth ideology.

By explaining why various sectors of local communities (including labour) support a growth agenda, the growth machine literature is useful for understanding how the systemic power of the business community (especially business people associated with land development) is maintained. It provides less insight, however, into the variations in approaches to growth politics or into the fact that local leaders also spend time and resources on what Paul Peterson (1981, 41–65) calls 'allocational' or 'redistributive' policies rather than development policies. Multiculturalism initiatives exemplify such allocational or social efforts. The growth machine perspective would lead one to expect that such policies would be pursued only to preserve the local growth consensus if it is threatened by local dissent. And the growth machine perspective does indeed explain a great deal of urban policy making, including the general orientation of local policies towards economic and population growth and thus towards development. However, because it focuses on how local communities converge on a growth agenda, it is less useful in explaining variations in local policy agendas – including the various types of growth initiatives and the social and allocational policies adopted to support growth.

The Importance of Relationships

By focusing instead on the relationships among participants in urban coalitions and the ways in which regimes shape the preferences of these participants, we can gain more insight into the micropolitics of policy making in cities. For example, the systemic power of the business community is central to urban regime theory. In fact, Karen Mossberger and Gerry Stoker (2001) argue in their review of the urban regime literature that if business does *not* participate in an urban governance arrangement, the urban coalition does not constitute a 'regime.' For Stone, business participation is privileged because of the resources possessed by the business community. However, because policy objectives – including economic-development objectives – require a variety of resources, the business community does not *control* local politics. Even economic-development objectives require the support of local political officials whose political careers are ultimately decided by voters.

Policies are negotiated within regime relationships. It matters who is 'in' and who is 'out' of the coalition, because regime partners negotiate with the business community to have their interests represented. Thus, unlike the 'growth machine' literature, which stresses the role of a broad ideological and cross-sectoral consensus among local leaders concerning the desirability of 'growth' – a consensus rooted in structural constraints of the political economy – urban regime theorists do not take policy preferences for granted. Rather, support for policies that a city's business community would like to see implemented must be negotiated among a group of local leaders whose combined resources are necessary to implement the local agenda. The policy-making process is shaped by the uneven distribution of resources in society. In this political process, various interests and identities negotiate and exchange support for policies – and sometimes support one another in the absence of a clear short-term exchange, in the interest of maintaining trust and an ongoing relationship.

In other words, urban regime theorists leave room for political agency. They acknowledge systemic constraints on local leadership as an imbalance in resource distribution: local leaders' choices are embedded in social structures and the political economy (Stone, Whelan, and Murin 1986, 203, in Orr and Johnson 2008, 17). These structures constitute their 'context of choice' – that is, they structure what is possible. However, as Stone and colleagues put it: 'At the same time, social structures and economies don't devise and install political arrangements. That is the role of political leaders. Political leaders must work with the resources they can mobilize (and anticipate what competing leaders might be able to mobilize). At the same time, they are not confined to a single pattern of arrangements. Leadership is part of a creative exercise' (Stone, Whelan, and Murin 1986, 203 in Orr and Johnson 2008, 18).

Stone (2005) has argued recently that though business people often participate in urban coalitions, business participation is not absolutely essential to urban regimes. Rather, the participants in regimes vary according to the policy objective. Stone's comments imply that urban regime theory can serve as an *analytical lens* through which one can ascertain whose participation would be necessary to achieve more progressive policy agendas or to 'reconstitute' (Imbroscio 1997) urban governance.

For Stone, the central question of urban regime theory is this: Who needs to be mobilized to take on a given problem effectively? The relative influence of regime participants depends on the importance of the resources they bring to the governing arrangement. The nature of the policy goal determines the requisite resources.

Urban Regime Dynamics: Regime Formation, Maintenance, and Change

Drawing from the rational choice literature, Stone (1989) explains that regimes are maintained by their ability to provide selective incentives to the partners. The idea that local leaders require either coercion or selective incentives to overcome the 'free-rider problem' originates in Mancur Olson's *The Logic of Collective Action* (1965). As in the group-politics literature that followed Olson's influential work, in urban regime theory the nature of the incentives varies with the regime and has implications for the ease with which that regime is maintained. Since politics at the local level often centres on economic-development or 'growth' objectives, early work emphasizes the importance of material incentives to regime formation and maintenance. More recent regime scholarship has expanded the range of motivations for regime participation from primarily economic ones to a broad range of 'purposive' incentives. For instance, in *Gay Politics, Urban Politics*, Robert Bailey (1999) argues that 'clashes over identities, values, and cultural attributes have taken center stage on the urban agenda' and that 'more than economic gain or even rational calculation, affirmation is the centerpiece of identity politics' (1999, 11, 4). Even Stone (2001, 2005) now attributes more importance to 'purposive' incentives than he did in his original *Regime Politics* (1989). For instance, ideas are resources with which to frame agendas that mobilize local elites to achieve particular policy goals; they are therefore an important part of the creative leadership process that leads to the development of productive urban coalitions. In this way, policy ideas are part of local capacity – 'a potential source of "power to"' (Stone 2005, 325). In other words, the way in which local leaders frame connections among identities, ideologies, and local agendas influences whether productive urban coalitions develop, the nature of the local agenda, and who is included in governance.

Furthermore, according to regime theorists, incentives for regime participation result from political agency (Stone 1989, 2001, 2005). For instance, in Stone's *Regime Politics* (1989), mayors play an important role in bringing local leaders together and helping them recognize the mutually advantageous nature of their partnership. Nevertheless, regime theorists do not preclude the possibility that leadership could originate elsewhere in the community. To build a successful regime, regime entrepreneurs must appreciate what kinds of resources and interests various actors bring to the arrangement and demonstrate how pooling these resources and exchanging support for various policies is in the interest of all members of the coalition. Most fundamentally, regime entrepreneurs need to frame an agenda that can attract the support of elites with the requisite resources to implement the agenda.

Structural factors also shape political choices. The way in which civil society is *organized* and *resourced* provides the context of choice for local would-be regime entrepreneurs; it also structures what can feasibly be accomplished at the local level through the building of coalitions. Problems of collective action affect the possibility of regime formation at two levels of analysis: first, at the individual level in civil society, where groups are formed; and second, at the 'regime' level, where bridges must be built among elites (who often represent important local organizations), both between sectors and between civil society and the local state. Stone's (1989) seminal work implies another manifestation of the systemic bias towards business participation – the fact that business communities are often well organized and, therefore, also able to participate in local coalitions. The 'downtown elite' was powerful in Atlanta because Central Atlanta Progress (CAP), its business organization, provided it with a strong, unified voice (Stone 1989, 169). Whereas Stone emphasizes the ability of business groups to generate a stream of selective material benefits that help keep the intersectoral coalition in place, it should be added that these resources are also important in generating the selective benefits that are necessary to overcome collective action problems within a single group or sector. Thus, the ability to overcome collective action problems at the intrasectoral (rather than the intersectoral) level is yet another form of structural business privilege.

Moreover, once local leaders form regimes, the governing arrangement structures policy development. At work in urban regime theory is an element of 'path dependent' (Pierson 1993) logic of the type theorized in the 'new institutionalism' literature. In other words, past policy decisions become self-reinforcing to a certain degree. Indeed, Stone uses the word 'path' in his description of regime development (Stone 1989, 10). For Stone, politics and policy mutually reinforce each other. He describes his approach to causation in this way:

> Social scientists are accustomed to an analytical framework where there is a clear distinction between independent and dependent variables ... The regime analysis I am employing offers a different dynamic. Politics in the form of the governing coalition shapes policy, and policy also shapes the regime. The reasoning here is not a simple reversal of the policy-causes-politics argument but rather that policy and politics are circular, each at various points causing and being caused by the other. In this view, causation is in part a matter of enacted change ... Sometimes changes in policy come first; sometimes politics (the character of the governing coalition) forges policy. Either can have a profound impact – illustrating that the interplay of event and structure is a process of structuring. (ibid., 164)

The line between structure and agency is blurred in Stone's model. The way in which he and other urban regime theorists conceptualize the causal role of ideas also reflects this tension between structure and agency. Ideas are seen variously as individual-level 'selective incentives' (what the collective action literature refers to as purposive incentives) and as general principles (or overarching policy goals). Stone (ibid.) refers to the latter as 'broad purposes.' In Atlanta, the city's slogan – the 'City Too Busy to Hate' – served as an ideological shortcut for regime actors, one that reduced 'transaction costs' among regime participants by expressing the regime consensus on broad goals. It served as an ongoing standard by which to evaluate the appropriateness of proposed solutions to urban challenges as they arose. Similarly, Bryan D. Jones and Lynn W. Bachelor (1993) developed the notion of 'solution set' to express the regime-maintenance function of policies. A 'solution set' constitutes a shared understanding of the nature of a policy problem and the types of solutions appropriate to such problems. Jones and Bachelor suggest that a great deal of policy making occurs through 'reasoning by analogy,' whereby local leaders adopt policies that are similar to their past policy choices because current policy challenges are interpreted through the lens of past 'solution sets' (Jones and Bachelor 1993, 249).

Creating and maintaining regimes is difficult. Over time, insiders develop relationships based on trust and establish broad purposes; this reduces transaction costs among regime actors. In other words, regime relationships are valuable and productive. Therefore, once one has been formed, outsiders have an incentive to join it, because the costs of challenging the existing regime and creating another one are significant. Thus existing regimes have what Stone (1989) calls 'preemptive power' over the municipal agenda. Regime participants negotiate and co-determine the municipal agenda. They decide who is 'in' and who is 'out' and shape the direction of regime change. Regime insiders have an incentive to 'manage' the regime to ensure its continued viability. If it falls apart, its capacity is lost and all regime participants lose.

Towards a Comparative Framework of Regime Politics in Ethnoculturally Diverse Contexts

To some, urban regime theory is more a 'concept' than a theory, because it cannot predict regime formation or explain regime change (Orr and Stoker 1994; Lauria 1997; Graham, Philips, and Maslove 1998; Mossberger and Stoker 2001). This limitation reflects the general preference for case-study analysis among urban regime scholars. Nevertheless, as Mossberger and Stoker note in their review of the literature on regime theory, taken together, existing case studies provide valuable insight into the factors associated with regime change. They identify *demographic shifts, economic restructuring, federal grant policies,* and *political mobilization* as central to regime formation and change (Mossberger and Stoker 2001, 811). Detailed case-study analysis is invaluable in generating hypotheses, and a great deal can be learned by comparing existing case studies. However, theory building and testing requires comparative studies specifically designed to test the causal effects of these factors.

In a recent article, Jon Pierre (2005) makes the case for a more comparative field of urban politics, arguing that 'there is much to suggest that one has come to the end of the line in terms of what urban regime theory can help uncover or explain' (2005, 450). With Jeffrey Sellers (2002a, 2002b, 2005), he suggests that urban scholars should examine how local political systems relate to their external environments and should also address normative and value-based issues surrounding policy agendas and policy styles. Unlike Sellers, however, Pierre contends that since the urban regime concept does not travel well outside the United States, urban scholars should focus on 'governance' rather than on urban regimes. Governance, he tells us, is a broader concept that incorporates policy agendas outside land-use and urban renewal agendas (2005, 450, 451). According to Pierre, a governance perspective does not prejudge who will participate in urban coalitions. Rather, it 'directs the observer to look beyond the institutions of the local state and to search for processes and mechanisms through which significant and resource-full actors coordinate their actions and resources in the pursuit of collectively defined objects' (ibid., 452). As a form of governance that privileges the business community, 'urban regimes' might be seen as one 'mode' of urban governance among many possible ones.

However, abandoning the concept of 'urban regime' in favour of a more broadly conceived notion of 'governance' sacrifices some precision. It also means abandoning the theorization of a systemic form of power that situates urban analysis within a political economy perspective.[1] Furthermore, the concept of 'urban regime' is more flexible than Pierre (2005) contends. It is embedded in a political economy perspective that acknowledges the privileged position of business in urban systems, given the business sector's overwhelming advantage in material resources, which it can use to 'encourage' other actors to participate in and maintain urban regimes. Nevertheless, urban regime theory does not preclude broader participation in the governing arrangement and is not limited to explaining land-use agendas (Stone 2005).

In addition, when considering the theoretical value of broadening urban analyses by conceptualizing urban decision-making structures as variable forms of 'governance,' one must consider the state of conceptual clarity of the literature on governance. Pierre (2005) admits that there is 'not as of yet a full-fledged theory of governance.' He himself identifies at least three ways in which the term is used – as a theory, as a normative model, and as 'an empirical object of study' (2005, 452–3). He also contends, with Gerry Stoker (1998), that the term is pre-theoretical. It is an empirical tool to assist the urban researcher in identifying what warrants study in cities (Pierre 2005). There is no reason why the urban regime concept cannot serve the same purpose. The concept draws our attention not only to informal arrangements but also to the political economy of cities. In particular, the urban regime 'lens' draws our attention to the possibility that the business community might be in a privileged position in urban coalitions when it comes to agenda

Table 2.1
Rodney Hero's (1998) ethnic configurations

| Racial/ethnic groups | State 'Types' | | |
	Homogeneous	Heterogeneous	Bifurcated
White (Northern and Western European)	High	Moderate	High
White ethnic (Southern and Eastern European)	Low	High	Low
Minority (Black/Latino/ Asian)	Low	Moderate	High
Type of political pluralism	Consensual	Competitive	Hierarchical/ Limited
Examples	MN, WI, WA, UT	NY, MA, NJ	SC, AL, MS, TX, CA, AZ

Source: This table (except for the last row) reproduces Figure 1.1 in *Faces of Inequality* (Hero 1998, 8).

setting, general decision making, and inclusion in 'governance' structures because it possesses a disproportionate share of resources in urban communities and because the institutional capacity of municipal governments is relatively weak.

Urban Regimes in Ethnically Diverse Contexts

The Social Diversity Perspective

Rodney Hero's 'social diversity perspective' shows promise in furthering comparative empirical research on the impact of demographic change on local policy making. In *Faces of Inequality* (1998), his pioneering work on American state and local politics, he develops a new interpretation of politically relevant variation across American states (and, to a lesser degree, counties), one that rivals dominant theoretical paradigms of American politics. In this work, Hero puts forward and tests the hypothesis that the ethnic configurations of political units affect their political processes, political institutions, and public policies. He explores this hypothesis through extensive, systematic, empirical analysis of a wide range of dependent variables in all fifty American states and some counties. For instance, he examines the relationship between the ethnic configurations of states on the one hand and, on the

other, voter turnout, strength of party organization, level of democratization, issue polarization in public opinion, interest-group strength,
formal governmental institutions, and public-policy outcomes in several policy areas (ibid., 22).

Hero develops a threefold typology of ethnic configurations – homogeneous, bifurcated, and heterogeneous – and theorizes about how
these configurations may affect the political dynamics or 'types of political pluralism' of states. Table 2.1 summarizes Hero's categories.

Hero also suggests how these configurations may exert their causal effects. For example, *homogeneous* states have mostly White populations that originate largely from Northern and Western Europe. He
hypothesizes that in these states, a 'consensual pluralism' is the norm
because whereas 'there might be high degrees of political competition
[in homogeneous states], including [for instance] high political party
competition,' in these states 'competition is tempered by an underlying consensus arising from homogeneity' (ibid., 16). In *heterogeneous*
states, where there are moderate levels of White residents from Northern and Western European backgrounds, a moderate number of racial
minorities (including Blacks, Latinos, and Asians), and high numbers
of what he refers to as 'White ethnics' (white residents with Southern
and Eastern European backgrounds), a 'competitive pluralism' emerg-
es. In his view, greater diversity in these states leads to greater competition among ethnoracial groups. He also notes that competition in these
states may be 'heightened by greater urbanization and factors such as
population density' (ibid., 16). Finally, *bifurcated* states, characterized
by a dualism between White Northern and Western Europeans on the
one hand and high numbers of racial minorities on the other, 'leads to
hierarchical or limited pluralism.' This form of pluralism is 'historically manifested in various legal and political constraints' in these states
(ibid.).

Hero's purpose is to develop a theory that offers a better explanation
of variations in state politics, policy making, and institutions than existing theories of state politics. More specifically, he developed his interpretation as both a complement *for* and a comprehensive alternative *to*
existing theories of state politics. For instance, in *Faces of Inequality*, he
claims to offer a 'clearer,' 'more precise,' and better account of change
(ibid., 10) than Daniel Elazar's widely held theory of state political cultures.[2] Indeed, to the extent that ethnic configurations of political units
matter to their politics, political outcomes, and institutional development, the social diversity interpretation is a powerful causal model. In

fact, one could predict change in these factors through demographic projections.

In *Racial Diversity and Social Capital* (2007), Hero takes on the social capital literature, arguing that it cannot sufficiently account for the influence of patterns of ethnic diversity on a variety of dependent variables. One of his central contributions is his explanation of state variation in ethnoculturally aggregated *and* disaggregated measurements of policy outcomes. He shows that aggregate measures of policy success often hide variations among policies in the way they affect the *relative equality* of minority racial and ethnic groups. Hero finds different 'faces of inequality' in political units with different ethnic configurations.

For instance, he shows that while social capital is highest in homogeneous states, which tend to produce superior policy outcomes on the aggregate level, homogeneous political units have the worst policy outcomes for racial minorities. In this vein, bifurcated political units tend to perform poorly in overall policy outcomes but do better when it comes to the relative equality of racial minorities. Hero's heterogeneous states tend to produce policy outcomes that fall between those of the two other categories (Hero 2003, 402). He concludes that there may be a 'dark side of social capital' insofar as social ties can be used to include *or* exclude – which appears to be the case for racial minorities in homogeneous settings.

In *Faces of Inequality*, Hero also examines the influence of ethnic configurations on policy debates about and general attitudes towards immigrants and ethnoracial minorities in the United States. For instance, he examines the adoption and support of 'official English' policies, which he describes as measures that are 'mechanisms of exclusion rather than assimilation [and that] condemn the multicultural traditions of minority populations.' He notes that such measures 'threaten the continuity of services that are necessary for participation in the political process' (Hero 1998, 108). (In the Canadian context, they would also threaten support for 'multiculturalism policies,' that is, for publicly led efforts to address the cultural biases in institutions – biases that underpin barriers to immigrant and ethnocultural-minority access to these institutions.) He finds that 'official English' measures are more likely to be supported and adopted in *bifurcated* and *homogeneous* locales than in heterogeneous ones (Hero 1998, 108).

Hero builds on Citrin, Rheingold, and Green (1990), as well as on others, who found that support for English-only policies was strongest in Southern states whose populations were primarily Anglo-Saxon, with few foreign-born residents, Hispanics, or Asians; and in four bi-furcated states – Arizona, California, Colorado, and Florida – that had experienced the largest influxes of immigrants between 1970 and 1980. In the homogeneous states the measures were adopted in the state legislatures; in the bifurcated states they were adopted through voter initiatives (ibid., in Hero 1998, 109). In addition, homogeneous states such as North Dakota, New Hampshire, Montana, and South Dakota all adopted 'official English' measures during the 1980s and 1990s (Hero 1998, 109).

Hero also discusses evidence that the ethnic configuration of a community affects individual-level policy preferences and attitudes. For instance, he draws from the work of Michael W. Link and Robert W. Oldendick (1996) regarding the impact of the social construction of race (by Whites) on support for equal opportunity and multiculturalism. This research shows that there are significant regional differences in how 'race' is socially constructed and in support for equal opportunity and multiculturalism. According to Link and Oldendick, 'social construction refers to the normative and evaluative images individuals hold concerning definable groups, such as the poor, the elderly, and racial minorities, whose behavior and well-being are affected by public policy' (Link and Oldendick 1996, 150). With respect to equal opportunity, Link and Oldendick found that White attitudes towards Blacks were a significant factor; at the same time, however, the effects of social constructions of differences between Whites and both Asians and Hispanic Americans were negligible. Furthermore, the effects of social construction were equal to those of socio-economic status and age and less than those associated with political orientation (ibid., 161). However, with respect to support for multiculturalism – defined broadly as 'the possible effects and consequences of increasing racial and ethnic diversity' (ibid., 154n2) – the effects of the social construction of race were clear. The 'social construction differential' – a measure of the 'difference (or differential) between white views of their own race and the views they hold of particular minority groups' (ibid, 153) – shapes Whites' attitudes about multiculturalism (ibid., 161). The social construction differential's impact on attitudes towards multiculturalism is significant for Blacks and Asians and especially strong for Hispanic Americans (ibid.). Furthermore, as Hero also points out, views about multiculturalism vary regionally. It is looked on less positively in the South, Midwest, and West (where bifurcated and homogeneous states are located) than in the Northeast, where Hero's heterogeneous states are located (see ibid., 161). Hero suggests that the ethnic configuration of states mediates these regional differences. The social diversity interpretation implies that 'the context within which individuals and/or groups are situated *is as, if not more, important* than the values or ideas that people "bring with them" or "have within"' (Hero 1998, 10; emphasis added). His work suggests that social context – and the ethnic configuration of a political unit in particular – influences social constructions of 'race,' 'immigrants,' and 'multiculturalism.'

By linking the ethnic configurations of societies with their types of political pluralism, the social diversity perspective offers a potentially fruitful approach to comparative studies of regime formation, maintenance, and change. One would anticipate that as local ethnic configurations change, so do local politics, policy outputs, and governance arrangements.

Clarence Stone's original regime analysis of Atlanta supports the idea that a demographic shift in the ethnic configuration of a local community will affect the local government's responsiveness to ethnocultural minorities. In Atlanta, a cooperative relationship (in the form of an urban regime) based on reciprocity and trust developed between Blacks and Whites, despite a deep history of racial oppression of Blacks. The formation of that city's 'biracial' regime was precipitated by a demographic shift that gave the Black community a majority. Urban regime theory helps delineate the circumstances in which intergroup cooperation can occur in an ethnically diverse and even divided context. Essentially, it posits that where the political will exists, local governments can serve as bridges between ethnic groups in cities.

Building Bridges

Marion Orr's (1999) case study of school reform in Baltimore develops an element of Stone's work that seems promising with respect to understanding the relationship between urban governance arrangements and policy outcomes in ethnically divided contexts. Orr chose to study Baltimore because he considers it an 'important center of African-American political and social life' and because of its Southern context and racial polarization (1999, xii). In his view, Baltimore's African-American community is exceptional among urban Black communities in terms of its 'level of sophistication and organization' (Orr 1999, 19). His research documents the historical development of what he calls 'Black social capital' in Baltimore and demonstrates how intracommunity 'social capital' is insufficient to achieve policy goals that benefit the

African-American community. Rather, education reform required that local leaders build an interracial 'bridge' between Whites and Blacks. In his view, the 'urban regime' literature conceptualizes how and why local leaders build these bridges.

Essentially, Orr makes two important and related theoretical points. First, he demonstrates that in an ethnically divided context, it is imperative to understand how to 'bridge' social capital. Second, he suggests that local institutions can be important bridges between cultural groups.

Orr's work shows that intragroup social capital is a necessary precondition for participation in governing regimes. It follows that levels of municipal responsiveness to immigrant communities in Canadian cities may be correlated with levels of intragroup social capital, such as 'Chinese social capital,' 'South Asian social capital,' and 'Black social capital' – the three most numerically significant visible-minority categories in Canada. This element of his theory suggests one way in which the ethnic configuration of localities may exert causal effects on regime building and ultimately also on policy outputs. When a single ethnoracial minority group is concentrated in a municipality, there is a greater likelihood that the group has created a range of institutions to support a strong sense of community and that it has developed the ability to mobilize collectively. This could explain why Hero found that policy outcomes were better for minorities in *bifurcated* settings than in homogeneous or heterogeneous locales. Bifurcated settings may provide a better opportunity for ethnocultural minorities to build and maintain ethnospecific social capital.

Nevertheless, though the ethnic distribution of social capital in civil society may be a precondition of the ability of urban governments to facilitate intergroup cooperation, developing a multiethnic regime also depends on the capacity and willingness of municipal officials and civil servants to serve as facilitators or 'bridges' and on the ability of these agents to *recognize opportunities for strategic cooperation*. In other words, the local state – which includes both elected officials and civil servants – is also an important factor in regime theory. As Orr demonstrates, the urban regime concept draws one's attention to the role of local political actors such as mayors in bringing together interethnic coalitions.

The Importance of Non-Electoral Arenas

Urban regime theory also explains a broader range of processes by which policy preferences enter policy making. Barbara Ferman (1996)

Table 2.2
Representation of visible minorities on eight Canadian municipal councils[3]

Municipalities (from most responsive to least responsive)	Size of council (excluding mayors)	Number of councillors who were 'visible minorities'	Percentage of Councillors who were 'visible minorities'	Percentage of visible minorities, in population, 2001/2006 censuses
Toronto, ON	44	5	11.4	42.8/46.9
Vancouver, BC	10	1	10	49/51
Richmond, BC	8	2	25	59/65
Markham, ON	8	2	25	55.5/65.4
Surrey, BC	8	0	0	37/46.1
Coquitlam, BC	7	0	0	34.3/38.6
Brampton, ON	5	1	20	40.2/57
Mississauga, ON	9	0	0	40.3/49

refers to the ways in which interests and identities might be represented as 'arenas.' She suggests four types of arenas (each with its distinct logic) from which regime builders draw – the business, civic, intergovernmental, and electoral arenas. Urban regime theory does not privilege the electoral arena, and political incorporation is not the only way to ensure that minority interests are represented in local governance. By contrast, in *Protest Is Not Enough* (1984), which compares the responsiveness of ten northern California cities to racial minorities, Rufus P. Browning, Dale Rogers Marshall, and David H. Tabb have argued that responsiveness occurs through the 'political incorporation' of minorities into a city's governing party or dominant coalition of *elected officials*. Unlike many American municipal governments, Canadian municipal councils are 'weak mayor' systems. As a consequence, it is more difficult to measure whether ethnocultural minorities have been politically incorporated into dominant coalitions on council. Indeed, in Canada, coalitions on a council may be a function of the issue at hand. But as Table 2.2 illustrates, the variation in municipal responses to immigrants and visible minorities is not correlated with the representation of racial minorities on local councils. All the mayors of the municipalities in the sample are White, and visible minorities do not represent more than 25 per cent of the councillors on any local council examined here. Note that in Canada, Toronto and Vancouver are the two most responsive municipalities to ethnocultural minorities. In those two cities, visible minorities are only 11.4 per cent and 10 per cent of the local councillors, respectively.

The reasons for the lack of political incorporation of immigrants and ethnoracial minorities into local councils are complex and require further study. However, one reason could be that non-citizens are not entitled to vote or run for municipal office. Canada has high naturalization rates – 85.1 per cent of eligible foreign-born individuals were citizens in 2006 (Statistics Canada 2007c, 23). Nevertheless, Myer Siemiatycki (2006) estimates that there are 263,000 immigrant residents in Toronto who are not entitled to vote (2006, 2). Given their concentration, 'White' local politicians also have incentives to respond to the preferences of ethnoracial minorities. However, in his study of the 2003 municipal election in Toronto – the municipality with the highest number of immigrants in Canada – Siemiatycki found that immigrants have significantly lower rates of voting than Canadian-born residents (ibid.).

Urban regime theory suggests why some municipalities respond to immigrant and ethnocultural concerns and policy preferences in the absence of equitable electoral representation. The theory posits that the electoral arena is only one entry point into the municipal policy-making process. Local leaders in the public *and* private spheres co-create and co-implement local agendas, which ensures that interests and identities are represented both within formal institutions (i.e., on council and in the municipal civil service) and through informal relationships with civil-society organizations that participate in the urban regime coalition. Furthermore, the policy preferences of regime participants – including those of White councillors – cannot be assumed, because they are negotiated within the regime and in the interest of regime maintenance. For instance, in Stone's case study of Atlanta, the downtown business elite needed the support of a Black-led council to pursue its urban renewal projects. In exchange, the business community provided Atlanta's Black community with jobs and supported integration. In Stone's words: 'Regime analysis instructs us that policy innovation is not only about individuals and their preferences. In Atlanta, for example, some business leaders personally would have preferred that racial segregation be perpetuated, but the business community embraced a policy of moderate change because that policy met their regime-building needs. As members of a biracial governing coalition, business leaders learned to link their desire for economic prosperity with abandonment of die-hard segregation' (Stone 1989, 160). In other words, the urban regime relationship shaped the preferences of regime participants: 'participation in the governing task and the quest for allies ... had an effect on the business elite, broadening its understanding of what constitutes a favourable economic climate' (ibid., 195).

Urban regime theory is the study of intersectoral, public–private co-operation and of 'how that cooperation is maintained when confronted with an ongoing process of social change, a continuing influx of new actors, and potential break-downs through conflict or indifference' (ibid., 9). In the urban regime theory model, one cannot predict policy outputs because they are products of negotiations among regime participants. In other words, it matters *who* participates in a regime. Municipal 'policy innovations – the critical decisions made in response to social change – emerge from and reflect the character of a city's governing coalition' (ibid., 160).

The immigrant population of Canadian municipalities has not yet translated its rising numbers into equitable electoral power. In the future, political incorporation could play a greater role in influencing municipal responsiveness to immigrants and ethnocultural minorities. The ethnic configurations of local communities could facilitate *or* impede the political incorporation of ethnoracial minorities. In Stone's study, a demographic shift in the ethnic composition of Atlanta led to Blacks becoming a majority in the city, which precipitated the development of a biracial regime. The authority inherent in controlling council and the government apparatus became a resource that enticed the cooperation of Atlanta's White business leaders into a regime relationship. However, urban regime theory suggests that the electoral arena constitutes only one venue of policy influence.

Urban Regimes, the Intergovernmental Context, and Globalization

Differences between the American and Canadian intergovernmental contexts as well as between the two countries' political cultures suggest that urban regime analysis may not apply as well in Canada as it does in the United States. The few comparative studies of Canadian and American cities tend to stress the differences between the two countries. For instance, in *The Myth of the North American City* (1986), Michael Goldberg and John Mercer argue that the way in which Canadian cities are governed reflects Canada's more collectivist and interventionist orientation relative to the United States.

One might argue that in a more collectivist political culture, urban regimes would be unnecessary, since the local state (or other levels of government) would be willing to fund urban initiatives as well as strong enough to do so. Political culture could override institutional and political-economy factors. One might expect a more progressive public-policy orientation at the local level in Canada. In such a public culture, public officials would be less likely to turn to the private sector to co-develop policy capacity. One might also expect more generous intergovernmental pooling arrangements in more collectivist political cultures and that upper levels of government would spend more in urban communities, negating the need for action by local governments. We do not, however, see these outcomes in Canada.

More recent and broad-based comparative work on political culture on the national scale suggests that differences between Canada and the United States have been exaggerated (Nevitte 1996). And if one includes European countries in the comparison, Canada and the United States stand out more for their similarities than for their differences.

In an article that 'reconsiders' the myth of the North American city thesis, David Imbroscio and Judith Garber (1996) argue that the development and 'growth' concerns of private property dominate Canadian urban politics as much as they do in the United States. These authors reject what they call 'cultural determinism' and stress the importance of differences in the two countries' institutions and constitutions. They argue that in the United States, cities construct their growth policies directly (at the city level), whereas in Canada, 'the locus of progrowth policy making is often the province rather than the city itself' (1996, 597). They develop the concept of 'constitutional regime' to explain the differences between Canadian and American cities' legal contexts, suggesting that Canadian local governments have little autonomy in policy making compared to American cities.

Similarly, institutional differences led Canadian urban scholar Andrew Sancton to conclude in a 1993 paper that 'the concept of urban political regimes is unlikely to be of much assistance in analyzing Canadian urban politics because massive provincial influence makes business involvement in such regime politics unnecessary' (1993, 20, cited in Urbaniak 2003, 11, and 2005, 6). In a strictly legal sense, municipalities are mere 'creatures of the provinces' – corporations whose existence depends on provincial will – and as such are subject to pervasive provincial policy interference. Given the highly restricted nature of local autonomy in Canada, one might expect business leaders not to expend resources on developing ongoing 'regime' relationships with a relatively powerless level of government. The forced municipal amalgamations in many of Canada's largest city-regions in late 1990s and early twenty-first century seemed to confirm the ideas of scholars who emphasize the institutional constraints on local agency.

Whether provincial officials respect municipal autonomy is also a matter of 'convention' and of dominant ideas regarding the role and democratic legitimacy of local governments. These ideas vary historically and across municipal systems in Canada. And as this chapter's opening quotation illustrates, many of Canada's most prominent urban scholars have noted that municipalities are increasingly being recognized as important democratic governments. Furthermore, in the absence of a comprehensive study demonstrating otherwise, one can justifiably assume that there is as much variation in growth politics and respect for municipal autonomy among provinces in Canada – and among states in the United States – as there is among provincial and state subunits in the two countries respectively. Indeed, there is evidence that this may also hold for Canadian and American cities' approaches to accommodating immigrants and ethnocultural minorities.

Though the United States is generally viewed as having a tradition of greater respect for municipal autonomy, especially in 'home-rule states' (Smith and Stewart 2006), trends in Canadian municipal systems support the notion that urban regimes might develop at the local level in Canada. There has been an increase in legislative autonomy in municipal systems across Canada, though this has not yet been coupled with additional fiscal policy instruments. Since the 1990s, beginning with Alberta's Municipal Government Act (1994), many provinces have introduced more permissive provisions into their municipal acts, such as ones relating to 'natural person' powers and spheres of jurisdiction. Furthermore, some provinces have made commitments to consult with municipalities on a variety of issues, including – most fundamentally – the issue of possible amalgamation (Tindal and Tindal 2009, 179).[4]

British Columbia's Community Charter (2003) recognizes municipal governments as an 'order of government' (ibid., 183). The City of Vancouver has been governed by its own City Charter[5] since 1886. The Ontario government's Stronger City of Toronto for a Stronger Ontario Act, enacted in 2006, is perhaps the most significant contemporary evidence of this trend. Donald Lidstone (2005), a constitutional lawyer and expert in municipal law in Vancouver, describes this act as a 'constitutional milestone [that] will help cities in the rest of Canada in their quest for palpable recognition as an order of government under our constitutional regime.'[6]

Urban scholars in Canada are also documenting examples of how municipal leaders overcome their formal limits through political will. Patrick Smith and Kennedy Stewart (2006) characterize municipal autonomy as existing in a 'mushy middle' between two poles – no local discretion and total local discretion. They demonstrate that municipal autonomy is a function not only of formal, legal frameworks but also of local leadership. Using as an example the implementation of Vancouver's drug strategy – which involved opening North America's first supervised heroin-injection sites in 2003 in the city's Downtown Eastside – they stress the importance of local officials' political will to increase local discretion. In this case, the Vancouver government strategically leveraged the support of upper levels of government for an initiative that was important to the city (2006, 259). This initiative required the participation of all levels of government – that is, what Smith and Kennedy call a 'whole of government' approach – which was possible only because of an exceptional leadership effort at the city level.

Municipalities now have more legal autonomy but fewer financial resources. This has created the conditions in which one might expect urban regimes to develop. Furthermore, in the context of globalization, many urban scholars have noted the emergence of more entrepreneurial forms of leadership in cities in different parts of the world (Clarke and Gaile 1998; DiGaetano and Strom 2003; Brenner 2004). 'Corporatist modes of governance' have become more common in both Europe and North America, according to DiGaetano and Strom (2003, 370).

Though much of the urban regime literature remains focused on American cities, a comparative literature is emerging (see, for instance, Sellers 2002a). The theory offers a fruitful starting point for analysing Canadian cases, given the many institutional and cultural similarities between Canadian and American cities. Canada and the United States are both federations, and their local governments are the exclusive constitutional responsibility of the provinces and states respectively. Furthermore, as in other British settler countries, local governments in Canada and the United States rely heavily on property taxes, though American municipalities are less dependent on this form of taxation than Canadian ones (Courchene 2007, 16). Thus the two countries share similar fiscal constraints. Canadian scholar Christopher Leo (1997) acknowledges the potential fruitfulness of the urban regime concept for the study of Canadian urban politics. However, with other urban scholars in the academic community outside Canada, he stresses that urban regime analyses must be placed in a global context as well as an intergovernmental one.[7]

According to DiGaetano and Strom (2003), in the United States the increase in 'corporatist modes of urban governance' (a mode that has much in common with urban regimes) 'reflects the dual conditions of federal withdrawal and an increasingly competitive urban economy' (2003, 370). These two conditions are common to the Canadian case. Upper levels of government have withdrawn from many policy areas, with important repercussions for cities. Furthermore, in the context of globalization, Canadian cities face more intense urban economic competition. Indeed, because they are on the same continent as American cities, and are part of a common free-trade regime through the North American Free Trade Agreement, Canadian cities can be viewed as the most direct competitors of highly competitive American cities.

The Research Design: Controlling Variables through Case Selection

Choice of Case Study Cities

This study compares eight highly diverse municipalities in Canada's two most significant immigrant-receiving city-regions in English-speaking Canada: the cities of Toronto, Mississauga, and Brampton and the Town of Markham in the Greater Toronto Area (GTA); and the cities of Vancouver, Richmond, Surrey, and Coquitlam in Greater Vancouver.

With a population of almost 5.1 million, the Toronto CMA is Canada's largest city-region. The City of Toronto is Canada's financial centre as well as its largest city, with a population of roughly 2.5 million. Mississauga is Canada's fifth most populous municipality and its most populous suburb, with more than 665,000 residents according to the 2006 Census. Markham and Brampton have populations of about 262,000 and 432,000 respectively. Markham is distinctive in that over 65 per cent of its people are visible minorities (Statistics Canada 2007b).

In the 1990s, Greater Vancouver received a disproportionate share of Canada's business immigrants. Furthermore, the GTA receives a diverse range of immigrants from around the world, whereas immigration to Greater Vancouver is primarily from Asian countries on the Pacific Rim. For this reason, Vancouver is often referred to as Canada's 'Pacific Rim Metropolis.' Richmond is the city-region's most non-White municipality: 65 per cent of its population falls into the 'visible minority' category (ibid.). Surrey is Greater Vancouver's largest suburban municipality, covering 317.4 square kilometres. Its population growth is expected to outpace that of all other municipalities in Greater Vancouver. Coquitlam is a relatively small municipality of just over 110,000 people. All of the municipalities in the sample are among their CMA's most numerically significant immigrant-receiving locales.

The research discussed here is the product of a series of embedded 'most similar systems' research designs, employing what Arend Lijphart (1975) refers to as the 'comparable-cases strategy in comparative research' (1975, 159). The strategy involves selecting highly similar cases that vary in terms of the political behaviour or policy output or outcome under investigation. Before the primary research was undertaken, to select the cases, an initial assessment of the variations among cases was made with the help of the limited secondary literature (Tate and Quesnel 1995; Wallace and Frisken 2000; Edgington et al. 2001; Edgington and Hutton 2002) as well as through website analysis. Then the categorization was refined and a typology of municipal responsiveness to immigrants and ethnocultural minorities was developed through more than one hundred key-informant interviews. The logic of all this is that if the researcher matches cases tightly, then the variations in the dependent variable (in this case, municipal responsiveness to immigrants and ethnocultural minorities) can be explained in terms of the remaining differences among cases.

In comparative politics, researchers often use 'most similar systems designs' to compare nation-states. Because the cases in this book are all located in Canada, they share many institutional and contextual features. It is worth making explicit some of these important similarities. Most fundamentally, all of the municipalities discussed here have limited formal autonomy. They lack independent constitutional status; under Section 92(8) of the Canadian Constitution, they are 'creatures' of their respective provinces. This means that their legal status is based in provincial legislation and that their responsibilities are delegated to them. In addition, all Canadian municipalities are highly fiscally constrained, relying mainly on provincial grants, property taxes, and user fees for their revenue (Slack 2005).

Furthermore, all cases in this sample share a national policy context that includes an official commitment to multiculturalism. Yet neither in Ontario nor in B.C. has the provincial government delegated to municipalities a formal role in crafting multiculturalism policies such as those touching on immigrant integration, employment equity, and anti-racism.

The number of immigrants and visible minorities in the population

Table 2.3
Profile of diversity at different scales

	Population		Foreign-born (%)		Visible minority (%)	
	2001	2006	2001	2006	2001	2006
Canada	29,639,030	31,241,030	18.0	19.8	13.0	16.2
Ontario	11,285,545	12,028,895	26.8	28.3	19.1	22.8
Toronto CMA	4,682,647	5,072,075	43.4	45.7	36.6	42.9
Toronto	2,456,805	2,476,565	49.4	50.0	42.8	46.9
Mississauga	610,815	665,655	46.8	51.6	40.3	49.0
Brampton	324,390	431,575	40.0	47.8	40.2	57.0
Markham	207,940	261,573	52.9	56.5	55.5	65.4
British Columbia	3,868,875	4,074,385	26.1	27.3	21.6	24.8
Vancouver CMA	1,986,965	2,097,965	38.7	39.6	36.5	41.7
Vancouver	539,625	571,600	45.9	45.6	49.0	51.0
Richmond	163,395	173,565	54.0	57.4	59.0	65.0
Surrey	345,780	392,450	33.2	38.3	37.0	46.1
Coquitlam	111,425	113,560	37.1	39.4	34.3	38.6

Source: Data compiled from the 2001 and 2006 Censuses (see Statistics Canada 2002, 2007b).

are well-documented factors in explanations of municipal responsiveness to immigration in Canada (Tate and Quesnel 1995; Wallace and Frisken 2000; Edgington et al. 2001; Edgington and Hutton 2002). A high level of those two population groups can be viewed as a necessary condition of municipal responsiveness to immigration, though not in itself sufficient.[8] Thus, in order to uncover the sufficient conditions for municipal responsiveness to changing ethnic demographics, this 'necessary' factor is held constant in all cases. Table 2.3 indicates the diversity of the eight municipalities in the sample.

Cases were also selected to explore how patterns of ethnocultural diversity affect the local politics of multiculturalism. All of the cases in the sample have characteristics that are very similar to those of what Rodney Hero calls 'bifurcated' political units. Cases with different configurations and concentrations of Canada's largest visible-minority populations were selected to explore the possible effects of differences in ethnospecific social capital. The cases are characterized by a diversity of visible-minority groups (Toronto, Mississauga, and Brampton in 2001), as well as by municipalities in which a single visible-minority group was numerically dominant (Vancouver, Richmond, Surrey, Coquitlam, Markham, and Brampton in 2006).

The book labels municipalities with a concentration of a single visible-minority group 'biracial' and those with a diverse visible-minority population 'multiracial.' Furthermore, drawing on Marion Orr's work on ethnospecific 'social capital,' municipalities with concentrations of either Chinese (Vancouver and Richmond) or 'South Asian' (Surrey and Brampton in 2006) visible-minority populations were chosen to explore the possible influence of ethnospecific social capital on municipal responsiveness.

This study's research design allows one to probe the influence of the intergovernmental context on the development of urban regimes and other local-governance arrangements from different vantage points. In light of the orthodoxy of the Canadian politics literature concerning the importance of provincial influence on municipal politics and policy making (Magnusson 2005), this research project is designed to test the extent to which municipalities are indeed beholden to their creators. This involves intraprovincial municipal comparisons. The intraregional comparisons provide another lens through which to examine provincial influence on local politics and policy making. They enable one to ask whether the differences are greater within or between to two city-regions. Moreover, the design allows one to explore the extent to which each region has cooperated to meet the challenges of immigration – specifically, whether the regional institutions of Metro Vancouver have facilitated intermunicipal partnerships relative to the GTA, which has no formal multijurisdictional mechanisms for regional cooperation. This book considers the effects of regional institutions in the Greater Vancouver–GTA comparison in light of the fact that urban scholarship has uncovered regional regimes in urban areas (Leo 1998; Clarke 1999).

Designing a project in which, with each comparison, all factors but one are common to the cases and in which the variation in that single factor (the independent variable) can be linked to variation in the dependent variable (in this case the level of responsiveness to increasing ethnic diversity) would be ideal. The inability of 'most similar systems designs' to do this has led Adam Przeworski and Henry Teune (1970, 34) to criticize them for not sufficiently falsifying rival hypotheses.

Such controls are possible through the manipulation of statistics in large data sets; but in the real world of politics and policy making, experimental controls are impossible. In Canada we simply do not have statistically significant data sets on local multiculturalism policies or on other factors that might permit us to test some of the hypotheses set forth in this chapter. Given the complexity of the social world, comparative research designs must be assessed according to what researchers can feasibly achieve by manipulating actual cases. Furthermore, those designs should be judged in relation to what they can offer in terms of theory building that large statistical analyses cannot. Benefits of such designs may include a more textured account of causal mechanisms, of the intersections of causal factors, and of dependent variables. Relative to many other 'most similar systems designs' – most of which are based on country-level comparisons – the one used in this study better controls for and isolates the possible causal effects of the independent variables because it compares subunits (municipalities) within a single country. A scientifically sound comparative design is one that can be held to reasonable standards, that controls for obvious and established rival explanations (here, the number of immigrants and ethnocultural minorities in the population), and that allows one to 'test' the relative causal influence of variables identified in established theory (here, urban regime theory, the social diversity perspective, and the intergovernmental context); it is also one that has the potential to generate rival explanations, to point to modifications in the theory, and to integrate theoretical approaches.

This study aims to balance the methodological values of a case-study–based 'regime analysis' with an attempt to build theory through the comparative method. According to Stone (1989), he based his original regime analysis on the historical method, which 'proceeds by analyzing the conjunction of factors, not by isolating single variables' (1989, 257). Therefore, because it examined more than one causal factor, Stone's method failed to meet Przeworski and Teune's (1970) standard. Stone describes the case-study method as a sort of longitudinal 'most similar systems' design whereby 'a historical sequence holds *some* set of factors constant, but it also allows for *others* (including the intentions of purposive actors) to change'; his argument is that 'the examination of a sequential process is a rough counterpart to laboratory control' (1989, 257; emphasis added). In this way, causality can be probed across both time and space. To the extent possible in a study of multiple cases, the present analysis offers the details and nuances of each case and highlights how factors seem to conjoin in causally relevant ways. Nevertheless, it relies not only on sequences of events, but also on examinations of differences among similar cases. In this way, it attempts to balance generalizability with parsimony and descriptive accuracy. This book's theoretical goal is not to offer a straightforward rejection or confirmation of a single hypothesis. Rather, it is to *develop a theory* of what causes municipal responsiveness to immigrants and ethnocultural minorities in Canada by drawing from the theory-building efforts of past scholars. As part of this process, it contributes to the development of the concepts and typologies that are necessary to building and refining such a theory through time.

Thus, readers who hope to see a clear-cut test of a hypothesis may be disappointed. Furthermore, scholars who prefer case studies may be disappointed with the level of detail offered for each case. But the author hopes that on reading this book, the reader will agree that steering a middle ground by employing the comparative method has established a solid foundation on which to build theory in a new empirical terrain.

Theoretical Beginnings: An Integrative Summary

What explains the variation in municipal responsiveness to immigrants and ethnocultural minorities in Canada's most significant immigrant-receiving city-regions in English-speaking Canada? How does the policy capacity to meet the challenges of large-scale immigration develop at the local level, where resources are so constrained and legislation is so constraining? Urban regime theory provides a possible answer to these questions: perhaps urban coalitions drive policy outputs in multiculturalism policy. The social diversity perspective further suggests that local context – specifically, the ethnoracial configuration of the municipality – matters as well.

On completing their review of the literature on urban regime theory, Karen Mossberger and Gerry Stoker summarized the core elements of regime theory in this way: '[1.] partners drawn from government and nongovernmental sources, requiring but not limited to business participation; [2.] collaboration based on social production – the need to bring together resources for the power to accomplish tasks; [3.] identifiable policy agendas that can be related to the composition of the participants in the coalition; [4.] a longstanding pattern of cooperation rather than a temporary coalition' (Mossberger and Stoker, 2001, 829).

Urban regime theory would lead one to expect that *how* municipalities respond to immigrants and ethnocultural minorities reflects the nature of each municipality's 'governing coalition' or 'regime.'

In their review of the largely case-study–based literature, Mossberger and Stoker also identify factors that seem to be associated with urban regime change. These factors include demographic shifts, economic restructuring, federal grant policies, and political mobilization (Mossberger and Stoker 2001, 811). This book examines the influence of these factors on the emergence of and changes to governance arrangements using an urban regime lens. Chapters 4 and 5 deconstruct urban regime theory by examining several factors related to the development of urban regimes and then filtering the findings through an urban regime analysis. Chapter 6 explores how demographic shifts have structured the politics of immigration and urban regime development in highly diverse cities. Chapter 7 explores how economic restructuring and federal grant policies (which, some argue, are rooted in global processes of 'rescaling') have led to changing patterns of political mobilization in ways that affect the municipal role in multiculturalism policy and initiatives. More broadly, it probes the intergovernmental context as a structural factor that shapes the development of local multiculturalism initiatives.

The next chapter begins the empirical journey through the politics of multiculturalism at the local level, asking how municipalities vary in their efforts to manage diversity and accommodate immigrants and ethnocultural minorities. Are patterns evident in municipal policy outputs and, if so, how might we characterize them? We will now turn to these questions and to the task of developing a typology of municipalities' role in official multiculturalism.

3 A Comparative Overview of Municipal Multiculturalism Policies

The Canadian municipalities in this study are at the forefront of social change and, as such, have become important innovators in multiculturalism policy development. Scholars rarely study policy making in local service areas such as planning, policing, recreation, and public-library services. Yet municipal governance and services play an important role both in the initial immigrant settlement process and in achieving the ongoing goals of Canada's official multiculturalism.

For instance, public libraries are among the first places new immigrants go to find information about their new community and to research employment opportunities (Buss 2004, interview; Harrison 2004, interview). Furthermore, as the democratic governments that are closest to newcomers (and to citizens generally), municipalities have a role to play in engaging them in community decision making and in the formal democratic process.

How are Canadian municipalities responding to immigration and to the ethnocultural diversity it creates? How do municipalities differ in their responsiveness to immigrants and to ethnocultural diversity? What does institutional 'responsiveness' mean in an ethnoculturally diverse context?

This chapter specifies what 'municipal responsiveness' means and introduces a typology of municipal responses to immigrants and ethnocultural diversity. However, the bulk of the chapter describes a range of municipal innovations in multiculturalism policy, clearly showing that municipalities play a crucial role in diversity management in Canada.

Official Multiculturalism as Institutional Responsiveness to Diversity

The term 'responsiveness' evokes notions of democracy and effectiveness in public administration when it comes to meeting citizens' and residents' needs and responding to challenges. The word is used to characterize many different aspects of institutional performance, including timeliness, creativity, innovation, and comprehensiveness in institutional responses.[1] And, as Canada's model of official multiculturalism implies, evaluations of institutional responsiveness must also assess the extent to which policy processes include immigrants and ethnocultural minorities.

In this study, municipal responsiveness to immigrants and ethnocultural minorities refers to *whether municipalities have adapted their services and governance structures to facilitate immigrant and ethnocultural-minority access to and participation in local governance.* In other words, the term refers to whether municipal policies and policy-making processes are consistent with Canada's policy of official multiculturalism.

What is 'official multiculturalism'? In Canada, it is a normative model that implies a positive role for the state in addressing barriers to ethnocultural-minority access to common political, social, and economic institutions. This model informs many public-policy initiatives at the federal, provincial, and municipal levels. These policies include, for instance, a variety of multiculturalism, immigrant settlement, and employment equity policies and initiatives.

The particular policies and initiatives associated with official multiculturalism have changed over time. Audrey Kobayashi has identified *demographic, symbolic,* and *structural* eras in the evolution of Canada's model of official multiculturalism (Kobayashi 1993, in Ley 2007, 10–11). Similarly, a Library of Parliament report describes Canada's commitment to official multiculturalism as comprising several stages: the 'Incipient Stage' (before 1971), the 'Formative Period' (1971–81), and the period of 'Institutionalization' (1982 to the present). In the current stage, 'multiculturalism serves as a positive instrument of change aimed at the removal of barriers that preclude the involvement, equity, access, and representation of all citizens in Canada's institutions' (Dewing and Leman 2006, 7). The authors of Parliament's report on official multiculturalism summarize the transition from symbolic to structural multiculturalism nicely: 'Where[as] early multicultural policies concentrated on cultural preservation and intercultural sharing through promotion of ethnic presses and festivals, the rejuvenated multiculturalism program emphasized cross-cultural understanding and the attainment of social and economic integration through removal of discriminating barriers, institutional change, and affirmative action to equalize opportunity' (ibid.). Since the entrenchment of the Charter of Rights and Freedoms in the Constitution, the courts have played an ongoing role in enforcing official multiculturalism by interpreting the Charter in a 'manner consistent with the preservation and enhancement of the multicultural heritage of Canadians' (Section 27) and by applying Section 15(1) of the Charter, which guarantees equal 'protection' and 'benefit' of the law 'without discrimination, and, in particular, without discrimination based on race, national or ethnic origin, colour, religion, sex, age, or mental or physical disability.'

Official multiculturalism is institutionalized and administered in a variety of ways that have changed over time in response to new challenges as well as to changes in politics and citizens' expectations. Federal programs with explicit multiculturalism-related purposes continue to be administered by a variety of government agencies. For instance, since the federal government adopted its policy of 'official multiculturalism,' its multiculturalism program has been moved several times (See Dewing and Leman 2006, 4–8; see also Abu-Laban and Gabriel 2002, ch. 4). From 1991 to 1993 the program was administered by a separate department called Multiculturalism and Citizenship. It was then moved to Canadian Heritage (ibid.), where it remained until the time of the interviews. A list of program guidelines produced by Canadian Heritage in 2003 indicates that the multiculturalism program has the following four objectives: to increase ethnoracial minority participation in public decision making; to combat racism; to eliminate systemic barriers to equitable access to public institutions; and to ensure that federal policies, programs, and services are responsive to ethnoracial diversity (Government of Canada 2003, 1). The federal government's immigrant settlement initiatives have also been informed by the norms of 'official multiculturalism' – norms that legitimize public support for immigrant integration and ethnoracial equity. At the time of the interviews, settlement programs were administered by a different department – Citizenship and Immigration Canada.[2] This administrative (and political accountability) structure led the federal government to distinguish between 'immigrant settlement' and 'multiculturalism' policies and programs. The former were designed to facilitate the initial settlement process (usually the first three years an immigrant spends in

Canada), whereas the latter were ongoing, long-term commitments to integrating all ethnocultural groups fairly into social, economic, and public institutions. This led many policy makers to speak of the policies separately, in terms of department silos. In high-immigration cities, local policy makers do not always make these types of distinctions as the connection between multiculturalism and immigration is clear on the ground. The common goals of multiculturalism and settlement programs are evident in the Conservative government's decision to move the multiculturalism program from Canadian Heritage to Citizenship and Immigration Canada in 2008.

The policy landscape is further complicated by the role provincial governments play in multiculturalism policy making (including what are referred to as 'multiculturalism programs' at the federal level and immigrant settlement). Furthermore, increased responsibility for immigrant settlement has been devolved to some provinces (including British Columbia) through immigration agreements in recent years.

In their cross-national study of whether multiculturalism policies erode support for welfare states, Keith Banting, Richard Johnston, and colleagues (2006) have observed: 'Unfortunately, there is no consensus in the literature on how to define the term "multicultural policies" ... The term has quite different connotations in different countries' (2006, 51). Contributing to this ambiguity, the policies and programs associated with Canada's official multiculturalism are constantly adapting to new social realities. Yet despite the dynamic nature of multiculturalism policies, they share a common normative core. For this reason, it is not surprising that Joseph Garcea (2006, 5) has found 'remarkable similarity' in *provincial* multiculturalism and interculturalism policies, which tend to be modelled on federal multiculturalism policy frameworks such as the 1971 policy and the 1988 Canadian Multiculturalism Act. In his survey he found that provincial multiculturalism policies focus on four primary goals: 'fostering awareness and appreciation regarding the multicultural ... nature of the province'; 'fostering cross-cultural understanding and social harmony within the province'; 'fostering participation by members of ethno-cultural groups in the economic, social, cultural, and political life of the province'; and 'fostering preservation, promotion, and sharing of cultural heritages' (ibid., 6). These goals are embedded in the federal policy infrastructure that has developed since 1971, the year that 'official multiculturalism' became government policy.

In this book a 'multiculturalism policy' includes any policy, initiative, or practice that addresses ethnocultural barriers to equitable access to social, economic, and political institutions. When such a policy is adopted by a municipal corporation, it constitutes a 'municipal multiculturalism policy.'

Note also that most immigrants to Canada are 'ethnocultural/ racial minorities.' As a consequence, multiculturalism policies and programs, which are designed to adapt institutions and governance processes to accommodate ethnocultural diversity, help manage the effects of immigration on cities. They amount to long-term immigrant-settlement policies. Some local leaders tend to adopt a longer view of the immigrant settlement process and, for this reason, do not distinguish between 'settlement' and other diversity policies.

The cities discussed here have become highly multicultural in a relatively short time as a result of immigration. Thus local leaders tend to blur the distinctions between 'immigrant settlement' and 'multiculturalism' policies. They also have added to the vocabulary used to describe Canada's 'multiculturalism model' of citizenship. Local leaders describe their multiculturalism policy efforts in a variety of ways: as 'diversity management,' 'access and equity,' 'interculturalism,' 'race relations,' and so on. Similar differences in language exist across countries. For instance, Britain tends to refer to its multiculturalism policies as 'race relations policies' (Banting, Johnston, et al. 2006, 55). This book employs the term 'multiculturalism policy' to refer to any policy that is informed by the norms of Canada's official multiculturalism, regardless of the language local leaders use.

Even so, the words that local leaders use to describe their multiculturalism policies are significant. For instance, the term 'diversity management' reflects the influence of the private-sector management literature and other neoliberal ideas on policy discourse (Abu-Laban and Gabriel 2002, 153). Moreover, the choice of language serves to frame the municipal role in a particular way. For example, Richmond has deliberately rejected the term 'multiculturalism,' which is associated with division in that city, opting instead for 'interculturalism,' a concept that expresses residents' and local leaders' desire for cultural bridging.

In other cases the language used to frame multiculturalism is intended either to keep the issue off the agenda or to claim a greater role in managing ethnocultural diversity. Because authority over immigration is clearly held by upper levels of government, Mississauga stresses that 'immigration' and 'immigrant settlement' are the responsibility of those upper levels. Yet for its part, Toronto has developed an 'immigrant settlement' policy, hoping to expand its role in multiculturalism policy and to be treated as a partner in intergovernmental negotiations surrounding immigration policy.

This chapter evaluates the extent to which three broad elements of policy respond to the concerns and preferences of immigrants and ethnocultural minorities. Those elements are (1) formal policy pronouncements and initiatives, (2) policy implementation, and (3) informal policies or practices. It measures policy outputs and implementation rather than policy outcomes.[3] It uses the following indicators to measure the responsiveness of Canadian municipalities:

- Councils' multiculturalism initiatives.
- Corporate multiculturalism initiatives.
- Policy pronouncements of municipal departments and agencies.[4]
- Informal policies or practices in all arenas (council and civil service).
- The views of leaders in the immigrant settlement sector and of ethnocultural organizations as to how responsive municipalities are to their concerns.

Using these indicators, a typology of municipalities' multiculturalism policy efforts has been developed: 'responsive,' 'somewhat responsive,' 'unresponsive.' This typology is organized around two primary axes – the *comprehensiveness* of municipal efforts to promote ethnocultural equity, and the extent to which the challenges of integrating ethnocultural minorities equitably are addressed in a *proactive* manner.

Policy *comprehensiveness* refers to the breadth, range, and depth of policies in place. This follows Rufus P. Browning, Dale Rogers Marshall, and David H. Tabb's (1984) approach in their classic work on the 'political incorporation' of Blacks and Hispanics into city politics in ten cities in northern California, *Protest Is Not Enough*. Though they do not explicitly discuss the principles guiding their operationalization of policy 'responsiveness' to Blacks and Latinos, in their evaluation of responsiveness (they use the word 'responsive') they do refer to the 'breadth,' 'range,' and 'effectiveness' (ibid., 143, 151, 161) of policy responses. Whereas their formal responsibilities vary, most municipal governments are involved in land-use planning and offer recreation services, and some are involved in policing and public health. The question then becomes whether they consider ethnocultural-minority and immigrant needs and preferences in all of their activities or only in some (and, if only some, which ones). Thus evaluating *comprehen-*

siveness entails judging the extent to which individual departments in a municipality have been responsive to immigrants and ethnocultural minorities in their policy making. However, municipalities are not simply service providers: as democratic governments, they also play an important role in engaging their diverse populations in decision making as well as in making all residents feel welcome and included in the community. Municipalities have a range of policy options from which to choose when deciding how to accommodate immigrants and ethnocultural minorities.

Municipal multiculturalism policies tend to fall into the following *policy types:*[5]

1 Municipalities may establish *a separate unit of government to manage diversity and organizational change* in response to immigration and dramatic increases in the ethnocultural diversity of their populations. These units then serve as a catalyst for change across all municipal departments by coordinating their efforts and by engaging with the community.

2 Municipal governments may provide *grants* to community organizations, offer *in-kind support* to community organizations (such as space and staff support), and conduct *research* on community needs.

3 Municipalities may develop *employment equity* initiatives to address systemic barriers to immigrant and ethnocultural-minority access to employment. The scope of these policies can vary. Municipalities may address these barriers within their own organization, and they may also take steps to encourage the fair integration of immigrants and ethnocultural minorities into the private sector.

4 Municipalities may develop an *immigrant settlement policy* that explicitly acknowledges their own role in managing immigration through their multiculturalism policy initiatives.

5 Municipalities may increase their *political inclusiveness* by establishing mechanisms whereby immigrant and ethnocultural-minority preferences enter council deliberations on policy matters. This may involve creating advisory committees that deal with immigrant and ethnocultural concerns specifically, offering interpretation services for citizens who wish to make deputations to council, or translating information on municipal elections.

6 Municipalities may make efforts to increase *access and equity in service delivery* through translation and interpretation, culturally sensitive services, or a communications strategy.

7 Municipalities may develop *anti-racism initiatives*, including efforts to improve intercultural relations, combat racism, and eliminate hate activities.

8 Municipalities may create an inclusive *municipal image* by establishing inclusive symbols and using inclusive language in key municipal documents.

9 Municipalities may support *multicultural festivals* and events.

Comprehensiveness also refers to the 'depth' of municipal responses to immigrants and ethnocultural diversity. Policy depth refers to the degree of institutionalization or organizational penetration, not only of formal policy initiatives but also of informal practices. In other words, policy depth refers to whether policies are well implemented.

In sum, a municipality that responds in a *comprehensive* way adopts a range of policies across its departments and agencies and implements them effectively. Such a municipality tries to engage ethnocultural minorities and immigrants in the political process and to create a welcoming environment. A municipality's comprehensiveness with respect to multiculturalism initiatives can be conceptualized along this continuum: *comprehensive*, to *limited*, to *highly limited*. This continuum is similar to how Browning, Marshall, and Tabb measured variations in the policy responsiveness of ten northern Californian cities in their seminal study: 'At its strongest the governmental response to minority interests extended across many programs and agencies of city government and permeated routine decision-making and service delivery. At its weakest, the response was sporadic, half-hearted, undertaken only under duress, and limited to verbal assurances and an occasional, isolated action. Across a wide range of issues and routine actions that never became issues, the responsive governments were pervasively different' (ibid., 143).

Following the approach developed by Marcia Wallace and Frances Frisken (2000), the 'amount of initiative' that municipal officials show in putting policies in place is also assessed.[6] Along this axis, municipalities can be *proactive, reactive,* or *inactive* in their responses to immigrants and ethnocultural minorities. According to Wallace and Frisken, 'proactive' policy making 'involves institutionalized efforts to identify and address immigrant needs *before* problems arise, using research, the collection and mapping of demographic information, and consultation with community groups and city departments' (ibid., 6; emphasis add-

Table 3.1
Typology of municipal responsiveness to immigrants and ethnocultural minorities

	Responsive	Somewhat responsive	Unresponsive
Breadth and depth	Comprehensive	Limited .	Highly limited
Policy style	Proactive	Reactive	Inactive
Immigrant settlement leaders' assessment	Positive	Varies	Negative
Policy types	1-9	5-9	9

ed). 'Reactive' policy making, on the other hand, 'entails setting up a unit of city government (an advisory committee, a local ombudsman) to hear demands and complaints from the community and to pass these on to the relevant municipal departments.' 'Reactive' policy making is 'passive' rather than anticipatory. The third category – 'inactive' – refers to 'a failure or deliberate refusal to acknowledge that immigrant settlement is affecting either the character of the municipality or the service needs of the local population' (ibid.). These categories are, of course, 'ideal types.' In reality, municipalities may proactively initiate some programs and policies while responding to other challenges reactively. Even so, these categories are useful in terms of characterizing the *overall policy style* of municipalities in multiculturalism initiatives.

In this book's conceptualization, 'responsive' municipalities are *proactive* and *comprehensive* in their responses to immigrants and ethnocultural minorities; 'somewhat responsive' municipalities are generally *reactive*, and their responses are *limited* rather than *comprehensive*; 'unresponsive' municipalities are largely *inactive* in multiculturalism policy, and their responses to immigration and ethnocultural diversity are *highly limited*. 'Responsive,' 'somewhat responsive,' and 'unresponsive' municipalities also tend to adopt a set range of policies (the above list). To a large degree, the range of their policy choices reflects their policy styles and level of policy 'depth.' Table 3.1 summarizes the categories.

One might question whether other combinations of policy styles (on the one hand) and of breadth and depth (on the other) are possible. For instance, a municipality could be proactive in its policy style but still be relatively limited in its levels of responsiveness. Or it might be reactive in its policy style but relatively comprehensive in the breadth and depth of its responses. In practice, however, the policy styles and levels of breadth and depth in municipal responses fell into the three bundles summarized in this table. In order to be 'proactive' a municipality must create institutions to support its policy style, and this tends to result in a greater level of policy comprehensiveness. Similarly, a municipality with a reactive policy style might develop a breadth of policies for responding to immigrants and ethnocultural minorities, but policy depth would require some form of institutionalization, which, in turn, would lead to a more proactive policy style. Though these categories do not perfectly summarize all of the fine-grained ways in which municipalities vary in their responses, they represent a useful analytical tool with which to characterize variations in municipal responsiveness.

Thus, these distinctions and evaluative criteria were employed to assess the nature and scope of multicultural policy outputs and implementation. The evaluation is based on data collected from available secondary sources, municipalities' websites and those of their agencies, local-government policy documents, and key informant interviews with more than one hundred local leaders.[7] Interviewees included mayors, city councillors, civil servants, leaders in the immigrant settlement sector, and other community leaders. Interviews with immigrant-serving community leaders were especially important for assessing the extent to which the policies in question were responding to the most important needs of immigrants and ethnocultural minorities and were being effectively *implemented*.

What is considered a 'responsive' policy is arguably a subjective judgment. However, there is considerable consistency between the 'objective' assessment of the extent to which municipal responses are equitable and the views of community leaders. In particular, community leaders in the immigrant settlement sector and in other sectors representing ethnocultural minorities tend to view municipalities that adapt their services and governance structures to accommodate diversity in line with the normative framework of Canada's official multiculturalism as 'responsive' to their concerns.

An Overview of Municipal Multiculturalism Policies

The findings of this study support earlier research (Tate and Quesnel 1995; Wallace and Frisken 2000; Edgington and Hutton 2002; Good 2004) suggesting that the extent to which municipalities are responsive to immigration varies widely, even among cities with similarly high levels of ethnic diversity. Thus the City of Toronto and the City of Vancouver are 'responsive' to immigrants and ethnocultural minorities; both have adopted a *comprehensive* range of policies that reflect the needs and preferences of these groups, and they have done so in a *proactive* way. The cities of Coquitlam, Richmond, and Surrey and the Town of Markham have been 'somewhat responsive' to their changing ethnocultural demographics; their policy responses have been *limited* and for the most part have been adopted *reactively*. Mississauga and Brampton have been 'unresponsive' to the particular concerns of immigrants and ethnocultural minorities; for the most part they have been *inactive* in multiculturalism policy. These groups will now be discussed in turn.

'Responsive' Municipalities

City of Toronto

The responses of the City of Toronto to the needs and preferences of immigrants and ethnocultural minorities are comprehensive insofar as they are relatively consistent across municipal departments and agencies, and insofar as the city has adopted a broad range of policies to accommodate the diversity of its population. Furthermore, the city has often planned its policies and has institutionalized a commitment to multiculturalism policy goals in the municipal organization. The City of Toronto, which was formed through the largest amalgamation in Canada's history in 1998, has built on the strong foundation of diversity policies that was developed in the former Municipality of Metropolitan Toronto and the former City of Toronto. The former City of Toronto and Metro Toronto were active in multiculturalism policy as early as the mid-1970s (Wallace and Frisken 2000, 22, Table 8). This section describes some examples of the most significant policy responses in Toronto to illustrate its proactive style and relatively comprehensive approach to adapting its services and governance structures to diversity.

The city's responsiveness to diversity is reflected symbolically in its motto 'Diversity Our Strength.' Toronto adopted the motto when its new coat of arms was approved by council in October 1998. It selected the motto after distributing a questionnaire asking for suggestions from Torontonians, which elicited 1,100 responses. The City's Access, Equity and Human Rights Awards (such as the William P. Hubbard Award for Race Relations, awarded yearly to a person who has contributed to improving race relations in the city) recognize the importance of diversity to the city. Moreover, the City of Toronto makes proclamations recognizing important ethnocultural events such as Black History Month and Asian History Month. Essentially, the city views diversity and multiculturalism as essential to its image.

When the new City of Toronto was formed in 1998 it embarked on a comprehensive exercise to develop a plan of action for access and equity by establishing the Task Force on Access and Equity, chaired by Councillor Joe Mihevc. Toronto City Council approved this group's recommendations in the form of an action plan in December 1999. The city's access and equity initiatives flow from this plan. The planned nature of the city's response reflects its proactive policy style.

Toronto's commitment to access and equity is institutionalized in a special unit – the Diversity Management and Community Engagement Unit (DMU), which is part of the City Manager's Office. The DMU supports several diversity-related advisory committees and working groups of council; it also provides leadership in diversity policy to line departments and agencies. It also supports the implementation of formal policies and initiates action when unanticipated needs arise. One community leader mentioned that her best experience with the City of Toronto was when the DMU hosted educational events about anti-Muslim discourse in response to the backlash experienced by Toronto's Muslim community after 11 September 2001 (Jamal 2003, interview). The DMU is designed to be a 'catalyst' and 'facilitator' for the entire corporation and to link the council to both the civil service and the community (Lee 2003, interview).

Since January 1998 the city has adopted a number of 'core policies' to guide policy making and planning in the city. These include its Workplace Human Rights and Harassment Policy (November 1998), its Hate Activity Policy and Procedures (December 1998), its Employment Equity Policy (May 2000), and its Multilingual Services Policy (February 2002). The former Metro Toronto and City of Toronto both had employment equity policies. The current city gathers data on the characteristics of its employees to develop proactive strategies for employment equity. The city has made significant progress towards the goal of providing multilingual services. Access Toronto, a public information service, offers information on city services in more than 140 languages, using interpreters provided by Language Line Services. Language Line Services is an interpretation and document-translation service based in Monterey, California, which provides over-the-phone service in 150 languages twenty-four hours a day, seven days a week without an appointment.

Unlike the other cities in the sample, the City of Toronto has institutionalized a monitoring process for all of these policies through its Human Rights Office. This office is located in the city's Human Resources Department and handles complaints about harassment, employment discrimination, hate-related activities, and lack of equity in employment practices and in accessing city services. The city has also made efforts to monitor the implementation of its diversity policies. For instance, in 2004 the city conducted a 'social audit' of its departments to assess the extent to which the recommendations of the Task Force on Access and Equity had been implemented (City of Toronto 2004).

The city includes ethnocultural minorities in political decision making through five access and equity policy advisory committees. One of these is the Race and Ethnic Relations Advisory Committee. All five consult formally with ethnocultural minorities on city issues. Advisory committees are composed of members of the community and at least one elected member of council (Siemiatycki et al. 2003, 448). On their own, such committees would usually reflect a reactive policy style. However, in Toronto, because other institutional supports (such as the DMU) are in place, the advisory committees represent a mechanism of community engagement that contributes to the city's ability to assess community needs and to plan for future challenges.

There is some debate in the literature and in the community regarding how appropriate and effective such committees are. For instance, Carol Tator argues that citizen advisory committees are based on an out-of-date conception of ethnic relations (Tator 1998, in Siemiatycki et al. 2003, 449). In Toronto, community leaders question whether it is more effective to have separate structures to address immigrant and ethnocultural-minority issues or to have these issues dealt with in a more integrated way. Debbie Douglas, the Executive Director of the Ontario Council of Agencies Serving Immigrants (OCASI) – the umbrella organization for Ontario's immigrant settlement agencies – recalled that when the city set up the Race and Ethnic Relations Advisory Committee in 1999, she opposed it because it suggested that the city was dealing with various diversity-related concerns through separate silos. However, she has since changed her mind, recognizing that when an integrated approach is adopted, race issues are lost (Douglas 2003, interview). Political leaders in unresponsive municipalities tend to make the argument that such committees are ineffective and unnecessary and that they sometimes create more problems than they solve. Despite the shortcomings of such committees, their value should be assessed in relation to feasible alternatives for addressing representational gaps on council, not according to unrealistic ideals.

The task force's recommendations also led to the establishment of two working groups: the Immigration and Refugee Issues Working Group and the Language Equity and Literacy Working Group. Citizens participate in these working groups, which are chaired by city councillors. Like advisory committees, working groups are a mechanism for engaging the community in the development of policy strategies. Toronto's first Immigration and Refugee Issues Working Group was chaired by Toronto's current mayor, David Miller, when he was a councillor. Councillor Janet Davis is the current chair. This committee was cited by a community leader who works with immigrants as an example of the progressiveness of the city with respect to addressing immigrants' concerns (Dunn 2003, interview).

The activities of the Immigration and Refugee Issues Working Group seem to have contributed to tangible policy change. In 2001, Toronto City Council adopted an Immigration and Settlement Policy Framework, which builds on all of the city's access and equity policy initiatives. Until recently, when Vancouver decided to emulate Toronto's initiative in this area, the City of Toronto was (according to this author's knowledge) the only city in Canada to have developed a policy that explicitly acknowledged its role in immigration and immigrant settlement policies. The policy has two primary and related goals: to 'attract newcomers,' and to 'provide supports to enable them to develop a sense of identity and belonging and fully participate in the social, economic, cultural and political life in the City' (City of Toronto 2001, 9). These goals reflect the city's proactive policy stance and the extent to which it values the contributions that immigrants make to the city. The city receives more immigrants than any other in Canada and is taking steps to ensure that it continues to attract them by creating an inclusive, welcoming environment. The policy framework has established the following priorities:

• To help immigrants integrate into the economy.
• To increase Toronto's role in intergovernmental discussions and decision making in immigration and settlement policy.
• To provide services that are accessible and equitable.

- To ensure that policies and programs are coherent and well coordinated across departments and intergovernmentally.
- To advocate on behalf of immigrants and educate the public.
- To build community capacity and civic participation. (City of Toronto 2001)

The policy was developed after extensive public consultations. The first two priorities represent a new direction for the city. The city has made some progress in implementing these policy goals by establishing, for instance, an immigrant mentorship pilot project. This project addresses what many community leaders have cited as the most significant barrier to immigrant integration – the recognition of foreign credentials and the requirement for Canadian experience in the job market. According to Rose Lee, Policy Coordinator with the city's DMU, 70 per cent of the twenty-nine participants in this project were employed in their fields by the time they completed the program (Lee 2005, e-mail correspondence). The city is also implementing its policy objectives by participating in the Toronto Region Immigrant Employment Council (TRIEC), a broad-based, intersectoral, multilevel coalition of prominent community leaders that has formed to address barriers to employment faced by immigrants. Finally, the city is advocating for new political, fiscal, and legislative relationships – or what has popularly been called a 'New Deal' – with upper levels of government in the fields of immigration and settlement.

In December 2000, under former Toronto mayor Mel Lastman (1998–2003), the City of Toronto created the position of Diversity Advocate on council. This person was to 'act as the City's primary spokesperson and advocate on diversity issues ... co-ordinate diversity-related activities with the Council representatives involved with each of the community advisory committees ... work with other institutions, community organizations, the private sector and the non-profit community to promote diversity principles and equity ... inform City Council on a regular basis on diversity issues and assist in organizing the chief administrative officer's annual report on diversity issues' (City of Toronto, 'Diversity Advocate'). However, according to Councillor Joe Mihevc, the Diversity Advocate can be effective only if a councillor with the ability to lead on these issues is appointed to the role. Lastman appointed Sherene Shaw, representative of the highly ethnoculturally diverse Ward 39, Scarborough-Agincourt, as Toronto's first Diversity Advocate; according to Mihevc, this choice was deliberately intended to limit progress on access and equity policy objectives (Mihevc 2003, interview). Sherene Shaw lost her seat in the 2003 municipal election. The position of Diversity Advocate remained vacant for some time until council appointed Mihevc to the position.[8]

The City of Toronto also conducts research on community needs to inform its policy making. For instance, in 2000 the city commissioned Professor Michael Ornstein of the Institute for Social Research at York University to study ethnoracial inequality in Toronto. The Ornstein Report (2000) was the first-ever study of its kind to be conducted at the municipal level in Canada. It revealed that recent newcomers to Toronto were taking ten years longer than previous immigrants to reach income parity with Canadian-born residents and that poverty in Toronto had been 'racialized.' For instance, Ornstein found that while 14 per cent of European-origin families were living below the low-income cut-off (LICO),[9] the figure was 35 per cent for South Asians, 45 per cent for Africans, Blacks, and Caribbeans, and 45 per cent for those of Arab and West Asian origin. Also, the poverty rate of non-European groups was twice that of European groups. African-born Toronto residents were the most disadvantaged; for instance, 87 per cent of Ghanaians were living below the poverty line (City of Toronto 2001). In response to this report, the city held community consultations, which resulted in the development of the Plan of Action for the Elimination of Racism and Discrimination in 2002. At the time of the interviews, the City of Toronto was having the findings of the Ornstein Report updated based on 2001 Census data. Ornstein has since produced an updated report (Ornstein 2006). However, it is unclear whether the city actually commissioned the update, since the new report is not available on the city's website and the report itself does not indicate that the research was commissioned by the city.

Several community leaders remarked during interviews that despite the stark findings of the Ornstein Report, the city initially shelved the findings (Casipullai 2003, interview; Shakir 2003, interview; Melles 2004, interview). Only after being pressured by community organizations did the city initiate community consultations that resulted in its Plan of Action for the Elimination of Racism and Discrimination (2002).

This plan reiterated the city's commitment to implementing the ninety-seven recommendations of the Task Force on Access and Equity. Initiatives included the following: promoting employment equity; publishing an annual diversity report card; developing indicators to monitor the socio-economic status of groups; identifying and addressing barriers to equitable participation in municipal elections; and advocating with upper levels of government to improve Toronto's social infrastructure. During interviews, several people pointed out that the plan to eliminate racism was vague (Douglas 2003, interview) and had not resulted in any new expenditure of financial resources (Shakir 2003, interview). Some community members wondered why the city needed to consult community groups again when it already had ninety-seven recommendations it could have implemented. According to Uzma Shakir, a prominent community activist in the immigrant settlement sector in Toronto, the plan was also based on a misconceived notion of the nature of the policy 'problem' – that is, it contained no financial commitments because the city perceived racism as a *behavioural* rather than a *structural* issue (Shakir 2003, interview). As Shakir points out, had the city viewed racism as a question of power, the solution would have had to involve the equitable inclusion of 'racialized' communities in power structures, which would have required financial resources (ibid.).

Nevertheless, the City of Toronto does fund initiatives to fight racism in the city through its Access and Equity Grants Program. It should also be noted that after the interviews with these community leaders in 2003, funding for access and equity programs increased significantly in 2004. That year, the city's budget to support emerging immigrant communities increased from just over $400,000 to $773,800 (Lee 2005, e-mail correspondence).

The Access and Equity Grants Program builds on a long history of community capacity-building programs in anti-racism offered by the former Metropolitan Toronto – specifically, the Multicultural Grants Program (1981) and the Multicultural Access Fund (1988). Through its grants program, the city encourages equity in two ways. First, it provides targeted funding to groups that represent ethnocultural minorities. Second, it requires that services provided by *all* community-grant recipients (including mainstream agencies) be accessible to all Toronto residents.

The Access and Equity Grants Program fills an important gap in community capacity in that it supports advocacy, public education, and community development – activities that many community organizations cannot carry out because their status as charitable organizations restricts their ability to engage in advocacy. The program most clearly reflects the proactive policy style of the City of Toronto insofar as it is based on a long-term strategy of community capacity building in 'access and equity' and in anti-racism initiatives (Siemiatycki et al. 2003, 445).

Toronto's responsiveness to its immigrant population is also apparent in the policies, practices, discourse, and governance structures of the city's departments and agencies. Interviews with officials in several city departments and agencies – including Toronto Public Health, Toronto Public Libraries, and Economic Development, Culture, and Tourism – revealed high levels of commitment to access and equity principles. However, as the city's social audit report notes, the city does not currently have an adequate ongoing system for monitoring its departments (City of Toronto 2004). According to the social audit, the Chief Administrative Officer's Office (now the City Manager's Office) was developing an Access Action Plan Guide to provide direction to departments and agencies in access and equity planning. However, even in the absence of firm direction from the CAO's office, two city departments – Toronto Public Health and the Economic Development, Culture, and Tourism Department – proactively developed their own access and equity plans in response to the task force recommendations (City of Toronto 2004).

The language used by the City of Toronto reflects its policy style. For instance, when asked what it means for a municipality to be 'responsive' to immigrants, Rose Lee noted:

> Being responsive has a positive connotation. But on the other hand, I feel that the word can mean being reactive. ... To me the city should be proactive. That's why research and planning play such an important role in being responsive. You have to be proactive in order to be able to respond, I think. We have to know the demographics [and] we have to know the socio-economic indicators that point to us whether there has been any progress made by immigrants and refugees in settlement and integration in the city. We need to have the research data so that we can plan proactively, to know whether we should keep going in this direction or we should steer in another direction or we should modify the services we deliver to a diverse population. (Lee 2003, interview)

Initiatives such as the Task Force on Access and Equity and the Ornstein Report are examples of how the City of Toronto has proactively gathered information about and from the community to learn about community needs.

Toronto's relatively high level of receptiveness to the needs and preferences of immigrants and ethnocultural-minority communities is also evident in community leaders' expectations. In general, community leaders in Toronto acknowledged that the City of Toronto is more responsive than other municipalities in the GTA; but they also stressed that much more needs to be done. In some respects, they were more critical of the City of Toronto than leaders in other municipalities were of their own local governments. One of the most interesting findings is the extent to which leaders in the immigrant settlement sector and other community leaders believed that Toronto should play a greater role in immigrant settlement than it currently does and, in a more general way, that it should have more power (Chatterjee 2003, interview; Dunn 2003, interview; Shakir 2003, interview; McIsaac 2004, interview; Melles 2004, interview). As Sam Dunn of Access Alliance Multicultural Community Health Centre put it: 'There is a disjunct between the locus of immigration and the frameworks of responsibility' (Dunn 2003, interview).

The view maintained by community leaders that the city has an important role to play in access and equity policy and in immigration and settlement belies long-held conceptions of Canadian municipalities as administrative 'creatures of the provinces.' More tellingly, the community leaders representing immigrants and ethnocultural minorities would not support an increased municipal role in immigrant settlement and multiculturalism policy if the city were not responsive to their concerns.

City of Vancouver

Like Toronto, the City of Vancouver has developed a range of policies to accommodate ethnocultural diversity and provides institutional support to facilitate organizational change.

The city's most important multicultural initiatives are associated with its Social Planning Department and its Equal Employment Opportunity Program and Office. At the City of Vancouver, social planning 'has the specific role within the civic system to address community and social issues and particularly as they affect disadvantaged groups and individuals' (City of Vancouver, 'Multiculturalism and Diversity'). Given the demographic changes in the city, the department views its role as one of 'ensuring that multicultural and diversity issues remain a corporate priority and to provide support to Council, other departments and community organizations in addressing those issues' (ibid.). The department's mandate supports a proactive orientation towards policy development. For example, the department provides recommendations to council and other stakeholder groups regarding the development of inclusive policies and strategies; identifies emerging issues; 'liaises with diverse communities and organizations'; and 'recommends funding or seeks resources' to address emerging needs and critical issues (ibid.). At the municipal level, social planning departments are seen as departments that generate new policy activity and thus as departments or functions that political leaders who want to limit their policy activity must manage carefully. Vancouver's social planning department has a full-time staff position – 'Multicultural Social Planner' – devoted entirely to social planning issues arising from the city's multicultural nature. Community leaders such as Timothy Welsh, the Program Director of Affiliation of Multicultural Societies and Service Agencies (AMSSA), the umbrella organization that represents B.C.'s immigrant settlement sector, emphasized how important it is that Vancouver has entrenched a commitment to multiculturalism in its infrastructure by designating a full-time social planner as a 'multicultural planner' (Welsh 2004, interview). The extent to which the city's Multicultural Social Planner is involved in the community was evident in the fact that all of the community leaders involved in the multiculturalism policy field knew Baldwin Wong, the person who held the position at the time the interviews were conducted.

The process for developing the city's official plan (1993–95) – the document that sets the tone for the entire municipality – reflected the city's proactive approach to engaging immigrants and ethnocultural minorities. Vancouver's Cityplan was developed after extensive community consultations (about twenty thousand Vancouverites participated in the process). To encourage newcomers' participation in the process, the city launched several innovative initiatives; for example, it recruited community facilitators, communicated through ethnic media, and established a variety of 'storefront' information booths in the municipality (Edgington and Hutton 2002, 18). The city translated key planning documents into Chinese, Hindi, Punjabi, Vietnamese, Spanish, and French and made them available at information booths (ibid.); it also established a multilingual phone line on which residents could leave a message in one of five non-English languages (Cantonese, Punjabi, Vietnamese, Spanish, or French) so that a city staff person could return the call in that language. Ten years after the Cityplan process, leaders in the immigrant community interviewed for this study were still pointing to it as an example of the city's responsiveness to immigrants (Chan 2004, interview).

The City of Vancouver is a national leader in employment equity policy. In 1977 it developed an Equal Employment Opportunity Policy, which it updated in 1986. That same year the city established an Equal Employment Opportunity Program, supported by the Equal Employment Opportunity (EEO) Office, a separate unit with full-time staff reporting directly to the City Manager's Office. The city seems to approach employment equity in a holistic way; that is, it attempts to create the conditions for fundamental change in the corporate culture of the municipality instead of focusing solely on hiring practices. The EEO office administers extensive programs in diversity training to city staff (especially managers).

Building on the success of these programs, the city created the Hastings Institute in 1989. This is an arm's-length, not-for-profit corporation that provides diversity training to outside organizations – including other municipalities, provincial ministries, Crown corporations, not-for-profit organizations, unions, and the private sector – on a fee-for-service basis. The City of Vancouver owns the corporation. The mayor and four members of council sit on the institute's Board of Directors to ensure that its directions reflect the city's priorities. The prestige of this organization is evident in the fact that Vancouver's City Manager at the time of the interviews, Judy Rogers (1999–2008), is a former director of the Hastings Institute. The institute's training programs are constantly changing to reflect new needs within the community.

According to a city report, the Equal Employment Opportunity Policy 'was a major change in direction for the City, and was the initiative from which other diversity policies followed' (City of Vancouver n.d., 1). These policies include the city's Civic Policy on Multicultural Relations (1988), which encourages city staff to make city services accessible to residents for whom English is a second language (City of Vancouver, 'Multiculturalism and Diversity'). The city developed its Diversity Communications Strategy in 1995–6 to begin realizing these goals. The Social Planning Department's Multicultural Social Planner, the director of the Corporate Communications Department, and the director of the EEO office coordinated the process leading up to the strategy by assembling a group of interdepartmental staff and citizens to identify the city's diverse communication needs (Wong 2005, interview). The process resulted in the implementation of a multilingual information and referral phone service as well as an inventory of city staff with minority-language capabilities. The multilingual phone line used for Cityplan became a regular service after this process (Wong 2005, interview).

Since 1985 the City of Vancouver has been making an effort to incorporate the policy preferences of newcomers and ethnocultural minorities into council deliberations by establishing advisory committees on multiculturalism-related concerns. Its current committee, established in 2003, is called the Special Advisory Committee on Diversity Issues. This committee is meant to serve as a resource to both council and city staff by helping with the development of policies and programs and with community events, and by allowing diverse communities to express their policy preferences. A representative from the EEO Office sits on this committee, as does the city's Multicultural Social Planner.

The City of Vancouver's responsiveness to its newcomer communities is also apparent in its Community Services Grants Program, which provides funding to about one hundred not-for-profit organizations in Vancouver. The program is responsive to immigrants in several ways. In 2005 more than 25 per cent of the city's direct service grants (which represent three-quarters of its total budget for grants of approximately $3.4 million) went to organizations serving ethnocultural and immigrant communities (Wong 2005, interview). In addition, within a second stream of funding, the city provides core funding to 'neighbourhood houses,' mainly on the east side of Vancouver, where many high-needs immigrants live. As well, the city uses the grant-application process as a means to monitor the progress of 'mainstream' organizations towards increasing ethnocultural minorities' access to their services (Wong 2005, interview).

The activities of the City of Vancouver's departments and agencies reflect a corporate commitment to multiculturalism. A progress report conducted by the EEO Office in 1997 documents an impressive array of multiculturalism initiatives in city departments and agencies (City of Vancouver 1997). The City Clerk's Department initiatives are worth particular mention, given that department's importance to the political process. According to the report, the city hires election staff with non–English-language skills to reach out to Vancouver's diverse communities; translates election materials into five languages; sets up an election-information line that can be accessed in five languages; produces an election-information sheet in fifteen languages; and makes an effort to disseminate election information not only through mainstream media but also in ethnospecific publications and broadcast media (ibid., 14). The city offered these same services in the lead-up to the referendum on whether Vancouver's electoral system should be changed from an at-large system to a ward-based system (Wong 2005, interview).

In general, the immigrant-serving sector seems well aware of the city's most important multicultural initiatives. All the community leaders interviewed for this study agreed that Vancouver is by far the most active of the municipalities in the region in terms of multicultural policy (Chan 2004, interview; Welsh 2004, interview).

Community leaders in Vancouver tended to make a distinction that was not made as clearly in Toronto: the fact that the city is responding to cultural diversity but not to immigration and settlement issues (Chan 2004, interview; Cheng 2004, interview; Welsh 2004, interview). Baldwin Wong, the city's Multicultural Social Planner, confirmed this impression in a qualified way. According to him, the city has a role to play in the longer-term integration needs of immigrants and ethnocultural minorities rather than in their short-term settlement and adaptation needs, which are met by more senior levels of government (Wong 2005, interview).

'Somewhat Responsive' Municipalities

City of Richmond

Of the six 'suburban' or 'edge' cities in the sample, Richmond, B.C., is the most responsive to immigrants and to ethnocultural diversity. However, its responses are limited by the fact that it does not have a separate administrative unit or department to coordinate its efforts. Instead, advisory committees play a central role in managing the city's response to social change.

The history of advisory committees in Richmond indicates varying levels of political support for a city role in intercultural relations (Sherlock 2004, interview; Huhtala 2005, interview). It also highlights the city's reactive approach to multiculturalism policy. The city established its first intercultural committee, the Coordinating Committee on Ethnic Relations (CCER), in 1990 in response to a large influx of Chinese immigrants. The CCER's mandate focused on encouraging organizational change in Richmond's civil service. The result was two significant policy changes: a Multicultural Policy (1991) and a Framework for Action (1992) to implement multiculturalism policy objectives.

The Framework for Action (1992) resulted in 'cross-cultural training for city staff, the provision of translation and interpretation services for key civic functions and documents; [and] the development of an inventory of staff with language abilities in addition to English' (City of Richmond 2002, 3). Participating departments and agencies (including Richmond Library and Richmond Hospital) adopted multiculturalism policies and introduced new multiculturalism programs. At the committee's request, the city also began funding two prominent community agencies that provide settlement services in Richmond – the Richmond Multicultural Concerns Society and S.U.C.C.E.S.S., a prominent Chinese settlement organization (Sherlock 2005, personal correspondence).

The Advisory Committee on Intercultural Relations (formed in 1995) adjusted its mandate in order to focus on 'promoting harmonious intercultural relationships' (ibid., 3). A staff report from 1994 suggests that the shift in the committee's mandate was precipitated by a backlash from long-term residents of Richmond:

> One of the important concerns that has surfaced in the past few months is the 'backlash' from, primarily, non-ethnic or long-term ethnic residents who are objecting about the time and money being spent on helping new residents adjust to life in Richmond. This 'backlash' is expressed over concerns of signage and service in the new Asian malls, translation services, the 'Christmas tree on City Hall' issue, the growing number of Chinese newspapers and Chinese signage in older institutions (banks, stores, etc.) and the mega house discussions. This 'backlash' is being felt by most ethnic and ethnic-serving agencies, as well as our City government. (City of Richmond 1994a, 3)

So in 1995 the city redirected its efforts in multiculturalism policy. Its new project was to facilitate intercultural bridges between the Chinese community and the original residents. The committee's activities reflect its mandate of promoting positive intercultural relations. It has established Good Neighbour Month, launched a street-banner program celebrating multiculturalism, hosted discussions with developers of Asian-style malls regarding English signage and service, and set up displays about the Official Community Plan in Aberdeen Centre, Richmond's first Asian mall. Aberdeen Centre was developed as an alternative to Vancouver's Chinatown (Huhtala 2004).

The city established its current committee, the Richmond Intercultural Advisory Committee (RIAC), in 2002 at the request of Malcolm

Brodie, the mayor.[10] However, RIAC's true genesis lies in a heated community conflict over the location of a group home in a predominantly Chinese neighbourhood in Richmond (Townsend 2004, interview). Essentially, the city established the committee in response to an intercultural misunderstanding about the nature of group homes in Canada (Townsend 2004, interview). The city resisted taking action for more than eight months before it was forced to establish a Group Homes Task Force (Huhtala 2005, interview). That task force became a public-education exercise. Of the task force's budget of about $150,000, about $50,000 was spent on translation, interpretation, and other initiatives aimed at reaching out to newcomer communities. Specifically, the city provided interpretation services at task force meetings and at some council meetings and published materials on the issue in multiple languages (Townsend 2005, e-mail correspondence).

Though the city established the RIAC reactively, there is some evidence that it has resulted in proactive policy making. After extensive community consultations, the RIAC has developed an ambitious strategic plan. The directions therein include the following: addressing language barriers that inhibit community building; launching anti-racism initiatives; facilitating information sharing in culturally sensitive ways; facilitating immigrant involvement at all levels of government; ensuring that the city and community partners' policies and planning reflect the RIAC's intercultural vision; acting as advocate to other levels of government; developing partnerships; and supporting the development and integration of Richmond's immigrant youth population (RIAC 2004, 6). The strategic plan also includes suggestions for specific initiatives, such as establishing 'a media watch mechanism with partners to monitor local media, City and community communication and work to redress misperceptions created by inaccurate or insensitive references' (ibid., 7). The plan contains many innovative ideas for implementing its strategic directions.

However, the plan reflects the concerns of the largely White, English-speaking, long-standing residents as much as those of immigrants and ethnocultural minorities. For instance, it identifies non-English signage as a key issue (ibid., 2), and it calls for a 'City bylaw that would require all public stores and businesses to have some basic level of signage in English' (ibid., 7).

Richmond adopted the concept of 'interculturalism' as a normative framework for policy making because the term 'multiculturalism' had become associated with division in Richmond. The RIAC's strategic plan notes that multiculturalism has been used to refer to immigrants rather than – more broadly and inclusively – to the overall population, which has always included ethnocultural minorities. The RIAC's strategic plan describes the new concept of 'interculturalism' as 'a culturally interactive and vibrant process [and as] the next step for Canadian multiculturalism' (ibid., 4). The plan's vision statement appears to strike a balance between the need for integration and a respect for diversity (ibid.). Though implementation of the plan is still under way at the time of writing, the process of developing the plan has already had a lasting impact on the city. According to Scott Schroeder, former coordinator of West Richmond Community Centre and a member of the RIAC, the committee had an 'indirect' influence on government departments and agencies almost immediately by supporting a corporate philosophy of interculturalism. In his view, 'quick wins' – such as being able to implement programs and services without having to ask council for approval – are important to maintaining interest in advisory committees. He suggested that the RIAC's lengthy deliberations about its philosophy of interculturalism, which brought clarity to the goals of the city, facilitated these policy victories in the city's line departments and agencies (Schroeder 2004, interview).

Richmond has also developed a communications strategy in response to ethnocultural diversity. The strategy is informal rather than a planned policy. For instance, the city regularly advertises in Asian-language newspapers. Moreover, according to Ted Townsend, Manager of Communications and Corporate Programs, the city does not have a comprehensive multilingual communications plan; instead it translates city plans and communications on an ad hoc basis, 'as need is perceived and resources are available' (Townsend 2004, interview). This is consistent with Edgington and Hutton's (2002) description of Richmond's approach to translating council material. They describe it as 'sporadic rather than systematic' (2002, 21). In any given month the city produces a variety of publications, advertisements, and media releases in Chinese and occasionally in Punjabi (Townsend 2005, e-mail correspondence). The city has also experimented with 'language banks,' consisting of lists of staff with language skills in languages other than English. However, it has had to approach this initiative cautiously, because it requires some employees to take on tasks beyond their job descriptions, raising the issue of supplementary compensation (Townsend 2004, interview). Also, the city meets its multilingual communication objectives in partnership with community organizations such as S.U.C.C.E.S.S., which in return for the city's 'financial and other support for a number of [its] programs and initiatives ... provide[s] assistance to [the city] in communicating with [its] client base, translation and supporting civic initiatives such as the Richmond Substance Abuse Strategy that cross cultural lines' (Townsend 2005, e-mail correspondence).

The Media Watch program is contracted out to a firm called Chinese InforMedia Services at a cost of $15,000 to $20,000 a year (ibid.). The service, which reports to the city twice a month, monitors articles written in Chinese about Richmond in the three daily Chinese newspapers for accuracy and potential controversies or misunderstandings; it also helps gauge the effectiveness of Richmond's efforts to reach out to the Chinese community (Townsend 2004, interview).

The City of Richmond has been quite responsive at the level of its agencies and departments. For instance, Richmond Library has four full-time staff who can serve residents in Chinese languages and has an extensive Chinese-language collection. It also offers extensive ESL programming, including programs in Mandarin on the Internet, the public-education system, wills and estates, and power of attorney. According to Greg Buss, the library's programs are about helping people acquire basic life skills such as taking the bus. Generally, they help immigrants make the transition into Canadian society (Buss 2004, interview). In other words, Richmond's library plays an important role in settlement services.

The RCMP's Richmond Detachment is also responsive to the local population's diversity;[11] for example, it maintains an Asian Advisory Committee (Hansen 2004, interview). In policing circles the Richmond Detachment is known to be a leader in 'bias-free policing,' an emerging approach to policing that acknowledges systemic racism in police services and that proactively attempts to eradicate it.[12] According to an article in the *Richmond News*, Richmond's Superintendent Ward Clapman has been vocal on the need for the local detachment to reflect its population. In 2003, 23 per cent of the 214-member contingent were visible minorities (Hansen 2003). Comparable figures for the other municipalities in the sample were not collected; that said, the proportion of visible minorities in the Richmond Detachment seems high, considering that Richmond's dramatic demographic shift in its ethnoracial composition is relatively recent and that police services have long resisted organizational change. For instance, ethnocultural minorities often face language barriers when trying to pass the RCMP's mandatory Police Aptitude Test. Moreover, some immigrants from countries where police corruption is widespread view the police with suspicion, and others do not attribute to the civil service the prestige attached to professions such as law and medicine (Hansen 2003, 3). It was clear during the interviews with Clapman and two of his staff that diversifying the RCMP was a priority for the Richmond Detachment, which addresses barriers to recruiting visible minorities proactively – for example, by asking members of the Asian media to attend training facilities and showing them what it means to become a police officer (Clapman 2004, interview; Hansen 2004, interview; Thiessen 2004, interview).

The City of Richmond's Parks and Recreation Department is also responsive to diversity. For instance, Richmond's community centres work with settlement agencies to welcome newcomers and provide tours of the city and City Hall (Schroeder 2004, interview). The city has recently conducted a sweeping service-delivery review; one of its objectives was 'to establish expanded and more formal partnerships with immigrant and multilingual groups in order to better service the entire community' (Townsend 2005, e-mail correspondence).

However, though its population is over 60 per cent non-White, the city does not have a corporate employment-equity policy. Essentially, while the city has played a role in 'managing' intercultural relations and has adapted its services, it has not proactively redistributed or reallocated the city's public resources equitably. The RIAC's Strategic Plan and Work Program begins by outlining a number of the city's perceived shortcomings and challenges, one of which is its failure to be a positive role model in equitable hiring (RIAC 2004, 3). It is noteworthy that when Richmond's first intercultural advisory committee began pushing for organizational change it was met by a backlash on the part of long-standing residents, as a result of which the committee's mandate was changed.

Leaders of community organizations tend to view Richmond's level of responsiveness to ethnocultural diversity in a positive light (McKitrick 2004, interview; Sanghera 2004, interview). Balwant Sanghera, the RIAC's chair as well as Executive Director of the Multicultural Concerns Society of Richmond, described Richmond as 'very receptive' to suggestions from the community concerning intercultural initiatives (Sanghera 2004, interview). Timothy Welsh, a program director with the Affiliation of Multicultural Societies and Service Agencies of B.C. (AMSSA), the umbrella agency representing settlement agencies in that province, commented that among the race relations committees in Greater Vancouver, the RIAC 'seems like a dynamic one' (Welsh

2004, interview). The Federation of Canadian Municipalities in 1998 recognized Richmond with an honourable mention in its annual Race Relations Award Competition for its efforts to promote intercultural understanding.

In general, in Richmond, civil servants and political leaders tend to make realistic assessments of Richmond's level of responsiveness to diversity. They do not overstate their accomplishments, and community perceptions support their observations.

City of Surrey

The City of Surrey appears to have been somewhat proactive in its response to immigrants and ethnocultural minorities insofar as it has commissioned a series of reports. However, its range of responses is limited, and it appears as though it has implemented the recommendations of its reports in only a superficial way. Moreover, some community leaders rate its level of responsiveness poorly. It does not have a separate advisory committee or an entrenched administrative structure to coordinate the municipality's responses to ethnocultural diversity. As a consequence, its policy responses lack depth.

Surrey's Human Resources Department has made an effort in recent years to reach out to the city's diverse communities. For instance, because South Asians represent its largest ethnoracial-minority group, the city has begun to advertise jobs in the *Indo-Canadian Times* as well as the *Vancouver Sun*. In addition, the city commissioned a report to provide recommendations on how it could increase its employee diversity: *Closing the Cultural Gap: The City of Surrey* (Ail, Dobson-Borsoi, and Eley n.d.). According to City Councillor Judy Villeneuve, the city has made an effort to increase employment equity, because the business community is diverse and Indo-Canadians are the main developers in the city. However, it is unclear how well the city has succeeded at increasing employee diversity.

Furthermore, the diversity committees that do exist serve specific functions instead of advising council or crafting plans for the municipality as a whole. For instance, the city had a Diversity Advisory Committee mandated to 'act as advisors to the Surrey RCMP and Surrey Parks, Recreation and Culture Department on intercultural matters' (City of Richmond 2002, 5). This committee dealt mainly with staff training and recruitment needs. According Laurie Cavan, the Manager of Community and Leisure Services in Surrey, this committee disbanded because

Parks and Recreation and the RCMP had different rationales for connecting with the community (Cavan 2004, interview). Also, in the late 1990s the City of Surrey had a Staff Multicultural Coordinating Committee (City of Surrey 1997, 10), but the research process was unable to unearth what became of this committee. The city recently established a Diversity Committee to promote city jobs within the community (Cavan 2004, interview), but its effectiveness must be considered questionable, considering that many of the civil servants interviewed for this study were unaware of its activities.

In the past, many of Surrey's most important initiatives in diversity policy have been initiated by agencies that deliver services directly. Surrey's Parks, Recreation, and Culture Department has been a leader. In 1996 it launched a Task Force on Intercultural Inclusivity through an initiative called Reaching Out in Surrey, whose mandate was to identify barriers to equal access to recreation services by minority ethnic communities and to develop a strategy to address those barriers (City of Surrey 1997). Edgington and Hutton (2002) report that 'based on these findings, in 1996 the Department developed a mandate on how city facilities (e.g., parks and community centres) might play a role in overcoming isolation among certain immigrant communities, and so facilitate social contact between the various groups in Surrey's diverse population.' Furthermore, 'the City council as a whole set out to develop further initiatives with regard to inclusive programs and service delivery' (2002, 22). Building up the findings of the task force, the City's Parks, Recreation, and Culture Department conducted additional research and consultations to develop an Intercultural Marketing Plan in 2000. According to Laurie Cavan, the manager of Surrey's Community and Leisure Services, Parks, Recreation, and Culture Department, the city has made considerable progress on the plan since 2000. All of the city's marketing materials now contain some multilanguage component. The city has also made efforts to expand access to recreation services for low-income groups, since the newcomer groups the city consulted identified cost as a significant barrier to using recreation services. And in response to the recreation preferences expressed by Surrey's South Asian community, the city was building a kabadi park at the time the research was being conducted (McCallum 2004, interview).

The city's Library Services Department has also made changes to increase access for ethnocultural minorities. For instance, Surrey's libraries have a Multicultural Outreach Librarian (one such position, held by Ravi Basi, serves all branches in the library system), multilingual collections, and a computer-based learning lab to serve immigrants. To reach its diverse community, Surrey libraries advertise in ethnic newspapers. A new library, the Strawberry Hill Library, was recently built in a neighbourhood that is 80 per cent South Asian. To promote cultural bridging, it has developed extensive collections in Punjabi, Arabic, Urdu, and Chinese as well as books about India in English. A local 'street level' bureaucrat says that despite concerns from council that this primarily South Asian neighbourhood would not use a library, it has always been extremely busy (Basi 2004, interview).

High-level civil servants tended to avow that Surrey is highly responsive to its population's diversity. In fact, according to one, Surrey is a model of ethnocultural relations because ethnic groups are integrated (Dinwoodie 2004, interview). According to several others, Surrey does not need to offer targeted services to ethnic groups or establish separate ethnocultural advisory committees, because ethnocultural minorities' interests and preferences are integrated into mainstream policy making. In their view, Surrey has 'moved beyond race relations' (ibid.; McCallum 2004, interview; Mital 2004, interview).

It is interesting that the perceptions of community leaders were very different. Leslie Woodman, Executive Director of Surrey-Delta Immigrant Services Society (SDISS), one of the largest immigrant settlement organizations in Surrey, said that the initiatives of the Parks and Recreation Department did not have the support of the corporate level, which made them less effective. Her impression of Surrey was that it was celebrating its diversity but had not embraced diversity as 'different ways of doing things' (Woodman 2004, interview). In fact, she painted a picture of ethnic solitudes, contending that the South Asian community was sharply isolated from the mainstream. She mentioned instances of South Asian peoples' houses being 'fire bombed,' and of drive-by shootings.[13] She added that such hate-inspired incidents had led to the development of the Progressive Intercultural Community Services Society (PICSS), one of the most prominent community organizations in the city (Woodman 2004, interview; Gill 2005, interview). She also described some of the newcomers in Surrey as in 'self-preservation mode' – by which she likely meant that many newcomers were dealing with poverty, high levels of crime, and systemic racism.

According to Woodman, the City of Surrey is biased towards mainstream agencies and sees SDISS[14] as a 'special-interest group' (Woodman 2004, interview). In her view, the city prefers to deal with mainstream organizations such as OPTIONS[15] rather than with organizations, such as hers, that serve newcomer communities exclusively. The interview with Bruce Hardy, Executive Director of OPTIONS, confirmed this impression to some extent. He said that two or three of the staff at his organization are on a 'first-name' basis with all council members (Hardy 2005, interview).

Hardy confirmed the impression that Surrey had done little substantively to respond to immigrants' needs or to ethnocultural diversity. He noted that the city does some basic diversity training, but as he himself pointed out, the Surrey website does not contain information in any language other than English. He also noted that the council is entirely White, as are the school board and the governing boards of community organizations (ibid.). Finally, he mentioned that Surrey had not hired a social planner until 2003 or 2004. 'Social planning leads to wanting to fund things,' he suggested as an explanation, '[and] we [City of Surrey] don't want to fund things' (ibid.).[16] According to community leaders, newcomers have been poorly integrated into community power structures.

Several informants mentioned an innovative annual business award that recognizes organizations (including businesses and not-for-profit agencies) that are leaders in promoting the value of cultural diversity. SDISS pioneered the award. According to Woodman, the city's lack of responsiveness to immigrants was evident in its refusal to give SDISS $2,500 to be a 'diamond sponsor' of the Cultural Diversity Award, even though its political leaders stress that Surrey is 'open for business.' Instead, in 2004, SDISS approached Telus and Alcan for sponsorships. In Woodman's view, the City of Surrey missed an important opportunity to support a diversity event that was in line with its business-oriented priorities. Her comments suggested that even the business community was more responsive to immigrant and ethnocultural-minority concerns than the city. In her view, 'The town is still very much behind the eight-ball in terms of a visionary kind of model of leadership' (Woodman 2004, interview).

Another leader in the immigrant-serving sector, who wanted to remain off the record, referred to Surrey as the 'Texas' or the 'Alberta' of Greater Vancouver. By this he meant that Surrey is more conservative politically than other municipalities in Greater Vancouver. He added that Surrey also has more 'flashpoints' of intolerance than other parts of Greater Vancouver. Hardy's comments support this assessment. In his view, in Vancouver and Richmond, 'people will practise the simple courtesy of at least pretending tolerance [whereas] in Surrey there is a significant part of the population that proudly resent multiculturalism' (Hardy 2005, interview).

To summarize, though some of Surrey's policy initiatives – such as the reports it commissioned – reflect a proactive approach to policy making, the lack of institutional support for diversity initiatives limits the city's responsiveness. Also, the view from the community is less generous than one might expect, given Surrey's apparently high level of activity at the policy level (as measured by the number of reports and consultations on diversity matters), because the policies have not been implemented effectively.

Town of Markham

The Town of Markham is the only suburban municipality in the GTA that has been 'somewhat responsive' to immigrants and ethnocultural minorities. At the symbolic level, Markham's City Plan includes 'embracing diversity' and 'fair integration' as central goals. However, the town has responded to immigration and ethnocultural diversity in a limited way, and its policy style has been reactive.

Like Richmond, Markham has a history of race relations advisory committees and special task forces. In 1988 the Town of Markham established two ethnocultural advisory committees: the Committee on Race and Ethnocultural Equity of Markham (1988), and the Heritage and Multiculturalism Committee (1988–91). In 1995 it reconstituted the former as the Race Relations Committee. These committees have had a turbulent past. In 1995 the Race Relations Committee disbanded when then Deputy Mayor Carole Bell made negative comments about the concentration of Chinese immigrants in Markham – comments that many in the community perceived as racist. Her remarks led to a massive mobilization of Markham's 'visible minority' community (see chapter 4). The way in which the conflict unfolded reflected the city's reactive policy style. The mayor convened the Mayor's Advisory Committee (1995) to study the issue. Following the Mayor's Advisory Committee's report (Mayor's Advisory Committee 1996), the Race Relations Committee was re-established in 1997 to manage ethnocultural relations as well as to help implement the report's recommendations.

In 2005 the committee's mandate was to 'foster harmonious community relations with the Town.' The committee 'is dedicated to creating an environment in which all residents are treated equally' (Town of Markham, 'Markham Race Relations Committee'). To this end, the committee organizes an annual festival called 'The Many Faces of Markham'; engages in public-education campaigns; offers diversity training sessions to town staff; and does 'corporate outreach' to strengthen relationships among the town, the business sector, faith groups, and other institutions in Markham (ibid.).

One of the recommendations of the task force was that the town provide diversity training for its staff. However, according to Marlene Magado, chair of the Race Relations Committee at the time of our first interview, the diversity training the committee offers is not mandatory, and town staff who wish to participate must do so on their lunch break (Magado 2004, interview). During her tenure as chair, one of the committee's most important accomplishments was the development of a dispute-resolution protocol to handle interethnic conflicts between neighbours that are brought to council.

In Markham, the Human Resources Department has taken the lead in responding to diversity. A civil servant in the department says that given Markham's size, it does not have the 'luxury' of dedicating a separate staff person or administrative unit to diversity-related initiatives (Markham civil servant 2004, interview). However, in this person's view, the municipality has still been relatively *proactive* in meeting the needs of its population; for example, it has conducted research, held committee meetings, and commissioned Environics polls to assess community needs. It is also developing a corporate 'diversity policy.' Also, it seems to be the only municipality in the present sample that provides ESL language training to its employees.

The town does not have a formal employment-equity policy; however, both Khalid Usman (a town councillor) and a human-resources employee described employment equity as an informal policy or practice of the town (Markham civil servant 2004, interview; Usman 2004, interview). For instance, the town sends staff to job fairs and advertises in ethnic newspapers to attract a diverse workforce. The fire department has been actively trying to recruit a more diverse staff in recent times (Sales 2004, interview). In addition, the town participates in TRIEC, a GTA regional coalition that works to facilitate immigrants' integration into the job market. Through a TRIEC-initiated program, Markham offers mentoring to immigrants who want to gain Canadian experience. Yet as Marlene Magado pointed out, not a single commissioner in Markham is non-white, even though these positions are appointed and therefore could very easily be made more representative if the political will existed (Magado 2004, interview).

Some departments and agencies seem to be launching initiatives to address access barriers to city services as well as to reflect the preferences of ethnocultural minorities. For instance, the town is currently building a cricket field in response to the changing recreation preferences of its population, and its libraries have Chinese and South Asian components (Usman 2004, interview).

In addition, like many suburban municipalities, Markham has developed an informal bank of people who can serve as interpreters and translate city documents as needed (Sales 2004, interview). This list, created by the Information Technology Department, lists employees with language skills in twenty-five languages other than English. In 2002 this practice was formalized and given the title Multilingual Services Policy (Town of Markham 2002). For the most part, though, multilingual services are available only to the Chinese, the town's largest immigrant community (Magado 2004, interview). Also, the policy is rather limited, as departments and agencies must work within their existing budgets when offering interpretation and translation services (Town of Markham 2002).

One community leader dismissed Markham's Race Relations Committee as serving a 'public relations role' (community leader 2004, interview), even though in an ethnically divided context, public-relations efforts can contribute to community harmony. Furthermore, at the time of the first interview with her, the former chair of the town's Race Relations Committee suggested that Markham Council is not overly receptive to and supportive of the committee's activities (Magado 2004, interview). The research supports this assessment to a certain extent. Regional Councillor Jim Jones, for instance, was openly dismissive of the committee, describing it as 'looking for injustices' (Jones 2004, interview). However, in a later interview, Marlene Magado offered a more positive assessment of council's receptivity to the initiatives of the Race Relations Committee (Magado 2005, conversation).

City of Coquitlam

The City of Coquitlam's response to its changing social demographics has been so limited that it is at the margin between the categories of 'somewhat responsive' and 'unresponsive.'

The city has a Multiculturalism Policy, initially adopted in 1994 through a community-based social planning committee (Kingsbury 2004, interview) and then officially adopted by council in 1999. The city had had a Multiculturalism Committee between 1999 and 2003. However, according to interviewees, very little came of this committee. For instance, Jon Kingsbury, who was mayor (1998–2005) at the time he was interviewed, mentioned that the committee had wanted the city to translate more of its publications into minority languages and to develop formal employment-equity policies, but council had not approved these initiatives (ibid.).

Between 2003 and 2005, multiculturalism issues were incorporated into the Liveable Communities Advisory Committee (City of Coquitlam 2003). According to the deputy clerk, the city reorganized its committee structure (which included eliminating the previously separate multiculturalism committee) because it was 'moving towards a more holistic or sustainable approach [and] trying to break down silos within the organization' (Innes 2004, interview). At the time of the interviews, the extent to which multiculturalism initiatives would be a priority of the committee remained to be seen.

Kingsbury also mentioned that the city had begun hiring people who can speak French and Mandarin, but that it had done more to accommodate diversity when Daniel Chiu, a councillor of Chinese background, was on council. Since his departure, what the city was doing had 'dropped off dramatically' (Kingsbury 2004, interview).

The research uncovered limited evidence of responsiveness to ethnocultural diversity in Coquitlam. The city is the primary funder of a long-standing multiculturalism festival called 'Faces of the World Arts and Culture Festival.' Also, the local library has a multicultural services librarian who can speak both Mandarin and Cantonese. The library organizes tours for groups that provide ESL services; it also has ESL and minority-language collections (Harrison 2004, interview). The library board (which consists of nine council-appointed community members) includes representatives of the two fastest-growing communities in Coquitlam – the Korean and Chinese communities.

But there was little indication of this kind of change in Coquitlam's RCMP detachment. Ric Hall, superintendent of the Coquitlam Detachment, said that they were staffed to the minimum and thus did not have the 'luxury' of appointing a staff member to deal with diversity issues (Hall 2004, interview). With respect to employment equity, he said that 'we have no control over who we get' because the federal government assigns officers. The contrast with Richmond superintendent Clapman's approach in this respect was striking.

When asked whether the lack of a police force that reflects Coquitlam's diversity affects the ability of officers to reach out to the community and to enforce the law, Hall said that when officers encounter linguistic barriers, they can draw from the language skills of other RCMP employees. If they do not have the needed language resources locally, they have lists of people with various language skills whom they can call for help. In sum, the Coquitlam Detachment does not have formal policies or entrenched practices to manage diversity and reach out to immigrants and ethnocultural-minority communities.

Similarly, there was little evidence of responsiveness in other departments and agencies. For instance, a manager in recreation services said that he did not think he would have anything to offer in an interview.

Even so, there is some evidence that the city is trying to facilitate interethnic networks in the community. For instance, at the time of the interviews, the city had just developed an Internet portal called 'City Soup.' This website provides information about Coquitlam's businesses and community events in English, Chinese, and Korean. According to Ansar Cheng, a program director for settlement and language training with S.U.C.C.E.S.S., City Soup is an example of how the city is trying to include immigrants in the business sector (Cheng 2004, interview). The initiative seems to be an effort to coordinate community resources and create intersectoral and interethnic bridges.

The community's social infrastructure appears to be relatively underdeveloped. S.U.C.C.E.S.S. has recently opened a branch office in Coquitlam; a representative of this organization sat on the former Multiculturalism Committee. This appears to be the only settlement agency in Coquitlam. For this reason, it was difficult to gather information regarding the city's responsiveness to immigrants and ethnocultural minorities from leaders representing those communities.

'Unresponsive' Municipalities

City of Mississauga

The City of Mississauga, just west of the City of Toronto, is Canada's most populous suburb. When Marcia Wallace and Frances Frisken conducted their pioneering research on multiculturalism policies in GTA municipalities, they found that Canada's largest suburb had been inactive in multiculturalism (Wallace and Frisken 2000, 19). Similarly, the present study found that for the most part, Mississauga remains inactive in this area. At the time of the interviews, the only 'corporate' responses to diversity in Mississauga were the mayor's annual multicultural breakfast and an annual multicultural festival called Carassauga. However, while Carassauga initially relied on grants from the city council, it has been financially independent since 1995 (Carassauga website). Carassauga's website notes that Mississauga's long-standing mayor, Hazel McCallion, is especially proud of this fact.

Municipal staff said that the city has a policy *against* translating documents into other languages. For instance, despite requests from various ethnic groups for it to be translated, the city's new Master Plan is available only in English (civil servant, City of Mississauga 2003, interview). The policy against translation is tacit and is reinforced by what is perceived to be Mayor McCallion's position on the issue (civil servants, City of Mississauga 2003, interview). Mississauga councillor Nando Iannicca confirmed this English-only policy to me, adding that if staff were to use other languages to deliver services it would be by 'happenstance.' More generally, Iannicca said that while existing resources (bilingual staff, for instance) might be marshalled to deal with diversity issues, no new financial resources would be expended (Iannicca 2004, interview). Many suburban municipalities maintain a list of employees' language skills as the basis of an informal 'language bank.' Mississauga has such a list, as do Brampton and Markham. McCallion confirmed this corporate policy, stating that Mississauga does not 'adopt language issues' because 'if they [immigrants] come to Canada, they should adopt the Canadian way' and because adapting services linguistically is 'a very costly item [which] would be another burden on the property tax' (McCallion 2004, interview).

Some evidence of limited responsiveness in some city agencies and departments was uncovered. However, these responses are largely ad hoc, uncoordinated, and not supported by any corporate policy. For instance, the city's Recreation and Parks Department has taken some initiative by planning venues for bocce, soccer, cricket, and kabadi (civil servant, City of Mississauga, 2003, interview). Also, that department has a close working relationship with the Carassauga Board. In addition, libraries in Mississauga provide some books in different languages and liaise with new immigrant groups (librarian, Mississauga, 2003, interview). Many leaders in the immigrant-serving sector expressed how important employment equity is to municipal responsiveness to their concerns. For instance, one leader of a well-known ethnoracial organization in Mississauga described employment equity as the 'fairest social policy one can adopt' and remarked that there is an expression in Mississauga (among immigrant-serving organizations) that the municipal civil service is 'lily-white' (Chaudhry 2003, interview). Leaders in the immigrant-serving sector interviewed for this study agreed that Mississauga has been unresponsive to the concerns of immigrants and ethnocultural minorities. As one settlement worker put it, the city's approach is: 'Yes, you're here, yes you can have your festivals, but no access to city hall or to money' (community leader 2003, interview).

City of Brampton

The City of Brampton's responsiveness to social change has been highly limited. On the surface it might appear that Brampton has been more responsive to ethnocultural diversity and to immigrants than has Mississauga. For instance, in 1990, Brampton established the Brampton Race Relations Action Committee (BRRAC), a citizens' committee that was to report to council on race relations issues. This committee led Marcia Wallace and Frances Frisken (2000) to describe Brampton as 'reactive' because it had set up an advisory committee to 'hear complaints and demands from the community [and to] pass these on to the appropriate municipal departments' (2000, 6). However, this committee – though it still exists on paper – does not appear to have produced any significant policy changes. In fact, the single Brampton councillor from a 'visible minority' group that was interviewed was unaware of its existence (Manning 2004, interview), and long-standing councillors told me that the committee never meets (Moore 2004, interview). The committee does not appear to have been appointed. It seems that interest in BBRAC waned when Mayor Peter Robertson, who pioneered the initiative, was defeated in the 2000 municipal election.

The only other initiatives by Brampton to include ethnocultural minorities in policy making are a monthly breakfast hosted by the mayor for community leaders representing various religions that are common in Brampton, and a multicultural festival called Carabram. The City of Brampton is one of several sponsors of Carabram (see Carabram website).

Several examples of unresponsiveness surfaced in the interviews in Brampton, many of them offered by political leaders. For instance, City Councillor Grant Gibson mentioned that Brampton's South Asian community has sent delegations to the city to advocate for the legalization of basement apartments or 'secondary suites.' Many South Asian families want their extended family to live with them semi-independently, and basement apartments are one way of accommodating this cultural preference. But the City of Brampton has long opposed basement apartments and has not changed its position on this issue to accommodate South Asian families.

Linda Jeffrey, the current MPP for Brampton Centre, remembered some serious problems in reaching out to the community when she was a Brampton city councillor. According to her, Brampton's Sikh community is served by about ten newspapers and a television station, yet the city did not advertise in these media when she was a councillor (Jeffrey 2004, interview).

The interview with Brampton councillor Garnett Manning, one of the few suburban councillors from a visible-minority background, was especially illuminating.[17] According to him, immigrants and ethnocultural minorities feel as though the city does not represent them. One fundamental issue is city employment: many ethnocultural minorities do not feel that they have fair access to city jobs.[18] According to Manning, employment equity is not just about fair distribution of relatively lucrative public-sector jobs; it shapes the city's ability to respond to minority groups in more subtle ways. Employees' understandings of the needs and preferences of residents are shaped by their cultural assumptions and affect many aspects of city governance, including service delivery, programming choices, and marketing.[19]

Manning stressed that it is the city's responsibility to reach out to the community and that cities cannot wait for ethnocultural communities to come to them. He underscored the importance of being proactive; yet the more passive approach reflected in Brampton councillor Grant Gibson's statement – 'unless they come to you, you don't really know their needs are' (Gibson 2004, interview) – appears to dominate in Brampton. Manning painted a picture of deep discontent among ethnocultural minorities with regard to being excluded from decision making in the city: 'We may be looking at a boiling point in this city' (Manning 2004, interview). His words serve as a warning that municipalities cannot afford to be complacent about including diverse groups fairly in city governance.

Summary of Findings

This overview of multiculturalism policy initiatives attests to the important role played by Canadian municipalities in this policy area. Cities are Canada's most important public-sector innovators in this domain, yet it should now be clear that this country's municipalities vary greatly in their responsiveness to dramatic social change. How immigrants to Canada experience public services and local democracy varies with where they choose to settle.

The cities of Toronto and Vancouver are both 'responsive' to the needs and preferences of immigrants and ethnocultural minorities. They are *comprehensive* in adapting their services and governing structures to immigrants and to ethnocultural diversity as well as *proactive* in their policy styles. Furthermore, leaders of ethnocultural and immigrant communities view the policy responses of these two cities favourably relative to leaders in the other municipalities in the sample.

The City of Toronto coordinated its responses to diversity through a comprehensive planning exercise: the Task Force on Access and Equity (1998). In addition, the Diversity Management and Community Engagement Unit (DMU) has institutionalized support for diversity initiatives at the apex of municipal power, the City Manager's Office. The city collects demographic data and has commissioned reports to identify the needs of its diverse communities. Its Access and Equity Grants Program reflects its long-term, proactive commitment to developing community capacity in anti-racism and multiculturalism initiatives.

Likewise, the City of Vancouver has institutionalized support for multiculturalism initiatives by placing a Multicultural Social Planner in its social planning department. The city's Equal Employment Opportunity Office and the Hastings Institute provide additional institutional support for the city's multiculturalism policy goals. These institutional supports coordinate efforts across departments and agencies and (in the case of the Hastings Institute) extend the institutional scope of municipal institutions into the private sector; the result has been a *comprehensive* and coherent municipal response. The city's *proactive* style in multiculturalism policy is evident in the fact that more than 25 per cent of its community-grant budget targets immigrant and ethnocultural-minority community organizations.

'Responsive' municipalities go well beyond their 'limits.' According to Peterson (1981), because cities compete with one another for investment, they must limit their policy making to policies that are in their 'economic interest.' This competition limits municipalities to 'development policies' and 'allocational policies' (i.e., policies that reallocate existing resources such as employment equity policies); it also precludes policies that would have a redistributive impact. For this reason, he predicts that local governments will not play a role in redistribution.

Canadian cities compete with one another for investment. And because they generally have access to fewer financial tools, and are more constrained legislatively than American cities, one might expect them to limit their policy activities to those which are provincially mandated. Yet among the municipalities in the sample, Vancouver and Toronto have exceeded such limits. These cities' community-grant programs are clear examples of redistributive policy activity.

Of the eight municipalities examined in this book, four – the cities of Richmond, Surrey, and Coquitlam and the Town of Markham – have been 'somewhat responsive' to immigrants and ethnocultural diversity. These municipalities have responded in limited, ad hoc ways. Their most important step has been to establish advisory committees (or, in the case of Surrey, a staff diversity committee). They have not institutionalized ongoing support for diversity initiatives in the civil service to the extent that Toronto and Vancouver have.

Leaders of immigrant-serving organizations in all four of these municipalities stressed the importance of employment equity. The lack of a diverse workforce has implications for a municipality's ability to be *proactive*. A diverse municipal staff – at *all* levels – is an important resource for multiculturalism policy development. None of the 'somewhat responsive' municipalities have formal employment-equity policies, though there is some evidence of movement in that area. For instance, while research for this study was under way, the Human Resources Department in Markham was developing an employment equity policy (civil servant 2004, interview).[20] In addition, Surrey has studied employment barriers, though it has not followed up with a formal policy. Richmond and Coquitlam have not developed employment equity policies.

Of the suburban municipalities in this study that fall into the 'somewhat responsive' category, Richmond and Markham have been more active in multiculturalism policy. However, many such initiatives in these municipalities might also be viewed as reactions to backlashes on the part of long-standing residents. In other words, the motivations for policy change vary across municipalities.

Coquitlam is the least responsive of the 'somewhat responsive' municipalities. The only relevant difference between Coquitlam and the unresponsive municipalities is that it has included multiculturalism goals in its Liveable Communities Advisory Committee. We must wait to see how important this response will be to capacity development in multiculturalism.

The final two municipalities in our study – the City of Mississauga and the City of Brampton – have both been 'unresponsive' to immigrants and ethnocultural diversity. Their responses are limited to cultural festivals and 'multicultural breakfasts.' Under the leadership of former mayor Peter Robertson, Brampton established a Race Relations Committee, but this committee no longer meets. Mississauga has never had a race relations committee. One difference between the two relatively 'unresponsive' cities that could lead to a divergence between the two municipalities is that Brampton mayor Susan Fennel currently sits on the council of TRIEC, a regional coalition that has emerged to deal with immigrant employment. Otherwise, there is very little evidence of immigrant settlement and 'access and equity' policy development in Brampton. Mississauga's mayor was asked to sit on TRIEC, but declined (McIsaac 2004, interview).

Concluding Thoughts

The eight cases in the sample represent a range in levels of responsiveness to immigrants and ethnocultural diversity. In his case study of Toronto, Myer Siemiatycki and colleagues (2003) assessed the city's responsiveness to diversity using a normative ideal developed by Leonie Sandercock – the idea of 'cosmopolis' (Sandercock 1998). The Siemiatycki study described this ideal city as 'a city characterized by genuine respect for differing human identities as well as a recognition of the common destiny and intertwined fate of diverse groups; a city devoted to inclusive democracy and the social justice claims of its more marginalized, less powerful communities' (2003, 376). Toronto falls short of this ideal.

The 'cosmopolis' is an ideal towards which municipalities might strive. All eight municipalities in the sample have failed to achieve this ideal. At the same time, the variations in levels of municipal responsiveness – even within the same province – point to the importance of local factors and governance in meeting Canada's multiculturalism goals. Comparing instances of relative success and failure in multiculturalism policy development at the local level opens a path to understanding how municipalities might come closer to the ideal of 'cosmopolis.'

However, the American literature on state politics indicates that policy change could also occur in the opposite direction. A fifth category – one might it call 'reactionary' – is also possible. This category suggests the possibility of proactively *anti*-immigrant and *anti*-multiculturalism policies such as 'English only' or 'official English' policies. Reactionary policies are hypothetical in Canada's large urban centres; however, a small town in Quebec – Hérouxville – passed a resolution in January 2007 establishing a reactionary code of conduct for would-be immigrants that was deeply rooted in stereotypes. For instance, the code included a rule against the stoning of woman. These rules were created in the virtual absence of an immigrant community.[21] In the United States, reactionary 'English only' policies became quite popular in the 1980s, with several legislatures in southern states adopting such measures and high-immigration states such as California and Florida enacting them through voter initiatives (Hero 2003, 109). Proponents of 'official English' claim that these policies speed up the assimilation of immigrants. However, some proponents also support these policies in the belief that they will discourage immigration (ibid., 108). According to opponents, in Rodney Hero's words, they are 'mechanisms of exclusion' and 'threaten the continuation of services that are necessary for participation in the political process' (ibid., 108). In other words, 'official English' measures threaten what Canadian policy makers refer to as multiculturalism policies.

The debates that led up to and then surrounded the Quebec government's Commission de Consultation sur les Pratiques Accommodement Reliées aux Differences Culturelles (Commission on Reasonable Accommodation) attest that Canada has not been immune to backlash and to vigorous debates about how far the state and society should go to accommodate immigrants and ethnocultural minorities. As we shall see, such debates are not limited to Quebec, where a sense of cultural threat has grown out of the province's status as a cultural and linguistic minority community within Canada. As well, in local communities in English-speaking Canada's largest city-regions – Greater Vancouver and the GTA – there has been a backlash against immigration along with evidence of nativist tendencies.

Interestingly, these tendencies have been most pronounced in Richmond, Vancouver, and Markham. In all of these communities, large and economically powerful immigrant Chinese communities have been perceived as a threat to English-language institutions and other cultural norms. As mentioned earlier, Mississauga has a tacit 'English-only policy.' However, this policy appears (on the surface at least) to be driven by a desire to avoid the costs of translation and interpretation, rather than by a general, community-based backlash against change in the ethnocultural make-up of the municipal population – a backlash of the sort one can observe in the municipalities mentioned above. The salient point, though, is that political leaders in Mississauga tend to emphasize the 'costs' of immigration rather than the benefits. Emphasizing the costs of immigration to municipalities could have the unintended effect of inciting a backlash against immigrants.

In the United States, public support for 'official English' policies was so strong that they were adopted in spite of widespread opposition from elites. Jack Citrin and colleagues (1990) found that support for such policies was driven by popular (citizen-based) American nationalism. The importance of language in the symbolic definition of the community is most evident in Richmond and Markham – two of Canada's Chinese 'ethnoburbs' (Li 1999), where some long-standing residents feel that their 'English-speaking' culture is under threat. Some members of the Chinese community view the concerns of English-speaking residents as racist and exclusionary.

Municipalities' policy initiatives play an important role in managing the direction of change in community race relations – change that results from wide-scale immigration. Such initiatives play a role in integrating newcomers; they can also help manage the reactions of long-standing residents to change. Understanding this role will be crucial to building cities that are 'socially sustainable.' From the perspective of a social scientist, this variation provides a virtual laboratory in which to test hypotheses and identify the causes and consequences of important differences in municipal behaviour.

The next chapter lays the foundation for explaining and understanding municipal responsiveness by asking why four municipalities – Toronto, Markham, Brampton, and Mississauga – in Canada's most numerically important immigrant-receiving city-region vary so dramatically in their levels of responsiveness to immigration and social change.

4 Determinants of Multiculturalism Policies in the Greater Toronto Area

Toronto is Canada's largest city. The Toronto CMA has a population of close to 5.1 million, just over 2.3 million of which is foreign-born (Statistics Canada 2007b). It is Canada's largest immigrant-receiving city-region by far. In fact, in 2002, municipalities in the GTA received 111,580 immigrants, or 48.71 per cent of all immigrants to Canada that year (CIC 2002). The foreign-born population of the municipalities of Toronto, Mississauga, and Markham is 50 per cent or over; in Brampton the figure is close to 50 per cent (Statistics Canada 2007b).

Toronto is Canada's most ethnically diverse city as well as one of the most ethnically diverse urban centres in the world. In fact, Toronto is so ethnoculturally diverse that an 'urban legend' has developed that the UN has declared Toronto the most multicultural city in the world (Doucet 2001, 4).[1] However, this was not always the case. Before 1961, the proportion of visible minorities in Metropolitan Toronto (now the City of Toronto) was less than 3 per cent and Toronto was known as a British Protestant bastion (Doucet 1999, 12). As late as 1961, 59.2 per cent of the City of Toronto (then Metro Toronto) was ethnically British (ibid., 42, Table 12). By 1996 this figure had declined to 9.6 per cent. The 1980s and 1990s were important years in this ethnic transition. In 1981, ethnically British residents still formed 42.7 per cent of Metropolitan Toronto's population (ibid.).

A similar ethnic transformation occurred in Toronto's suburban municipalities. In 1981, British residents constituted 49.5 and 58.1 per cent of Mississauga and Brampton's populations, respectively. By 1996, only 9.7 per cent of Mississauga's and 12.7 per cent of Brampton's residents were British. Similarly, in Markham, 52 per cent of residents were British in 1981 but only 8.2 per cent in 1996 (Doucet 1999, 43, Table 13). Municipalities in highly diverse city-regions such as the GTA play important roles in multiculturalism policy. However, the extent to which they have shown leadership in responding to ethnocultural diversity and immigration varies. This means that how immigrants experience local government in Canada varies depending on the city in which they settle. Different 'citizenship regimes' operate at the local level in Canada.

The degree to which municipalities vary in their approaches to the challenge of accommodating diversity is puzzling in light of limited conceptions of municipal autonomy in Canada. Municipalities are sometimes portrayed in Canadian political science as nothing more than 'creatures of the provinces.' This principle would lead one to expect policy convergence among municipalities – at least those within the same province. Yet municipal autonomy indeed exists in a 'mushy middle' between legislative frameworks that provide little local discretion to municipalities and forms of 'home rule' – what Patrick Smith and Kennedy Stuart (2006) label systems of 'beavers' and 'cats' respectively. Some Canadian municipalities have become what Patrick Smith and Kennedy Stuart (2006) refer to as 'eager beavers,' municipalities that have exceeded their formal levels of autonomy through local leadership efforts.

This chapter explores the microdynamics of policy innovation at the local level by comparing four highly diverse municipalities in Ontario. To this end, it examines the governance patterns of some of the most important immigrant-receiving municipalities in the GTA – Toronto, Mississauga, Brampton, and Markham.

It addresses the following questions: How do local actors view their role in immigrant settlement and integration? Where does local leadership come from in ethnic relations? Given Canadian municipalities' tight legislative and fiscal constraints, how are municipalities able to respond to large-scale immigration? In other words, how does the policy capacity develop to respond effectively to dramatic ethnocultural social change at the local level, where the political will exists?

The politics of suburban local governments is an underexplored yet important area of inquiry in Canada. Understanding the role of suburban municipal-governance structures in immigrant integration is imperative, given that immigration is increasingly a suburban phenomenon.

Toronto has been 'responsive' to its immigrant and ethnocultural-minority population; Markham has been 'somewhat responsive' to ethnocultural diversity; and Mississauga and Brampton have both been 'unresponsive' to the dramatic demographic change in their populations. Following the logic of a 'most similar systems design' (Lijphart

1975), this chapter explains the variation in municipal responsiveness to immigrants and ethnocultural minorities by exploring the key empirical differences among these highly similar cases. Thus it considers how Toronto's politics and policy-making processes differ from the politics and policy-making processes in highly diverse suburbs in the GTA. Are there stark differences between Toronto on the one hand and Mississauga and Brampton, the two relatively 'unresponsive' municipalities, on the other?

The differences in levels of responsiveness are not simply a question of divergence between the GTA's urban core – the City of Toronto – and its suburbs, since Markham has been more active in multiculturalism policy and initiatives than have Mississauga and Brampton. Why has Markham responded differently? What is common to Mississauga and Brampton that makes them unresponsive to ethnocultural change? What distinguishes these two unresponsive suburbs from the 'somewhat responsive' suburb of Markham (at least with respect to local multiculturalism policies)?

The chapter begins by describing key empirical differences among the cases that could affect urban regime development. It then filters the findings through an urban regime analysis. This body of theory emphasizes the importance of public–private relationships to building policy capacity, thereby shedding light on how the empirical differences between the cases matter. As the literature on urban regime theory suggests, municipal responsiveness to the concerns of ethnocultural minorities requires strong political will and exceptional leadership. In addition, the effectiveness and scope of municipal responsiveness is both shaped by and limited by contextual factors, including, for instance, how civil society is organized and the resources available in the public and private spheres.

Toronto's relative responsiveness to immigrants and ethnocultural minorities is the result of the efforts of political and community leaders to build and maintain a network of productive governance arrangements and resources to support multiculturalism and settlement-policy development. Mississauga and Brampton's inactivity in multiculturalism can be understood in terms of both the absence of political leadership in this area and a lack of pressure on the part of civil society to intervene. Markham demonstrates the independent importance of community leadership and immigrant 'social capital' to municipal responsiveness, as well as the role of community backlash in municipal agenda setting in multiculturalism and race relations policy.

Characterizing Key Differences in Multiculturalism Policy Making

Competing ideas concerning the scope for municipal action in Canadian federalism characterize the Canadian political science literature. The orthodox conception views municipal agency through a constitutional lens, emphasizing municipal constitutional subordination and the constraints in municipalities' provincially provided legal framework. The constitutional doctrine of 'creatures of the provinces' is cited regularly to downplay the importance of local democracy and municipal autonomy (Magnusson 2005).

More recently, there appears to be greater recognition that there is some room for autonomy in municipal decision making. For instance, the sixth edition of Richard Tindal and Susan Nobes Tindal's classic *Local Government in Canada* (2004) describes, for the first time, the scope for municipal action as a 'mushy middle' situated between the strictures of Dillon's Rule,[2] which limits municipal action to powers expressly delegated to them by provinces through their incorporation, and forms of 'home rule.'[3]

In Canada, provinces delegate municipal mandates through provincial statute. Ontario has not delegated a role in multiculturalism initiatives to its municipalities (Wallace and Frisken 2000, 1). Therefore, though a countrywide entrenched normative framework exists, in the absence of federal and especially provincial direction, municipal officials are very much on their own in their decisions on multiculturalism policy development. According to David Edgington, Bronwyn Hanna, and their colleagues (2001), the tight legislative constraints under which municipalities operate condition the attitudes of municipal officials and in this way limit the extent to which municipalities respond to immigration (Edgington, Hanna, et al. 2001, 18). However, the ways in which municipal officials in Toronto, Mississauga, Brampton, and Markham describe their role in immigration and settlement and in 'managing' social change varies considerably – a reflection of competing conceptions of the scope of municipal agency that now permeate the Canadian political science literature. The fact that the four municipalities are located in the same province and face similar institutional (legal, fiscal, and – ultimately – constitutional) constraints highlights the political nature of the way in which local leaders 'frame' the municipal role.

Political Leaders' Ideas Concerning the Municipal Role in Multiculturalism

Toronto is the only GTA municipality in the sample that has been 're-sponsive' to immigrants and ethnocultural minorities. Its responsiveness is related to the presence of a strong group of political leaders who envision a broad role for Toronto in immigration, settlement, and multiculturalism policy. For instance, Toronto councillor Joe Mihevc, who chaired Toronto's Task Force on Access and Equity (1998), believes that municipalities have at least six roles to play in immigration, settlement, and multiculturalism policy. First, they are *facilitators,* which includes everything from connecting immigrant organizations with one another to connecting those organizations to job-training organizations and school boards. Second, they are *funders* of ethnocultural organizations and social service agencies that cater to ethnocultural needs. Third, they are *advocates* on behalf of immigrants to other levels of government. Fourth, elected municipal officials are *present in the community* and at ethnocultural events, helping make immigrants and ethnoracial minorities feel that they belong. Fifth, they *encourage immigrant integration into the labour market* and, more generally, promote their contributions to economic development. Sixth and finally, they are *service providers* and thus have a role to play in offering services in culturally appropriate ways (Mihevc 2003, interview). In addition, Toronto's deputy mayor, Joe Pantalone, has stressed the importance of Toronto having a seat at the intergovernmental table when immigration and settlement issues are discussed (Pantalone 2004, interview).

Compared to those in other municipalities, political leaders in Toronto tend to emphasize opportunities for municipal action and to downplay their jurisdictional limitations. They are more entrepreneurial and have a greater sense of efficacy than other municipal political leaders in the GTA sample in terms of confronting public-policy challenges both in multiculturalism policy and more generally. For instance, when Mihevc was asked how the city was able to launch what it calls its 'access and equity' initiatives despite its tight, provincially imposed legislative constraints, he replied:

> That's the beauty of local government. That's why we do feel we are a level of government. The legislative framework that allows local government to exist is so broad you really have a lot of scope for whatever you want to do. Just pick a different piece of legislation – or you just do it because there's a legislative vacuum at the provincial level. And this is one area,

access and equity, where they [provincial leaders] don't care. They don't know they don't care. In many ways that's federal stuff ... who's coming into the country. So ... this area has a lot of scope for imagination, creativity, and variation. (Mihevc 2003, interview)

Toronto councillor Kyle Rae offered a similarly dynamic account of the scope of municipal agency:

I would suggest that a city that wants to move into an uncharted sector will get away with it, because I think the provincial government is inadequate or inept at managing their responsibility. Although we are seen to be creatures of the province, they take very little interest in what we do. And they would, I think, prefer that we don't rock any boats. And if we feel that we [would like to] make immigrant issues a priority, as long as it doesn't bother them, they couldn't care less. They have a very lackadaisical approach to us as being their 'children.' As long as there isn't a dollar figure [attached] to it they couldn't care less what we do. Part of it is irresponsibility on the part of the province. (Rae 2004, interview)

In other words, according to Mihevc and Rae, Toronto's initiatives in access and equity were facilitated by the lack of political leadership in this area from upper levels of government. Their impression is that municipalities are free to act as they wish, as long as they do not ask the province for more money.

When asked how the city responds in the context of tight fiscal constraints, several Toronto councillors described Toronto's role in immigration and settlement policy and in access and equity[4] as a matter of 'necessity' (Pantalone 2004, interview). Rae contended that activity in multiculturalism policy has been 'generated by activist councillors [who] push the envelope because of need' (Rae 2004, interview). In other words, activity in multiculturalism initiatives required strong political leadership. Though there was some variation, many of the Toronto councillors who were interviewed took for granted the value of adopting diversity policies. Deputy Mayor Pantalone put it bluntly, stating that Toronto has a philosophy that diversity is 'healthy, adds value, and we should foster it' (Pantalone 2004, interview).

Even so, not all Toronto councillors agree that the city should play a role in immigration and access and equity policies. One councillor told me off the record that 'the city wastes a huge amount of money on multicultural initiatives for the sake of political correctness and for the sake of feeling good.' This person also suggested that multiculturalism policy is the responsibility of senior levels of government, and felt that municipalities should not be acting in policy areas for which they do not have funding from upper levels of government:

> I think that municipalities have really been sucked in. Instead of trying to take up the slack of the other levels of government shirking their responsibilities we should hold them accountable. Right? We take the bait, we play into their hands ... and we're not very good at it, because we're not built for it when we try and take up the lack of resources that the other levels of government have not provided for us. (Toronto city councillor 2004, interview)

Though the councillors who were interviewed for this book tended to see an important role for the city in immigration, immigrant settlement, and other multiculturalism-related initiatives, the sample of interviewees was no doubt biased by the fact that councillors who support activity in these policy fields were more likely to accept a request for an interview than those who do not. A core group of Toronto's political leaders do support access and equity initiatives as well as an increased role for Toronto in immigration policy (including a seat at the intergovernmental table when immigration policy is being addressed).

In the GTA, the attitudinal differences of local political leaders in relation to Toronto were most stark in Mississauga, where leaders tend to 'frame' immigration and immigrant settlement as federal responsibilities and to describe the municipal role in terms more in line with traditional conceptions of municipal agency. According to long-serving Mississauga councillor Nando Iannicca (1988–present), municipalities do the 'grunt work for the castle' (Iannicca 2004, interview). In his view, municipalities are 'pure administrators' that plough snow, remove garbage, and ensure that sewage is treated; it follows that immigration and settlement are not on their 'radar' (Iannicca 2004, interview). When asked why Toronto has taken on a role in immigration and settlement and Mississauga has not, Iannicca said that it was because 'party politics has permeated [Toronto] at the local level ... [In Toronto] people will say, "he's the new NDP member of Council." ... What the hell is that? Does a socialist take garbage from the curb differently?' (ibid.). Essentially, he offered a highly apolitical account of municipal responsibilities and decision making.

Relative to those in Toronto, political leaders in Mississauga were more inclined to highlight financial constraints as a reason for their inability to respond to immigration (ibid.; McCallion 2004, interview). Yet Mississauga's financial position is relatively strong. It is debt-free (Stobie 2004, interview) and has not borrowed money since Hazel McCallion was first elected mayor in 1978 (Chin 2008). Toronto, on the other hand, has had to go to the province at budget time every year to cover a perpetual budgetary shortfall. In 2007 it succeeded in balancing its budget only after the province delegated new taxation powers to it as part of a broader process of legislative reform.

Iannicca stressed that municipal policy making is guided by a strict financial imperative, which in turn is structured by a heavily constrained revenue base. According to him, his city cannot increase commercial taxes for fear of commercial flight. He also pointed out that property taxes are regressive and that the city does not want to force residents out of their homes owing to tax increases. Essentially, he argued, 'growth' (much of which is driven by immigration) 'does not pay for itself.' In his view, upper levels of government benefit (through increased revenues) from growth induced by immigration, whereas municipalities must cover the costs (Iannicca 2004, interview).

In general, Mississauga's political leaders were inclined to emphasize the costs of immigration and to point out that the federal government has abdicated its financial responsibility for supporting immigrants (McCallion 2004, interview). In Mississauga, the refusal on the part of city councillors to respond to immigration appears to be partly a political strategy – in other words, the city is standing its ground against upper levels of government, which have downloaded additional services onto municipalities without transferring additional resources. Ontario municipalities are in a unique position: ever since a local services realignment in 1997, they have been faced with the responsibility to take on additional responsibilities in social service areas (Tindal and Tindal 2009, 174–5).[5] As Iannicca stressed, municipal roles and financial capacity 'go hand in hand' (Iannicca 2004, interview). Mississauga refuses to embrace an 'unfunded mandate' in immigrant settlement and other multiculturalism-related initiatives.

Similarly, councillors in Brampton stressed the importance of federal and provincial financial support for municipal responses to immigration (Moore 2004, interview; Jeffrey 2004, interview). Echoing Iannicca and McCallion, Peel regional councillor[6] Elaine Moore said that the property tax should not be used to 'subsidize' federal immigration decisions (Moore 2004, interview). In Mississauga and Brampton, political leaders view municipal roles as inseparable from financial capacity.

With the support of both Mississauga and Brampton, every year Peel Region sends a 'ceremonial' invoice to the federal government to recover the costs of immigration to the region (Kolb 2004). At the time of the interviews, the latest invoice, dated 19 August 2004, was for $836,017.29, which included $563,474.34 for assistance payments to refugees and $272,542.95 for administration costs (Region of Peel Invoice no. 114330 2004). The region has been sending such invoices to the federal government since November 1990. The 'total amount now due' in 2004 was $39,198,073.95. This figure includes interest charges on the federal government's outstanding balance (ibid.). According to Moore, the action is 'ceremonial' in the sense that political leaders recognize that the federal government will not transfer the money to them. The idea is to send a message (Moore 2004, interview).

Political leaders in Brampton also had a 'small-c' conservative view of municipal agency. According to former Brampton councillor Linda Jeffrey, municipalities are risk-averse and 'often only do what they're required to do [by the province].'[7] She elaborated: 'Councils are paralysed by the thought that they're going to set precedents that they have to continue later on. We can't do that, because if we do that, then we have to do that for everybody.' At the municipal level, 'it's risky behaviour' to enter new territory, and councils are simply 'not risk takers' (Jeffrey 2004, interview). Long-time Brampton councillor Grant Gibson described the municipal dilemma in this way: 'We're the lowest level of government, we have nowhere to download. We have to go to the taxpayer' (Gibson 2005, interview).

Nevertheless, despite this general 'small-c' conservatism, at least two Brampton councillors, including Elaine Moore (regional) and Garnett Manning (local), said that the municipality should do more to accommodate immigrants and ethnocultural minorities. Moore mentioned the need for the city to begin advertising in ethnic newspapers, and to include diversity management in the city's employment practices and in the design of the city's buildings (Moore 2004, interview). Similarly, Manning, who is Jamaican-born, underscored the importance of organizational change in Brampton; this must include injecting diversity measures into its employment and communication policies (Manning 2004, interview). All told, however, in Brampton there appeared to be insufficient political will to respond.

Markham has been 'somewhat responsive' to changes in the ethnocultural demographics of its population. There, municipal leaders vary in their perceptions of the municipal role. For instance, one regional councillor framed the issue of immigration purely as a question of managing growth. He felt that the municipality should treat everyone the same way and that planning and building Markham well would avert racial conflict. In his view, when public space is available for community interaction, one does not have to worry about multiculturalism. He was saying, in effect, that responding to immigration does not require *proactive*, targeted local leadership in multiculturalism policy (Jones 2004, interview).

Markham councillor Khalid Usman described the municipal role as one of making immigrants feel welcome. He mentioned several initiatives of the Markham Race Relations Committee (of which he is a member), including the 'Many Faces of Markham Festival.' But he also stressed the Region of York's responsibility in immigration and settlement, since in his view services such as public health, welfare, and policing are more relevant to the immigrant settlement process than those which are the municipality's responsibility.[8] In addition, he noted that the city has an important indirect role to play in immigration-driven growth by planning for services, and he mentioned that affordable housing is a priority in his ward. The city is now working on rental apartments – something that was unheard of in Markham until recently (Usman 2004, interview).

Strength, Style, and Ideas of Municipal Mayors

In Canada, mayors possess very little power relative to most mayors in the United States, especially those who operate under 'strong mayor systems.'[9] In most Canadian cities, local councils have both legislative and executive power – a type of system called a council–mayor or 'weak mayor' system. In many Canadian municipalities,[10] mayors are one among equals on council. As Andrew Sancton has observed, in Canada, 'if a mayor has any real power, it derives from political alliances and connections rather than from the official job description' (Sancton 1994, 175).

Though all the municipal systems discussed in this chapter are weak-mayor systems in a formal sense, there were variations in the sample regarding how and where informal political power was concentrated. Hazel McCallion, Mississauga's mayor, is one of the most powerful and vocal municipal leaders in the GTA. She has been mayor since 1978, having been re-elected eight times and acclaimed twice. She has consistently received over 90 per cent of the popular vote in recent elections. Charles Stobie was Vice-President of Government Relations for the Mississauga Board of Trade (MBT) at the time of the interview with him in 2005. He put it this way: 'Hazel McCallion is an institution in this City and she really isn't beholden to anybody' (Stobie 2005, interview). 'Anybody' here includes the business community. Her opinion is decisive on most policy matters. Essentially, though Mississauga is a weak-mayor system in a formal sense, the city operates as though it had a strong-mayor system; effectively, McCallion holds a veto on local decisions (Urbaniak 2005). There is evidence that power is even more concentrated in Mississauga under McCallion's leadership than it would be in a formal strong-mayor system: her power seems to extend not only to executive functions on council and into the upper echelons of the civil service, but also into the informal channels of community decision making.

Because her influence is so pervasive, McCallion's opinions on matters of public policy carry a great deal of weight. As we have seen, she has a highly limited conception of the municipal role in immigration and diversity management. She does not agree with the normative framework of Canada's countrywide model of ethnocultural relations and immigrant integration – that is, official multiculturalism. In her view, immigrants themselves bear sole responsibility for their own integration: 'If they [immigrants] come to Canada, they should adapt to the Canadian way' (McCallion 2004, interview). Her opinion on this issue is rooted both in her general desire to limit municipal policy activity and in her ideas about the state's obligation to help immigrants integrate. Essentially, she believes in a 'melting pot' model of integration, one that stresses private responsibility for assimilation rather than public support for integration. Furthermore, in her view, it would be fruitless to develop diversity policies; she deems such policies ineffective. For instance, she believes that one cannot eliminate employment discrimination or racism with government policy and that formal policy responses to diversity can have the opposite effect of what was intended: 'Sometimes with the structures we set up, we create racism, we create division rather than integrating' (ibid.).

McCallion's influence seems so pervasive in Mississauga that people in all sectors are aware of her personal opinions on issues and tend to defer to them. In fact, some civil servants in Mississauga reported that, ultimately, McCallion's view is the only one that matters on council

(Mississauga civil servant 2003, interview). This perception is consistent with the rationale provided by Councillor Iannicca for not creating a race relations committee in Mississauga. According to him, McCallion has a very strong view that municipalities are not in the 'business' of race relations (Iannicca 2004, interview). Similarly, as MBT representative Stobie put it, the biggest question in the 2003 municipal election in Mississauga was, 'How long was it going to take for Hazel McCallion to crack the whip and get Eve Adams [who was the only new councillor on Mississauga's eleven-member council in 2003] to toe the line?' (Stobie 2005, interview). Interestingly, some civil servants referred to Mississauga's laissez-faire role in ethnocultural relations as 'policy.' When pressed as to what this meant, one civil servant explained that the policy was informal and was grounded in McCallion's personal opinion on such matters (Mississauga civil servant 2003, interview). These findings are consistent with Tom Urbaniak's (2005) in-depth study of McCallion's mayoralty, which includes case studies of decision making in several policy fields. He has found that McCallion's leadership in Mississauga is 'preemptive' and 'overriding' (2005, 477).

Outside observers, too, recognize McCallion's power in Mississauga. According to Uzma Shakir, a prominent activist in the immigrant-serving sector in Toronto, Mississauga is 'run like a personal fiefdom ... with personal dispensations' (Shakir 2003, interview). According to her, despite McCallion's lack of support for diversity policies, as many ethnocultural communities would defend her as would speak up against her. From the perspective of several Toronto-based immigrant-serving organizations, this support was apparent when they organized a rally in Mississauga in response to comments made by McCallion that portrayed immigrants and refugees as a burden on municipalities and on public services generally. In an interview with Diane Francis (2001), McCallion revealed her attitude towards refugees and her interpretation of immigration's impact on public services:

> 'Refugees' are not people who have been displaced and are brought in for humanitarian reasons into Canada. Only a few are in that category. Most are smuggled in or are queue-jumpers who lie their way into the country by pretending they cannot go home and get all the entitlements they need immediately ... The motels around the airport [which is located in Mississauga] are filled with so-called refugees.
>
> If you go to the Credit Valley Hospital the emergency is loaded with people in their native costumes. A couple will come here as immigrants

and each bring over their parents. Now you have four people who never contributed a nickel toward our medical system using it at an age when they will cost everyone a great deal of money. No wonder we have to worry about our medical system looking after everyone.

Political leaders in other GTA municipalities have made inflammatory remarks about immigrants and ethnocultural minorities. However, the responses of civil-society leaders in Mississauga were very different from those in the other municipalities. By one leader's account, several immigrant-serving organizations in Mississauga showed no interest in participating in rallies organized in response to the mayor's comments. According to several informants, the Executive Director of India Rainbow Society – a prominent immigrant settlement agency in Mississauga – went out of her way to publicly dissociate her organization from protests organized by Toronto-based agencies. In fact, she purportedly went to the rally at City Hall to declare that her organization did not support it.

When pressed about why Mississauga's immigrant-serving organizations might behave this way, Shakir suggested that local agencies were concerned that McCallion might withdraw scarce sources of funding, including money associated with advertising in local ethnic media (Shakir 2003, interview). Similarly, a civil servant with Peel Region suggested that civil-society groups do not oppose McCallion because they believe she could make a phone call to the appropriate decision maker at the regional level and have that organization's community grant withdrawn (civil servant, Region of Peel, 2004, interview). However, this research did not uncover any instance of McCallion ever having acted in such a way. Furthermore, according to McCallion herself, the City of Mississauga has a policy against advertising in ethnic media as well as in the *Mississauga News* (the 'mainstream' community paper); in her view, it would be unfair to do so unless the city advertised in all ethnospecific community newspapers (McCallion 2004, interview). In other words, municipal advertising cannot be used to co-opt Mississauga's immigrant-serving and ethnocultural organizations.

Nevertheless, what is important for this discussion is that perceptions of McCallion's power and of her personal opinions on issues appear to affect the behaviour of community leaders. More specifically, it appears as though some actors in civil society do not want to challenge McCallion, fearing the financial consequences of her disapproval.

What is more, McCallion derives power not only from her perceived ability to punish, but also from a deep respect for her strong leadership and political success. Tindal and Tindal describe how her image as a strong leader was enhanced by the way she handled an evacuation of the city in 1979 (after a Canadian Pacific Railway accident) and by the way she returned to work several days after being hit by a pick-up truck in 2003 (Tindal and Tindal 2009, 254). McCallion is also a Member of the Order of Canada and placed second in the World Mayor Contest in 2005 (ibid., 254). Many community leaders stated that despite their differences on policy, they liked 'Hazel.' Because she is liked, people in the community tend to make allowances for her. Charles Stobie described how he once attended a gathering at which citizens were being sworn in. With him was a friend who was a public relations person for Citizenship and Immigration Canada. McCallion, who was also in attendance, was asked to say a few words. As Stobie recounts:

> Hazel basically stood up there and told these people [newly naturalized Canadian citizens] I expect you to assimilate into our population, become good Canadians, to adopt certain Canadian traits and practices. [She] sort of went completely contrary to this 'salad bowl' type, multicultural type of atmosphere that the federal government wants to cultivate. And they all sort of cringed and, of course, she gets away with it. But at the end of the day when all the proceedings were over with and there was a photo op for everybody, who did everyone want to get their picture taken with? Hazel McCallion. (Stobie 2005, interview)

According to Stobie, McCallion 'has a bit of a Teflon quality' on the ethnic relations 'score' (ibid.).

Why is McCallion so popular? One widely accepted explanation is that she has reigned over a period of exceptional growth in the city and, in the process, has generated considerable revenue in the form of development levies. The city did not raise property taxes for twelve consecutive years (1990–2001), though with rising costs and decreasing revenues, it has since been forced to do so. Nevertheless, in 2004, Mississauga had the lowest residential tax rate among the large cities in the GTA, excluding Toronto.[11] The 2005 increase on residential assessment was 5.8 per cent (ibid.). McCallion is also known for being a strong advocate for the municipality and for 'showing up' regularly at community events (Seepersaud 2003, interview). An outside observer confirmed this, stating that the fact that she could withdraw her 'presence' from events was an important incentive for complacency on the part of community leaders in Mississauga (community leader 2003, interview). In addition, when McCallion was interviewed, it was apparent that she is highly knowledgeable about Mississauga society, including about ethnic community organizations and events, and that she participates in many community activities (McCallion 2004, interview).

These personal connections are valuable when community conflicts arise. In fact, McCallion's description of how ethnic relations are 'managed' in Mississauga supports to some extent the suggestion that she runs Mississauga like a 'personal fiefdom.' McCallion's own description of how community conflicts are handled reveals her personal involvement in disputes. According to her, when conflicts arise between ethnic groups, she makes personal phone calls to the relevant community residents and, in her words, 'tells them' how to resolve the conflicts. During the interview with her, she mentioned an example of two Sikh factions in Mississauga that were arguing: one faction did not want to let the other on their property for a parade. In her words:

> It's a different approach [in Mississauga in relation to other GTA municipalities that have policies and committees to deal with such issues], and it's an open approach. If you've got a problem, if anyone is treated with disrespect or indication of racial discrimination, the way we operate is: I want them in my office, I want to know why, and I want to investigate. I investigate every issue. (McCallion 2004, interview)

She stressed that she does not want city staff handling such issues and that she handles them personally (ibid.).

Essentially, under McCallion's leadership, the City of Mississauga is at the stage of celebrating multiculturalism in the private sphere. Indeed, it was McCallion who first organized Carassauga, Mississauga's multiculturalism festival. As the Carassauga website notes, the celebration 'was developed in response to a challenge put forth by Mississauga Mayor Hazel McCallion to all ethnocultural groups during a meeting in the old City Hall in the fall of 1985.' City Council originally supported the festival through corporate grants. However, the festival has been completely self-supporting since 1995 – a development that the mayor is especially proud of, as the website notes.

According to informants interviewed for this study, the importance of mayoral leadership is also apparent in Toronto, in the transition from former mayor Mel Lastman (1998–2003) to the current mayor, David Miller. Both Lastman and Miller might be considered 'strong' leaders.

However, Miller's leadership style is very different from Lastman's. In particular, Miller is more cooperative than Lastman.[12] This difference has been evident since the beginning of his tenure, when he asked prominent community leaders to participate on his 'transition team,' a non-partisan group of public- and private-sector leaders whom he selected to advise him on the direction the city ought to take. It was also evident in the participatory budget process that he introduced. A senior civil servant in Toronto's CAO's office (now the City Manager's Office) told the interviewer that unlike under Lastman, the Toronto City Summit Alliance – an elite coalition of public- and private-sector actors in Toronto and other networks in civil society – is now deferring to Miller's leadership (Abrahams 2004, interview).

Furthermore, Miller seems to take a special interest in immigrant settlement and multiculturalism policy. As a city councillor, he championed immigrant and refugee issues and chaired Toronto's Immigration and Refugee Working Group. He also sat on the Toronto Regional Immigrant Employment Council (TRIEC) – a regional coalition of GTA leaders that emerged to tackle the issue of immigrant integration – with mayors and regional chairs of other highly diverse municipalities. He had the opportunity to develop and solidify relationships with civil-society leaders in this sector; as a result, today he can call on these leaders to help him develop local capacity in immigrant settlement and multiculturalism policy.

But in Toronto, given the size of council[13] and the extent to which it is politicized,[14] a mayor cannot be as strong as McCallion has become in Mississauga. At the time of the interviews, power was less concentrated in Toronto's municipal system than in Mississauga's. This could change, since Toronto's governance institutions have been reformed in such a way as to strengthen the power of the executive through an executive committee that provides leadership to council. This committee includes the following members: the mayor, the deputy mayor, the chairs of standing committees (which are appointed by the mayor), and four members-at-large appointed by council. These changes came into effect in January 2007 and are part of the reforms introduced with the new City of Toronto Act, formally titled the Stronger City of Toronto for a Stronger Ontario Act.

Though the Brampton and Markham councils are similar in size to Mississauga's, the interviewees in these cities did not point to a single political leader as 'all powerful' on council. Wallace and Frisken (2000) noted the importance of mayoral leadership in their study; they also cited the leadership that Mayor Peter Robertson showed in Brampton's Race Relations Action Committee (which no longer meets). Yet on his own, Robertson was unable to maintain council's support for that initiative. In Mississauga, by contrast, all of the local leaders and civil servants cited the importance of McCallion's personal opinions on matters of public policy, including the issue of the municipality's role in multiculturalism. Relative to Mississauga, political power seems more dispersed in other GTA municipalities in the sample.

Community Capacity in Multiculturalism

The research also uncovered significant differences in the extent to which municipalities in the sample possessed well-developed immigrant settlement, anti-racism, and other multiculturalism-related community infrastructures. Toronto's high level of responsiveness is correlated with an abundance of well-resourced organizations in the immigration, settlement, and multiculturalism policy fields. The city has many immigration and settlement agencies and ethnospecific planning councils, as well as other organizations that provide services to immigrants and refugees and represent their interests. Indeed, a recent study of services for newcomers in the GTA found 197 Toronto agencies that serve immigrants (Lim et al. 2005, 19, Table 5).

More recently, the City of Toronto has benefited from having the Centre of Excellence in Research on Immigration and Settlement (CERIS) locate in Toronto. This centre is one of several federally funded research partnerships under the Metropolis Project – an international initiative meant to bring together academics and not-for-profit agencies in collaborative research dealing with the effects of immigration on cities. The federal government has established research centres across the country, including one each in Montreal, Toronto, Edmonton, Vancouver, and, more recently, Halifax. CERIS's mandate covers the GTA and the Province of Ontario as a whole. Nevertheless, because many of the participants are Toronto-based (from the universities and not-for-profit agencies), much of CERIS's research focuses on Toronto. During the period in which interviews were conducted in Toronto, CERIS's board members were solely from partner organizations in Toronto. This continues to be the case (CERIS, 'Governance Board and Directors'). Similarly, all but one of the members of the CERIS Partnership Advisory Council are from Toronto (one is from Mississauga). The fact that CERIS is located in Toronto means that a great deal of its research focuses on Toronto. That location also facilitates the development and maintenance of social networks among stakeholders in immigration policy in Toronto.

By comparison, Mississauga, Brampton, and Markham have fewer immigrant settlement organizations. According to a recent study, there are twenty immigrant-serving agencies in Mississauga, eight in Brampton, and six in Markham (Lim et al. 2005, 19, Table 5). Similarly, a study by Lucia Lo and her colleagues (2007) of the distribution of settlement services in the Toronto CMA concluded that the current distribution of settlement resources has not caught up with the trend towards the sub-urbanization of immigrant settlement (2007, 56). They hypothesized that the mismatch between settlement need and the availability of settlement services is the result of 'a widespread misconception among both the general population and policymakers that suburban regions are more affluent and do not have to deal with homelessness and other festering problems that exist in the city' (ibid.). This perception affects funding allocations in social services as well (ibid.).

Informants for this project pointed out that Markham's few settlement agencies are not home-grown; rather, they are branches of settlement agencies established elsewhere. For instance, COSTI, a prominent settlement organization in Toronto, has opened an office in Markham and provides language services to newcomers. The Catholic Community Service of York Region (which serves the entire region of York, not only Markham) provides the federal government's Immigrant Settlement and Adaptation and HOST programs in Markham through a local branch. The Markham African Caribbean Association and the Toronto Chinese Community Services Association also provide settlement services in Markham.

Markham does not seem to have interethnic umbrella organizations that coordinate efforts in the settlement and multiculturalism-related sectors and that serve an advocacy function. Mississauga and Brampton have two such agencies: the Peel Multicultural Council (PMC) and the Multicultural Inter-Agency Group of Peel (MIAG). Local leaders established the PMC in 1977 after the publication of a report by the Social Planning Council of Peel on immigrants' needs in Peel Region. The MIAG evolved from a task force of the Social Planning Council of Peel in 1982.

According to Marlene Magado, a community leader in Markham's immigrant-serving sector, Markham's most prominent local ethno-cultural organizations are the Federation of Chinese Canadians in

Markham (FCCM), the Markham Federation of Filipino Canadians, and the Markham African Caribbean Association (Magado 2004, interview). These organizations do not provide settlement services as defined by upper levels of government, but their programs help integrate immigrants by engaging them in community activities. Of the three organizations, the FCCM is clearly the largest and most active, with four divisions: the Markham Chinese Seniors Association, the Chinese Sports and Recreation Club of Markham, the Chinese Chamber of Commerce in Markham, and the Markham Chinese Cultural Club. Though the FCCM is ethnospecific, there is evidence that it is moving in a more multicultural direction. In 2001 the Chinese Chamber of Commerce supported the development of a multicultural professional association, one that would include members of the wider Asian community, to be called Asian-Canadian Entrepreneurs and Professionals (ACEP). This effort built on the efforts of Dr Ken Ng and Eric Viola, who launched an *Asian-Canadian Business Directory* in 1993 and 1994 (Federation of Chinese Canadians in Markham, 'Homepage').

Multiculturalism and the Business Community

The involvement of the business community and private foundations in multiculturalism policy development and in managing intercultural relations also differed among the cases in the GTA sample. In Toronto, private foundations support organizations representing immigrants, refugees, and ethnocultural minorities through many community foundations such as the Maytree and Laidlaw foundations. Foundations offer financial *and* in-kind support; they also conduct valuable research in the sector.

The Maytree Foundation deserves particular mention. Alan Broadbent, a prominent Toronto businessman and philanthropist, established it in 1982 and is its current chair and CEO. Facilitating capacity building in immigrant and refugee settlement in large urban centres is one of the foundation's priorities. In 2001 the foundation's assets were worth close to $24 million and its total grants to community organizations were close to $1.4 million (Grantmakers Concerned with Immigrants and Refugees website[15]). Leaders in Toronto's settlement sector consider the Maytree Foundation an important catalyst for change in the city, as well as an ally. The foundation is viewed as bold and progressive. Broadbent's philosophy is one of 'venture philanthropy,' which involves taking high risks in exchange for high returns in successful ventures. He disagrees with funders who try to leverage their grants by asking community organizations to match contributions, preferring instead to ensure that enough money is available to implement the organization's goals (Broadbent 2001).

The Maytree Foundation influences change in Toronto by providing grants to community agencies, offering management training to employees of community organizations, developing community leaders in partnership with York University through its Leaders for Change program, and providing loans to immigrants for credential assessment and short-term training needed to enter their occupation (Maytree Foundation 2004). Several leaders in the immigrant settlement sector who were interviewed for this study were graduates of Maytree's Leaders for Change program. Maytree has also launched special projects such as TRIEC and the Funders' Network on Racism and Poverty. More recently (and since the interviews were conducted), the Maytree Foundation and the TCSA have partnered to launch a new project called 'Diverse City: The Greater Toronto Leadership Project.' This project aims to integrate Toronto's diverse population into leadership positions in the private sector and not-for-profit sectors (Diverse City website).

Since 2001, Toronto's business community has taken a more visible role in immigration and settlement by allying itself with the city to advocate for new fiscal, political, and legislative relationships – popularly referred to as a 'New Deal' – between the City of Toronto and upper levels of government. The business community plays a prominent role in the Toronto City Summit Alliance (TCSA), which is devoted to this goal. The TCSA developed at a conference convened by former Toronto mayor Mel Lastman in 2001, which was attended by prominent community leaders representing various sectors in Toronto. The alliance that developed after the conference has drawn together representatives from business, labour, the not-for-profit sector, cultural industries, and universities; also participating are past mayors and a past premier of Ontario. The alliance has made 'becoming a centre of excellence in the integration of immigrants' one of its top five policy priorities (TCSA 2002) along with a 'New Deal' in immigration and settlement from upper levels of government. The TCSA has established the Toronto Region Immigrant Employment Council (TRIEC) to create local capacity to integrate immigrants into the city's economy.[16] The Maytree Foundation supports the administrative costs of the TCSA and its related working groups and alliances. Alan Broadbent's recent book *Urban Nation* (2008) advocates city-state (provincial) status for Canada's largest and most important immigrant destinations – Montreal, Toronto, and Vancouver. In his book he links immigration to the need for greater urban autonomy and, ultimately, to the future economic success of Canada's largest cities.

In contrast, in Mississauga, the mainstream business community, as represented by the Mississauga Board of Trade, has not taken an active interest in immigration issues (Stobie 2005, interview).

Brampton's business community seems to be making efforts towards integration. The Brampton Board of Trade (BBOT) website has a multilingual portal with information available in Punjabi, Portuguese, Italian, and French. Also, the BBOT has recently begun participating in TRIEC (Leiba 2005, interview). Its current general manager, Sheldon Leiba, was executive assistant to former Brampton mayor Peter Robertson, whose leadership was key to establishing the former Brampton Race Relations Action Committee. According to its own website, the BBOT has established a Multiculturalism Committee.

In Markham, the mainstream business community does not appear to have been as proactive as Toronto in supporting social initiatives and community development for the immigrant community. However, the Federation of Chinese Canadians of Markham (FCCM) has taken a leadership role in developing the Chinese community's social and economic integration into Markham. The FCCM houses a prominent Chinese business association (the Chinese Chamber of Commerce) and offers a variety of social services to the local Chinese community.

The business community's important role in intercultural relations in Markham became apparent in 1995 during the Carole Bell controversy. The Chinese business community helped pressure the city to respond to Bell's comments through its connection with Dr Ken Ng, who at the time was president of the FCCM and co-chair of the Coalition of Concerned Canadians. On 29 August 1995 the Markham Board of Trade issued a media release stating: 'We invite and encourage the Chinese business community to join our organization and work with us towards the common goal of harmony and prosperity ... We hope reciprocal invitations will be forthcoming as well.' The Board of Trade also took a conciliatory position on the issue of English-language signage in Asian malls: 'We support the view that all signage and public literature contain English [but] the Markham Board of Trade believes that this should be voluntary, not legislated' (Markham Board of Trade 1995).

Ten years later, the Markham Board of Trade is trying to encourage the integration of the business community, which continues to be fragmented ethnically. It has a diversity committee that advises the board and staff on cultural issues. Representatives of both the Town of Markham and York Region sit on this committee. In addition, the

Markham Board of Trade has a partnership with the Scarborough–York Region Chinese Association. But despite these efforts, the Chinese business community continues to operate somewhat independently. According to Keith Bray, president and CEO of the Markham Board of Trade, it is 'very hard to cross-pollinate' with the Chinese community in Markham and there are times when 'one might get the feeling that Chinese business is not interested in serving the clientele from the existing community' (Bray 2005, interview). As discussed earlier, the Chinese Chamber of Commerce remains independent of the Board of Trade but seems to be reaching out to the larger Asian business community. Bray would like to see the business community become more integrated with Markham:

> Our job here [at the Markham Board of Trade] is to be the voice of business for Markham. And, to speak for the business community, there's no place for race and creed. And there's too many splinter groups that have formed, ethnic-driven organizations that all want a piece of time [from the city] and yet our issues are common. There's probably three Chinese organizations that work independently of each other in this area ... If you think of it at a town level, town official level, each group thinks their issues are unique and want a piece of time. All of them should be part of the big picture too. And we're the umbrella. We're working very hard to make sure that we're an appropriate umbrella for them. That we're welcoming. (Bray 2005, interview)

In Markham, the mainstream business community recognizes that it has a clear stake in community integration, because business interests cannot be effectively represented when the business community is divided.

The Municipal Civil Service and 'Street-Level' Bureaucrats

Significant differences are apparent in the extent to which commitment to, and supports for, multiculturalism policy development and implementation exist in municipal civil services.

In Toronto, the DMU plays an important role in coordinating diversity policies across municipal departments. Also, civil servants with a keen commitment to diversity issues can be found in many departments and agencies and help ensure that the DMU's objectives are implemented at the departmental level.

Furthermore, from what was uncovered during the research, Toronto is the only municipality in Canada to have an intergovernmental relations unit. This unit reflects the higher level of municipal policy-making capacity in Toronto. It has been instrumental in supporting the city's efforts to secure new fiscal and political relationships with both upper levels of government – for example, in immigration policy.

Mississauga has a few advocates on behalf of immigrants and ethnocultural minorities within individual departments and agencies, including the recreation department. According to the Carassauga website, the festival has 'always enjoyed' a close working relationship with the city's Parks and Recreation Division. Community leaders in Mississauga's settlement sector identified one employee in that division as an especially strong advocate. In general, where advocates for immigrants and ethnocultural minorities existed in municipal civil services, they were easy for the researcher to identify. People in community organizations were usually aware of them, since in order to be responsive to immigrant communities, civil servants must first contact immigrant-serving organizations for advice.

But even when a few advocates for multiculturalism policies can be found in the civil service, if political support and a broader commitment to multiculturalism are both lacking, it is local politicians who drive local decision making. In Mississauga, a common theme in the interviews with Mayor McCallion and Councillor Iannicca was that politicians cannot let the civil service take over decision making (Iannicca 2004, interview; McCallion 2004, interview).

It is possible that Brampton, too, has 'street level' bureaucrats who support multiculturalism policy development. However, these individuals could not be identified, since community organizations were ambivalent about a municipal role in immigrant settlement and other multiculturalism initiatives.

In Markham there is no independent unit or separate staff person whose job it is to ensure that a multiculturalism lens is applied to policy making. At the time the interviews were conducted, the town's Human Resources Department was taking a leadership role in this respect. Markham was developing a diversity policy as well as an employment equity policy. However, it is the town's Race Relations Committee that appears to be driving changes in multiculturalism policy.

The Role of the Media

Interviewees were not asked about the role of the media. However, in Toronto, several interviewees noted the importance of the *Toronto Star* to agenda setting in the city. In a 2002 article, *Star* reporter Sonia Verma referred to the newspaper as a 'fearless crusader,' tracing its activist history as far back as 1920 (2002, A1). Several councillors who were interviewed referred to the *Star* as an ally. Deputy Mayor Joe Pantalone described the *Star* as 'responsive to airing city issues' (Pantalone 2004, interview). Councillor Brian Ashton called the *Star* a resource for the city and a means for Toronto to get its message to Ottawa (Ashton 2005, interview). Also according to Ashton, the city cannot lobby Ottawa on its own, and the *Star* helps it do so to a certain extent.

Under the leadership of its former publisher, John Honderich (1994–2004), the *Star* was a key player in raising the issue of a 'New Deal' for cities on the national and provincial agendas. Many New Deal activists trace the movement's rise to a page-one editorial that Honderich wrote on 12 January 2002, which described what he perceived as an urban crisis (Gillespie 2005, B1). In May 2004, Toronto's new mayor, David Miller, appointed Honderich to be his 'special ambassador on the cities agenda' (Gillespie 2004, B1). The *Star*'s editorial position on the 'New Deal' issue continued after Honderich's departure in 2004. For instance, in 2005, then editor-in-chief Giles Gherson wrote a piece that urged political leaders at all three levels of government (federal, provincial, and municipal) to 'push [the] pedal to the metal on [the] New Deal campaign' (Gherson 2005, A2). The TCSA's website indicates that Gherson participated in one of the alliance's initiatives – the Emerging Leaders Network. He spoke to the network on 6 June 2006 on the subject of 'how news about Toronto and city building is made' (TCSA 'Emerging Leaders Network').

The *Star* is also reputed to be more progressive in certain respects than Canada's national newspapers. For example, it has assigned a reporter to cover the diversity and immigration beat (currently that reporter is Nicholas Keung). The paper also played a key role in bringing the issue of racial profiling in police services to the forefront of public debate. Between 19 and 27 October 2002, the *Star* published a series of controversial articles suggesting that Blacks in Toronto were victims of racial profiling by Toronto police. The Toronto Police Association responded by filing a class action suit against the *Star* for $2.7 billion. Justice Maurice Cullity dismissed the case in June 2003. The issue of racial profiling remains on Toronto's local agenda (Mascoll and Rankin 2005).

Politicians in suburban municipalities mentioned the impact of a well-circulated local paper as a possible reason for Toronto's higher level of activity in multiculturalism policy, but for different reasons. According to one informant, because the *Star* politicizes local issues in Toronto, local politicians must posture for the public; at times, this involves developing policies in areas outside local jurisdiction (Fisch 2004, interview).

In Markham, the *Markham Economist and Sun* played a key role in documenting the conflict between former deputy mayor Carole Bell (and her supporters) and the Coalition of Concerned Canadians (CCC). However, according to a community leader in York Region, the local newspapers are not generally directed towards immigrants (community leader 2004, interview). In the Carole Bell incident, the newspaper reported what had become a community-wide issue of importance to both long-standing residents and the immigrant community.

The *Mississauga News* seems to support Hazel McCallion, perhaps because of personal connections between the mayor and the newspaper owner. One informant described that paper's owner as a 'good friend' of McCallion (Peel Region civil servant 2004, interview). An archive search on the *Mississauga News* website for 'Hazel McCallion' brought up several articles praising the mayor. Over the course of the research, no articles in the *News* that were critical of McCallion were found; indeed, most references to her were congratulatory. For instance, one article written by Karen Bridson-Boysczuk (2004), titled 'Business Leaders Singing City's Praises: Business Leaders Still Bullish About City,' mentioned several times how important McCallion has been to the city's economic success. Since McCallion is so highly respected (or greatly feared) in the community, it would likely be difficult to uncover a local story that portrays her in a negative light or that criticizes her decisions. In particular, given her power, it would be hard to find a member of the community who would want to be quoted as disagreeing with her.

Local leaders did not mention the *Brampton Guardian* as significant to multiculturalism policy in any way.

A Qualitative Analysis of Local Political Cultures

American urban scholar Barbara Ferman (2002) defines political culture as 'the collective expectations of the population about the roles and behavior of their government and political system' (2002, 7). She identifies some broad traits of local political cultures that influence community mobilization at the local level. Generally, some local cultures 'emphasize communalism, collective enterprise, trust, reciprocity, and social networking,' whereas others are 'characterized by cynicism, mistrust, competitiveness, and strong individualism' (ibid., 7–8).

In *Making Democracy Work* (1993), Robert Putnam argues that a community's level of 'social capital' explains the extent to which institutions perform well or are responsive to community concerns. Social capital refers to interpersonal relationships of trust and reciprocity that facilitate community organization. In other words, social capital facilitates collective action. Communities vary in the extent to which they possess strong and socially productive stocks of relationships built on interpersonal trust.

Urban regime analyses of American cities have found that the ethnic and racial composition of cities influences how social capital is distributed in local communities. Marion Orr (1999) found that Blacks in Baltimore possessed ethnospecific social capital – what he calls 'Black social capital.' Orr's case study implies that to determine whether institutions are responsive, it is not enough to measure levels of social capital across entire communities. Instead one must examine which groups possess social capital and how patterns of social capital determine who benefits from urban policies. Furthermore, where interpersonal networks of social capital are fragmented, one must also pay attention to bridging between groups. According to Orr, the 'urban regime' concept characterizes the role that city governments can play in creating bridges between groups. Intergroup policy preferences are negotiated within the regime.

Clarence Stone and his colleagues (2001) have developed the concept of 'civic capacity' to describe the capacity of an intersectoral group of local leaders to cooperate in efforts to solve significant urban challenges (2001, 4). The 'concept of civic capacity has roots in some broader theoretical discussions about urban politics, social capital, problem definition, and nonincremental policy change,' but unlike the concept of 'social capital [, which] concerns behaviour that is largely interpersonal and private ... civic capacity centers on activities that are squarely in the public arena and involve governance institutions and major group representatives' (ibid., 5). The concept of 'civic capacity' shares theoretical ground with that of 'social capital' but differs in that it emphasizes productive relationships among elites and their significance for public policy rather than simply interpersonal relationships. In this way, it draws our attention to the role of elites in intra- and inter-sectoral cooperation as well as in interethnic cooperation.

Putnam's work measured social capital by examining the preponderance of organizations that had little direct relevance for public policy (such as bowling leagues). One could argue that patterns of organization in social service agencies and other agencies that serve immigrants are a better measure of the social capital of immigrant communities (Douglas 2003, interview). Furthermore, such organizations represent potential partners in multiculturalism policy development.

The concept of 'civic capacity' offers an observable way of measuring political culture by drawing attention to the relations among leaders of established organizations in civil society. Political cultures and levels of civic capacity differed across the four GTA cases. Important differences emerged regarding how immigrants and ethnocultural organizations were organized, the extent to which they were capable of cooperating, the strategies they used to influence local governance, and their general expectations of the local government's role and behaviour. Furthermore, across the four communities, there were differences in how long-standing residents – the 'majority population' – reacted to large-scale immigration.

Markham stands out among the cases insofar as immigration generated a widespread community backlash. No evidence of a backlash towards immigrants was found in Toronto, Mississauga, or Brampton. As Hazel McCallion put it in 2004, Mississauga simply does not have the 'racial confrontation' that exists in Markham (McCallion 2004, interview).

In Toronto, leaders of immigrant settlement and other ethnocultural organizations said they found it relatively easy to cooperate with one another (Douglas 2003, interview; Shakir 2003, interview; Melles 2004, interview). Some leaders mentioned that cooperation among immigrant-serving agencies builds on a long tradition of cooperation among community organizations in Toronto more generally (Melles 2004, interview). As needed, coalitions develop among organizations on issues of common concern. These coalitions are sustained for varying periods of time depending on the issue, and they tend to draw in familiar groups of actors. A good example of such a coalition was the Elections Equity Coalition, which formed during the 2003 municipal election campaign to ensure that issues of concern to immigrants and ethnocultural minorities were on the agenda of the various candidates for municipal office. The effectiveness of that coalition can be seen in the fact that they organized a debate of mayoral candidates which five of the leading candidates attended: David Miller, Barbara Hall, John Tory, John Nunziata, and Tom Jacobek.

In general, the City of Toronto's political culture is highly dynamic. Organizations in Toronto expect a great deal more of their local government than do organizations in other GTA municipalities. As a result, leaders in the immigrant-serving sector are more critical of the city than one might expect, given the city's level of responsiveness to multiculturalism. Differences in political cultures between Toronto and the other GTA municipalities sample are also evident in the strategies community organizations deploy to influence local decision making. According to Debbie Douglas, President of the Ontario Council of Agencies Serving Immigrants (OCASI) – Ontario's umbrella organization representing immigrant settlement agencies – in Ontario these organizations generally follow two strategies to influence the political process: either meeting 'in the boardroom' or meeting 'on the street.' According to her, organizations in Toronto employ both strategies, whereas organizations in suburban municipalities like Mississauga, Brampton, and Markham tend to prefer the former (Douglas 2003, interview).

It is interesting that in Toronto, organizations that one would expect to be 'small-c' conservative employ these grassroots, less conventional advocacy strategies. For instance, in its recent campaign to educate the public about the need for new political, fiscal, and legislative relationships between the City of Toronto and upper levels of government, the Toronto Board of Trade used grassroots strategies. As Toronto councillor Shelley Carroll described it: 'When we had the "Enough Of Not Enough" campaign with the Board of Trade, that was so uniquely Torontonian because it's businesses saying that "Yeah, we'll help you out," but they did it in an activist sort of way. To be going out to subways and handing out postcards and things, it was like the Board of Trade had become "People for Education"[17] or "Citizens for Local Democracy"'[18] (Carroll 2004, interview).

Carroll gave the impression that there was strong solidarity among a broad range of organizations in Toronto that wanted Toronto to thrive as a city (ibid.). The strategies of local leaders reflect fundamental differences in political culture between Toronto and the three suburban municipalities in the GTA sample.

However, local leaders' expectations are the most striking indicator of Toronto's dynamic political culture. These people expect the city to overcome its jurisdictional and resource limitations and provide leadership in multiculturalism policy. They do not accept the argument that these policy areas are provincial and federal responsibilities and, therefore, beyond the scope of local mandates. As Uzma Shakir put it: 'One of the reasons I do believe that municipalities must play a role is because people settle in municipalities, they live in cities, they don't live in jurisdictions, they don't define themselves in constitutional jurisdictional things, they don't care. Immigrants have come here, they have come to Canada, they have chosen Toronto or Mississauga or Markham and that's where they're living their lives and the nearest level of government to them is the municipal government' (Shakir 2003, interview).

Instead of accepting the established framework of decision making and the division of powers between levels of government, local leaders in the immigrant-serving sector in Toronto have chosen to challenge them. This orientation towards upper levels of government and the City of Toronto is not unique to the immigrant settlement and other multiculturalism-related sectors. A broad intersectoral alliance of local leaders (which includes the business sector) has developed around the goal of increased local autonomy for the City of Toronto.

In contrast to Toronto, a culture of competition rather than cooperation pervades the immigrant-serving sector in Mississauga. Andrea Seepersaud, the executive director of the largest immigrant settlement organization in Mississauga, described relations among immigrant-serving organizations in Peel Region as a 'back-biting, back-stabbing affair' because of the scarcity of funding. She put it bluntly: 'I don't see that spirit of cooperation.' She added that even when it occurred, co-operation led to a dead end. She contrasted Mississauga with Toronto, where, in her experience, organizations were willing to share information and partner and where the approach to delivering services centred on clients instead of being driven by organizational interests (Seepersaud 2003, interview). Another representative of the sector said: 'We're all trying to get money from the same pot' – a circumstance that made it hard to partner with those who were applying for the same grants (Mississauga community leader 2003, interview).

Seepersaud also tied Mississauga's inaction to a more general lack of political efficacy among the city's residents: 'The people in Mississauga don't think much can be done by themselves. It's sort of relax and let others do it for them. So if they don't like the way garbage is picked up, they're not thinking, "We can change this by doing things differently, by getting somebody who is more with the community to sit on the council that actually makes decisions around these kinds of things." ... Let's start getting our people in there!' (Seepersaud 2003, interview).

Other leaders of immigrant-serving organizations in Mississauga said that newcomers were themselves partly 'responsible' for the lack of municipal responsiveness to their concerns. One of them suggested that immigrants tend to feel that they are responsible for participating only in federal and provincial elections (Chaudhry 2003, interview). Seepersaud agreed that low voter turnout among immigrants was part of the problem: 'We have become an extremely diverse community where the advantage in being in this community is the diversity itself and you've got these square pegs ... getting elected because we don't go out and vote.' She also cited conflict and competition among ethnic groups that had been transferred from other countries as a barrier to the electoral success of newcomers in municipal elections. She suggested that if an Indian candidate were to run in a municipal election, Pakistanis would mobilize against that person (Seepersaud 2003, interview). This research indeed found evidence that conflict was being transferred from immigrants' countries of origin. One example, already mentioned, was McCallion's intervention in a conflict between two Sikh factions over a parade route. In general, the evidence indicated that the immigrant population was more divided in Mississauga than in Toronto.

Also, community organizations in Mississauga did not appear to expect the same level of responsiveness by the city to the concerns of immigrants and ethnocultural minorities, and they were more cynical about the likelihood that the city would take on a significant role in immigration-related policy. Furthermore, community organizations representing immigrant concerns were not proactive in their approach to putting immigrants' concerns on the agenda. Naveed Chaudhry, Executive Director of the Peel Multicultural Council, who is an immigrant from Pakistan, noted the wisdom of an expression in his mother tongue that translates: 'Even mothers only feed their [own] babies when they cry' (Chaudhry 2003, interview).

There is similar evidence of a culture of competition among ethnocultural organizations in Brampton. On 17 September 1992, an article in the *Toronto Star* reported some 'in-fighting' between two of the region's most prominent ethnocultural organizations: the Peel Multicultural Council (PMC) and the Brampton Multicultural Centre. The Executive Director of the PMC reported that the Brampton Multicultural Centre had split off from the PMC, which was worried that the centre intended to take over its advocacy functions in Brampton. In the article, the mayor at the time, Peter Robertson, referred to the issue as one of 'jealousies between the two groups' (Robertson in White 1992b).

More recently, a community leader interviewed for this study seemed not to have considered the city's role in facilitating immigrant settlement in Brampton (Nuss 2004, interview). Perhaps for this reason, the response rate to requests for interviews with leaders of community organizations was very low in Brampton. Local leaders in Brampton did not seem to expect the municipality to play a role in multiculturalism policy.

In contrast, Markham's newcomer community seems to possess considerable capacity for cooperation and collective political action. This culture of cooperation became evident in the summer of 1995, when the community organized spontaneously in response to comments made by the deputy mayor, Carole Bell, at a regional meeting – comments that many people in the community perceived as racist. Her comments were directed primarily at the Chinese community. In the context of a discussion of the strengths and weaknesses of York Region, she said: 'The growing concentration of ethnic groups is causing conflicts in Markham ... The weakness of multiculturalism ... comes when there is a concentration, when you are getting only one group of people' (Queen 1995). She then added a more personal statement: 'I wouldn't come to the region and I would go because of it – and I'm saying that truthfully' (Queen 1995).

An ad hoc community committee, which would later become the Coalition of Concerned Canadians (CCC), sprang up a few weeks after Bell made her comments to demand that she apologize, retract her statement, and publicly recognize the contributions of Chinese Canadians to Markham. She refused to apologize, instead choosing to 'clarify' her position by writing a series of letters to the editors of community newspapers that contained comments that further offended many Markham residents. She stated: 'When dozens of individuals who are the backbone of Markham say they are moving away, as dozens of other neighbours and friends have, then we have a problem that must be addressed.' Also, 'We once had one of the finest communities in North America with enviable business parks and the top corporations in the land. Now all we get are theme malls to serve people way beyond our borders' (Bell 1995). According to many in Markham, her comments implied that immigrants to Markham – Chinese immigrants in particular – were not part of the 'backbone' of Markham society. In these letters, Bell also raised concerns about the lack of English signage in Asian malls.

What became the CCC was co-chaired by two leaders in Markham's ethnocultural 'minority' community: Dr Ken Ng, President of the Federation of Chinese Canadians in Markham (FCCM) and the current chair of its board; and Marlene Magado, then chair of the Markham

Federation of Filipino Canadians. In other words, the incident led to an interethnic coalition to fight the racialization of the Chinese community and to press the deputy mayor for an apology. The CCC had many allies, and its support grew as the conflict unfolded. The Harmony Movement, a prominent national organization devoted to creating interracial, interethnic, and interreligious harmony, circulated a petition that was endorsed by more than one hundred organizations. These organizations represented many sectors and had varying degrees of clout. For example, they included prominent organizations such as the Toronto-Dominion Bank and the Canadian Auto Workers Union. Signatories to the petition also included prominent individuals, including many mayors of other GTA municipalities.

The Carole Bell controversy illustrated how local councillors can politicize community-based networks in local communities. Her comments resulted in a massive mobilization of ethnocultural minorities; it also politicized long-standing residents who were opposed to (or, at least, concerned about) some of the changes occurring in Markham. The latter group was largely invisible,[19] yet it seems to have possessed high levels of social capital – or perhaps more accurately, 'antisocial capital' (Levi 1996) – which it was able to translate into political influence. Throughout the storm, Bell insisted repeatedly that she was simply representing the views of these long-standing residents. There is a great deal of evidence to support her contention. Bell reported that she received 500 letters of support and overwhelming support through phone calls (Krivel 1995, A6). Newspapers reported residents expressing cultural insecurities. As one resident put it: 'We don't mind sharing, but we don't want to be taken over by other cultures' (Belgrave 1995, A1). According to a *Markham Economist and Sun* report, about four hundred supporters attended a council meeting on 28 August, and stood and applauded as Deputy Mayor Bell entered the council chamber. The previous week, the CCC had made deputations to council in a chamber crowded with its own supporters. The rest of the council, however, refused to denounce Bell's comments. Only Alex Chiu, who is ethnically Chinese and who represented the highly diverse ward of Milliken Mills, spoke out publicly against the deputy mayor after initially remaining 'neutral.' In fact, Mayor Don Cousens not only failed to denounce Bell's comments, but also came to her defence: 'I have known Carole Bell for many years, and I know her not to be racist' (Cousens, quoted in Krivel 1995). According to Marlene Magado, co-chair of the CCC, Cousens conceded in a private meeting that the CCC was right in principle, but added that he could not denounce Bell's remarks because of his political 'friends' (Magado 2005, personal communication).

To summarize, immigration and the social change it brought about affected the four local communities differently. We see evidence of differences in levels of 'civic capacity' in the cases as well as the introduction of new community and political dynamics. In the next section these differences are filtered through an urban regime framework to show how they matter when it comes to municipal responsiveness to immigrants and ethnocultural minorities.

Understanding How Differences Matter: Looking at the Cases through an Urban Regime Lens

The urban regime literature sheds light on how the differences among these four highly diverse municipalities have interacted to lead to the various policy outputs discussed in chapter 3. Urban regimes have three interdependent components: a set of actors, a set of relationships, and a capacity (Stone 1989, 179). A regime's policy capacity is a function of who participates in the regime network and the resources they bring to bear on the regime's policy goals. As we have seen, the actors who support multiculturalism policy and who view themselves as stakeholders in positive ethnocultural relations and in immigrant settlement vary across municipalities. We have also seen notable differences in relationships among various public- and private-sector actors. Moreover, the findings reveal disparities with respect to community capacity in immigrant settlement and other multiculturalism-related endeavours.

Urban regime analysis is valuable in terms of explaining regime development and maintenance. Moreover, this theoretical model stresses the immensity of the challenge of creating and maintaining intersectoral relationships, as well as how the requisite resources can be pooled for effective policy responses to complex urban policy problems. So it is also useful as a theoretical tool for understanding why cooperative relationships fail to develop around some urban agendas and in some contexts.

In their article on urban governance in Detroit during the period of Coleman Young's mayoralty, Marion Orr and Gerry Stoker (1999) applied urban regime theory to investigate why an effective public–private partnership did not emerge as a revitalization strategy and to suggest a new way to analyse local politics (1999, 50). This section examines instances of regime development as well as reasons why a regime fails to develop multiculturalism policy.

The Toronto Regime: 'Diversity Our Strength'

Urban regime theory helps one understand the City of Toronto's relative responsiveness to the concerns and preferences of ethnocultural minorities and of immigrants. The City of Toronto has *chosen* to develop policy capacity to respond to ethnocultural change in its population by developing local capacity in access and equity policy over time. It has helped form and then participated in coalitions of public- and private-sector actors, and it has advocated among upper levels of government on behalf of immigrants. Toronto's relatively comprehensive approach to including immigrants and ethnocultural minorities' needs and preferences in local governance can be understood in terms of its own capacity in multiculturalism policy, the breadth of its intersectoral participation in governance, and its regime's resources. Besides developing locally based cooperative relationships, Toronto has been seeking new modes of cooperation with upper levels of government to meet newcomers' needs.

Toronto's current capacity in access and equity policy builds on the policy capacity of the former City of Toronto and former Metro Toronto. The city's choice of 'Diversity of Strength' as its official motto expresses its commitment to access and equity. Like Atlanta's motto, 'The City Too Busy to Hate' (Stone 1989), Toronto's motto has served to reduce 'transaction costs' among regime participants by formalizing the regime's broad purposes. Its Task Force on Access and Equity (1998) involved wide-scale public participation, which helped consolidate the access and equity policy networks that existed in some pre-amalgamation municipalities (especially the City of Toronto and Metro Toronto).

For this reason, in Toronto, the access and equity policy framework continues to serve as a 'solution set' – that is, as a dominant understanding of the nature of a policy problem and the types of solutions appropriate to such problems (Jones and Bachelor 1993). In Toronto, past policies do indeed shape current diversity policies, which have been perpetuated not only by the ideas and understandings of city officials, but also by a well-organized immigrant settlement sector and by active ethnocultural community organizations and coalitions. In other words, policy ideas have been institutionalized both in the city's formal institutions and in its informal networks. It is especially noteworthy that the access and equity policy framework survived amalgamation.

However, in the newly amalgamated Toronto, another way of framing immigration and multiculturalism, one that stresses the benefits of diversity to economic development, has risen to prominence. This new framework is consistent with a broader trend in Canada towards a neoliberal policy discourse that ties immigration, multiculturalism, and employment equity to success in a global economy. Yasmeen Abu-Laban and Christine Gabriel (2002) have characterized this shift in policy discourse at the national level as one that now emphasizes 'selling diversity.'[20]

The 'selling diversity' policy framework has not displaced the access and equity framework of the pre-amalgamation City of Toronto and Metro Toronto. However, there is some evidence of a shift in policy discourse in the naming of the department responsible for multiculturalism initiatives: the DMU. As Abu-Laban and Gabriel (2002) explain, the idea of 'managing diversity' originated in the human-resources and management literature of the 1980s. According to this model, a diverse workforce becomes a comparative advantage in a global economy (2002, 153). Ethnocultural diversity is not accommodated out of fairness and principles of justice; rather, it is 'managed' in order to (a) promote economic growth, and (b) avoid race relations problems that could threaten business investment.

The prominence of the link between immigration and ethnic diversity on the one hand and economic development on the other has broadened the scope of Toronto's governance arrangements. Because the prevailing economic wisdom is that Toronto's economic performance in a global economy is tied to its ability to 'city build' and be diversity friendly, the Toronto regime has acquired new and highly powerful partners in capacity building in immigrant settlement, including the Toronto Board of Trade and Manulife Financial.

The Toronto case illustrates the importance of the local state's capacity for regime responsiveness and maintenance. In Toronto, the DMU in the CAO's office plays an important role by serving as a bridge linking the city bureaucracy to council and civil society. It is also an important repository of policy expertise and of research in access and equity policy. Local capacity in access and equity has given Toronto a partial autonomy that allows it to take a more proactive role in immigration and multiculturalism policy.

The participation of the immigrant settlement sector and of ethnoracial community organizations in municipal decision making is sustained through working groups and committees that provide regular communication between the public sector (both elected and administrative) and the private sector. Toronto's diverse regime builds on the capacity of a strong immigrant-settlement sector and on a range of eth-noracial advocacy organizations.

As regime theory would predict, the private sector plays an important role in immigrant settlement and in access and equity policy in Toronto. Foundations such as the Laidlaw Foundation and the May-tree Foundation provide the regime with important resources in the form of research, community capacity building grants, and leadership training in civil society. More recently, under the regime's leadership, prominent private-sector companies, such as Manulife Financial, have been serving as mentors to new immigrants with foreign credentials and experience.

In 1996 the federal government began funding the Metropolis Project and its local research branch in Toronto (CERIS) as a means to bring together networks of government officials at all three levels of govern-ment and a cross-sectoral group of leaders in civil society who have a stake in immigrant settlement in Canada's urban centres. Toronto hosted the international Metropolis annual conference in October 2005. This initiative strengthened existing networks and built new ones. It is an important example of how upper levels of government can help steer change in local governance without violating the division of pow-er (which grants provincial governments exclusive responsibility for municipalities).

A network of councillors who are strong advocates of immigrant set-tlement and diversity policy provide political leadership to the regime. Also, the particularities of Toronto's institutional structure have facili-tated the maintenance of urban regime relationships, even when may-ors change. The relatively weak mayoral system – even since measures were introduced to strengthen the role of the mayor and executive on council – and the relatively large council allow community leaders to maintain 'socially productive' relationships with like-minded council-lors, even when a mayor who does not make access and equity a prior-ity is in office. One community leader in the immigrant-serving sector mentioned that under Mel Lastman's leadership, the city was not as responsive to the concerns of her organization, but she could still con-tact particular councillors with whom she had established relationships (community leader 2004, interview).

Toronto's access and equity regime follows a pattern of policy change described in Stone's *Regime Politics*. To a certain extent, urban regimes are self-perpetuating or 'path-dependent.' The policy responses and initiatives of the past result in the emergence of a certain form of politics that, in turn, fosters related policies. Thus, while Toronto's DMU is an example of responsiveness, it now supports stakeholders in these policies and thus is both a 'dependent' and an 'independent' variable.

Stone's (1989) earlier work emphasized the role of selective material incentives in regime maintenance and attributed an important role to the business community in providing these incentives. Material selective incentives do play a role in maintaining informal cooperative efforts at the local level; however, Toronto's local regime is also maintained by what interest group scholar Jack Walker (1983) calls state sponsorship, with both purposive incentives and material incentives serving as 'side payments.' For instance, the city's Access and Equity Grants Program has an important regime maintenance function. Through this program, the local state not only supports existing interest groups and movements, but also shapes the structure of civil society and in this way develops and extends the regime.

Alan Cairns, a prominent Canadian political scientist, developed the concept of the 'embedded state' to describe the interdependent relationship between the Canadian state and civil society as well as to convey the idea that institutions can shape civil society and, through incentives, 'create' identities (Cairns 1985). The concept of the 'embedded state' describes some aspects of the relationship between the City of Toronto and civil society, such as its interdependent nature. However, whereas Cairns's concept of 'embeddedness' evokes images of stasis, coercion, and dependence, the Toronto case evidences a more dynamic, variable, and purposive relationship between the municipality and civil society. As regime theory implies, at the local level, local leaders must actively and *purposively* maintain relationships with local political officials, civil servants, and civil-society organizations. Local leaders across sectors choose whether to foster interdependence between the state and civil society and which policy ends to pursue.

In Toronto, local leaders have chosen to develop governance arrangements that respond to the city's changing ethnocultural demographics. The city supports new groups, and these groups in turn pressure the state for policy change in a dynamic that Stone (1989) describes as 'structuring' (1989, 10). The resources that local leaders bring to the governance arrangement and the extent of intersectoral consensus on policy goals together shape the power dynamics of governance relationships. One cannot assume that the state possesses a disproportionate level of power over civil society. In the Canadian municipal environment, the question of 'power to' is more important than the question of 'power over.'

Some of the literature on the effects of state funding on community organizations stresses the coercive nature of such relationships. However, the Toronto experience appears to support Leslie Pal's (1995) more balanced assessment of the power dynamics inherent in state funding of community organizations.[21] The nature of the power relationships depends on the 'interests' of the state and the extent to which they coincide with the interests of the funded organizations. Furthermore, as regime theorists argue, regime arrangements reshape or structure the policy preferences of all regime participants, including those of local political officials and civil servants (state actors).

Toronto's community grants program is designed to support community organizations that help immigrants and address issues of interethnic equity. Access and equity funding fills gaps in community capacity and allows organizations to advocate. Indeed, Rose Lee of Toronto's DMU remarked that many of the community organizations funded by the city are the same ones that pressure the city to become more active in access and equity policy. In other words, the city does not fund only those organizations that are willing to manage social change without challenging the status quo. Lee joked about the pressure that city-funded community organizations bring to bear on the city; these organizations in effect tell the city: 'We are paid to be belligerent to you' (Lee 2003, interview).

Similarly, Toronto councillor Maria Augimeri acknowledged that there are many social service organizations that are 'progressive in nature [and] help lead us [the City of Toronto]' (Augimeri 2004, interview). The relationship between community organizations and the local state is best described as co-leadership on diversity-related issues. In other words, as regime theory predicts, the local state does not *control* regime participants but rather co-produces policy capacity *with* them.

It is also in the interest of local officials to strengthen the ability of immigrant settlement organizations to advocate, because it increases the effectiveness of these groups in extracting resources from 'state sponsors' at other levels of government. In other words, supporting community organizations can lead to more resources being transferred from upper levels of government to the municipality.

Furthermore, the municipal government's support of community organizations strengthens its ability to get funding from the private sector. As governments, municipalities have the ability to confer legitimacy on organizations and networks in civil society. Thus, while city budgets are limited, the city can implement its multiculturalism objectives by facilitating the ability of the private sector to participate in the 'regime.' According to Councillor Shelley Carroll, the city's vetting process makes private foundations more comfortable funding community organizations. For instance, the Maytree Foundation supports many of the same organizations that the City of Toronto funds through its community grants (Carroll 2004, interview).

In 2002, local leaders formed the TCSA, a coalition of what are popularly referred to as 'blue chip' influencers, to provide leadership on several community issues in Toronto and the metropolitan region. This alliance arose owing to a perceived lack of political leadership from upper levels of government on pressing issues in the city (Good 2004). Some community leaders also felt that former mayor Mel Lastman was not providing sufficient municipal leadership. However, Lastman and community leaders found common ground in their desire to 'take on' upper levels of government (Crombie 2003, interview). In Toronto, when political leadership wanes, the community tends to fill the gap and exert pressure for necessary policy changes. The city is truly co-led.

The *Toronto Star* participates in the city's regime on access and equity; it also crusades on the issue of the need for new relationships among the three orders of government. Unlike the editors of Canada's Toronto-based national newspapers (such as the *Globe and Mail* and the *National Post*) or the editor of the *Toronto Sun*, the *Star*'s former and current editors are personally committed to Toronto's New Deal agenda. However, while the *Star* is often an ally of the city, like community organizations, it is also a source of regime dynamism. The *Star* uncovers new issues and challenges in the city and frames them in ways that, while often supporting regime goals, also challenge local governance arrangements to respond to emerging issues. By drawing attention to particular city concerns (such as the New Deal agenda and racial profiling in police services), it plays a key role in establishing city priorities. In other words, the *Star* plays an important role in setting the city's agenda.

In this way, the *Star* serves the role that John Logan and Harvey Molotch (1987) describe in *Urban Fortunes* – it supports and maintains the city's general disposition towards growth (1987, 213). In their words, 'the media have a special influence simply because they are committed to growth per se, and can play an invaluable role in coordinating strategy and selling growth to the public' (ibid., 213). The *Star* helps promote the business case for immigration and successful settlement of highly skilled immigrants, as well as the more general message that a New Deal for cities is needed to attract more investment to Toronto.

Toronto's policy goals reflect the composition, scope, and dynamics of its regime. For instance, it is the only city in our sample of eight to have developed an Immigration and Settlement Policy Framework, because of its tight connections with leaders in a relatively well-resourced immigrant settlement sector. These leaders include people such as Debbie Douglas, Executive Director of OCASI, and Uzma Shakir, Executive Director of the Council of Agencies Serving South Asians (CASSA). When Toronto frames its multiculturalism initiatives as immigration and settlement policies, it is sending a message to upper levels of government that it is active in a policy field that formally belongs to the provincial and federal governments.

Remarkably, Toronto is the only city where members of the business community and prominent community foundations and community leaders in the settlement sector would all like to see local government take on an increased role in immigration and settlement policy. Furthermore, these stakeholders organized to pressure upper levels of government to negotiate a tri-level agreement in this policy field. (The fruits of their labour are discussed in chapter 7.) In other words, this policy reflects a broad-based intersectoral consensus on the current and emerging roles of the city in immigration policy and immigrant settlement (as defined by upper levels of government). The policy also brings together many years of policy expertise developed in the City of Toronto and the previous Metropolitan Toronto. In fact, the City of Toronto is arguably the most knowledgeable government in Canada with respect to settlement needs and other multiculturalism challenges (Ashton 2005, interview). This policy expertise is housed in the city's major institutions (both public and private) and is pooled within its urban regime.

In sum, Toronto's responsiveness to immigrants and ethnocultural minorities can be understood in terms of its public- and private-sector participation and the nature of the resources brought to the regime by local leaders in both sectors. The concept of 'growth machine' is also useful to understanding local governance in Toronto. With the rise to prominence of the idea that diversity is a comparative advantage in a global economy, and with the realization that failing to settle skilled immigrants adequately leads to billions of dollars of lost GDP, immigration politics have become central to growth machine politics. However, the growth machine framework does not help us understand why and how local leaders pursue growth the way they do. This is why it is important to examine the microdynamics of urban regimes. In Toronto, local business leaders such as Alan Broadbent have made the business case for immigration, and the settlement sector is included in the re-gime. In addition, local leaders have tied these issues to a broader de-bate and reform movement concerning the rising importance of cities in Canada. Local initiatives and politics matter.

Mississauga: Hazel McCallion's Personal Fiefdom

Mississauga's inactivity in multiculturalism policy needs to be under-stood as a political choice *not* to innovate in this area. Regime analysis pushes one to ask why there has been no cooperation on multicultural-ism initiatives in Mississauga. The case demonstrates how important political leaders are to incorporating new interests into municipal gov-ernance arrangements – and to keeping issues off the agenda.

Mississauga is led by a powerful mayor who does not see a role for municipalities in immigrant settlement and who believes in a 'melting pot' model of immigrant integration. Her influence is so pervasive that her personal opposition to municipal action in diversity policy virtu-ally pre-empts any city involvement in this area. Mayor McCallion's personal belief that employment equity and anti-racism policies are ineffective keeps these policy options off the municipal agenda. In ad-dition, local political leaders tightly limited the powers of municipali-ties while framing immigrant settlement as a federal responsibility. In Mississauga, both these factors have enabled Mississauga's politicians (including, most obviously, McCallion) to avoid directing their atten-tion towards immigration and multiculturalism issues.

In Mississauga, potential regime participants, such as the leaders of immigrant settlement organizations and of organizations that represent ethnocultural minorities, do not collaborate. The lack of collective ac-tion on the part of immigrant settlement agencies and other ethnocul-tural organizations can be explained in terms of selective disincentives for cooperation. Government grant programs can encourage organiza-tions to compete for scarce funding rather than cooperate with fellow agencies. In Mississauga the immigrant settlement sector is largely dis-engaged from local politics, focusing instead on service delivery and on securing resources from upper levels of government.

Of course, immigrant-serving agencies compete for funding in all municipalities in the sample. Therefore, other dynamics are also at work in Mississauga. As the literature on collective action suggests, rational individuals will not expend resources to act collectively to pursue goals that are perceived as unattainable (Chong 1991; Stone 2005). Councillors, civil servants, community leaders, and the business community in Mississauga all defer to McCallion's leadership. Given her strength, community leaders in Mississauga consider it fruitless to challenge her personal opinion that the city does not have a role to play in immigrant settlement and multiculturalism policy. In this sense, the city's immigrant settlement agencies and ethnocultural organizations are behaving rationally by not expending their scarce resources on efforts to influence the city. From the perspective of the immigrant settlement sector, it makes more sense to focus on upper levels of government.

However, there is also evidence that the immigrant community is divided at a more fundamental level. A community leader referred to a competitive dynamic between Pakistanis and Indians (Seepersaud 2004). McCallion also mentioned infighting among Sikhs in Mississauga to illustrate how she approaches ethnic conflict in the city. These comments suggest that Mississauga's immigrant community lacks the capacity to act collectively.

McCallion's leadership is reinforced by an invisible power structure that represents Mississauga's 'old guard.' Though direct evidence of this was not unearthed, some interviewees suggested that McCallion could 'punish' organizations and individuals that challenged her. One civil servant mentioned the perception that McCallion could have an organization's Peel Region grant withdrawn if it spoke out against the city. The threat of McCallion's personal disapproval divides the immigrant community and thus is a barrier to coordinated political pressure on the municipality. Immigrant communities fear the withdrawal of her presence at ethnocultural events. Indeed, some ethnocultural communities invite municipal officials to private celebrations, such as weddings. When interviewed, McCallion mentioned that she had attended a Sikh wedding in the community. Some community leaders are more willing than others to challenge McCallion (at least publicly).

Thus, in Mississauga, multiculturalism is mainly a private matter. McCallion holds an annual multicultural breakfast with leaders of ethnocultural communities, and a private multiculturalism festival called Carassauga is held every year. This limited responsiveness reflects a lack of leadership in the multiculturalism field, as well as a political choice to take a laissez-faire approach to demographic change. The priorities in Mississauga are to keep property taxes low and to create an environment that attracts and retains businesses. Until recently the fiscal management philosophy there was 'pay as you go' (Chin 2008). At the time of the interviews, the political leadership prided itself on running a debt-free municipality. These concerns trump multicultural-ism initiatives in the city as the business community does not appear to make a connection between multiculturalism initiatives and economic development.

Brampton: The Failure of a Budding Multiculturalism Agenda

Under former mayor Peter Robertson's leadership, Brampton created a Race Relations Committee. According to Wallace and Frisken (2000): 'The idea for a Brampton Race Relations Action Council (BRRAC) origi-nated with a voluntary group of citizens that assembled to address race relations issues. After it had been in existence for a year or two, BRRAC approached the city council about the possibility of becoming a for-mal municipal structure, and the council agreed to formalize it' (2000, 32). However, the committee no longer meets, though it has not been formally disbanded. Brampton councillors interviewed for this study were unsure what became of it.

The Brampton example demonstrates how ongoing leadership is required in order to maintain productive governance networks. There appear to be three main reasons why the committee failed. First, there seems to have been a culture of competition among ethnocultural or-ganizations. Second, the committee's mandate seems to have been un-clear, so it was unable to engage the interest of Brampton's citizens. Third, there seems to have been insufficient political will to support an ongoing role for the city in multiculturalism policy. In the absence of municipal leadership in such policy, leaders of settlement organiza-tions seem not to have considered the importance of municipal govern-ments to immigrant settlement.

On 17 September 1992 the *Toronto Star* reported that some councillors were concerned that the BRRAC might be providing services that over-lapped with services offered by the Peel Multicultural Council (PMC) and the Brampton Multicultural Centre. According to the article, the committee seemed to have a vague mandate, one that was delineat-ed by Everett Biggs, then chair of the committee, in this way: 'within the context of being a Canadian first, to eliminate racism in the city of Brampton' (Biggs, in White 1992a).

Moreover, around this time there was infighting between the PMC and the Brampton Multicultural Centre, two of the most prominent community groups in Brampton, over their respective mandates. An-other article in the *Star* on the same day reported that interest in the committee varied among ethnocultural groups. Biggs was quoted that 'the Hindu, Sikh and black communities tend to support these initiatives more. But we need other people – from the French, German and Croatian, Greek and other communities' (ibid.). Essentially, besides facing power struggles within the multiculturalism community, the committee seemed to be having difficulty building bridges to connect Brampton's multicultural groups. In particular, racial minorities were interested in creating capacity in race relations initiatives, whereas the 'White' immigrant communities were not. Linda Jeffrey's observation that there are ten newspapers that serve Brampton's Sikh community suggests that significant intra-group divisions might exist as well. These divisions all impede the ability of Brampton's immigrant community to act collectively.

It is difficult to find reliable information on the precise reasons why the committee failed. However, the city's interest in multiculturalism seems to have faded after Mayor Robertson lost the 2000 municipal election to Susan Fennel, the current mayor. Regional Councillor Elaine Moore's more recent comments offer another possible explanation. In her view, the committee's mandate was outdated and the city should instead have entered the field of 'diversity management,' which involves incorporating diversity-friendly practices in employment and the design of city buildings (in other words, in mainstream city functions). In Moore's words: 'The City of Brampton of 400,000 people is well beyond the race relations [mandate]. We should be into what I call diversity management, what the City of Toronto calls diversity management. This is not race relations, this is not "everyone have a group hug and let's get along" which, when Brampton first started to grow and the different groups were moving into this community, probably worked ... That is kindergarten stuff' (Moore 2004, interview).

Mobilizing governance arrangements to support multiculturalism requires a strong sense of purpose. Thus, Brampton's relative lack of responsiveness can be understood in terms of local leaders' inability to sustain cooperation around multiculturalism goals. There has been community infighting in Brampton, and multiculturalism has not been framed in a way that engages the broad community. Let it be added, though, that there does not seem to have been any overt backlash against immigration.

In some ways, Brampton is poised to become more responsive to its ethnocultural diversity. Two crucial conditions for regime development exist. As we saw above, municipal political leaders (such as Moore, and former councillor Garnett Manning) recognize the need for their city to do more to adapt to ethnocultural diversity, and the business community seems to be taking an interest in the issue. With a renewal of purpose, local leaders could build an urban regime whose goals include managing diversity through multiculturalism policies.

Markham: A Race Relations Mandate

In Markham, local leaders have developed and maintained productive urban governance arrangements around the goal of managing race relations. These relationships are anchored to a certain extent in the town's advisory committees. Markham has had a race relations committee since 1985. However, the summer of 1995 marked an important turning point in its role in race relations and other multiculturalism challenges, when the Carole Bell incident triggered the dynamics that led to a more effective race relations committee.

In reaction to comments by Bell, a former deputy mayor, about the Chinese in Markham, a broad intersectoral alliance of community leaders representing the town's largely newcomer and 'visible minority' communities forced the issue of intercultural relations onto the town's agenda. Contributing to this was a backlash among long-standing community residents against immigration and the changes it was bringing to their community. The Coalition of Concerned Canadians (CCC) did not extract an apology from Bell, nor did it convince council to denounce her comments. But its pressure led Markham's mayor to take a leadership role in managing the conflict. He issued a letter of community reconciliation and established a task force to recommend steps to improve intercultural relations in Markham. According to the former chair of the CCC, who was chair of the Markham Race Relations Committee at the time of the first interview with her, Markham's current race relations committee is more effective than past committees because of these events (Magado 2005, personal communication). Carole Bell has since left Markham, but many political figures from that period remain on Markham Council, including Mayor Don Cousens, who continued as mayor until stepping down in 2006.

In fact, there appears to have been a rapprochement between Markham's political leadership and its visible-minority communities, especially the Chinese community. For instance, in 2003, Markham Council appointed Marlene Magado, a local leader in Markham's Filipino community and CCC co-chair, as chair of the Markham Race Relations Committee. And in 2004, Markham councillor Alex Chiu was made an Honorary Chairman of the FCCM (the most prominent Chinese organization in Markham). Frank Scarpitti, the town's deputy mayor at the time, was co-chair of the FCCM's 'Taste of Asia Annual Festival,' and Mayor Don Cousens was an Honorary Patron of the FCCM.

The concepts developed in Marion Orr's 1999 study of education reform in Baltimore, *Black Social Capital*, contribute to our understanding of the Markham case. The intense pressure placed on the town would not have been possible without high levels of ethnospecific 'social capital' in the newcomer communities, especially the Chinese community. Just as the Black community benefited from its strong informal networks and 'institutional completeness' in Baltimore, the Chinese community is well organized and well resourced in Markham. Some would suggest that there are 'two solitudes' in Markham, owing to the development of many parallel Chinese institutions. Indeed, the three most prominent ethnocultural organizations in Markham are ethnospecific. According to Orr, these ethnospecific stores of social capital can create barriers to interethnic cooperation.

Orr also stresses the importance of 'bridging' social capital to achieving outcomes that benefit ethnocultural minorities (ibid.). In Markham, the Carole Bell incident demonstrates how buy-in from both newcomer communities and long-standing residents is necessary in order to encourage positive intercultural relations. The long-standing, largely White, English-speaking community also appears to have a great deal of 'social capital.' One of the most striking elements of the Markham case is the extent to which the long-standing community, which is largely White, coalesced in support of Carole Bell's discriminatory comments. The case illustrates Orr's point that 'where local groups are polarized, social capital within groups is often promoted at the expense of intergroup cooperation … Participation in associational life sometimes serves to fragment, rather than to integrate, a society' (1999, 6).

It seems that prior to the Carol Bell incident, Markham society was characterized by fragmentation and segregation. That society continues to be fragmented along ethnic lines to some extent (Bray 2005, interview); even so, the incident led to the development of bridges linking Markham's visible-minority communities, which collectively formed the CCC and opened a dialogue between long-standing residents and Markham's newcomer communities. Markham's Race Relations Committee has since become more effective, and there seem now to be ongoing relationships between local political leaders and Markham's visible-minority communities. As does Orr's case study, the Markham case illustrates the important role of municipalities in bringing together disparate community networks (Orr 1999). In other words, a regime can bridge a municipality's ethnospecific social networks.

The literature on urban regime theory assigns a prominent place to the business community in urban governance, because that sector possesses a disproportionate share of society's material resources. The business community enters the story of the development of Markham's race relations regime in several ways. At the most basic level, poor intercultural relations are bad for business; therefore, the business community is an important stakeholder in the issue of race relations. This was evident in the Markham Board of Trade's decision to enter the debate by issuing an official position on intercultural relations shortly after the Carole Bell incident. Today the Markham Board of Trade participates in the informal governance of intercultural relations through its diversity committee, which has both municipal and regional participation (Bray 2005, interview).

In some ways, however, the incident also illustrates the limits of business influence on the municipality. At the time, a great deal of the investment flowing into Markham was coming from the largely immigrant Chinese community. A tarnished municipal image in the area of race relations could have jeopardized future business investment. According to Marlene Magado, reporters in China covered the Carole Bell controversy (Magado 2004, interview). In fact, given the importance of Chinese immigrant investors to municipal economic growth, and Chinese immigration to population growth, making negative remarks about the impact of Chinese immigration to Markham amounted to challenging head-on the basis of the immigration-driven growth and the 'growth machine.' In Markham, local residents challenged this notion because of the cultural changes taking place in the community. Even so, Markham's political leaders were reluctant to alienate longstanding residents and Carole Bell's supporters.

The Markham case highlights the independent importance of *race, culture,* and *identity* to understanding community power structures. It also underscores the importance of electoral resources (voting power) to local decision making. As the urban regime model suggests, various types of resources matter and electoral power is only one form of resource.

In Markham the business community's influence also intersected with race and culture, highlighting another important community resource – the ability to define the community's identity. Specifically, developers (both Chinese and non-Chinese) and Chinese retailers who cater to Chinese consumer tastes and preferences have reshaped the cultural symbols of some of Markham's public spaces by, for instance, developing Asian-style malls such as the Pacific Centre. Economic power, coupled with the high numbers of Chinese immigrants to Markham, instilled a sense of cultural threat among long-standing residents of Markham. In other words, backlash towards immigration was part of the Markham's growth process.

Opposition by long-standing residents to changes in the community highlights a point made by theorists of multicultural citizenship – that all public institutions are culturally biased (Kymlicka 1995; Carens 2000). Cultural neutrality is impossible. Private organizations and companies are culturally biased as well. While long-standing residents of Markham might say that Asian-style malls are exclusive because they do not have English-language signage, one could equally well say that Canadian municipal institutions are biased towards English-speaking residents – for instance, towards residents with recreational preferences for hockey. The question then becomes: What should one reasonably expect a municipality to do in order to include immigrants and ethnocultural minorities in governance and to accommodate their service preferences? Furthermore, if intercultural bridges are to be maintained and strengthened in Markham, both public institutions and private organizations will have to accommodate long-standing residents *as well as* the largely Chinese immigrant community. Yet local governments are incapable of dealing effectively with intercultural relations on their own, since the scope of the challenge extends into the private sector. Thus, local leaders in Markham have created regime relationships to build policy capacity in this area.

Comparing the Local Governance of Multiculturalism in the GTA

Toronto and Markham have responded to immigrants and ethnocultural minorities by adapting their services and governance structures. This can be understood as political choices to incorporate multiculturalism policy goals into urban governance arrangements. In Toronto, the principle of valuing diversity permeates many departments. Toronto responds to immigration by taking measures to encourage organizational change and by adopting access and equity and social policies to help immigrants integrate into Toronto society. In addition, local officials consider immigration a fundamental pillar of the city's economic-development strategy (Brown 2003, interview). The comprehensiveness of Toronto's response relative to Markham's can be understood in terms of the broader scope of participation in the Toronto regime, and its resources.

Markham's governance arrangements that support multiculturalism policy development are not as well resourced as Toronto's. The town does not have the institutional capacity to coordinate informal networks to the extent that Toronto does. Markham does not have a separate unit equivalent to Toronto's DMU to engage the community, and it has few immigrant settlement agencies and ethnocultural community organizations. Nor does it have private foundations that support multiculturalism policy goals. Unlike Toronto, Markham's multiculturalism policy development is not tied to a proactive economic development agenda and urban autonomy goals.

However, access to community and state resources does not entirely explain the policy differences between Toronto and Markham. Mississauga and Brampton have more community capacity in immigrant settlement and multiculturalism than Markham, yet they are less responsive to demographic change. As the Carole Bell incident brought to light, Markham's policy responses were largely a reaction to a community consensus that there was a race relations 'problem' in Markham. Race relations made it onto the municipal agenda in that town because of a nativist backlash against Chinese immigration and a counter-reaction on the part of Markham's visible-minority community. The CCC, co-chaired by leaders of the Chinese and Filipino communities, was a multiethnic alliance.

Comparing the dynamics of the Markham case with Mississauga's experience tempers the widespread impression in Mississauga that Hazel McCallion is the only 'independent variable' influencing agenda setting in multiculturalism policy. Rather, McCallion is located within a community power structure that supports her autonomy. In Markham, the Carole Bell incident suggests that concentrated power of the type evident in Mississauga is more widespread than first appears. The resistance that several political leaders showed in responding to the CCC during the incident (e.g., refusing to apologize or denounce her comments) is in some ways surprising. It was not until the CCC had broadened its support base regionally, nationally, and even internationally (Magado 2004, interview) that the town (and the mayor in particular) responded by establishing a task force to study race relations. Essentially, it took supralocal alliances, in addition to the economic strength and social capital of the Chinese community, to force a response from the town. In the end, the town never did formally apologize or denounce Bell's comments.

McCallion is arguably more influential and powerful in Mississauga than Markham's political leaders are on their own turf. Even so, the comparison highlights the importance of *how* civil society is organized in Mississauga. Essentially, Mississauga's immigrant and ethnocultural-minority communities do not have sufficient levels of 'bridging social capital' to pressure the municipality to respond. When McCallion made controversial remarks about both refugees and the South Asian community in Mississauga, it triggered a reaction from the immigrant settlement sector, but some immigrant-serving organizations later back-pedalled and disassociated themselves from protests against McCallion's comments. Mississauga's immigrant community does not speak with a unified voice.

It is possible that McCallion's personal influence was instrumental in 'containing' the protests. One potential explanation is that she made phone calls to some leaders in the community following the publication of her controversial remarks in the *Financial Post*, since her approach to 'managing' ethnocultural relations in Mississauga is to handle issues personally. In contrast, the CCC refused to accept a private apology from Carole Bell (which was offered) but rather insisted on a public retraction and apology for her statements. According to the coalition, a public apology was necessary for community healing. Thus, the differences in levels of responsiveness to immigrants and ethnocultural minorities in Mississauga and Markham might be explained by differences in both community capacity and political leadership. Indeed, the two factors are interdependent. Regime theory draws one's attention to the relationships among local leaders in the public and private spheres, which suggests why outcomes differed in these two cases.

The comparison between Markham and Brampton also illustrates the importance of social capital to municipal responsiveness within and across ethnocultural communities. Both Brampton's former Race Relations Action Committee and Markham's Race Relations Committee 'evolved out of a committee established by interested citizens' (Wallace and Frisken 2000, 32). In both Brampton and Markham, race relations committees were first established because the local council was receptive to citizens' concerns. Why, then, did Markham's Race Relations Committee persist while Brampton's faded? There seem to be two primary reasons. First, in Brampton, there seems to have been a lack of interorganizational and intercultural social capital. Second, there does not seem to have been a widespread backlash against the changing social demographics in Brampton on the part of long-standing residents, as there was in Markham. It follows that race relations were less of an issue in Brampton than in Markham. Brampton's Race Relations Action Committee failed to engage either Brampton's long-standing White residents or its White immigrants. Furthermore, these two factors appear to be common to both Mississauga and Brampton, tempering once again the local impression that McCallion's personal power alone explains the lack of multiculturalism initiatives in Mississauga.

The variations in the extent to which municipalities in the same province have adapted their services and governance structures to include immigrants and ethnocultural minorities tell us that local politics do affect municipal responsiveness to constituents. Local leaders make genuine choices about whether to develop capacity in multiculturalism policy. That said, more structural factors shape local politics as well. For instance, the way in which civil society is organized and resourced, the resources of the municipality, and the relationships among local leaders across sectors all affect a municipality's willingness and capacity to develop effective urban regimes with multiculturalism goals. These factors provide the 'context of choice' in which local leaders manoeuvre.

The next chapter explores the politics surrounding the accommodation of immigrants and ethnocultural minorities in Canada's second-largest immigrant-receiving city-region – Greater Vancouver. It explores the differences among the cases in the region (Vancouver, Richmond, Surrey, Coquitlam) to explain variations in their responses to immigration and ethnocultural change. The chapter concludes with a regime analysis of the four cases and describes emerging patterns.

5 Determinants of Multiculturalism Policies in Greater Vancouver

Greater Vancouver's immigration experience is in some ways unique. Greater Vancouver has attracted a disproportionate share of Canada's business immigrants (Olds 2001, 81). Relative to Toronto and Montreal, Vancouver's immigrant population is mostly Asian, especially Chinese. Between the 1991 and 1996 censuses, Greater Vancouver received a staggering 44,700 immigrants from Hong Kong, which was returned to the People's Republic of China in 1997 (GVRD 2003, 1). Many Hong Kong immigrants settled in Richmond, one of Greater Vancouver's most popular suburban destinations for immigrants (Ahn 2004, interview). Vancouver's non-European population increased by 422 per cent between 1971 and 1986 (Olds 2001, 85). Since the early 1970s, shortly after Canada's immigrant selection practices changed, social change has been dramatic in Vancouver.

The 2006 census indicated that 778,555 immigrants, representing 38.7 per cent of the population, lived in the Vancouver CMA. Within Greater Vancouver, the four largest municipalities – Vancouver, Surrey, Burnaby, and Richmond – receive the bulk of the region's immigrants. In fact, in 2001, 73 per cent of the region's foreign-born individuals lived in these four municipalities alone (GVRD 2003, 3). However, immigrants are increasingly moving outside the regional core to suburban municipalities such as Coquitlam, Port Moody, North and South Langley, and the North Shore (ibid., 4).

The Province of British Columbia neither mandates a municipal role in multiculturalism policy development nor provides funding to support such a role (Edgington, Bronwyn, et al. 2001, 10). The lack of provincial guidance in this important policy area has provided room for local innovation and variation. Vancouver, the region's core city, has been responsive to its changing ethnic demographics, whereas Richmond, Surrey, and Coquitlam have all been somewhat responsive to the changes in their populations.

This chapter explores the empirical differences among the cases to investigate possible factors associated with municipalities' differing levels of responsiveness to immigrants and ethnocultural minorities. It then filters these factors through a regime analysis to explain how and why the cases vary. Finally, it compares the four cases and summarizes the key explanatory factors.

This chapter shows that Vancouver's greater responsiveness to immigrants and ethnocultural minorities compared to other case-study municipalities in Greater Vancouver can be explained by the fact that immigration is tied to a proactive economic-development regime and to the concentration of resources in the urban core. In Vancouver, Chinese business people are important players in growth politics. In the suburban municipalities of Greater Vancouver, resources and patterns of political mobilization explain the varying levels of municipal responsiveness to immigrants and ethnocultural minorities.

Characterizing Key Differences in Multiculturalism Policy Making

Political Leaders' Ideas Concerning the Municipal Role in Multiculturalism

Restrictive ideas about the scope of municipal autonomy affect how municipalities in Greater Vancouver respond to ethnocultural change (ibid., 6). However, elected officials in Greater Vancouver vary in the extent to which they have internalized these ideological constraints.

Councillors in Vancouver tended to agree that the municipality has an important role to play in facilitating immigrants' integration with the community. They were inclined to see an important municipal role in public education, community engagement, and facilitating immigrants' access to city services. For instance, Councillor David Cadman mentioned numerous municipal roles in accommodating ethnocultural diversity, including reaching out to the community, attending events, and ensuring that everything having to do with community life was communicated to immigrants and ethnocultural minorities (Cadman 2004, interview). He stressed the importance of the city's public-education role, and he mentioned how the city had worked closely with the Chinese community on the Downtown Eastside[1] safe injection sites issue[2] 'because [the Chinese community's] ability to tolerate that [facility] is dependent on how well it is understood' (ibid.). Councillors in Vancouver also stressed the city's role in facilitating employment equity within the city and beyond through the Hastings Institute (Louis 2004, interview; Woodsworth 2004, interview).

Similarly, in Richmond, Councillor Linda Barnes stressed the importance of the city's public-education role in facilitating the successful settlement of Richmond's immigrants. To illustrate the nature of the challenge, she mentioned that the fact that one's neighbours have a legal say in whether one can rezone one's property is a new idea to many immigrants (Barnes 2004, interview). Problems have already arisen in Richmond with respect to newcomers building large homes (often called 'monster homes' by detractors) that diverge from the traditional architectural style of Richmond's neighbourhoods. Barnes also noted that some newcomers are fearful of certain social practices they do not understand. The recent 'group homes' controversy is a good example. Many Chinese-speaking residents were opposed to the plan to site a group home in a primarily Chinese neighbourhood. This opposition resulted in a massive mobilization of Chinese residents (and some long-standing residents) to pressure the municipality to intervene. In Richmond, political leaders view the municipal role primarily as one of facilitating intercultural understanding.

Another theme that emerged in the interview with Barnes is that Richmond councillors are aware of their financial limitations. In Richmond, only the mayor's position is full-time. According to Barnes, this limitation is maintained because residents fear that if all council positions were full-time, it would generate more activity than the municipality could afford. Because of financial limitations, municipal officials must be cautious about initiating new municipal programs – especially programs that engage the community. As she put it: 'If you start something, be prepared for what you've created' (ibid.). In other words, municipal councils must manage citizens' expectations. Local leaders cannot launch costly programs that citizens will come to expect to continue.

Surrey's former mayor, Douglas McCallum, 'called the shots' in Surrey at the time of the interviews (Houlden 2004, interview). The way in which he perceived the municipal role was an important measure of Surrey Council's receptivity to multiculturalism initiatives. McCallum presented immigration primarily as an economic-development opportunity (McCallum 2004, interview). In other words, according to him, immigration was a positive force that brought growth and investment to Surrey. However, he did not feel that this required a new role for the municipality in terms of facilitating the integration of immigrants. His comments suggest that city services could contribute to the integration process unintentionally; in other words, integration could occur even without proactive city efforts to adapt services and accommodate cultural preferences (ibid.).

The role of Surrey's Parks and Recreation Department appears to be a partial exception to this passive approach. This department has consulted with immigrant groups and ethnocultural minorities and developed a multicultural marketing strategy. These initiatives are consistent with the fact that the mayor has stressed the importance of encouraging a physically active city as a way of integrating newcomers into the community (ibid.). In general, however, the interview with McCallum suggested that his view of Surrey's role in immigrant settlement and multiculturalism initiatives is laissez-faire.

McCallum's view in this respect is consistent with his idea of the role of government more generally. His political philosophy is expressed by a sign on his office wall: 'Government is best which governs least.' As McCallum put it: 'If you run it [the city] like a business, then the simple fact is that we provide police, fire, parks and rec, and engineering (the roads, sewers and water) and that's it' (ibid.).

However, a minority of Surrey councillors support a more expansive municipal role in social issues. According to interviewees, Councillor Judy Villeneuve is one such councillor (Basi 2004, interview; Houlden 2004, interview). Villeneuve herself acknowledged that she had always been in a minority position in terms of her attitude towards social issues (Villeneuve 2004, interview).

In Surrey, perceptions of the municipal role are very much tied to local leaders' concerns about municipal finances and the appropriate division of powers and financial responsibility among the three levels of government. As Villeneuve explained:

There is a big reluctance on the level of city government to take on responsibility for social issues because ... those are the issues that the federal and provincial governments.are responsible for and we don't have a taxing ability. And so they're very nervous in stepping in that direction, because we have no way of funding programs and supporting it, and they don't want to send a message that we will take on those responsibilities, because the governments are tending to download or cut programs, but we're facing the problems on our streets. We're the closest level of government to the people and their problems ... It's a challenging time right now for cities, and that's why there's so much discussion during this federal election[3] about ... urban infrastructure and what the federal government's going to do, because they used to support housing initiatives, and they used to give money to the provinces to play a role. (Villeneuve 2004, interview)

Similarly, Bruce Hardy was asked whether municipalities have a role to play in immigrant settlement. Hardy is the Executive Director of OPTIONs, a prominent social-service agency in Surrey. He replied:

It's a tough question, because in B.C., the municipalities do not have a formal role in integrating newcomers. That's a provincial role, and to some degree a federal role. Municipalities out here have been very, very cautious of investing in programs for fear of setting a precedent. So what they've done out here, they've worked hard to be accommodating, they've worked hard to try and be welcoming, but the reality is that it is not viewed as a municipal initiative per se. (Hardy 2005, interview)

For the most part, in Surrey, local political leaders consider integrating and accommodating immigrants to be a provincial and federal government role.

The former mayor of Coquitlam, Jon Kingsbury, views immigration as an important economic-development opportunity. He stressed the potential of the Asian community to connect Coquitlam to the Pacific Rim economy. However, it is difficult to pioneer new initiatives in Coquitlam, because political will is lacking. Kingsbury maintained that Coquitlam Council was dominated by an old guard of retirees who had been elected by the established neighbourhoods in the city.[4] He seemed frustrated that councillors did not support popular municipal initiatives, such as twinning cities internationally to create social and economic ties. In particular, he would have liked Coquitlam to develop relationships with Chinese cities. He also wanted to see more Chinese and Japanese[5] councillors elected to council, because he felt these groups recognized the value of trade (Kingsbury 2004, interview).

Also according to Kingsbury, Coquitlam residents were not sufficiently engaged in local affairs: 'The sad part is that not enough people are getting involved.'[6] He noted that newcomer communities had been more engaged in local affairs when Daniel Chiu, a councillor of Chinese background, was on council.[7] He attributed this to the fact that Chinese residents were more comfortable contacting Chiu, because they could speak to him in their mother tongue. However, in Kingsbury's assessment, Chiu was 'not as popular with White people.' Kingsbury did not seem to consider it a municipal responsibility to proactively engage the community in Coquitlam (ibid.).

Kingsbury felt that the city's failure to engage newcomer communities was not the only problem. He contended that the city needed to do more to involve young people in local politics, for they would bring new ideas to council. He viewed the fact that two 'young people' had been elected in the last election as a step in a positive direction.[8] He suggested that municipal priorities were misplaced in part due to a lack of fresh ideas of the sort that community engagement generates. For instance, he remarked that 'we [the city] spend a third of our budget chasing crime,' though the money would be better spent on recreation and library programs (ibid.). Several councillors were contacted in Coquitlam; none responded to the requests for interviews.

In sum, local political leaders in Vancouver and Richmond stressed municipalities' role in public education and in facilitating intercultural understanding. In Surrey, political leaders viewed immigration as a positive force driving economic development, but they also considered immigrant integration and settlement to be responsibilities of upper levels of government. Coquitlam's mayor admitted that immigration, settlement, and multiculturalism policy was not on the city's agenda, even while stressing the potential economic-development opportunities associated with immigration to Coquitlam.

Partisan Politics in Metro Vancouver: Do Parties Matter?

Greater Vancouver is one of the few places in Canada where partisan politics have developed at the local level. Vancouver, Richmond, and Surrey all have political parties at the local level. Nevertheless, parties and party ideology do not appear to affect municipal responsiveness to immigrants and ethnocultural minorities.

At the time of the interviews, Vancouver had two political parties: the Non-Partisan Association (NPA) and the Coalition of Progressive Electors (COPE).[9] The former is a right-wing party representing business interests; the latter is a left-wing party supported by unions and progressive social movements. Within COPE were two main factions, popularly called 'COPE Classic' and 'Diet COPE.' At the time of the interviews, under the leadership of Mayor Larry Campbell, COPE had a majority on council.

Evidence that ideological differences had an impact on the extent to which parties developed policies responsive to immigrants and ethnocultural minorities was not found. Both major parties in Vancouver have supported the city's objectives in multiculturalism policy. Mike Harcourt (1980–6), an independent mayor with COPE support, governed Vancouver in the early to mid-1980s, a time of major change for the city,[10] when it was preparing for Expo 86, an event that would raise its international profile. As mayor, Harcourt was known for Pacific Rim initiatives. More specifically, one of his primary goals during his tenure as mayor was to realize Vancouver's economic potential in the Pacific Rim (Edgington, Goldberg, and Hutton 2003, 31).

According to political scientist Patrick Smith, under Harcourt's leadership the City of Vancouver developed a clear economic rationale for its emerging internationalist stance, engaging in 'paradiplomacy' with Pacific Rim cities (Smith 1992, 93–6). Vancouver's economic-development policies during this period were tied visibly to immigration. For instance, the city established formal links with Guangzhou in southern China, because of Vancouver's large Cantonese population, which has strong ties to its homeland (ibid., 93). To support investment from the Pacific Rim, Harcourt successfully lobbied the federal government to have Vancouver designated one of Canada's two international banking centres (ibid., 96).

Harcourt was also personally committed to social planning and to supporting multiculturalism initiatives (Edgington, Hanna, et al. 2001, 17). In many ways, these policies were natural complements to his economic-development strategy. Under his mayoralty in the 1980s, the City of Vancouver established an anti-racism advisory committee on council; it also institutionalized support for multiculturalism initiatives by establishing the Equal Employment Opportunities (EEO) Office.

Policy innovation in employment equity policy was also evident during NPA mayor Gordon Campbell's tenure as mayor (1986–93). In particular, under his leadership the highly innovative Hastings Institute was born. This institute is a not-for-profit arm's-length corporation of the City of Vancouver that provides diversity training to public- and private-sector organizations. According to Thomas Hutton (1998), under Campbell's leadership the city developed a new policy focus on the integration of immigrant and domestic migrants (1998, 96). Under Harcourt the city had actively fostered relationships with Pacific Rim countries in order to encourage foreign investment; under Campbell the city's new focus involved, in Hutton's words, 'reallocating resources to social planning, adopting regulatory rather than developmental policy approaches and giving less priority to economic policies and programmes' (ibid., 97). Citing an interview with Campbell, Smith noted that Campbell himself acknowledged that 'Harcourt was ... much more active in generating global activities for the City than the Campbell Administration was' (ibid., 94). In other words, Harcourt, the mayor who led the left-wing coalition on Vancouver's council in the 1980s, was more focused on encouraging foreign investment and economic-development objectives than was Campbell, the leader of the right-wing NPA. It was Campbell who shifted the city's focus from economic development to community integration.

In Vancouver, then, there is no clear link between partisan politics and support for multiculturalism policy (though political leaders on the left, such as Councillor Ellen Woodsworth, viewed themselves as particular champions of multiculturalism initiatives). Both COPE-led and NPA-led councils have innovated in multiculturalism policy. Support for multiculturalism policies continued under NPA mayor Philip Owen's leadership (1993–2002), and multiculturalism policies continue to have the support of both COPE and NPA councillors (Kohli 2004, interview). Informants for this study did not mention political leaders or their party stripes as a significant factor in Vancouver's responsiveness to immigrants and ethnocultural minorities.

In May 2005, Vancouver's independent (but COPE-supported) Mayor Larry Campbell (2002–5) established a working group on immigration in Vancouver as part of a strategy of the 'Charter 5 (C5)' coalition of cities to negotiate new relationships with upper levels of government in immigration policy (City of Vancouver 2005).[11] Vancouver has developed a cross-party consensus that the municipality has a role to play in facilitating immigrants' and ethnocultural minorities' access to city services. Also, under both NPA-led and COPE-led councils the city has adopted new policies designed to respond to immigrants' needs and preferences.

Similarly, in Richmond and Surrey there is no clear relationship between partisanship and multiculturalism policy development, though councillors affiliated with the provincial NDP seemed somewhat more interested in the municipal role in this area. Richmond's most important responses to diversity (e.g., its long history of race relations advisory committees) do not appear to be driven by ideology. Not a single informant mentioned the ideological leanings of Richmond's councillors as affecting how Richmond has responded to the city's changing ethnocultural demographics. Even in Surrey, where local leaders were more likely to suggest that former Mayor Doug McCallum and his right-of-centre Surrey Elections Team drove the municipal agenda, party-based ideological preferences were not always decisive. In B.C., municipal politicians who want to stay in power must accommodate both the political right and the political left, because the province is so 'political' (Hardy 2005, interview). Municipalities must manage their relationship with a province that oscillates between right-wing and left-wing governments. Bruce Hardy, the Executive Director of OPTIONs, remarked about the right-leaning former mayor of Surrey: 'Doug [McCallum] is a smart, smart, political guy. He is not going to alienate 30 to 40 per cent of his population base. If people come to him and say, "These are important considerations, you need to look at it," he will do that both because it's the right thing to do politically and − I know him reasonably well − he also does it because it's the right thing to do, period' (Hardy 2005, interview). Hardy knows the mayor reasonably well, as his organization is part of Surrey's governing coalition.

The Municipal Civil Service and the 'Street Level Bureaucrats'

In Vancouver, the municipal civil service plays an important role in multiculturalism policy and in shaping intercultural relations in Vancouver through its Social Planning Department, the EEO, and the Hastings Institute. The City of Vancouver employs a full-time multicultural social planner whose job it is to keep abreast of the needs of Vancouver's diverse communities. That person also creates capacity in managing the ethnic and racial dimensions of social change by developing policy, conducting research, and building and maintaining community networks. More generally, according to Councillor David Cadman, the city is well served by staff who understand the importance of helping Vancouver's diverse population understand what the city is trying to achieve (Cadman 2004, interview).

The EEO has been an important catalyst of progressive organizational change in the City of Vancouver. According to Rajpal Kohli, a policy adviser with the city's Equal Opportunity Program, senior management has played a crucial role in the city's responses to ethnocultural diversity (Kohli 2004, interview). A former city manager, Kendar Bell, pioneered the city's initiatives in diversity training. Bell had completed the Kingswood Management Program, a well-known cultural-sensitivity training program. The Kingswood Management Program identifies and trains champions of change, who then serve as catalysts within their departments. Staff of the former Metro Toronto developed this program and offered it to senior managers in their municipality between 1987 and 1995. The City of Vancouver then purchased the program from Metro Toronto and tailored it to Vancouver (City of Vancouver 1999). Bell delivered the program to the city's senior managers – first, mainly to senior-level civil servants. The program was then adapted to other kinds of organizations. The initial program was based on a 'fictitious City of Kingswood [and] mimicked a civic bureaucracy' (ibid.). The program was so successful that outside agencies, including provincial and federal government agencies, wanted to receive the training. The Hastings Institute was established to provide external training of the type the city was offering internally through its EEO Office. For instance, the institute developed the Pacific Management Training Program, which was offered from 1991 to 1994 to the not-for-profit sector (ibid.). A city document reports that in Vancouver the Kingswood program was offered between 1987 and 1995 and produced 451 graduates from a variety of agencies, including 'the City of Vancouver, other municipalities, provincial government ministries, crown corporations, non-for-profit organizations, unions and the private sector.' Graduates became catalysts of change in their organizations; they 'developed personal contracts to undertake changes in their workplaces that would lead to greater accessibility, more equitable hiring and promotion practices, more meaningful and respectful dialogue with the diverse community, and more flexibility in service delivery' (ibid.).

The Hastings Institute has been fundamental to building policy capacity in employment equity that bridges the public–private divide. Essentially, it has extended the scope of employment equity and diversity-friendly organizational change from the public sector into the private sphere by creating partnerships with prominent organizations in Vancouver. An administrative report described the Hastings Institute model:

> From the beginning, one of the unique attributes of the Hastings Institute has been its focus on forming partnerships and developing allies to effect change. The fundamental partnership is between the Hastings Institute and the City of Vancouver; without this partnership and the continuing support of Council, the Hastings Institute would not exist. Other key partners include the Vancouver Foundation, the Vancouver School Board, BC Building Corporation and CUPE Local 1004. In addition, during its initial

three years of operation, the Hastings Institute received core funding from the Secretary of State – Multiculturalism and Citizenship Canada, and financial support for program development from provincial ministries and agencies. (City of Vancouver 1999)

The EEO Office and the Hastings Institute have a relatively high profile at the City of Vancouver. Judy Rogers, Vancouver's current city manager, was director of the EEO program when the city established the Hastings Institute. In other words, the EEO Office appears to be considered a stepping stone to the apex of power in Vancouver's civil service. The institute's profile is evident in the fact that both the city manager and the mayor sit on the institute's Board of Directors.

In Richmond, at the corporate level, a social planner from the Planning Department provides support to the Richmond Intercultural Advisory Committee (RIAC). However, responding to ethnocultural diversity is only a small part of this person's responsibilities. The city's communications manager also plays a role in managing intercultural relations. Overall, however, there are fewer city resources devoted to citywide multiculturalism initiatives in Richmond than there are in Vancouver.

The City of Richmond's decision to limit the public resources it devotes to multiculturalism initiatives was a calculated one. According to Terry Crowe, the Manager of Planning, the city could play two roles in intercultural relations: as a leader or as a facilitator. According to him, while the city has provided leadership in intercultural relations by establishing RIAC, in the longer term it is pursuing the latter role (Crowe 2004, interview). This is why the city engaged in extensive consultations to develop RIAC's strategic plan and mandate (Crowe 2004, interview). In other words, instead of investing in new municipal institutions and staff to address intercultural concerns, the city is facilitating the development of socially productive coalitions. RIAC delegates various aspects of intercultural relations to organizations in civil society; it also coordinates efforts across the public and private sectors.

In Richmond, leaders in city agencies such the Richmond Library and the RCMP also play an important role in crafting multiculturalism policy. 'Street-level' bureaucrats have expressed a willingness to change and to accept new municipal responsibilities. Richmond's municipal agencies are less likely than those in other suburban municipalities in the sample to worry about 'jurisdiction.' For instance, Ward Clapman, Superintendent of the RCMP's Richmond Detachment, has embraced what he views as a new role for police officers in community development. During an interview he remarked that municipal roles had become 'blurry' (Clapman 2004, interview) and that the formal role of municipalities was outdated. Municipalities were, he said, 'playing from a playbook or a framework that was designed a long, long time ago [and] things have changed.' For him, municipal roles are 'about flexibility today, so responsiveness is about how flexible you're willing to be or how rigid are you going to be back to the old playbook' (ibid.). Similarly, Greg Buss, the Chief Librarian in Richmond, stressed how flexible municipal organizations must be. Both the Richmond Detachment and Richmond's library have adapted their services to ethnocultural change in the community.

In Surrey there is little targeted support for diversity initiatives at an organization level. The Human Resources Department has made some effort to reach out to Surrey's diverse community, especially its South Asian population. However, Surrey's leadership seems to believe that little effort to adapt is required of the municipality, because the city has moved beyond race relations. Murray Dinwoodie, the city's General Manager of Planning and Development, described Surrey as a model of successful municipal adaptation to ethnocultural change (Dinwoodie 2004, interview). In Surrey, managers of 'street-level' departments and agencies such as Parks and Recreation and Libraries appear to be the most important leaders in multiculturalism policy. Surrey's most important responses have been launched by these agencies.

In Coquitlam, when the multiculturalism advisory committee was meeting, the deputy clerk played an important support role. In addition, Coquitlam's libraries have taken some significant steps to accommodate diversity. However, at the time of the interviews, there was very little corporate-level activity in multiculturalism policy in Coquitlam. Recall that Coquitlam is a borderline case between the two categories of 'somewhat responsive' and 'unresponsive.'

Community Capacity in Multiculturalism

Vancouver is the most well-resourced municipality in the Greater Vancouver sample.[12] There are several large and prominent settlement organizations in Vancouver; there is also an umbrella organization – the Affiliation of Multicultural Societies and Services Agencies of B.C. – that represents the sector provincially. The largest settlement organizations are the Immigrant Services Society, the Multilingual Orientation Service Association for Immigrant Communities (MOSAIC), and S.U.C.C.E.S.S. (United Chinese Community Enrichment Services Society). Mainstream organizations such as the United Way also play an important role in community development (Woroch 2004, interview).

S.U.C.C.E.S.S.'s role in immigrant settlement in Metro Vancouver is worth particular mention. This group is one of the most prominent and entrepreneurial settlement agencies in Greater Vancouver. It was founded in 1973 to offer settlement services to Chinese immigrants and has evolved into a multicultural agency that serves immigrants and citizens alike. It has an operating budget of $17 million. Only 60 per cent of its funding comes from government; the remaining 40 percent comes from fund-raising events, donations, membership dues, and user fees (S.U.C.C.E.S.S., 'Donations').[13] It has eleven offices in Vancouver, Richmond, Burnaby, Coquitlam, Surrey, and Port Moody, as well as at Vancouver International Airport. The organization's ability to set up offices in new cities is exceptional within the competitive and somewhat territorial settlement sector. Unlike other agencies, which are perceived as competitors by local agencies, new branches of S.U.C.C.E.S.S. are welcomed into communities because of the organization's ability to raise a great deal of its own money (Hardy 2004, interview). In other words, S.U.C.C.E.S.S. is not viewed as a competitor for scarce government funds in the same way as other organizations.

Vancouver and Richmond both report close ties with S.U.C.C.E.S.S. For instance, representatives of S.U.C.C.E.S.S. sit on both Vancouver's and Richmond's multiculturalism-related advisory committees. Furthermore, Richmond libraries work closely with both the Richmond Chinese Society and S.U.C.C.E.S.S. on responding to the needs of the Chinese community (Buss 2004, interview). In Richmond, the Multicultural Concerns Society and S.U.C.C.E.S.S. are the two most prominent settlement organizations, and both organizations have close relationships with the City of Richmond.

Coquitlam's Mayor Kingsbury mentioned the importance of S.U.C.C.E.S.S. in his city. He contended that because of the organization's access to federal funds, it was more effective to support the organization than to take on an independent city role in multiculturalism policy (Kingsbury 2004, interview).[14] In acknowledgment of the resources that S.U.C.C.E.S.S. brings to the community, the City of Coquitlam provides the organization with free office space. At the time of the interviews, S.U.C.C.E.S.S. seemed to be the only organization offering settlement services in Coquitlam.

In Surrey, immigrant settlement services are offered primarily by three organizations: the Surrey-Delta Immigrant Services Society, Progressive Inter-cultural Community Services, and OPTIONs, a mainstream community organization offering settlement services. Of these three, only OPTIONs has developed close relations with Surrey's political leadership.

The extent to which immigrant settlement resources explain how municipalities respond to immigration depends on the relationship between settlement organizations and municipalities. Also, the nature of the relationship between the wider community and organizations within the settlement sector tells us something about the opportunities for creating inclusive governance arrangements at the local level.

Multiculturalism and the Business Community

Vancouver's business community plays both direct and indirect roles in multiculturalism policy development. A network of private foundations, business associations, banks, and credit unions is contributing to Vancouver's responsiveness to immigrants and ethnocultural minorities. Vancouver's business community recognizes the importance of immigration to Vancouver's economic growth and to its international competitiveness. In her book-length study of the transformation of Vancouver in the 1980s and 1990s, Katharyne Mitchell (2004) suggests that a powerful coalition of local leaders and government officials supported the investment of funds in multiculturalism initiatives; the goal in this was to create the conditions for the unfettered flow of capital into the city.

VanCity, a socially progressive credit union in Vancouver, is one of the most active business-sector participants in community-development activities related to immigrant settlement (Woroch 2004, interview; Vescera 2005, interview). For instance, VanCity sends representatives to one of Vancouver's leading settlement agencies – Immigrant Services Society (ISS) – to help refugees set up new bank accounts. The organization also provides financial support to ISS's Refugee Children's Christmas Party (Woroch 2004, interview). In addition, in partnership with MOSAIC – another prominent immigrant settlement agency in Vancouver – VanCity lends money to immigrants who need to pursue further education to become accredited in their professions (Vescera 2005, interview).

Another organization, the Vancouver Foundation,[15] plays two primary roles with respect to immigrant settlement and multiculturalism initiatives: as a funding agency, and as a convener (ibid.). For instance, the foundation participates in a multiculturalism 'funders' network' with the City of Vancouver, the province, and the United Way. It served as convener on 27 October 2003, when it launched an event called Immigration and Migration: A British Columbia Dialogue, which brought together a broad cross-sectoral group of community leaders; and on 14 February 2005, when it co-sponsored an event called Dialogue on the Future of Multiculturalism in British Columbia. The Hastings Institute, the Laurier Institution, the B.C. Ministry of Community, Aboriginal, and Women's Services (MACWS), and Canadian Heritage were other sponsors of the 2005 event.

The Laurier Institution is another private-sector leader in multiculturalism initiatives in Greater Vancouver. Its primary contribution to policy development is through research and public education. The institution is a national not-for-profit organization based in Vancouver. Business and community leaders established the Laurier Institution in 1989 to increase awareness of and knowledge about the social and economic implications of diversity. The institution's website does not list its founders; however, as Mitchell observes, the foundation's Board of Directors reflects an affinity with Hong Kong business and investment concerns (Mitchell 2004, 109). Mitchell is critical of many multiculturalism capacity-building efforts in Vancouver, because she associates the growth of efforts to address issues related to multiculturalism in the 1980s and 1990s with a neoliberal project of facilitating the circulation and accumulation of capital. She considers the Laurier Institution to be 'the most prominent and well financed' of the groups in Vancouver that want to reduce racial friction through public-education campaigns. She also notes that it has commissioned reports in the interest of capital accumulation (ibid., 106). For example, when conflicts concerning rising housing costs emerged in the city, the institution commissioned reports which were meant to show that it was not immigration that was driving up costs (ibid., 107). The language of these reports had the effect of silencing voices that were critical of rising housing costs and unfettered growth, implying that such concerns were racist and unpatriotic because they went against Canadian multiculturalism (ibid., 108). Mitchell describes the Laurier Institution's report as such: 'The Laurier reports are indicative of a virulent form of neoliberal urban discourse in Vancouver in the late 1980s and 1990s. In addition to the rhetoric that labeled any form of state intervention problematic, as causing unnecessary blockages and costs by disrupting market forces, these reports portrayed the city as rife with entrenched anti-immigrant and racist superstitions. The struggles over housing prices, affordability, livability, and quality of life – the literal spaces of the city – were inescapably racialized' (ibid., 109).

Its motives may be less than altruistic; even so, it is clear that the Laurier Institution has contributed to building multiculturalism capacity in Vancouver. The institution was involved in diversity-related education programs as part of Vancouver's successful bid for the 2010 Winter Olympic and Paralympic Games. Currently it is working on a project called Diversity 2010: Leveraging the 2010 Olympics and Paralympic Games to Brand and Make Greater Vancouver a Truly Multicultural City (Laurier Institution 2005). It has proposed to hold a summit on this issue and has called for the creation of a task force with representation from business, the media, all of Vancouver's cultural communities, and other major stakeholders. The goals in this are to assist in the city-branding process and to foster Vancouver's reputation for excellence in the integration of immigrants (ibid., 2–3). The report draws clear connections between multiculturalism and economic growth, and it stresses that the 2010 Olympics are an opportunity to further brand Vancouver globally as a city whose diversity is a competitive advantage (ibid., 4).

According to David Edgington, Michael Goldberg, and Thomas Hutton (2003), the Hongkong and Shanghai Bank of Canada (HSBC) is also playing a role in fostering intercultural understanding in Vancouver. Their 2003 study reports that HSBC has supported social and cultural programs, 'typified by periodic festivals and celebrations of the growing Hong Kong community in Vancouver' (2003, 31). According to them, HSBC undertook these initiatives in 'close cooperation with local governments, non-government organizations (NGOs) and Vancouver's Chinese Community, but with openness also extended to the broader public' (ibid., 31).

Informants interviewed for this study downplayed HSBC's role in multiculturalism initiatives in Vancouver. They said that of the city's financial institutions, VanCity rather than HSBC has done more to help settle immigrants (Woroch 2004, interview; Vescera 2005, interview). Nevertheless, the importance of HSBC to the city's response to immigration must be understood in terms of a broader understanding of the relationship between immigration and business interests in Vancouver. In Vancouver, multiculturalism initiatives, as well as social initiatives related to immigrant settlement, complement the city's economic-development objectives. Among powerful members of Vancouver's business and political elite, a consensus exists that the city's economic strength is linked to its relationships with Pacific Rim countries (Olds 2001). This consensus links the long-standing business elite to Vancouver's new Asian business elite (Olds 2001). According to Hutton (1998), HSBC is one of the three or four most important local institutions involved in Vancouver's relationship with the wider Asia-Pacific region (Edgington, Goldberg and Hutton 2003, 31). HSBC played a pivotal role in the establishment of the Hong Kong–Canada Business Association, the second largest bilateral business association after the Vancouver Board of Trade/World Trade Center (ibid., 32). When the economic rationale for the City of Vancouver's Pacific Rim focus was developed and implemented under Mayor Mike Harcourt (Smith 1992), HSBC played an important role in implementing the strategy. As David Edgington and his colleagues describe it:

> Implementation of the new strategy, with its assertive Asia-Pacific orientation, included a series of social, cultural and educational exchanges between Vancouver and Asian cities. Furthermore, the city's strategy incorporated a sequence of municipal business and trade missions to selected Asia-Pacific business centres, including Hong Kong, Singapore, Kuala Lumpur, Bangkok, and Guangzhou in southern China. Senior Hong Kong Bank of Canada representatives participated in a number of these missions. They were designed both to increase Vancouver's profile within Asia, and to introduce Vancouver business people to prospective opportunities and partners in the region. Importantly, the HSBC provided significant logistical support, market intelligence, and introductions to key Hong Kong business interests and individuals. (ibid., 31)

In Richmond, the business community has played a remarkable role in intercultural relations. The leadership of prominent Chinese developer Thomas Fung in facilitating positive intercultural relations warrants particular mention. Fung is a son of the late Fung King Hei, who owned Sun Hung Kai Securities, one of Hong Kong's largest securities firms (ibid.). *Time* magazine (Canada) has called Thomas Fung one of Canada's most influential individuals (Young 2004).[16] His development company, The Fairchild Group, developed a series of Asian-style malls in Richmond, beginning with the Aberdeen Centre, which opened in 1989.

However, Asian malls such as the Aberdeen Centre soon acquired a reputation for being 'unfriendly to non-Asians' in Richmond because shop owners erected Chinese-only signs (Pynn 1997). Richmond's long-standing community[17] complained to council that the city's malls were exclusive. In consultation with the City of Richmond, Fung decided to tear down the Aberdeen Centre and to redevelop it at a personal cost of millions of dollars in order to re-establish the mall a way that would accommodate both Asian and Western cultures. According to Kari Huhtala, a senior policy planner with the City of Richmond: 'The decision to rethink the concept, and rebuild the structure, comes from the vision that Aberdeen's creative concept could accommodate both Asian and Western cultures. Fung's vision resulted in a new Aberdeen Centre four times larger than the original, including a hotel. The Centre brings together a fusion of Asian and North American brand-name out-lets [and will] celebrate public holidays such as Christmas, Halloween and Valentine's Day, as well as traditional Asian celebrations, such as Chinese New Year and mid-Autumn festival' (Huhtala 2004).

The Aberdeen Centre's commercial tenant legal agreement, which 'obliges merchants not to use permanent Chinese-language signs inside or out, and to maintain Aberdeen for English-language use' (ibid.), is one of the most interesting aspects of the development from the per-spective of intercultural relations. Furthermore, in 1997, six of Rich-mond's largest Asian malls (all also owned by Thomas Fung's Fairchild Group) – Aberdeen Centre, Fairchild Square, Parker Place, President Plaza, Yaohan Centre, and Central Square – jointly created a market-ing arm to change their image as 'Chinese-only' malls, the goal being to attract people of all cultures. The aim is to promote the six malls as 'Asia West.' According to Asia West's chair, Harvey Lowe, the mar-keting group pushes shopkeepers to accommodate non-Asians by in-cluding English on their signs and carrying clothing in sizes suited to non-Asians (Pynn 1997). Tourism Richmond, a not-for-profit agency es-tablished to market Richmond as a tourist destination, uses the concept of 'Asia West' in its marketing materials.

The business community in Richmond also participates in the city's race relations committees. Richmond has an economic advisory task force that fosters an ongoing relationship with the business community, including members of the Richmond Chamber of Commerce and also of two ethnospecific business associations – the Taiwanese Chamber of Commerce (formerly called Sunbright) and the Richmond Asian Pacific Business Association.

According to Linda Barnes, a Richmond councillor who was the Richmond Intercultural Committee's liaison at the time of the interview with her, the city used these networks to appoint people to RIAC, because municipal politicians wanted to ensure that the 'movers and shakers' were represented on the committee in addition to a broad spectrum of community interests (Barnes 2004, interview). Past race-relations committee minutes indicate that Richmond's business community has participated in the city's intercultural committees for some time. For instance, Harvey Lowe, chair of Asia West, sat on a previous intercultural advisory committee as a representative of the Richmond Chamber of Commerce (City of Richmond 1996).

The Chinese community has also taken leadership in both pressuring and assisting city agencies to adapt to their community. According to Greg Buss, the manager of Richmond's library, Richmond's Chinese community worked hard to bring forward its needs (Buss 2004, interview). 'In our situation,' Buss said, 'we were very fortunate because the community came to us and basically said, what you're doing is a total embarrassment and it's totally unacceptable.' The Chinese community was willing to assist the city in its response through donations from Chinese community organizations and individual Chinese philanthropists. For instance, one member of the community – Mr Kwok-Chu Lee – donated close to $750,000 in cash and Chinese-language materials. According to Buss, such donations helped the library respond to Chinese needs and preferences; they also helped pre-empt any backlash against change in the community, by avoiding a dynamic that might have led to ethnocultural competition for scarce library resources. As Buss put it: 'It was more like a dollar spent here might attract two dollars [and] so the positive cycle starts building up.' Because Chinese donors paid for the bulk of Chinese-language materials, the library was able to focus on purchasing English-language materials, which are important to the Chinese community in Richmond as well as to the long-standing one (ibid.).

In other words, the library's budget – which is derived in large part from the city's property tax revenue – is used for English-language resources, even though a large proportion of the taxpayers' mother tongue is Chinese. The politics of library collections could have become a zero-sum game; instead, with the help of Chinese donors, it has become a 'win-win' situation.

This study found little concrete evidence that the business community in Surrey was pressuring the city to accommodate newcomers (at least in a sustained and visible way). However, according to Surrey councillor Judy Villeneuve, the city's employment equity initiatives are partly a reaction to the fact that many developers in Surrey are of South Asian origin. According to Murray Dinwoodie, Surrey's city manager, between 30 and 50 per cent of all applications for development projects are from Surrey's Indo-Canadian community (Dinwoodie 2004, interview). In his view, for this reason the city does not have to find ways to proactively include the South Asian community in the planning process – they are included 'by default, because they are the developers' (ibid.).

Balwant Sanghera, a community leader in Richmond of South Asian origin, acknowledged that there are a lot of South Asian business people in Surrey. But in his view, 'they interact with [the City of Surrey] on an individual basis, so collectively there are very few initiatives that the city has been forced to take' (Sanghera 2004, interview).

The Surrey-Delta Immigrant Services Society (SDISS) encourages businesses to accommodate and reflect ethnocultural diversity through its Diversity Awards. This annual event began as an initiative to educate business about the value of hiring newcomers and encourage businesses to embrace diversity (Woodman 2004, interview). SDISS has an ongoing relationship with the business community through this initiative. In fact, the Surrey Chamber of Commerce coordinated the event for two years while SDISS's former executive director was on sick leave (ibid.). SDISS created a Leadership Council to identify small businesses with innovative practices. Participants on this leadership council include the *Surrey Leader* (the local newspaper), Surrey Libraries, Parks and Recreation, the Surrey Chamber of Commerce, Kwantlen University College, and the Surrey Detachment (ibid.). City agencies participate in this initiative even though, at a corporate level, the city was unwilling to be a 'diamond sponsor' of the event by contributing $2,500 (ibid.). There is also an ethnospecific business association in Surrey – the Indo-Canadian Business Association – which Woodman described as 'insular ... a sort of counter-movement' (ibid.). It is notable that this organization was not part of the Leadership Council that sought potential Diversity Award winners for the former SDISS's business award. Furthermore, Woodman was the only community leader to mention this association, and even then only in passing.

There was some evidence of the business community's influence in Coquitlam's library services. For instance, the Taiwan Economic Development Office and the Council of the People's Republic of China approached the library's management to discuss diversifying its collection. According to Karen Harrison, these groups donated significant amounts of materials. These donations were orchestrated by Salina Leung, a Chinese member of the Library Board who is involved in the Chinese Parents' Association in Coquitlam's schools (Harrison 2004, interview).

The Role of the Media

As mentioned in chapter 5, local leaders were not asked about the role played by local media. Furthermore, with one exception, local leaders in the media were not interviewed. Nevertheless, the importance of the media's interpretations of immigration, intercultural relations, and local politics was clear in several examples that local leaders offered of intercultural conflicts and misunderstandings. Furthermore, geographer Katharyne Mitchell's (2004) research suggests that the media played an important role in mediating the transformation of the city-region in the 1980s and 1990s.

Local leaders in Vancouver did not mention the *Vancouver Sun* as affecting in any way their responsiveness to immigrants and ethnocultural diversity. This might have been because Vancouver had already weathered many of its 'growing pains.' However, Katharyne Mitchell describes a variety of roles that the *Vancouver Sun* played in supporting Vancouver's global transformation in the 1990s. Initially, in the late 1980s, according to her, it published 'lopsided' articles that reinforced the link between immigration from Hong Kong and both rising housing prices and unpopular changes to established neighbourhoods. These articles fuelled a citywide racism in the Vancouver in the late 1980s (Mitchell 2004, 70–1). Following these controversial articles, which played on already existing community sentiments and fears, the *Sun* helped legitimize unfettered development and population growth in the region. It commissioned articles by academics that discredited slow-growth ideas and that presented development and high population growth as inevitable. Here Mitchell refers to the articles in a series titled 'Future Growth: Future Shock,' for which the newspaper commissioned two UBC professors – Alan Artibise and Michael Seelig – to promote a growth agenda (ibid., 132–4). In her words, 'the authors used various forms of ideological persuasion to win consent for their neoliberal, pro-growth agenda'; this included presenting growth as inevitable and rational (ibid., 134). As she describes it, the series began with an article that painted slow-growth movements as childish and that compared their adherents to

Peter Pan: 'Lock the gates. If the choice were ours, we could stop people from moving into the Pacific region ... We are the Peter Pan of urban regions. Like Peter Pan, we would simply like to declare: "We won't grow up." But locking the gates is not a realistic option' (Artibise and Seelig 1990, in Mitchell 2004, 134). The newspaper also played an important role in disseminating the pro-immigration research that foundations such as the Laurier Institution produced (ibid., 106–8). In a more minor sense, the newspaper also served as a vehicle for expressing opposition to growth. However, after the controversial series in the late 1980s, these views were not expressed in articles by journalists but rather by community members through letters to the editor (ibid., 139).

In Richmond, civil servants attributed misinformation disseminated by the Chinese-language media to the Chinese community as a significant trigger to the explosive 'group homes controversy.' This controversy led to the development of a new communications strategy that includes a media watch program whereby the city monitors Chinese-language newspapers for inaccurate content and potential controversies.

In Surrey, the only mention of the media was in the context of the need to advertise city jobs in ethnic media. In addition, Leslie Woodman mentioned that the *Surrey Leader* was a member of the Leadership Council established by the city to identify businesses that might warrant recognition for their innovative approaches to including diversity in their business practices. The vehicle for this recognition was the SDISS's (now DiverseCity)'s annual business award.

In Coquitlam, informants did not mention the role of the local media – including *Coquitlam Now* and the *Tri-City News* – in community debates about social change and multiculturalism policy processes.

A Qualitative Analysis of Local Political Cultures

The research uncovered evidence of differences in 'political culture' among the four cities in the Greater Vancouver sample. In interviews, community leaders in Vancouver said they found it relatively easy to cooperate with one another and that the sector was well organized (Chan 2004, interview; Woroch 2004, interview). However, there was some evidence of discord among organizations. At the time of the interviews, the Multilingual Orientation Service Association for Immigrant Communities (MOSAIC), one of the largest settlement agencies in Vancouver, had withdrawn from the Affiliation of Multicultural Societies and Service Agencies of B.C. (AMSSA), the province's umbrella organization for immigrant settlement groups. Apparently, MOSAIC had disagreed with the structure of AMSSA's board and with its decision to offer services in competition with those of its member agencies. In addition, according one informant, community leaders with MOSAIC felt that AMSSA should be 'making more noise on issues' than it was (community leader 2004, interview). In this regard, Timothy Welsh, Program Director for AMSSA, said that in its advocacy strategies, AMSSA 'has to walk a fine line so that it doesn't lose its [provincial] funding' (Welsh 2004, interview).[18]

In the GTA, organizations that represent immigrants and ethnocultural minorities vary in their advocacy strategies: in suburban municipalities they prefer to negotiate 'in the boardroom' whereas in Toronto they also engage in contention 'on the streets' (Douglas 2003, interview). Welsh suggested that there is little variation in the strategies that MOSAIC and AMSSA follow to influence the political process. He described the common approach of immigrant organizations in Greater Vancouver: 'They [settlement organizations in Vancouver] try to achieve active communication with governments, not letting them rest comfortably, seeking info when [governments are] veering off in some direction, [and] giving them info ... It is advocacy but a different approach.' Settlement organizations in Vancouver are 'very diplomatic' and 'cautious.' In Welsh's assessment, neither MOSAIC nor AMSSA is like the Ontario Council of Agencies Serving Immigrants (OCASI, the umbrella organization for settlement agencies in Ontario),[19] which 'stood up to' Ontario's Conservative government during the Mike Harris years and lost a large portion of its provincial funding as a result (Welsh 2004, interview).

At the time of the interviews, the settlement sector did not expect a great deal from the City of Vancouver in immigration and settlement policy. That sector perceived the city as a junior partner in immigration and recognized its limitations as a municipal government. Several community leaders noted that Vancouver was responding to 'diversity,' not 'immigration' (Chan 2004, interview; Welsh 2004, interview). They did not appear to expect the city to do more than adapt its own services or to become a major player in immigration policy. Nevertheless, all of the immigrant settlement leaders interviewed for this study had ongoing relationships with Baldwin Wong, the city's Multicultural Social Planner.

A new node in the city's immigration and other multiculturalism-related networks emerged in Vancouver in 1996, when the federal government launched the Metropolis Project. B.C.'s Metropolis research centre – Research on Immigration and Integration into the Metropolis (RIIM) – has its headquarters in Vancouver.[20] RIIM fosters the development and maintenance of intersectoral networks in Vancouver as well as networks across levels of government. RIIM's management board includes university professors, community leaders, and representatives from all three levels of government, and the board members have ongoing relationships with immigrant settlement agencies. For example, Patricia Woroch, the Executive Director of the Immigrant Services Society (ISS) noted that Jennifer Hyndman, a RIIM management board member and a geography professor at Simon Fraser University, sits on the board of her agency as well (Woroch 2004, interview). The City of Vancouver's representative on RIIM's management board is Baldwin Wong. Because of Metropolis networks, leaders in the immigrant settlement sector and Baldwin Wong were familiar with the academic and community research on immigration's impact on Vancouver.

In sum, the settlement sector in Vancouver is fairly cooperative. It is generally 'cautious' and 'diplomatic' in its advocacy strategies and focuses on provincial policy. The sector's expectations of local government are lower than its expectations of the provincial government.

At a broader level, immigration has changed Vancouver's political culture by introducing new community cleavages. In interviews, political leaders and community leaders alike acknowledged that at first there had been tensions surrounding immigration owing to cultural differences between long-standing residents and the primarily Hong Kong Chinese immigrants who arrived in the 1980s and 1990s. Many informants for this study made a point of mentioning immigrants who tore down existing homes and built 'monster homes,' thereby creating tensions between immigrants and the long-standing community (Cadman 2004, interview; Cheung 2004, interview, Wong 2004, interview). David Edgington and Thomas Hutton (2002) describe the 'most pejorative connotation of the "monster home" usage [as] related to what many viewed as outlandishly ostentatious and unsympathetic design values – such as "cathedral style" front entrances, and paved front yards, with little or no landscaping' (Edgington and Hutton 2002, 19). Informants also mentioned 'tree cutting' as a source of significant interethnic strain (Cheung 2004, interview, Wong 2004, interview).[21]

According to David Ley and his colleagues (2001), resistance to the housing preferences of newcomers to Vancouver was general, and in some neighbourhoods, such as Shaughnessy and Kerrisdale, that resistance was 'sustained' (Ley et al. 2001, 13). The conflict over housing in these neighbourhoods led to a public hearing in 1992 that pitted 'Caucasian' residents against primarily Hong Kong–born newcomers (2001, 13). Shaughnessy and Kerrisdale are upscale, well-established neighbourhoods in Vancouver, and for that reason many expected that the preferences of long-standing residents in these neighbourhoods would prevail. But owing to the strength of the Hong Kong residents' intervention, the public hearings led to unexpected compromises:

> Though the City had expected an outcome favouring the longer-established residents, the strength of immigrant intervention precluded a simple decision. The stalemate led to a joint planning process and the eventual recommendation that traditional designs would be preferred but not mandatory in new construction, though builders would receive a density bonus if they built in a traditional neighbourhood idiom. This solution seems to have satisfied most parties, enough anyway that the problem has disappeared, and a new style, a reworked Tudor revival, has become the builder's choice for a new vernacular. (ibid., 14)

Such incidents suggest that immigration can alter local political cultures by introducing new political cleavages. It also indicates how intraethnic patterns of mobilization matter to policy outputs. In Vancouver, the powerful Hong Kong Chinese immigrants were able to challenge the zoning preferences of the city's long-standing socio-economic elite.

Several informants mentioned that Richmond has a long history of community engagement and community cooperation. According to Terry Crowe, Manager of Planning in Richmond, these traits are rooted in Richmond's history as a fishing and farming community in which people helped one another and developed strong interpersonal networks of support. In general, informants described a community with high levels of social capital. Crowe also mentioned that Richmond as a community has a reputation for being 'rebellious [and] a little feisty.' For example, the city insisted on having its own library board when the province did not want to allow it. And unlike other municipalities in Greater Vancouver, Richmond entered the field of affordable housing as well as establishing both a child-care board and a seniors' advisory board. It also had the 'vision' to hire a social planner (Crowe 2004, interview), even though provincial legislation does not require municipalities to engage in social planning.[22]

Similarly, Annie McKitrick, a well-known community leader in both Richmond and Surrey, suggested that Richmond's decision to take on a role in multiculturalism policy reflected a 'long volunteer history in Richmond [and a culture of making] things happen' (McKitrick 2004, interview). A culture of cooperation also characterizes the city's immigrant settlement sector, as well as its community organizations representing ethnocultural minorities (Sanghera 2004, interview).

However, some immigrant and ethnocultural-minority communities in Richmond are more organized than others. The Chinese community, which accounted for 67 per cent of the city's visible-minority population in 2006 (see Table 6.2), is well organized; smaller groups are 'having a tougher time' (Schroeder 2004, interview). Richmond's Chinese community is also highly engaged in community affairs. Community leaders in neighbouring municipalities recognize this level of engagement; Surrey's Multicultural Librarian noted that 'the Chinese community is very vocal in Richmond' (Basi 2004, interview). Informants also remarked that, from the municipality's perspective, the Chinese community appears to be cohesive. Greg Buss, the Chief Librarian in Richmond, mentioned that the Chinese community speaks with a 'unified voice,' which helps the library respond to its concerns (Buss 2004, interview).

Richmond's Chinese community is so well organized and 'institutionally complete' (with shopping centres that cater to Chinese residents and other Chinese-specific amenities) that in 2002 some community leaders feared that two solitudes were developing in the city (Edgington and Hutton 2002, 20). Balwant Sanghera noted the fear of ghettoization when a single immigrant group comes to a city in large numbers (Sanghera 2004, interview).

In Richmond as in Vancouver, some 'growing pains' have been associated with the large-scale influx of Chinese immigrants (Hardy 2004, interview). Among other things, these pains relate to 'monster homes,' inflated housing prices, and local property taxes. Edgington and Hutton described the situation: 'In this way the more affluent new immigrants were perceived as displacing existing households, and thus dramatically reshaping the social morphology of the community. The vehemence of some of these objections (perhaps predictably) invoked a vigorous counter-reaction among new immigrants, including accusations of racism and discrimination, and indeed the controversy was largely structured around (if not defined by) race-situated constituencies' (2002, 20).[23]

The lack of English-language signage in Asian malls also caused strain in the community. As Hardy put it, when large-scale change happens, 'people feel they're losing something' (Hardy 2004, interview). As in Vancouver, immigration to Richmond has changed the local political culture by introducing new ethnocultural cleavages and by reshaping the community's identity.

According to informants, immigrants are not as engaged in Surrey, in part because that city does not have a tradition of engaging with the community (McKitrick 2004, interview). One leader in the immigrant settlement sector in Greater Vancouver described Surrey in the following way: 'Culturally Surrey is a very different place from Burnaby[24] and Vancouver. Burnaby and Vancouver share a lot culturally in terms of what it means to be an urban government and "Who are we?" and "What do we do?" Where[as] [in] Surrey ... they just view themselves as different. We're on the other side of the river. We're an agricultural community. And we aren't the same as Vancouver. We're intentionally different. We have bigger properties. They're kind of like the hinterland of Greater Vancouver' (community leader 2004, interview).

According to the same community leader, there are more 'flashpoints of intolerance' in Surrey than in the other municipalities in the sample. Richmond also had some 'growing pains,' but it learned to value its diversity very quickly (community leader 2004, interview).

Other community leaders described Surrey's political culture less positively. A local leader outside Surrey who preferred to remain anonymous made comments such as 'it is so dysfunctional there ... [the city is run by] bully leadership.' Balwant Sanghera mentioned that Surrey still has 'quite a few rednecks' and that 'Surrey Council has some people like that' (Sanghera 2004, interview). Bruce Hardy, a community leader in Surrey, observed: 'There is relatively rampant racism in most of the lower mainland. We have the feeling on the one hand that the visible minorities get a better shake than Caucasians, and of course, the visible minorities know that it's not true.' Hardy agreed that racism is more of a problem in Surrey than in Vancouver or Richmond. In Vancouver and Richmond, 'people will practise the simple courtesy of at least pretending tolerance. In Surrey there is a significant part of the population that proudly resent multiculturalism' (Hardy 2004, interview).

South Asians are the largest immigrant and visible-minority group in Surrey. The population is largely Indo-Canadian (Villeneuve 2001, interview), and the Sikh religion is the most common religion among Surrey's South Asians. In 2001, 56,330 Sikhs lived in Surrey but only 10,000 Muslims and 9,620 Hindus – the other two religions that are common in South Asia (Statistics Canada n.d.b).

Though they do not examine Surrey specifically, the findings of Gurcharn S. Basran and B. Singh Bolaria (2003) support community leaders' perceptions as they relate to religious divisions within Surrey's Sikh population (divisions which, they argue, are simplified and exaggerated in the local media) and to the majority community's response to the concentration of Sikhs in Surrey. Citing an Angus Reid survey conducted in 1991, they note that Canadians' 'comfort level' with Sikhs is lower than it is for all other visible-minority groups: a mere 43 per cent for Sikh immigrants (and slightly higher for Canadian-born Sikhs) (2003, 179). The comparable figure for Chinese immigrant groups – the group that is concentrated in the other Greater Vancouver municipalities – is 69 per cent (ibid).

Several informants suggested that the South Asian community is fragmented and poorly organized. For instance, Ravi Basi, the Multicultural Librarian for Surrey, noted that the Punjabi community is somewhat 'vocal' in Surrey, and also 'very political ... We began to wonder whether they [the South Asian leaders who approach the library with their service preferences] were speaking for the whole community.' In her view, 'they do make their needs known,' yet at the same time, there are various South Asian 'interest groups' in Surrey (Basi 2004, interview). By this she meant that there are many different interests and identities in Surrey's South Asian community (and not formal interest groups in the political science sense of the term). In this vein, another civil servant in Surrey said that the city has had a difficult time identifying the leaders of immigrant and ethnocultural minorities (Cavan 2004, interview).

Factions within Surrey's South Asian community seem to coincide with religious cleavages. Balwant Sanghera, a community leader in Richmond of South Asian ethnic origin, said that the South Asian community in Surrey is divided between modern and fundamentalist groups (Sanghera 2004, interview). Leslie Woodman referred to moderate and radical Sikh factions (Woodman 2004, interview). Ric Hall, Superintendent of the RCMP's Coquitlam Detachment, who previously worked with the Surrey Detachment, noted that 'Surrey is unique unto itself' because of its size and concentration of 'East Indians' (Hall 2004, interview). He described a highly divided South Asian community plagued by intragroup violence. In his words, there is 'fighting in temples, if they're not shooting at each other in the streets ... There is always a strong police presence at [East Indian] events' (Hall 2004, interview).

In general, Leslie Woodman painted a picture of a highly isolated South Asian community with many social problems. For instance, she mentioned that many South Asians in Surrey were in their forties and did not speak English very well. She also noted that some children who were born in Canada access ESL classes in the community because they don't speak English at home. And she suggested that some of Surrey's South Asian youth join gangs because of an identity crisis arising from the South Asian community's conservatism. She said that though India had adapted many conservative customs, Surrey's Indian community had not (Woodman 2004, interview). Other informants mentioned street racing and youth gangs as issues in Surrey's South Asian community.

In *The Sikhs in Canada* (2003), Basran and Singh Bolaria argue that the image of Sikh communities in B.C. as violent is perpetuated by the local media. That coverage 'characterizes the community as conflict ridden, with a tendency to settle disagreements and disputes through violence; one with no aptitude for reasoning and democracy, as a "troubled" community requiring inordinate use of public resources including policy and courts to maintain harmony and peace within it and to reduce its threat to the general public' (2003, 168). Conflicts are generally simplified into conflict between moderates and radicals (ibid.), and headlines are sensationalized – for example, 'Saturday's Bloody Riot in Surrey' (ibid., 170). Media coverage of conflicts within the community has 'shaped public opinion and the perception of a community' (ibid., 167).

There is also evidence of competition and conflict within the immigrant settlement sector in Surrey. Bruce Hardy, Executive Director of OPTIONs, a mainstream organization with close ties to Surrey's council, described the settlement sector as highly competitive in Surrey. There were rivalries among community organizations, each of which tended to defend its turf. For example, immigrant settlement agencies appeared to resent mainstream organizations that offered immigrant settlement services. In Bruce Hardy's words: 'There's been a little bit of a community pissing match [between service agencies in Surrey], because the belief is in some parts that they [organizations that specialize in immigrant settlement services, such as SDISS] should be the only voice of immigrants in the community. Although many agencies that are multi-service offer multicultural programs as part of their services.' Hardy was straightforward about the competitive relations among community organizations in Surrey: 'Whenever agencies come sniffing in your territory for contracts, we [community agencies in Surrey] go ballistic.' S.U.C.C.E.S.S. is unique in that community organizations invite it into their communities, because it raises about forty cents of every dollar it spends on services (Hardy 2005, interview).

Surrey-Delta Immigrant Services Society (SDISS), which is located in Surrey and was one of the three largest settlement organizations in Greater Vancouver when the interviews were conducted, does not have an ongoing relationship with Surrey Council's 'power brokers' – a term that Hardy used when interviewed. According to Lesley Woodman, Executive Director of SDISS, Surrey's council perceives organizations that specialize in immigrant settlement (such as SDISS) as 'special-interest groups' (Woodman 2004, interview). In her view, the city prefers to deal with mainstream organizations – the ones that provide services to immigrants in addition to services to the larger community. SDISS has a relationship with Surrey's more left-wing councillors, such as Judy Villeneuve. But according to Woodman, Villeneuve was not influential on council at the time of the interviews.

The 'power brokers' on council at the time of the interviews – including the mayor and members of the Surrey Election Team (the governing party) – chose to develop ongoing relationships with OPTIONs rather than with SDISS. In fact, two or three of the staff of OPTIONs (including its executive director, Bruce Hardy) were on a first-name basis with everyone on council at the time of the interviews (Hardy 2005, interview). The Surrey leadership's preference for mainstream organizations seems to be related to the fact that such organizations are less likely to pressure the municipality to enter new service areas or to adapt their current services. According to Hardy, OPTIONs is 'very moderate' and does not lobby the municipal government to adjust its role in the community. The organization respects the municipal leaders' argument that immigration policy is not their area of responsibility. Instead, OPTIONs works with the city on issues that the city itself identifies as priorities (ibid.).

Civil society in Coquitlam is less developed than in any of the other municipalities in the sample. It remains a 'bedroom community'; roughly 70 per cent of its residents work outside the city (Jones 2004, interview). However, there is a network of volunteers and community 'insiders.' Simon Ahn, a Korean-born immigrant who sits on the Library Board, observed that one 'see[s] the same people everywhere'

(Ahn 2004, interview). Similarly, for the most part, an old guard of retirees governs the city (Kingsbury 2004, interview).

According to Ahn, some immigrant groups are more organized and influential than others. In particular, the Chinese and Indo-Canadian communities are more engaged in local affairs than Koreans 'due to [their] numbers' (Ahn 2004, personal communication). The Chinese community's influence can be seen in the city's library, which has a Chinese-language collection. According to Karen Harrison, who manages Coquitlam's library, both the Taiwan Economic Development Office and the Council of the People's Republic of China approached the library to discuss how they could improve its collection (Harrison 2004, interview). Nevertheless, the research did not uncover evidence of large-scale community mobilization to pressure the municipality to respond at a more corporate, citywide level. Rather, it seems that the immigrant community's pressure was limited to the Coquitlam Library.

In general, informants described Coquitlam as tolerant and free of major ethnic-relations controversies (Ahn 2004, interview; Jones 2004, interview). The issues that sparked controversy in Richmond are absent in Coquitlam. Coquitlam has no separate Asian malls. Its two major 'Asian'[25] markets are located within its two major, 'mainstream' malls, Coquitlam Centre and Henderson Centre, where – as noted by Warren Jones, Coquitlam's city manager – there is a real mix of people (Jones 2004, interview). Furthermore, Chinese immigrants generally have not moved into established neighbourhoods. Rather, a new residential development called Westwood Plateau has attracted Chinese immigrants to Coquitlam. In the absence of a clash of community preferences and goals, Coquitlam's community cleavages remain latent.

Understanding How the Differences Matter: Looking at the Cases through an Urban Regime Lens

Vancouver: The Pacific Rim Consensus

Urban regime theory draws one's attention to the informal governance arrangements that create and sustain the capacity to achieve local policy goals. Vancouver's responsiveness to immigrants and ethnocultural minorities can be explained by the presence of leaders who support these goals in the public and private sectors and by the resources they bring to the governance arrangement. The city's responsiveness to immigrants and ethnocultural minorities can also be explained by the way in which local leaders connect multiculturalism goals to economic-development objectives. The regime recognizes that immigration and investment from Pacific Rim countries drives growth in the city and that positive ethnic relations are crucial to maintaining community consensus around immigration and growth.

The ways in which local leaders frame policy goals constitute a source of 'power to' (Stone 2005). As in Toronto, 'a new justification for multiculturalism and anti-racism emerged in the 1980s and 1990s – such measures were good for business and good for trade' (Abu-Laban 1997, 83). Similarly, in Vancouver, immigration and foreign investment became the city's key economic-development strategy. As we saw above, establishing Vancouver as the 'gateway' to Pacific Rim countries became the city's overriding economic-development objective in the 1980s. The idea persists that immigration and multiculturalism are good for economic growth. As Vancouver councillor Jim Green put it: 'Diversity is our key to success ... Most people on this council believe that it is our diversity that gives us our competitive edge internationally' (Green 2004, personal communication).

The City of Vancouver has played an important role in the city's new Pacific Rim economic-development activities. As Abu-Laban (1997) observes: 'Vancouver has now emerged as a "global city,"[26] in part because successive municipal governments have actively cultivated cross-border relations not only at provincial and federal levels, but also at the international level' (1997, 83). International cross-border relationships focus primarily on Pacific Rim countries.

A clear public–private consensus among Vancouver's elite on policy goals has made possible the development of an internationalist economic-development regime with a Pacific Rim focus. As David Edgington and Michael Goldberg (1990) argue, 'the Pacific is one area where there is extraordinary consistency of vision among public and private sector organizations and individuals' (1990, 40, in Olds 2001, 92). The private-sector participants in the Pacific Rim coalition are powerful and cohesive.

Geographer Kris Olds (2001) observes that Pacific Rim–specific institutions (such as the Asia-Pacific Foundation of Canada, the International Financial Centre Vancouver, and the Hong Kong Business Association), as well as more mainstream institutions (such as the Greater Vancouver Real Estate Board and the Vancouver Board of Trade), are linked and 'command considerable public and private resources that are used to structure the nature of policies and processes which influence Vancouver's future ... Taken together, the reach and influence of the Pacific Rim contingent is long, sinuous, and hegemonic' (2001, 92). From the start, the city tied its multiculturalism initiatives to its Pacific Rim economic-development initiatives. The city now uses its diversity to market Vancouver internationally. For instance, local leaders used Vancouver's diversity as a selling point for its successful Olympic and Paralympic bid (Green 2004, interview).

Thus the City of Vancouver's multiculturalism initiatives are, to some extent at least, by-products of what Patrick Smith (1992) describes as a new internationalist, Pacific Rim policy stance. Though the city had an Equal Employment Opportunity Policy as early as 1977, it updated this policy significantly in 1986, at a time of massive flows of immigration to Vancouver and at the tail end of Mayor Harcourt's Pacific Rim initiatives. The city continued to innovate in this area under Mayor Gordon Campbell by establishing the Hastings Institute. The city's commitment to multiculturalism continues to this day.

Furthermore, both parties supported this economic-development model and the multiculturalism policy responses that accompanied it. What Kris Olds (2001) refers to as the 'Pacific Rim Consensus' is a cross-party consensus. Katharyne Mitchell (2004) notes that by supporting unfettered development, the NPA undermined an 'unspoken pact' between Kerrisdale residents and NPA councillors that west-side neighbourhoods would be protected (2004, 78–9). The historic zoning restrictions in this well-established community became an impediment to growth and went against the Pacific Rim Consensus. A cynical reading of the motives underpinning multiculturalism policies would dismiss those policies as devices to facilitate the flow of capital into the city and its accumulation there.

Vancouver's civil service plays an important role in providing resources to the regime; it also serves an important regime-maintenance function by providing selective incentives to regime participants. The city houses many of its resources in its EEO Office, the Hastings Institute, and the Social Planning Department. City programs, such as its Community Services Grants Program, are used to develop and maintain ongoing relationships with immigrant settlement groups as well as with other organizations that have multiculturalism-related mandates. These grants also help fill gaps in community capacity.

The city also shapes the direction of change in mainstream community organizations through its requirement that multiculturalism goals be incorporated into service planning and delivery. The Hastings Institute extends the local state's employment equity initiatives into the private sector by offering diversity training programs to private organizations. And the city's Multicultural Social Planner maintains ongoing relationships with leaders in the immigrant settlement sector and with other regime participants.

Private foundations and institutions also participate in multiculturalism policy development. The Laurier Institution conducts important research on multiculturalism; it also plays a regime-maintenance function by addressing community backlash towards immigration through reports and public-education campaigns (Mitchell 2004). The Vancouver Foundation sponsors and convenes community multiculturalism events. VanCity plays an important role in community development by sponsoring events as well as by offering loans to new immigrants who want their foreign credentials validated.[27] These private-sector organizations offer an important pool of resources – a local-level 'multiculturalism infrastructure.'

Vancouver's responsiveness to immigrants and ethnocultural minorities can be explained by the presence of a strong regime. There is a broad consensus among elites in Vancouver that immigration is a positive force in the city. Intercultural conflicts are managed with the goal of maintaining this consensus. Thus, even while large influxes of Chinese immigrants have created new community cleavages, ethnic conflicts have been managed with the overall goal of maintaining the regime.

As geographers David Ley, Michael Goldberg, and Thomas Hutton (2003, 16) observe, citing Ley, Hiebert, and Pratt (1992), when some Vancouver-area residents became concerned about rising costs of housing caused in part by immigration, 'neither the provincial nor city governments showed much enthusiasm for controls on real estate that might adversely affect either flows of people or investment to Vancouver, either from Hong Kong or from the wider Asia-Pacific region.' In other words, the Vancouver regime's commitment to attracting immigrants and investment from the Pacific Rim took priority over addressing the concerns of some long-standing residents about the impact of immigration on housing affordability. Opposition to growth was labelled racist, which undermined neighbourhood movements that developed to challenge the 'value-free development' (Mitchell 2004) of Vancouver's globally embedded 'growth machine.' Furthermore, as Mitchell demonstrates, the resources of the city's powerful business community – including the Hong Kong contingent – were brought to bear on the issue of managing community backlash. Racialization of the conflict was a challenge to the regime; but if Mitchell (2004) is correct, it was also a way to silence dissent (and thus a regime-maintenance strategy).

Thus the city's policy responses to periodic interethnic community conflict must be understood in the context of its entrenched, well-resourced regime. For instance, when the influx of immigrants into some of Vancouver's established neighbourhoods resulted in intercultural conflicts over housing preferences, the city's local planning processes mediated the conflict in the interest of regime maintenance. In this instance the city passed compromise by-laws that accommodated both immigrants and long-standing residents. David Ley and his colleagues (2001) attribute the compromise to the organizational strength of Vancouver's Hong Kong immigrants and suggest that the fact that the city did not favour long-standing residents was surprising. The residents were the upper class (mainly Whites), whose preferences had long been influential in the city.

When one looks at this issue through a regime lens, however, one would – in retrospect – expect such an outcome. Intercultural compromise is necessary to long-term regime maintenance and to maintaining a consensus on the importance of the city's international relationship with the Pacific Rim. Sustained intercultural conflict would jeopardize not only the city's 'social sustainability' but also its economic development. In addition, since the Hong Kong business elites are powerful in Vancouver's regime, a compromise that accommodated their housing preferences (and the housing preferences of the Hong Kong Chinese community generally) was necessary.

In fact, given the central role played by immigrants from Hong Kong to the local 'growth machine,' one might have expected the city to disregard the concerns of long-standing Whites in favour of 'value-free development.' Growth machine theory would explain the compromise by-laws by arguing that compromise is necessary when an issue threatens growth. However, urban regime theory offers a more precise explanation of policy outcomes. The long-standing White residents possessed an important resource: their ability to punish local politicians in the electoral arena. That democratic resource also mattered to local politicians. Important as well was the organizational strength of the Hong Kong Chinese. Urban regime analysis draws our attention to the broader structures of community power as well as to the need to maintain a local consensus concerning development and multiculturalism. As Stone (1989) explains, the study of urban regimes is not simply about 'who cooperates [and] how their cooperation is achieved across institutional sectors of community life'; it is also 'an examination of how that cooperation is maintained when confronted with an ongoing process of social change, a continuing influx of new actors, and potential break-downs through conflict or indifference' (1989, 9). Governing decisions in urban regimes 'have to do with *managing conflict* and *making adaptive responses* to social change [; they] are not a matter of [a single sector] running or controlling everything' (ibid., 6). Here, neither the Hong Kong economic elite nor Vancouver's politically influential long-standing residents were able to control the municipality's response. Urban regime theory leads one to expect a compromise solution in the interest of regime maintenance, which is precisely what occurred.

In the 1980s and 1990s conflicts of this sort injected an observable vitality into Vancouver's regime. Community resistance was relatively widespread. In this way, the Vancouver case illustrates the importance of elite–mass relations to understanding urban regime dynamics. Local elites had to manage the reactions of the community in the interest of maintaining the regime's integrity. Nevertheless, beyond these conflicts, Vancouver's regime seems to have followed a path-dependent form of development; put another way, incremental changes and improvements in multiculturalism policy occurred owing to institutionalized leadership in Vancouver's civil service, a climate of receptivity to multiculturalism initiatives on council, and entrenched relationships among a variety of public- and private-sector leaders. Those relationships are based on a consensus that multiculturalism is a fundamental strength of the city. Vancouver's diversity is a source of economic development and contributes to its international profile. Multiculturalism is part of Vancouver's globally saleable 'brand' (Laurier Institution 2005).

Leaders in Vancouver's civil society do not seem to apply sustained pressure on the city to respond to multiculturalism. Leaders in the immigrant settlement sector have ongoing relationships with leaders in the city and with the city's Multicultural Social Planner, yet they are not pressuring the city to take on a more expansive role in developing immigration and multiculturalism policy. In part this is because many leaders in the immigrant settlement sector do not perceive the city as an important policy actor in immigration and immigrant settlement policy (which, as defined by upper levels of government, covers only the first three years of settlement). Several leaders, when interviewed, clearly articulated the view that the city is responding to *diversity*, not to immigration (Chan 2004, interview; Welsh 2004, personal communication).

In other words, the city has made efforts to accommodate immigrants in its governance structures and when delivering its services, but does not view those efforts as an incursion into immigration policy.

The city is not resisting such a role, since the immigrant settlement sector has not pressured the city to enter this policy field. For the immigrant settlement sector, the province is clearly the most important government actor. The sector's approach is 'cautious' with respect to advocacy with governments (Welsh 2004, interview). To the extent that the sector engages in limited advocacy, it is directed at the province, which is the sector's primary government financial patron. In the absence of sustained and vocal pressure, the city has responded to the community's ethnocultural diversity by adopting multiculturalism policies on its own. Its responses are consistent with the consensus view of its regime partners. No pressure is needed where a consensus already exists.

Owing to the absence of sustained pressure on the part of the immigrant settlement sector in Vancouver's regime, the city had not developed an immigrant settlement policy when the interviews were being conducted. Vancouver differed from Toronto in this respect. This difference may also reflect differences in the provincial context. Overall, the Province of British Columbia has been more consistently supportive of multiculturalism policy goals. In Toronto, in the absence of provincial support, the settlement sector had an incentive to join forces with other local leaders to lobby for a greater role for the city in immigrant settlement. Nevertheless, there is evidence that the ways in which municipal leaders in Toronto and Vancouver frame their responses to immigrants are converging. Recall that former Mayor Larry Campbell established the Mayor's Working Group on Immigration in 2005 after interviews were conducted in the city-region.

As urban regime theory suggests, electoral politics is only one arena in which policy decisions are made. Policy actors' preferences cannot be assumed; rather, they are products of regime dynamics. Both the left and the right in Vancouver support a municipal role in multiculturalism policy. There appears to be a consensus that foreign investment and ethnic accommodation are interlinked. Because of this consensus, multiculturalism policy goals have made it onto the Vancouver council's agenda, even though few immigrants or ethnocultural minorities are represented on council (only one councillor out of ten was a visible minority when the interviews were conducted in 2004). White, non-immigrant local leaders provide political leadership in multicultural policy development. Regime theory also helps us understand why, despite their heavier electoral weight in municipal politics (since immigrants without citizenship cannot vote in municipal elections), local decisions do not necessarily favour the interests of long-standing residents. There is a systemic bias towards business interests, and electoral resources are only one type. Regime relationships structure local decision making.

In sum, Vancouver's multiculturalism policy networks are linked to wider economic-development networks. There is a strong consensus among Vancouver's business and political elite that diversity is a source of economic and social strength in the city. Within this consensus, policy changes occur in an incremental fashion. In the 1980s and 1990s, when Vancouver's cultural and racial composition went through its most dramatic changes, intercultural conflicts punctuated this relatively linear form of policy development. However, the idea that immigration (and the ethnocultural diversity it implies) is an important strength of the city was firmly embedded in the regime. As new challenges and opportunities arise, these networks continue to shape Vancouver's responses. For instance, Vancouver capitalized on these networks in its successful bid for the 2010 Olympics by using its ethnocultural diversity as a selling point.

Richmond: The Architecture of an Intercultural Regime

In Richmond, governance relationships have emerged to manage race relations – what local leaders have recently reframed 'intercultural relations.' Over time, Richmond's race relations committees have been important anchors of the regime. The race relations committee was reconstituted in 2002 as the Richmond Intercultural Advisory Committee (RIAC). The rationale behind the founding of RIAC clearly reflects a 'regime building' mandate. For instance, the goal is to encourage 'Richmond's diverse cultural and community organizations to pool and co-ordinate their activities, experience, knowledge, skills, abilities and resources' (City of Richmond 2002). RIAC is designed to create capacity to manage ethnocultural diversity in a highly resource-constrained environment by pooling resources across the public and private sectors.

Current cross-sector capacity building in race relations builds on past efforts and networks. The predecessor to RIAC explained the need to extend the scope of formal local institutions to address ethnic relations challenges:

While many of the issues that Council deals with have ethnic relations implications, in my view, there are many ethnic relations issues that belong to or are better dealt with by other organizations. The whole issue of ethnic relations between school age children and the possible culturally based schisms that may be occurring in that age group seems to be something the School Board would be better equipped to address than Council. Ethnic relations in the business world, such as linguistic issues in signage and cultural expectations in styles of personal service, might be an area the Chamber of Commerce could profitably address. Multicultural needs and sensitivities in the area of community recreation programs is an area that in the Richmond system would be appropriately addressed by the Council of Community Associations. The Sports Council and Arts Council could fulfill similar roles in the areas of sport and the arts. The Library is particularly active in the area of multicultural information needs. And of course the various volunteer and service agencies fulfill roles appropriate to their particular mandate. The whole notion of an Ethnic Relations Co-ordinating Committee is based on the idea that there are many agencies involved in ethnic relations and that some problems or opportunities overlap and benefit from a co-ordinated approach. (City of Richmond 1994b, 3–4)

RIAC's chair put it this way: 'City resources are limited and organizations too are limited but when you put everything together – businesses, organizations, and the city, then it increases your capacity to help serve the people' (Sanghera 2004, interview). Race relations committees coordinate and help foster existing productive and informal networks in civil society as well as in street-level agencies in the city. They represent intentional efforts on the part of local leaders across the public and private sectors to co-manage the city's response to its changing ethnocultural demographics.

The extent to which urban regimes are socially productive is structured by the availability of resources across sectors and by the extent to which local leaders have mobilized around the regime's goals. In Richmond, city officials at all levels are receptive to immigrants' concerns and preferences. Also, Richmond's efforts to adapt to and accommodate ethnocultural diversity have been facilitated by the fact that elite members of the Chinese community have been willing to devote personal resources to facilitate the city's responses to the concerns of its primarily Chinese immigrants. A single member of the Chinese community donated three-quarters of a million dollars in cash and books to the Richmond Public Library; and members of the community's busi-ness elite, such as Thomas Fung, were willing to provide co-leadership with the city to resolve interethnic tensions in Richmond.

Indeed, Richmond's Chinese community not only has facilitated the city's response to its community's own cultural preferences, but also is willing to accommodate English-speaking, non-Chinese residents of Richmond. Wealthy immigrants such as Thomas Fung have the capac-ity to redefine the cultural identity and the public face of Richmond. For this reason, intercultural accommodation is not just about address-ing the needs and preferences of immigrants with respect to municipal and community services; it is also about facilitating long-standing resi-dents' access to private developments (such as Asian-style malls) that are important privately owned 'public' meeting places in the city.

To facilitate mutual accommodation, the city has extended the scope of municipal institutions to the private sector by developing urban re-gime coalitions. These coalitions serve as bridges between Richmond's immigrant Chinese community and long-standing residents. However, though the city has been receptive to taking on a role when pressured to do so by the community, it has not adopted a role in race relations proactively. Two main factors have pushed the issue of race relations onto the city agenda: a proactive Chinese immigrant community, and backlash on the part of the long-standing residents. In a volatile envi-ronment, the city has chosen to play a facilitative role in race relations. The city's policy style in intercultural relations is reactive.

Managing race relations in a city that has experienced a dramatic shift in its population's ethnic composition is a difficult task. The city's political leaders and civil servants have had to walk a fine line in re-sponding to pressure from immigrants (primarily Chinese) to adapt city services to their needs and preferences. According to Greg Buss, Richmond's Chief Librarian, the generous donations the Chinese com-munity made to the library meant that it could use its existing budget to purchase English-language materials. In Buss's view, when making decisions about how to distribute city resources in an ethnically divid-ed context such as Richmond, the key is to prevent competition from developing among cultural groups (Buss 2004, interview). Since the Chinese community was willing to donate library materials and money to the library if the city were receptive to accommodating the needs of the Chinese community, a dynamic of 'increasing resources rather than depleting resources' developed (ibid.).

The City of Richmond's overall policy style with respect to intercultural accommodation is evident in how it facilitated a community resolution to the 'monster homes' controversy. Recognizing the 'particularly divisive and destructive nature of the monster house conflict,' Richmond Council and its planning staff 'undertook a series of public meetings (including a special community task force) to address the issues, culminating in no fewer than seven residential by-law amendments implemented between November 1993 and June 1995' (Edgington and Hutton 2002, 20). The by-laws dealt with required setbacks, landscaping, and building envelopes. 'The City was instrumental in largely shifting the locus of the debate from a hostile interethnic arena to a "normal" community planning process, resulting in a series of compromise by-law amendments which, while not totally satisfying to either principal party, comprised a mutual accommodation of interests' (ibid., 20). In other words, the City of Richmond played an important mediating role in this controversy and brought a resource to the regime that only a municipal government could offer – the established authority of a planning process that was flexible enough to allow interethnic compromise.

In Richmond, more recently, cultural misunderstandings on the part of newcomers have triggered policy changes at the municipal level. When Chinese newcomers reacted negatively to the locating of a group home in a mainly Chinese neighbourhood, the city at first resisted taking action; eventually, though, it established the Group Homes Task Force to manage the controversy. The task force became a public-education exercise about group homes in Canada. The city spent $150,000 on this initiative, including $50,000 on translation, interpretation, and outreach to the Chinese community. In response to this controversy, Mayor Malcolm Brodie decided to renew Richmond's race relations committee by establishing RIAC. Another response to the group homes controversy was the city's launching of a media monitoring program.

Currently, the City of Richmond's role in managing intercultural relations is one of facilitator or enabler – a role adopted deliberately by the city to avoid expending too many resources. Terry Crowe, Richmond's Manager of Planning, explained that the city considered two possible roles for itself in intercultural relations: it could lead, or it could facilitate. It chose the latter (Crowe 2004, interview).

Richmond's political leaders acknowledge that the city has an important role to play in intercultural relations, especially in educating the public. However, they also point out that their city is fiscally constrained and must limit the extent to which it commits financial resources to this goal. The city's decision to pool resources to encourage positive intercultural relations reflects its receptivity to a role in multiculturalism policy development as well as its reluctance to devote extensive public (i.e., financial and staff) resources to meeting these goals. The city's decision to facilitate rather than 'lead'[28] is also shaped by a belief that if the city takes complete ownership of a policy field such as multiculturalism policy, the community will not feel the same sense of ownership. Instead of developing new initiatives, the city prefers to engage with and support community leaders who are working towards interculturalism goals. Scott Schroeder, Community Coordinator of Diversity Services with the city's Parks and Recreation Department, says that many community organizations in Richmond are taking a leadership role and that the city's approach is to support their efforts (Schroeder 2004, interview). For instance, local leaders have initiated city festivals, which the city supports. In other words, like a good manager, the City of Richmond delegates responsibilities within the community where possible and rewards community initiative.

The city's decision to play a role in intercultural bridging has been facilitated by its political culture as well. Many informants mentioned the city's tradition of community engagement. One legacy of this tradition is a community that is both proactive and able to cooperate. When faced with emerging community tensions, the city's natural inclination has been to open a dialogue between community leaders and the city. For instance, the city's political leaders decided to talk to Thomas Fung about the controversy over Chinese-language signs in Aberdeen Mall. The city could have passed a by-law[29] to regulate the signage; instead it handled the issue informally. In Balwant Sanghera's view, the city has been effective at managing intercultural relations because of this 'common sense' approach (Sanghera 2004, interview).

Informal public–private networks support Richmond's 'common sense' approach. Informal channels of communication whereby local leaders can navigate delicate ethnocultural issues serve as an important resource. Instead of legislating simple, 'once and for all' solutions to ethnic controversies, the city negotiates with leaders in the community.

The case of Richmond also illustrates the importance of 'framing' to regime maintenance and renewal. According to Schroeder, the federally developed idea of official multiculturalism lost meaning in Richmond because it became associated with tolerance rather than interethnic bridging and the embracing of diversity (Schroeder 2004, interview). Most important, the frame did not express the true ethnic-relations challenges faced by a community that had received immigrants largely from a single group. So the city renamed the committee and reframed the issue as one of 'interculturalism.' Members of RIAC have spent a great deal of time deliberating about the 'new'[30] concept – interculturalism – that underpins the regime's mandate.

As Stone (1989) explains in *Regime Politics*, 'small wins' are important to regime maintenance. In Richmond, informants mentioned several ways in which RIAC facilitates 'small wins.' For instance, in Lesley Sherlock's view, it is important to have city staff on the RIAC so that they can update committee members on the tangible (even if incremental) progress the city is making towards interculturalism goals. This 'keeps morale up' among community members (Sherlock 2004, interview). In Schroeder's view, the time that RIAC members invested in deliberating about the committee's normative underpinnings was well spent, as it facilitated 'quick wins.' He explained that though the committee cannot establish new programs or set up new administrative structures without council's approval, civil servants can put 'philosophies' such as interculturalism into practice through the city's existing programs. In other words, a consensus exists around 'broad purposes,' and that consensus then shapes the daily decisions of regime members. For instance, in Richmond, interculturalism shapes how council-approved recreation programs are implemented, with no requirement for council approval for additional money (Schroeder 2004, interview).

In sum, Richmond has developed a regime in which the city plays mainly a coordinating role. Yet despite the city's desire to limit its role to that of facilitator, community dynamics have compelled the city to take leadership on certain issues. Many city initiatives (including its first race relations committee) have been reactions either to intercultural misunderstandings or to backlash among long-standing residents regarding changes in the community. The 'monster home' issue, the controversy over English-language signage in Asian malls, and the 'group homes' debate all led to reactive policy changes in Richmond. The group homes controversy also led the city to begin monitoring ethnic media to pre-empt community conflict based on intercultural misunderstandings.

In the absence of these conflicts, policy changes to address multiculturalism-related policy goals would have been limited and incremental. In Richmond, regime maintenance is facilitated by a community consensus on the nature of the ethnic-relations challenge and by a well-articulated 'broad purpose' that responds to that consensus. The legacies of the city's past responses to community controversies – such as its decision to establish its first race relations committee – also facilitate regime maintenance.

Surrey: A Narrowly Conceived Development Agenda and the Absence of Political Mobilization

In Surrey, corporate responses have been highly limited. Policy innovation in Surrey has taken place in agencies that provide services on the ground, such as libraries and the Parks and Recreation Department. Immigration and immigrant settlement issues are a low priority on the municipal council's agenda. According to one observer, land development is the 'number one' issue; crime, keeping taxes low, homelessness, and the city's image are other items high on the agenda (Basi 2004, interview).

Surrey's focus on land development likely has the support of a large number of local residents. As Surrey councillor Judy Villeneuve pointed out, 80 per cent of Surrey residents are involved in development as either developers or as tradespeople (Villeneuve 2004, interview). Surrey's mayor, Doug McCallum, maintains that development is the number-one priority of Surrey residents. In the interview, he recounted how he was walking one day through a Surrey neighbourhood and a tradesperson working nearby almost fell off a roof while thanking him for encouraging development in the city (McCallum 2004, interview).

However, a municipality's focus on development is not necessarily incompatible with a municipality taking a leadership role in multiculturalism policy. A municipal role in the latter can be framed as part of an economic-development strategy. McCallum recognizes that immigration gives Surrey a competitive edge in attracting businesses. For instance, he mentioned that Chase Bank had recently moved its headquarters to Surrey to take advantage of its multiculturalism; specifically, Chase Bank wanted to draw from Surrey's multilingual[31] workforce. Even so, according to many political leaders in Surrey (including the mayor), the municipality need not intervene in order to benefit economically from immigration. According to McCallum, Surrey is benefiting from immigration 'naturally'; it is 'not a planned thing' (ibid.).

By drawing our attention to the importance of informal, 'governance' relationships to understanding policy outcomes, urban regime theory helps us understand why multiculturalism policy remains a low priority on Surrey's municipal agenda, despite that city's relatively large foreign-born population. As mayor, McCallum was the most powerful political leader in Surrey. His priority was to limit government, and he does not believe that municipalities should involve themselves in social planning. His desire to limit the municipality's role in social issues is shared by a majority of Surrey councillors (Villeneuve 2004, interview). Thus, Surrey's political leaders have chosen not to develop relationships with community organizations that would pressure the city to expand its mandate. Instead of fostering a relationship with the immigrant-specific agency – Surrey-Delta Immigrant Services Society (SDISS) – the city's political leaders have chosen to maintain a relationship with OPTIONs, a less radical mainstream community organization.

That said, SDISS has developed relationships with at least some street-level bureaucrats in Surrey. Ravi Basi and Melanie Houlden, two employees of Surrey's libraries, used to sit on SDISS's board. Also, street-level bureaucrats in Surrey's libraries consult with immigrant-specific organizations such as Progressive Intercultural Community Services, S.U.C.C.E.S.S., and SDISS.

There is evidence pointing to the development of what some regime theorists call 'subregime' or 'microregime' relationships. The former term refers to coalitions in specific policy arenas such as housing. Microregimes are a subcategory of subregimes: the term refers to specific functions within the policy arena (Owens 2001). Agency-specific coalitions support multiculturalism policy goals in Surrey's libraries. The business community does not participate directly in these subregimes. For instance, officials at Surrey's public libraries said that they were introducing SDISS's ESL classes to immigrants who use library services. In addition, according to a librarian, the library pools 'brainpower' and marketing resources with community organizations (Houlden 2004, interview). Community organizations also do translations and provide interpretation services for the library. Members of community organizations have translated the libraries' summer reading newsletters into Chinese and Punjabi. As Houlden put it: 'It's almost like because we know what they do, we know how to get what we need' (ibid.). In other words, Surrey's ongoing relationships with immigrant organizations are valuable and contribute to social production.

Meanwhile, Surrey's Parks and Recreation Department, which has launched many of the city's most important responses to immigrants and ethnocultural minorities, has an ongoing relationship with OPTIONs. The Parks, Recreation, and Culture Commission has recently been renamed the Parks and Community Services Committee and has been given a broader mandate to examine social issues and 'cultural inclusivity' (Cavan 2004, interview). Delegating responsibility for the city's community initiatives – such as efforts to engage the city's diverse communities – to the Parks and Recreation Department is consistent with former Mayor McCallum's opinion that encouraging a physically active city is an effective way to integrate the community.

Surrey's Parks and Recreation Department does not seem to have ongoing relationships with immigrant-specific organizations. Perhaps this has affected its capacity to implement 'cultural inclusivity' initiatives. For instance, the department considered establishing a diversity committee with which it would work directly. However, the proposal did not attract participation from either the immigrant community or the community at large (ibid.). The department simply does not have the networks through which to implement its initiatives.

This situation seems to be related in part to the department's decision to develop relationships with OPTIONs rather than SDISS. It may also be that the city's response to immigrants and ethnocultural diversity is limited by the South Asian community's diversity. Because of that diversity, civil servants in Surrey do not know who the leaders of immigrant groups are (ibid.).

In Surrey, many developers are of South Asian origin. These people do not seem to be pressuring the city to adopt a more expansive role in multiculturalism policy. A power struggle over the evolving cultural definition of Surrey is absent, and there is no community consensus that there is an ethnic-relations 'problem.' Ethnic-relations challenges have not been politicized; nor are they broached in a way that would imply that the municipality should intervene. Some informants indicated that racism is a problem in Surrey (Sanghera 2004, interview; Welsh 2004, interview) and that the South Asian community is socially isolated (Woodman 2004, interview). Yet long-standing residents do not perceive immigration as a threat to the community's cultural identity. Hardy observes: 'The power brokers [in Surrey are about] what's good for business and keeping everything on a smooth keel' (Hardy 2005, personal). In the absence of a race relations crisis, and of politicized backlash on the part of the long-standing community, multiculturalism policy goals are a low priority.

Coquitlam: The Persistence of an 'Old Guard'

Immigration is relatively new to Coquitlam. Its immigrant population 'exploded' when the Westwood Plateau, an upscale residential area, was developed (Ahn 2004, interview). Edgington and Hutton (2002) attribute Coquitlam's lack of policy responsiveness to immigration to the fact that 'because social planning was not a compulsory service under section 530 of the BC Municipal Act (now the Local Government Act, 2000), neither council members nor taxpayer groups recognize it as a priority' (2002, 16).[32] In their study of the 'multicultural readiness' of municipalities in Greater Vancouver, Edgington, Hanna, and their colleagues (2001) noted that 'in many of the smaller "outer" municipalities there was especially a feeling that multicultural problems were too complex and expensive to be borne by local government alone without further budgetary assistance from the provincial government. Because of a much smaller rate base than the larger "core" councils, there was little ability (or even willingness) to take on additional responsibilities beyond the traditional range that municipalities were already expected to provide' (Edgington, Hanna, et al. 2001, 17).

The decision not to respond to immigration by adapting city services in a *proactive* way is a political one. As Mayor Jon Kingsbury admitted, an 'old guard' governs Coquitlam with the support of 'small-c' conservative retirees (Kingsbury 2004, interview). Furthermore, in the absence of sustained community pressure, the city has not been forced to *react* either. In Coquitlam there is little pressure from community organizations on the municipality to change.

Coquitlam's libraries, where policy change is evident, are an exception to this. The impetus for policy change came from the Chinese-speaking business community, including representatives of the Taiwan Economic Development Office and the Council of the People's Republic of China. Both have donated significant amounts of Chinese-language materials to the library. Salina Leung, a member of Coquitlam's Library Board who is ethnically Chinese, brokered these donations. According to Karen Harrison, Daniel Chiu – an ethnically Chinese councillor who was defeated in the 2002 municipal election – was also well connected in the Chinese community (Harrison 2004, interview). In the absence of community engagement in local affairs, of electoral renewal, and of community pressure, the existing governance arrangement persists.

One unique theme to emerge from the research on Coquitlam is that the city lacks its own independent identity. Coquitlam is one of three municipalities in Greater Vancouver – the others are Port Coquitlam and Port Moody – that local leaders tend to refer to collectively as the 'Tri-Cities.' Also, Coquitlam itself is a 'community of communities' with four primary neighbourhoods – Maillardville (the historic French-speaking community), Westwood Plateau (where many of Coquitlam's Chinese-speaking immigrants have settled), West Coquitlam, and Northeast Coquitlam, a relatively new area. The lack of a cohesive identity in Coquitlam may be one barrier to the development of a co-ordinated policy agenda to address the city's changing social demographics (along with other policy challenges). It was difficult to assess the impact of this variable, because it is associated with the possibility of amalgamation – an extremely sensitive topic in Coquitlam.

In Greater Vancouver, local leaders' tendency to view Coquitlam as part of the Tri-Cities has affected the development of civil society. The city is not involved in social planning functions, which are provided by the Society for Community Development, which plans for Tri-Cities as well as Amora and Valcarra. When asked about community capacity in immigrant settlement in Coquitlam, Rob Innes, Coquitlam's deputy clerk, answered that the Tri-Cities share community and family services, MOSAIC, S.U.C.C.E.S.S., and the Immigrant Services Society (Innes 2004, interview). Coquitlam does not have a city-specific immigrant settlement agency. At the time of the interviews, S.U.C.C.E.S.S., a powerful Chinese settlement agency with offices in many municipalities throughout Greater Vancouver, had opened an office in Coquitlam. However, it has since lost its provincial grant (Hardy 2005, interview). Since S.U.C.C.E.S.S. is an entrepreneurial settlement agency that raises 40 per cent of its funding on its own and that is federated across Greater Vancouver, it may continue to operate in Coquitlam nonetheless.

Comparing the Local Governance of Multiculturalism in Greater Vancouver

Several factors are associated with municipal responsiveness to immigrants and ethnocultural diversity in Greater Vancouver. At the most basic level, municipal responses are shaped by the ways in which local leaders frame the immigration challenge. In Vancouver, the most 'responsive' municipality in the Greater Vancouver sample, multiculturalism policy responses are part of an overall strategy of economic development through investment and immigration from Pacific Rim countries. Multiculturalism policies were developed in the City of Vancouver within a broad public–private 'Pacific Rim Consensus.' The city began acting in multiculturalism policy in the 1970s. These efforts were strengthened dramatically in the 1980s when, under a city council led by Mayor Mike Harcourt, the city began engaging in 'paradiplomacy' (Smith 1992) with Pacific Rim countries. As part of a comprehensive

Pacific Rim economic-development strategy, new institutions developed in the civil service to support the integration of immigrants into Vancouver society. In Greater Vancouver, Vancouver is unique in that its multiculturalism policies are clearly connected to a proactive economic-development regime.

In Richmond, a municipal role in managing diversity emerged on the city's agenda as a reaction to a backlash. The Richmond case highlights the importance of 'framing' and community consensus regarding the nature of the policy 'problem' to a municipality's decision to engage in multiculturalism policy. The large-scale influx of Chinese immigrants to Richmond led to cultural misunderstandings and tensions between immigrants and the long-standing community. It became clear that there was a race relations 'problem' in Richmond. In response, Richmond Council decided to establish its first race relations committee and began speaking with Chinese developers such as Thomas Fung about the concerns of long-standing residents. In other words, in Richmond, multiculturalism policy development was not a by-product of economic-development objectives; rather, it was based in more grassroots concerns.[33] This case suggests that the municipal role in multiculturalism policy originates in the impact of immigration on community dynamics.

In Vancouver the municipal role in multiculturalism policy developed more proactively in the context of a broad growth and economic-development paradigm. However, the city's role in multiculturalism policy was also influenced by community dynamics and ethnic conflicts. Similar community dynamics and issues emerged in Vancouver and Richmond with respect to differences in housing preferences – the so-called 'monster homes' debate. The municipal responses were also similar. Conflicts were normalized through the planning process, and the two municipalities adopted compromise by-laws. The Vancouver and Richmond cases illustrate the importance of elite–mass relations – with elites managing the community's reactions to social change – as well as the importance of public decision-making processes for managing interethnic relations.

Vancouver's superior level of responsiveness to immigration and ethnocultural diversity is a result of its political leadership's decision to play a proactive role in community integration as an aspect of managing the social effects of the Pacific 'growth machine.' The city was willing to devote more public resources to community integration than were other municipalities in Greater Vancouver. Beyond the dynamics of planning-based conflicts, evidence of community pressure on the municipality to adapt services and governance structures to ethno-cultural diversity was not uncovered. Instead, Vancouver's responses must be understood as part of an implicit understanding that it is the municipality's role to engage with its diverse community and that this role complements economic growth. In Richmond, by contrast, the city took on its role in multiculturalism policy reactively. While the city is now committed to playing an ongoing role in facilitating intercultural harmony, it has decided to limit its role to 'facilitator.' Unlike Vancouver, the city is unwilling to devote significant public resources to multiculturalism policy objectives and has chosen instead to encourage intersectoral pooling in civil society.

Richmond was the most responsive of the 'somewhat responsive' municipalities in the sample. It seems that a key difference between Richmond on the one hand, and Surrey and Coquitlam on the other, is the absence of politicized race-relations conflicts. In Richmond, conflicts surfaced over the development of Asian-style malls and over housing. Given the numbers of immigrants coming into Richmond, long-standing residents had a sense that they were losing something. Many of their concerns were rooted in issues surrounding the municipality's cultural identity, such as the architectural style of new development and housing, and also the language of work and leisure. In Surrey and Coquitlam, no evidence was found of politically channelled backlash against changes to local communities as a result of immigration. Several informants mentioned that racism is a problem in Surrey. However, the terms 'racism' and 'discrimination' are too general to mobilize groups politically. In Richmond, community tensions had a specific focus (planning decisions, for instance) and became political because they were about the power to define or redefine the community's cultural basis.

The community dynamics that result from immigration are therefore related to the relative power of immigrants and of long-standing residents and to the extent to which cultural change is visible in the public sphere. Richmond's Chinese community is well-organized and has leaders in many sectors. It is also 'vocal' (Basi 2004, interview). Richmond's Chinese community has the capacity to redefine the city's public face. That community's high level of organization and its economic power together mean that it can pressure community agencies to accommodate Chinese residents. What is more, as we saw with Richmond's library services, the Chinese community has offered generous donations to the city in exchange for a willingness to adapt its services along cultural lines.

However, in Richmond, accommodation is a two-way process. As we saw with the case of Aberdeen Centre, the elite of Richmond's Chinese community are willing to accommodate the long-standing community. The city's decision to rename its race relations committee the Richmond Intercultural Advisory Committee reflects the regime's primary goal – intercultural accommodation. Moreover, the development of an intercultural regime in Richmond has been facilitated by a council that is generally receptive to the idea of playing a role in facilitating intercultural understanding. Many informants suggested that Richmond Council's ability to engage the community is deeply rooted in that city's cooperative political culture.

The case of Coquitlam illustrates the importance of the strength and resources of immigrant communities to municipal responsiveness. As in Richmond, Coquitlam's Chinese community pressured the library to adapt its services culturally, and it made donations to facilitate the process. However, owing to the lack of 'backlash' on the part of long-standing residents, the municipality has yet to feel pressure to involve itself in intercultural relations at a more corporate level, at least in a sustained way. In the absence of a clear race relations 'problem' and of proactive leaders, Coquitlam folded its Multiculturalism Committee (1999–2003) into its Livable Communities Advisory Committee.

Similarly, evidence was not found that Surrey's immigrant community applied sustained pressure on the city to adapt its services. While there is evidence that racism is a problem in Surrey, the change in the ethnic demographics of the city does not seem to have mobilized the long-standing community politically. In the absence of conflicts over development, it seems that any problems of racism in Surrey remain under the surface.

In sum, community mobilization appears to be a central factor driving municipal responsiveness to immigrants and ethnocultural minorities in suburban Greater Vancouver. Immigrant communities pressure municipal agencies to respond to their service needs; at the same time, conflict between a powerful immigrant group and the long-standing community appears to be associated with broader, corporate-level responses to ethnocultural diversity. In other words, 'somewhat responsive' municipalities vary in terms of the intensity of the problems to which they must 'react.'

Vancouver is somewhat exceptional. Its multiculturalism policy objectives seem to be connected (through an urban regime relationship) to economic-development objectives and – more generally – to the idea that diversity is Vancouver's most important strength. The city therefore does not have to be pressured to the same degree to respond to the needs and preferences of its immigrant population. In addition, past policies tend to shape future policies. Adapting city services to ethnocultural diversity in Vancouver is part of an entrenched 'solution set' (Jones and Bachelor 1993) to the challenges of immigrant integration and community engagement. That solution set has been institutionalized in the city's EEO office, the Hastings Institute, and the position of Multicultural Social Planner. Absent exceptionally strong leadership opposed to the municipality's proactive role in multiculturalism policy, Vancouver's commitment to multiculturalism will continue.

Local politics do indeed matter. It is clear that immigration has changed community dynamics by creating new cleavages in municipal societies. The next chapter compares all eight municipalities in the sample, looking for patterns across cases. Specifically, it probes for patterns in levels of municipal responsiveness, governance dynamics, and the ethnic configurations of municipal societies. It also considers whether the 'social diversity perspective' can help explain why regime relationships to manage the social change that results from immigration develop or fail to develop. Finally, the chapter explores whether creating a dialogue between the literature on urban regime theory and the social diversity perspective is a fruitful way to develop an explanation of how municipalities govern demographic change.

6 The Relationship between Urban Regimes, Types of Social Diversity, and Multiculturalism Policies

Municipalities vary significantly in their responses to the ethnocultural diversity that results from immigration. In chapters 4 and 5 we saw that local patterns of coalition building – or in some cases, the failure of local leaders to build socially productive urban coalitions that include multiculturalism policy goals – help explain these differences. Urban regime theory suggests that policy outputs are products of local coalition-building processes; that is, they are products of *who participates* and of the *resources* that local leaders bring to bear on the governance arrangement. In tightly constrained fiscal environments, cities must extend the scope of local institutions in order to build the capacity to implement local agendas effectively. *How* local leaders frame policy goals affects *which* local leaders and interests will be included in the regime. Since local leaders tend to govern in the interest of growth (Molotch and Logan 1987) and the business community possesses a disproportionate share of the resources in local communities (Stone 1989), linking multiculturalism purposes to broader city-building and development agendas is a particularly effective strategy to develop productive governance arrangements in multiculturalism policy.

As we have seen, local leaders in *responsive* municipalities developed lasting relationships through which they pooled resources to create capacity in multiculturalism policy. In these cases, multiculturalism objectives were part of the regime's central policy agenda and were tied to the city's growth objectives. In *somewhat responsive* municipalities, local leaders also developed productive governance coalitions to create the capacity to respond to demographic change. Their governance arrangements, however, were significantly weaker than the relationships in responsive municipalities. To a certain degree, the governance arrangements among somewhat responsive municipalities varied in scope and strength as well. In *unresponsive* municipalities, leaders failed to develop productive public–private coalitions to address multiculturalism policy objectives.

This chapter compares the eight municipalities by exploring the relationship between the ethnic configuration of a municipality and the local governance of multiculturalism. It investigates whether the ethnic configuration of a municipal society shapes urban regime development and, ultimately, policy decisions. It seeks answers to the following two questions: Can patterns of demographic change in municipalities help explain the likelihood that an urban regime that includes multiculturalism policy objectives will emerge? And how (if at all) do immigrant settlement patterns affect local governance dynamics in ways that are significant for multiculturalism policy development?

The urban regime literature stresses the fragmentation of resources across the public and private sectors. However, local communities are also more or less fragmented ethnically. The ethnic configuration of a municipal community influences regime development by structuring how civil society develops. Changing ethnocultural demographics have the potential to fragment community resources and complicate the collective action problem, and this has an impact on the capacity to govern. Dramatic social change also introduces new community dynamics between long-standing residents (the 'majority' community) and new immigrant minorities as well as within immigrant communities. Community dynamics within immigrant communities can introduce community cleavages, which must be managed in the interest of growth. To understand how changing ethnic configurations influence local politics and coalition building in urban Canada, we must explore the intersection of the fragmentation of resources across sectors as well as how this type of fragmentation intersects with the ethnocultural fragmentation of communities (Good 2005). Urban regime theory is the study of intersector, public–private cooperation and of 'how that cooperation is maintained when confronted with an ongoing process of social change, a continuing influx of new actors, and potential breakdowns through conflict or indifference' (Stone 1989, 9). Municipal 'policy innovations – the critical decisions made in response to social change – emerge from and reflect the character of a city's governing coalition' (ibid., 160). Ethnic configurations shape urban regime development and policy outputs in a systematic way.

The next section outlines two ethnoracial configurations in the eight cases in the sample: biracial and multiracial. It then examines the findings of previous chapters through a social-diversity lens. In particular, it explores patterns between community dynamics, urban governance arrangements, and the level of policy responsiveness on the one hand and the ethnic configuration of municipal societies on the other. It then summarizes how a municipality's ethnic configuration shapes the *likelihood* and *nature* of urban regime development. It also discusses comparative literature that contributes to the theoretical weight of a social diversity perspective.

The chapter concludes that the ethnic configurations of municipal societies are contextual variables that help shape the *political choices* of local leaders. However, other elements of the social context matter as well – for example, the pattern of resource distribution in the municipality. In addition, the chapter argues that the social diversity interpretation must take into account the systemic power of the business community in municipalities. One needs to understand how ethnic configurations shape power relationships. In this way, urban regime analysis sheds light on how and why ethnic configurations exert their effects on municipal governance. Ultimately, though the municipality's ethnic configuration is important, it is simply one structure within which local leaders make their governing decisions – including the decision to form an urban regime with multiculturalism purposes.

Towards a Canadian Social Diversity Interpretation of Urban Politics in Canada's Immigrant-Magnet Cities

This chapter builds on Rodney Hero's 'social diversity interpretation,' which he developed in *Faces of Inequality* (1998). Hero argues that the ethnic configurations of American states influence their political processes, political institutions, and public policies, all of which he explores through extensive, systematic empirical analysis. For instance, he examines voter turnout, strength of party organization, level of democratization, issue polarization in public opinion, interest-group strength, formal governmental institutions, and public-policy outcomes in several policy areas (1998, 22). As we saw in chapter 2, Hero develops a threefold typology of ethnic configurations – *homogeneous, bifurcated,* and *heterogeneous* – and hypothesizes that they affect the political dynamics of states. Specifically, he finds a 'consensual pluralism' in homogeneous states, a 'competitive pluralism' in heterogeneous states, and a 'hierarchical or limited' pluralism in bifurcated states.

This chapter builds on Hero's work in several ways. It explores the fundamental hypothesis of the social diversity interpretation – that different ethnic configurations result in different types of political pluralism. Hero considers this idea a 'general expectation' of his social diversity interpretation (ibid., 15). This chapter also examines the relationship between ethnic configurations of political units and types of political pluralism, policies, and institutions – in this case, informal governance institutions or 'urban regimes.'

This analysis diverges from Hero's work in its empirical and theoretical objectives, in its typology of ethnic configurations, and in its methodology. Hero's main objective was to develop a better explanation of variations in state politics, policy making, and institutions than those offered by existing theories of American state politics. His interpretation was developed both as a comprehensive alternative and as a complement to existing theories of state politics. One of his central contributions is his use of both aggregated and disaggregated measurements of policy outcomes. He shows that aggregate measures of policy outcomes often hide the fact that policies vary in ways that affect the relative equality of racial and ethnic groups. A homogeneous setting produces the best overall policy outcomes, but the worst policy outcomes for racial minorities; bifurcated states do poorly on aggregate measures of policy responsiveness, but better on the issue of the relative equality of racial minorities; and heterogeneous states tend to be located in between these two categories (ibid., 22; 2003, 402). He also finds that official-English movements in the United States are more common in homogeneous and bifurcated states (1998, 108). Furthermore, social context can shape White attitudes towards racial minorities in ways that support the social diversity interpretation (ibid., 122).

Can a Canadian-made social diversity perspective offer a useful approach to studying the politics of multiculturalism in high-immigration cities and how they affect social production? Though the number of cases discussed here is statistically insignificant, a small comparative-research design is an appropriate way to begin exploring the value of a social diversity perspective in Canada. Owing to the quantitative nature of the data he presents, Hero can only establish correlations between ethnic configurations and hypothetical forms of political pluralism[1] on the one hand and dependent variables on the other. While his evidence is compelling, he does not explain precisely how ethnic configurations exert their causal effects. In other words, he cannot provide a textured account of the political dynamics of his cases. We do not have a sense of what one would expect 'on the ground' from his theory.

A qualitative study such as this one has the benefit of more precisely describing how ethnic configurations affect political dynamics (what Hero calls the nature of political pluralism). Furthermore, a smaller study directs attention to other contextual variables that may affect how a social diversity interpretation applies to both the local scale and the context of another country. The downside, of course, is that the findings are less generalizable. Yet in the interest of cross-national theory building, this design is a reasonable way to begin examining the effects of immigration on cities by looking at how ethnic configurations shape the politics of multiculturalism. The findings discussed here might then be tested cross-nationally and extended across Canada.

Moreover, though Hero devotes one chapter to local governments, his primary focus is on state politics. The focus here is on the responsiveness of *municipalities* to ethnocultural minorities (most of whom are immigrants). In particular, whereas the theoretical ideas discussed here might have more general implications, the primary goal of this book is to contribute to our understanding of municipal variations in multiculturalism policy development.

Local governments are qualitatively different from central governments in both the United States and Canada. City politics is a limited politics (Peterson 1981). The most fundamental question is how local political units develop the capacity to govern (Stone 1989). Local leaders develop governance arrangements to develop and implement local agendas. We should see this exercise as an examination of the findings – the patterns of policy outputs and processes of regime building – through a social diversity 'lens.'

At the end of *Faces of Inequality*, Hero offers a few hypotheses and areas for future inquiry. He raises the issue of intragroup and intergroup differences in his threefold categorization of ethnoracial diversity – White, White ethnic, and minority – stating that 'this complexity, the circumstances under which group competition is more or less likely, and a host of related considerations should be addressed as the social diversity interpretation is extended' (1998, 151). He also mentions that it might be not only the proportion of the group that matters, but also the absolute numbers, because this would affect a group's ability to achieve a critical mass to mobilize politically (ibid., 152). Moreover, large numbers can 'make the group more visible and more likely to be threatening and/or singled out' as well as give the group in question a 'greater ability to act in defense of group concerns' (ibid.). Furthermore, he mentions 'population concentrations,' hypothesizing that when groups are more concentrated within a state, they may be more threatening (ibid.). In addition, 'the recent arrival of a group in a state, the rate of change, and the presence in large numbers are important' (Hero 1998). The qualitative, small-sample, comparative approach is used here to explore these factors. These caveats are important in a Canadian social-diversity interpretation, and these hypotheses inform the categories of ethnic configuration.

Hero's three categories of ethnic configurations in the United States are *homogeneous*, *heterogeneous*, and *bifurcated*. To a certain extent, Hero's (1998) ethnic configurations are particular to the United States. Most important, in his typology of ethnic configurations he does not separate *immigrants* from *African-Americans*. Rather, states and localities with high numbers of ethnoracial minorities (defined as African-American, Latino, and Asian) are all considered bifurcated in their ethnic configurations (Hero 1998, 11). The cases in this sample all have very high numbers of what Hero calls 'minorities' and what Canadian scholars call 'visible minorities,' a defining feature of Hero's 'bifurcated category.' Two broad categories emerge from the data on the distribution of visible-minority populations in the eight municipal cases: *biracial* and *multiracial*.[2] The former refers to municipalities in which there is a high concentration of a single visible-minority group. More precisely, in biracial municipalities, a single visible-minority group constitutes more than 50 per cent of the total visible-minority population, or the second-largest visible-minority group is less than 50 per cent of the dominant visible minority group. These municipalities are 'biracial' in the sense that there are two main 'racial' groups in the population: a large 'White' population and a large number of residents from a single visible-minority group. The second category refers to municipalities in which a multitude of visible-minority groups have settled. These categories represent two subtypes of bifurcation in relation to Hero's (1998) conceptualization.[3]

Contextual differences between the cases and American states require that one proceed both deductively and inductively in the development of any typology of ethnic configurations. These differences are another reason to begin with qualitative research. We must develop the typology by comparing theoretical hypotheses with qualitative data.

Tables 6.1, 6.2, and 6.3 represent the ethnoracial configurations of the municipal populations in the eight cases. The tables are organized into their ethnic configurations. The biracial municipalities are in two groups (by city-region), given the space limitations in a single table. The bulk of the interviews were conducted in 2004, which was in be-

Table 6.1
Multiracial municipalities

City	Toronto		Mississauga		Brampton
Census year	2001	2006	2001	2006	2001
Total pop.	2,456,805	2,476,656	610,815	665,655	324,390
Foreign-born pop. (%)	49.4	50.0	46.8	51.6	40
Visible min. pop. (%)	42.8	46.9	40.3	49.0	40.2
Visible min. pop.	1,051,125 (100)	1,162,630 (100)	246,330 (100)	326,425 (100)	130,275 (100)
Chinese	259,710 (24.7)	283,075 (24.3)	35,955 (14.6)	46,120 (14.1)	5,445 (4.2)
South Asian	253,920 (24.2)	298,370 (25.7)	91,150 (37.0)	134,750 (41.3)	63,205 (48.5)
Black	204,075 (19.4)	208,555 (17.9)	37,850 (15.4)	41,365 (12.7)	32,070 (24.6)
Filipino	86,460 (8.2)	102,555 (8.8)	24,615 (10.0)	30,705 (9.4)	6,965 (5.3)
Latin American	54,350 (5.2)	64,855 (5.6)	9,265 (3.8)	12,410 (3.8)	5,225 (4.0)
Southeast Asian	33,870 (3.2)	37,495 (3.2)	10,015 (4.1)	14,160 (4.3)	3,005 (2.3)
Arab	22,355 (2.1)	22,485 (1.9)	11,415 (4.6)	16,785 (5.1)	1,850 (1.4)
West Asian	37,205 (3.5)	42,755 (3.7)	4,200 (1.7)	6,015 (1.8)	1,085 (0.8)
Korean	29,755 (2.8)	34,220 (2.9)	5,175 (2.1)	6,865 (2.1)	615 (0.5)
Japanese	11,595 (1.1)	11,965 (1.0)	1,980 (0.8)	2,425 (0.7)	535 (0.4)
Other VM	37,987 (3.6)	25,195 (2.2)	9,950 (4.0)	5,715 (1.8)	8,180 (6.3)
Multiple VM	19,855 (1.9)	31,000 (2.7)	4,755 (1.9)	9,100 (2.8)	2,110 (1.6)

Source: 2001 and 2006 census data (Statistics Canada 2002 and 2007b).

Table 6.2
Biracial municipalities (Greater Vancouver)

City	Coquitlam		Richmond		Surrey		Vancouver	
Census year	2001	2006	2001	2006	2001	2006	2001	2006
Total pop.	111,425	113,560	163,395	173,565	345,780	392,450	539,630	571,600
F-B (%)	37.1	39.4	54	57.4	33.2	38.3	45.9	45.6
VM pop. (%)	34.3	38.6	59	65	37	46.1	49	51.0
VM pop.*	38,190 (100)	43,875	96,385 (100)	112,955 (100)	127,015 (100)	181,005 (100)	264,495 (100)	291,740 (100)
Chinese	19,940 (52.2)	19,580 (44.6)	64,270 (66.7)	75,725 (67.0)	16,480 (13.0)	20,210 (11.2)	161,110 (60.9)	168,215 (57.7)
South Asian	3,280 (8.6)	4,185 (9.5)	12,120 (12.6)	13,860 (12.3)	75,680 (59.6)	107,810 (59.6)	30,655 (11.6)	32,515 (11.1)
Black	1,130 (3.0)	1,005 (2.3)	1,470 (1.5)	1,390 (0.8)	3,810 (3.0)	5,015 (2.8)	4,780 (1.8)	5,290 (1.8)
Filipino	2,570 (6.7)	3,050 (7.0)	7,190 (7.5)	9,555 (8.5)	10,235 (8.1)	16,555 (9.1)	22,085 (8.3)	28,605 (9.8)
Latin American	1,110 (2.9)	1,530 (3.5)	1,165 (1.2)	1,265 (1.1)	3,315 (2.6)	3,785 (2.1)	6,490 (4.0)	8,225 (2.8)
Southeast Asian	1,140 (3.0)	1,060 (2.4)	1,255 (1.3)	1,480 (1.3)	6,205 (4.9)	9,240 (5.1)	14,670 (5.5)	14,850 (5.0)
Arab	385 (1.0)	635 (1.4)	875 (0.9)	960 (8.5)	1,115 (0.9)	1,805 (1.0)	1,465 (0.6)	1,875 (0.6)
West Asian	2,580 (6.8)	4,250 (9.7)	1,155 (1.2)	1,155 (1.0)	1,185 (0.9)	1,790 (1.0)	3,160 (1.2)	5,355 (1.8)
Korean	4,240 (11.1)	5,990 (13.7)	900 (0.9)	1,290 (1.1)	5,195 (4.1)	7,665 (4.2)	6,130 (2.3)	8,780 (3.0)
Japanese	850 (2.2)	1,140 (2.6)	3,615 (3.8)	3,230 (2.9)	1,925 (1.5)	2,090 (1.2)	8,280 (3.1)	9,730 (3.3)
Other VM	125 (0.3)	80 (0.2)	335 (0.3)	295 (0.3)	555 (0.4)	655 (0.4)	1,115 (0.4)	990 (0.3)
Multiple VM	845 (2.2)	1,375 (3.1)	2,045 (2.1)	2,745 (2.4)	1,325 (1)	4,395 (2.4)	4,550 (1.7)	7,320 (2.5)

Source: 2001 and 2006 census data (Statistics Canada 2002 and 2007b).

Table 6.3
Biracial municipalities (Greater Toronto Area)

City	Markham		Brampton
Census year	2001	2006	2006
Total pop.	207,940	261,573	431,575
Foreign-born pop. (%)	52.9	56.5	47.8
Visible min. pop. (%)	55.5	65.4	57.0
Visible min. pop.*	111,485 (100)	170,535 (100)	246,150 (100)
Chinese	62,355 (54.0)	89,300 (52.4)	7,805 (3.2)
South Asian	26,360 (22.8)	44,995 (26.4)	136,750 (55.6)
Black	7,860 (6.8)	8,005 (4.7)	53,340 (21.7)
Filipino	5,265 (4.6)	7,370 (4.3)	11,980 (4.9)
Latin American	1,055 (0.9)	1,385 (0.8)	8,545 (3.8)
Southeast Asian	955 (0.8)	1,970 (1.2)	6,130 (2.5)
Arab	1,660 (1.4)	2,540 (1.5)	2,600 (1.1)
West Asian	2,305 (2.0)	4,975 (2.9)	2,875 (1.2)
Korean	2,265 (2.0)	3,225 (1.9)	580 (0.2)
Japanese	670 (0.6)	850 (0.5)	545 (0.2)
Other VM	2,725 (2.4)	1,895 (1.1)	8,900 (3.6)
Multiple VM	2,005 (1.7)	4,025 (2.4)	6,095 (1.4)

Source: 2001 and 2006 census data (Statistics Canada 2002 and 2007b).

tween the two census years. The 2006 census data had not been collected at the time of the interviews, and the data on visible-minority
populations in cities were not released until 2008. Nevertheless, these
data have been included to indicate the direction of change in the cases
and so that a few initial comments can be offered regarding what one
might expect from our cases. Except for one municipal community –
Brampton – the ethnic configurations of all of the cases remained stable
through the 2001 and 2006 censuses. Brampton shifted from a multiracial to a biracial municipality in between the two censuses. Because
the interview and other data were collected before 2006, Brampton is
treated as a 'multiracial' community here.

How might the ethnic configuration of a municipal society influence
policy development, institutional ('regime') development, and community dynamics? A number of hypotheses can be derived from the social
diversity interpretation and the American urban politics literature from
the caveats that Hero identifies.

First, one might expect the ethnic configuration of a municipality to
affect the nature of *collective action problems* in the community. For in-

stance, where there is a large number of a single ethnoracial-minority group, that group might more easily develop an array of ethnospecific community institutions and social ties to overcome collective action · problems. To the extent that numbers and spatial concentration affect the ability of ethnoracial minorities to develop social capital and ultimately 'civic capacity' (Stone et al. 2001, 4–5) through community institutions, the dominant immigrant community in a biracial municipality might have an easier time mobilizing for political action. This could influence the immigrant community's ability to pressure a municipality to respond to its concerns or to elect members of its community to local councils. Furthermore, 'raw numbers,' not just the immigrant group's proportion of the population, might matter as well.

Second, the ethnic configuration of a municipality might influence whether and how urban regimes emerge at the local level. Thus we should be aware of how the ethnic configuration of the municipality affects the distribution of resources in civil society as well as patterns of community organization. Since the business community is a central partner in urban coalitions, we should pay particular attention to how ethnic configurations affect the organization of the business community in a local community and how the business community perceives immigration.

Third, according to the social diversity interpretation, one would expect to observe changes in local community dynamics – and in *types of political pluralism* – as ethnic configurations shift. Canada's immigrant-magnet cities have been especially dynamic places. This gives the researcher the benefit of observing the effects of changes in the ethnic configuration of local communities through time. According to Hero's social diversity interpretation, differing forms of political pluralism constitute a 'causal mechanism' that explains variations in policy outcomes and institutions. We see this 'causal mechanism' in action as ethnic configurations change in Canada's immigrant-magnet municipalities.

Fourth, since *multiculturalism policies* are designed to address barriers to ethnoracial equity in access to public, social, and economic institutions, one might expect a relationship between local leaders' decisions to adopt such policies and the ethnic configuration of a municipal society. Multiculturalism policies assume that if one were to disaggregate policy outcomes and to assess the extent to which ethnoracial minorities benefit from public policies, then the level of benefit would vary. Multicultural policies are therefore meant to address the very disparities that Hero (1998, 2007) documents in his work. Thus, if the ethnic configuration matters to the relative equality that ethnoracial minorities experience in policy outcomes, one might expect to find patterns in the relationship between the ethnic configuration of local communities in Canada and their decisions to adopt multiculturalism policies. However, according to Hero (1998), though bifurcated contexts resulted in overall better outcomes for ethnoracial minorities, they were also associated with negative White attitudes towards ethnoracial minorities. Furthermore, Hero found lower levels of White support for multiculturalism initiatives in these political contexts and a greater likelihood that states and counties in these locales would adopt reactionary official-English measures. In other words, if Hero is right, we might expect a backlash against immigration in all of the cases in the sample, even if general policy outcomes in areas such as graduation rates and incarceration rates are better for minorities in these places.

Looking at the Findings through a 'Social Diversity Lens'

The eight municipalities in the sample vary in many ways. By looking at the findings through a 'social diversity lens,' we will discover that these forms of variation are related. In chapter 3 we found that the municipalities varied in the following ways:

1 In the extent to which their multicultural policies are *comprehensive* – that is, in the range of such policies and in the extent to which they are institutionalized in the municipal civil service.
2 In their policy styles – that is, whether such policies are *proactive, reactive,* or *inactive* in the multiculturalism policy field (Wallace and Frisken 2000).

These two elements are related insofar as the institutionalization of comprehensive support for adapting municipal services and governance structures fosters a proactive policy style, and insofar as the failure to do so is associated with reactive or inactive policy making.

Furthermore, in chapters 4 and 5 we discovered that municipalities varied in the following ways:

1 In how their *civil societies* have developed (the organizations and patterns of resources in local communities).
2 In the extent to which they have developed governance relationships or *urban regimes* to build the capacity to manage immigration

and ethnoracial change. In other words, they vary in terms of who participates in governance, the resources that are pooled in the local community, and the relationships among local leaders.

3 In the *types of political pluralism* – or political cultures – that have emerged as a response to changing ethnocultural demographics, as well as in the *nature of political debates* over multiculturalism.

The first two forms of variation constitute a measure of municipal responsiveness to immigrants and ethnoracial minorities. This measurement also takes into account the extent to which immigrant settlement leaders consider each municipality's approach to be responsive to the concerns of its communities.

To what extent do local communities' ethnic configurations explain variations in municipalities' multiculturalism policy-making processes and in how Canada's immigrant-magnet municipalities have responded to large-scale immigration? Do municipalities with 'biracial' and 'multiracial' configurations respond to immigration in similar enough ways to constitute a 'bundle'? And, if so, how does the ethnic configuration of a local community matter? The next section explores the commonalities among biracial and multiracial municipalities as well as the differences between the two in order to assess the value of a social diversity interpretation of the local politics and governance of multiculturalism.

Biracial Municipalities

MUNICIPAL RESPONSIVENESS

All of the biracial municipalities in the sample are either responsive or somewhat responsive to ethnocultural minorities. In other words, they are all active in the making of multiculturalism policy. The City of Vancouver has developed a comprehensive range of multiculturalism policies and has institutionalized support for its multiculturalism policy efforts in the civil service. Support for its many multiculturalism initiatives is institutionalized in several ways, including through the EEO Office, the Social Planning Department (which employs a Multicultural Social Planner), and the Hastings Institute. Furthermore, its community grants address both the immediate settlement needs of immigrants and the development of community capacity in the longer term. These initiatives reflect the city's *comprehensive* approach and support its *proactive* policy style in multiculturalism policy.

The four suburban biracial municipalities – the Town of Markham and the cities of Richmond, Surrey, and Coquitlam – have all taken a more limited, ad hoc approach to multiculturalism policy development. For the most part, they have developed multiculturalism policies reactively, in response to 'race relations' crises, intercultural misunderstandings, and social isolation.

In Richmond and Markham, race relations advisory committees play a central role in managing responses to social change. These two municipalities have also begun to translate some city information into Chinese; and they are developing communications strategies to respond to their diverse communities.

In Surrey, departments and agencies that deliver services on the ground have initiated the most important initiatives in diversity policy. In 1996, Surrey's Parks, Recreation and Culture Department launched its Task Force on Intercultural Inclusivity: Reaching Out in Surrey, in order to identify and address the barriers to equal access that minorities confronted in recreation services. And in 2000, Surrey developed a marketing plan to target ethnocultural minorities. Similarly, the city's libraries have adapted their services and play a part in community engagement.

Furthermore, Surrey has an interdepartmental staff committee (though it was difficult to find information about its activities) and appears to be making some efforts to address employment equity at the corporate level. However, a broad corporate commitment to address multiculturalism concerns proactively is lacking. Most informants noted that racism is a problem in Surrey, which indicates that its policies have also been developed 'reactively' in the sense that they are responses to a perceived 'race relations' problem in the community – in particular, to a profound social isolation of the city's South Asian community.

With the help of its Chinese community, Coquitlam's library has adapted its collections in response to immigrants and provides tours of the library to ESL organizations. Coquitlam also has a history of corporate multiculturalism advisory committees (1999–2003), though at the time of the interviews the multiculturalism 'function' was part of the Liveable Communities Advisory Committee.

The four suburban biracial municipalities have been 'somewhat responsive' to immigrants and ethnocultural minorities in their communities. Their policy responses are limited and ad hoc – that is, they respond to the ethnic relations challenge of the day.

COMMUNITY DYNAMICS AND TYPES OF POLITICAL PLURALISM

In several of the biracial municipalities, similar changes in community dynamics are apparent. Vancouver, Richmond, and Markham experienced a communitywide politicized backlash against the visible changes brought about by immigration – changes such as 'monster homes,' tree cutting, the rising costs of housing, and English-language signage in Asian malls.

Richmond and Markham's reactive policy styles and the ways in which immigration changes the nature of political pluralism in these locales are most evident in their histories of race relations advisory committees and task forces, which are these municipalities' primary responses to diversity. In 1995, Richmond's race relations committee redirected its multiculturalism policy efforts from organizational change to building bridges between the two segments of its bifurcated community in response to a backlash on the part of long-standing residents. The same year, the controversy sparked by Carole Bell's comments about the concentration of Chinese immigrants erupted in Markham.

Surrey's community dynamics have changed in response to immigration. Community leaders in Greater Vancouver note the prevalence of racism in Surrey and in Greater Vancouver more generally. Nevertheless, the new dynamic between the long-standing residents, who are largely 'White,' and the large South Asian immigrant community describes only part of the new community dynamics. Many informants described a highly diverse and even divided South Asian immigrant community. According to community leaders, religious cleavages seem to be a central source of these divisions – divisions that include intragroup violence. Owing to intragroup divisions, the South Asian community seems to lack sufficient social capital to organize to exert pressure on the municipality. Furthermore, Surrey's South Asian community is socially isolated.

Coquitlam's political dynamics do not seem to have been affected in the same way as happened in the other biracial municipalities. To date, the transition to a highly diverse municipality seems to have been relatively smooth. Evidence of a community-wide backlash against immigration in Coquitlam was not found, though the mayor at the time of the interviews attributed the defeat of a Chinese municipal politician to the fact that White voters opposed him (Kingsbury 2004, interview). Because many members of the Chinese immigrant community moved into a new development, they did not challenge the planning norms of established neighbourhoods. Furthermore, Coquitlam has no Asian malls, developments that have tended to channel underlying community tensions. Instead, there are Asian markets within mainstream malls. As in Surrey, Coquitlam's foreign-born and visible-minority communities are smaller both as a proportion of the overall population and in numerical terms. As (and if) Coquitlam's Chinese community grows, we may yet see a reaction from long-standing residents, especially if developers build malls that long-standing residents perceive as catering to Asians exclusively. Coquitlam may yet experience community debates similar to those that developed in Richmond and Markham in the 1990s. Changes in the built environment that run counter to the established cultural norms of a community appear to increase cultural insecurities and to politicize tensions.

INFORMAL URBAN GOVERNANCE RELATIONSHIPS AND
MULTICULTURALISM GOALS

In all the biracial municipalities, new governance arrangements have emerged to create a joint public–private capacity to accommodate and manage changes in ethnocultural demographics.

In Vancouver, the governance arrangements that have emerged to manage immigration and multiculturalism policy are stronger than those in the suburban biracial municipalities. First, the city has many more settlement and multiculturalism resources. Second, Vancouver's innovations in multiculturalism policy are linked to a proactive economic-development agenda that focuses on the city's ties with Pacific Rim countries (Hutton 1998, 97). Vancouver's powerful business community participates in developing the capacity to manage social change, because that change supports its economic growth objectives. Kris Olds observes that in Vancouver, the Pacific Rim–specific institutions (such as the Asia-Pacific Foundation, the International Finance Centre Vancouver, and the Hong Kong Business Association) and the mainstream institutions (such as the Greater Vancouver Real Estate Board and the Vancouver Board of Trade) are interlinked and 'command considerable public and private resources that are used to *structure the nature of policies and processes* which influence Vancouver's future' (Olds 2001, 92; emphasis added). The city's institutionalized commitment to supporting multiculturalism, coupled with a strong, proactive group of private-sector leaders, has contributed to its 'power to' manage ethnocultural relations.

In Markham and Richmond, lasting public–private governance relationships have developed around the goal of fostering positive relations between the largely Chinese immigrant community and the long-standing (and largely White) community. These informal institutions developed out of race relations crises and intercultural misunderstandings – that is, out of changing forms of political pluralism. In

Markham and Richmond, governance relationships are anchored in advisory committees but are also supported by strong informal channels of communication, as well as by resource pooling between the city and leaders in civil society. As in Vancouver, the city and the business community work together in managing race relations.

In Richmond and Markham, the emergence of governance arrangements to manage social change has been facilitated by the development of strong community-based institutions representing the local Chinese community. The strength of that community in Richmond (and in other municipalities in Greater Vancouver) is evident in the strength of S.U.C.C.E.S.S. Similarly, in Markham, the Federation of Chinese Canadians commands extensive resources. The leader of that organization (Dr Ken Ng) was one of the co-chairs of the ad hoc committee and its successor, the Coalition of Concerned Canadians, which organized in response to Carole Bell's controversial remarks.

Furthermore, in Richmond and Markham the business community supports a municipal role in managing race relations. In both places, many prominent developers and other business owners are members of the largely Chinese immigrant community. Work remains to be done in integrating various sectors of the local bifurcated community (including the business community) – recall the president and CEO of the Markham Board of Trade's comment that it is 'very hard to cross-pollinate' with the Chinese community in Markham and that there are times when 'one might get the feeling that Chinese business is not interested in serving the clientele from the existing community' (Bray 2005, interview). However, it is clear that the business communities in these locales recognize that poor ethnocultural relations are simply bad for business. And in both places, a great deal of the new business activity and development has been spurred by immigration (on the demand *and* supply sides).

In Surrey, public–private relationships have emerged at the departmental level. However, these relationships are more limited than those in Richmond and Markham, as well as more tenuous. Cleavages within Surrey's largely South Asian immigrant community make it hard for civil servants and 'street-level' bureaucrats (Lipsky 1976) to identify the community's leaders. The lack of cohesion among Surrey's large South Asian immigrant population seems to explain why stronger governance arrangements have not emerged. In addition, because of these divisions, the community has not been able to translate its numbers into collective action to pressure the city to respond more comprehensively to its concerns. Furthermore, whereas backlash against immigration is clearly a problem – a community leader commented that some long-standing residents 'proudly resent multiculturalism' – in the absence of intragroup solidarity, the South Asian community has been unable to fight its racialization in the community.

Though many developers and other business people in Surrey are of South Asian origin, they do not seem to be pressuring the municipality to adapt its services and governance structures to Surrey's new demographics. As one community leader in Greater Vancouver observed, developers in Surrey 'interact with [the city] on an individual basis' rather than as a cultural community (Sanghera 2004, interview).

Governance arrangements were limited in Coquitlam as well. However, this was not owing to divisions within the immigrant community. Rather, civil society remains underdeveloped, and the city is largely a bedroom community. Nevertheless, the strength of the Chinese community elsewhere in the Greater Vancouver area has spilled over into Coquitlam to a certain extent. S.U.C.C.E.S.S. has opened a branch there. A representative of S.U.C.C.E.S.S. had a seat on Coquitlam's Multiculturalism Advisory Committee (1999–2003). Furthermore, the willingness of the Taiwanese and other Chinese communities to donate books to the library facilitated the city's efforts to adapt library services.

The 'social diversity interpretation' leads one to expect a correlation between the ethnic configuration of a municipality and the way in which institutional goals are oriented (Hero 1998, 20). Like multiculturalism policies in other locales and at other levels of government, the goal of biracial municipalities' multiculturalism initiatives is integration. However, given the concentration of a single immigrant community in the city, fears of ethnic segregation and a perceived unwillingness among the immigrant community to integrate have emerged. Thus, biracial municipalities' initiatives address these goals. Multiculturalism policies must respond to majority concerns as well. For instance, Richmond's multiculturalism policy mandate is just as much a response to the concerns of long-standing residents as it is to the concerns of immigrants and ethnocultural minorities. For instance, the issue of non-English signage is one of its key communications issues (RIAC 2004, 2). Markham's Task Force on Race Relations identified similar community goals following the race relations crisis that was triggered by Carole Bell's comments in 1995 (Mayor's Advisory Committee 1996). Members of Richmond Intercultural Advisory Committee spent time debating the philosophy that should guide ethnic relations in Richmond, opting to reject *multiculturalism*, a term that in their view had become synonymous with ethnic segregation, in favour of *interculturalism* to reflect the need for bridges between communities and, most important, integration (Schroeder 2004, interview). Similarly, the report of Surrey's Parks and Recreation Department uses the word 'interculturalism' in its title. In Coquitlam the city's main concern is to create a bridge between its newcomer community and the municipality to encourage access and equity with respect to municipal services. In all cases, governance arrangements help broker intercultural groups and stress integration into a common local community. Influenced by neo-liberalism, multiculturalism policy discourse has shifted to the private sector concept of 'managing diversity' (Abu-Laban and Gabriel 2002). In biracial contexts, a great deal of what municipalities do involves 'managing' social conflict and cultural insecurities.

Multiracial Municipalities

MUNICIPAL RESPONSIVENESS

Multiracial municipalities are at one end or the other of the 'responsiveness' spectrum. The City of Toronto has been responsive to immigrants and ethnocultural minorities, whereas the cities of Mississauga and Brampton have both been unresponsive.

The City of Toronto has developed a comprehensive range of multiculturalism policies and institutionalized supports for those policies at the apex of power in the municipal civil service – the City Manager's Office. In Toronto, the Diversity Management and Community Engagement Unit (DMU) in the City Manager's Office supports and monitors the implementation of the city's multitude of formal (written) multiculturalism policies; the DMU is also a flexible unit that launches action when unanticipated needs arise.

In sharp contrast, the primary responses to social change in the suburban multiracial municipalities of Mississauga and Brampton are community festivals and annual 'multicultural' (Mississauga) and 'multifaith' (Brampton) community breakfasts with the local mayor. Responses in these suburban municipalities are mainly symbolic.

COMMUNITY DYNAMICS AND TYPES OF POLITICAL PLURALISM

It seems that in Mississauga and Brampton, neither immigration nor multiculturalism has altered community dynamics in an obvious way. In general, the community and local officials seem indifferent to the dramatic changes that have occurred in their populations. There has been no general backlash against immigration. Hazel McCallion, the mayor of Mississauga, has observed that Mississauga simply does not have the 'racial confrontation' that exists in Markham (McCallion 2004, interview).

One can observe some competition in the immigrant settlement sector, owing largely to the scarcity of settlement funding (Seepersaud 2004, interview). A *Toronto Star* article described a 'turf war' between Brampton's two most prominent ethnocultural organizations over which organization will do what in the settlement field (White 1992b). However, this competition for resources does not reflect a more general debate about the impact of immigration and multiculturalism on the community.

Also, in Mississauga and Brampton as in Surrey, there seem to be significant religion-based cleavages within the South Asian communities. McCallion mentioned a conflict between two Sikh factions in Mississauga's South Asian community when illustrating her approach to race relations (McCallion 2004, interview). A community leader suggested that if an Indian candidate were to run in a municipal election, Pakistanis would mobilize against that person (Seepersaud 2003, interview). Local municipal officials in Brampton cited the tendency of the South Asian community to run many candidates in each ward in municipal elections as a reason for the community's lack of electoral success (Moore 2003, interview). Another community leader remarked on the number of newspapers in Brampton that serve the Sikh community (Jeffrey 2004, interview). Unfortunately, the statistical category 'South Asian' is a too vague to allow the tracking of changes in the ethnoracial composition of Canada. Municipalities with large concentrations of 'South Asians' may not have cohesive immigrant communities.

In Brampton, former mayor Peter Robertson (1988–2000) was unable to sustain community interest in the Brampton Race Relations Action Committee because of the city's diversity. There was more interest in the committee within Brampton's Hindu, Sikh, and Black communities than there was within the French, German, Croatian, Greek, and other communities (Biggs, in White 1992a). Note that the Hindu and Sikh communities – two religions that are common in South Asia (though they constitute a single group in Statistics Canada's South Asian category) – are mentioned separately. Brampton's diversity was a barrier to developing a local agenda for multiculturalism policy. In addition, unlike the biracial municipalities, Brampton's 'White' community did not seem to see the value in a multiculturalism policy agenda.

Thus, at the time of the interviews, pluralism in Mississauga and

Brampton appeared to be competitive rather than cooperative, as well as highly limited.

In contrast, Toronto is characterized by a dynamic form of pluralism. Its political pluralism is conducive to both competition and cooperation, as evidenced in the strong governance arrangements that have developed there as well as in the city's broad-based urban autonomy coalition. The political strategies of local leaders in Toronto are more radical than those of leaders in other municipalities in the sample. For instance, unlike organizations with ethnocultural equity mandates in other locales, which prefer to influence the political process through informal communication channels and quiet negotiation, in Toronto these organizations meet both 'in the boardroom [and] on the street' (Douglas 2003, interview). As a community leader in Greater Vancouver noted, the Ontario Council of Agencies Serving Immigrants (OCASI), the umbrella organization for settlement organizations in Ontario, stood up to the province during the conservative era and lost a significant portion of its funding (Welsh 2004, interview). Toronto city councillor Shelley Carroll described the more general tendency of organizations – even small-c conservative organizations like the Toronto Board of Trade – to engage in such strategies, especially in their efforts to secure a 'New Deal' for the city from upper levels of government. She gave the impression that there is a great deal of cooperation and solidarity among a multisectoral group of local leaders and organizations in Toronto (Carroll 2004, interview). Toronto's diversity does not appear to be a barrier to cooperation.

In addition, though there are surely cleavages within immigrant communities in Toronto, ethnic conflicts have not become citywide issues. Furthermore, in Toronto there is strong evidence of ethnospecific social capital. Strong organizations represent the city's major visible-minority and immigrant communities. There are so many such organizations that they are impossible to list. Furthermore, the leaders of these organizations know one another and cooperate to advocate collectively on behalf of immigrants.

INFORMAL URBAN GOVERNANCE RELATIONSHIPS AND MUNICIPAL
INSTITUTIONAL PURPOSES

Multiracial municipalities diverge in yet another respect. Urban governance arrangements to respond to multiculturalism did not emerge in Mississauga and Brampton, whereas in Toronto, local leaders built strong and inclusive governance arrangements – an urban regime – to create the capacity to respond.

Toronto has strong immigrant settlement organizations and other multiculturalism-related community organizations. Furthermore, its business community views the successful settlement of immigrants as central to the city's global economic competitiveness. As in Vancouver, Toronto's multiculturalism policies are tied to a powerful economic-development agenda. The consensus in Toronto – as its motto, 'Diversity Our Strength,' implies – is that multiculturalism is a competitive advantage in the global marketplace. Also, attracting and retaining highly skilled immigrants is considered central to Toronto's growth agenda. Its urban regime includes city officials, prominent leaders in the business community, and representatives of labour, the social service sector, immigrant settlement organizations, and other groups. Under the umbrella of the Toronto City Summit Alliance (TCSA), high-powered leaders have cooperated to address a number of challenges, including 'becoming a centre of excellence in the integration of immigrants' (TCSA 2003). The TCSA established the Toronto Region Immigrant Employment Council (TRIEC) to address barriers to immigrant integration into the labour force. The council is co-chaired by the president and vice-president of Manulife Financial, one of Canada's most powerful financial institutions.

As in Vancouver, Toronto's business leaders and city officials have tied immigrant settlement goals to the city's economic-development objectives. Local community and municipal resources are pooled within its public–private governance arrangements to address policy goals. However, coalitions in the city are not just concerned with developing cooperative responses to diversity at the local level. Rather, Toronto's urban regime has expanded to encompass the regional and cross-provincial scales. Regime partners are fighting for greater levels of autonomy for the municipality and for a new status for the City of Toronto within Canadian federalism – a New Deal for the city (Good 2007). The lobbying efforts of this dynamic alliance of city leaders did a great deal to push the 'New Deal for Cities' onto the national agenda (Broadbent 2003). Immigrants' leaders, including their policy preferences, are included in the process of setting the local regime's agenda, including its urban autonomy goals.

In Brampton and Mississauga, immigrant settlement organizations operate in a resource-scarce environment that inhibits cooperation. Also, diversity seems to prevent immigrants from forming a common front to pressure those municipalities to respond. In Mississauga, immigrant integration and multiculturalism did not seem to be on the business community's agenda. In Brampton, the business community seemed interested in helping integrate immigrants into local governance. The city may be poised to become more active again in multiculturalism policy making.

Summarizing the Lessons

To what extent does the social diversity interpretation contribute to our understanding of the politics of immigration and multiculturalism at the local level? We can observe some clear patterns (albeit imperfect) in the biracial municipalities. However, in some ways the multiracial municipalities seem to fall into two distinct groups. Table 6.4 summarizes the findings.

What lessons can one draw from the findings discussed in this chapter and throughout this book? First, there is evidence that the collective action problem within immigrant populations is more easily overcome in biracial municipalities. Concentration appears to facilitate the development of community. For instance, in municipalities with a concentration of Chinese residents in Greater Vancouver we see strong community settlement capacity in the form of S.U.C.C.E.S.S. In Greater Vancouver, this capacity was so strong that it 'spilled over' into newer immigrant-receiving communities in the region. The organization began in Vancouver and then opened satellite locations in Richmond and (more recently) in Coquitlam, which did not yet have home-grown capacity in immigrant settlement. Thus, ethnic social capital seems to be an intervening variable that explains how ethnic configurations influence policy responsiveness. The importance of ethnospecific social capital to a group's capacity to influence local politics was one of Orr's (1999) main points in his work on the Black community in Baltimore.

Second, one can observe the emergence of new community dynamics – a backlash on the part of long-standing residents – in most biracial municipalities. In three of the biracial municipalities with a concentration of Chinese immigrants, a power struggle between the long-standing and ethnoracial-minority communities developed that centred on changes in the built environment that became symbols of the cultural evolution of the municipality. In Surrey, too, there was backlash against immigration, but a power struggle was absent, as the South Asian community had not mobilized against its racialization to the same degree. Thus, a dynamic of community backlash and – where the immigrant community possesses sufficient social capital to mobilize – a counter-reaction from the immigrant community, appears more likely to de-

Table 6.4
Summary of patterns of influence of ethnic configurations in multiculturalism policy making

Types of ethnic configurations	Multiracial	Biracial
Visible minorities (as proportion of population)	High	High
Composition of visible minority population	Diverse	Homogeneous
Backlash	No	Yes
Types of political pluralism	Competitive	Limited
Active in multiculturalism	No	Yes
Urban governance relationships to support multiculturalism initiatives	No	Yes
Dominant multiculturalism purposes	Celebrating multiculturalism Equitable access to services and inclusion in governance	Bridging, manage backlash, avoid segregation/social isolation Equitable access to services and inclusion in governance (to varying degrees)
Municipalities	Mississauga and Brampton (2001) Toronto	Vancouver, Richmond, Surrey, Coquitlam, and Markham

velop in municipalities where there is a large concentration of a single ethnic group. These new community dynamics in biracial municipalities increase the likelihood that the community will agree that there is an ethnic relations problem, which pushes the issue onto the municipal agenda. Rather unexpectedly, backlash leads to greater levels of responsiveness in biracial municipalities. As Orr (1999) also found, ethnospecific social capital solves only one element of the local collective-action problem. In order to achieve education reform that benefited Baltimore's Black community, local leaders had to build bridges among interethnic pools of 'social capital.' According to his study, 'bonding' (ethnospecific) social capital is insufficient. In his view, processes of urban regime building are one way in which interethnic bridging occurs. The new community dynamics in many biracial municipalities create incentives for local political leaders to intervene. Furthermore, the business community tends to support initiatives that will lead to resolving any conflict that might undermine the local community's economic well-being. Poor ethnic relations are simply bad for business.

Third, when a single group settles in a municipality, there is less of an immediate need for it to integrate, since it is more likely that the group will develop an extensive array of ethnospecific institutions. This has positive and negative implications. On the one hand, it seems to contribute to backlash on the part of long-standing residents, who contend that the immigrant group is not integrating. On the other, it provides the immigrant community with resources with which to organize to pressure the municipality to respond to its concerns and to counter backlash if it occurs. However, concentration can also result in exclusion and marginalization, which seems to be the case in Surrey, where, according to one informant, many in the South Asian community are in 'survival mode' owing to their social isolation (Woodman 2004, interview).

Finally, in biracial municipalities it is easier and potentially also less costly for local leaders to respond to a single immigrant group or ethnoracial minority than to a multiplicity of groups. For instance, translations have to be made in only one language, interpretation is in a single language, and employment equity efforts have to address barriers for only one group. Bridging through regime development is also easier in biracial contexts than in multicultural ones.

Nevertheless, though the municipality's ethnic configuration matters, the clear lesson to emerge is that it is not the sole factor. The *distribution of resources within the municipality and among ethnic groups* is important as well (Good 2005). At the local level, given municipalities' institutional limits, lack of resources, and perceived need to compete with other municipalities for residents and business investment (Peterson 1981), cities require the support of the business community to manage ethnoracial change. Clarence Stone (1989) has observed that 'as a practical matter, given the important resources and activities controlled by business organizations, business interests are almost certain to be one of the elements [of an urban regime], which is why regimes are best understood as operating within a political economy context' (1989, 179). Thus, municipalities in which the business community supports the development of multiculturalism policies are more responsive.

The importance of this factor is constant, regardless of the municipality's ethnic configuration. However, its importance to multiculturalism policy is structured by the community's ethnic configuration. A biracial municipality in which there is a prominent and cohesive immigrant business community provides an especially powerful combination – one that brings the weight of the business community *and* the weight of numbers to bear on municipal responsiveness to immigrants. This suggests why, in the present sample, biracial municipalities in which the ethnocultural 'minority' is predominantly Chinese have been more responsive than those in which the ethnocultural minority is South Asian. Specifically, in municipalities where Chinese immigrants predominate, there is a powerful and cohesive Chinese business community (one that includes developers). In addition, the Chinese business community is willing to facilitate municipal responsiveness to the Chinese community as a whole by donating or pooling resources. In Vancouver, multiculturalism policies are a by-product of a dominant, even 'hegemonic' (Olds 2001) economic-development model. In Toronto, too, we see how powerful the business community's support of multiculturalism can be and how this has influenced the city's capacity to respond to ethnocultural change. Tying immigrant settlement outcomes to the objectives of economic development has strongly propelled collective action around multiculturalism policies in that city, which has had to mobilize a highly diverse community, including a business community. In the Toronto case we also see the impact of tying issues to growth coalitions.

The *ethnic distribution of resources in civil society* also affects how the long-standing community perceives large-scale immigration. In all biracial municipalities with a concentration of Chinese immigrants, the ability of the Chinese business community to alter the cultural face of

220 Municipalities and Multiculturalism

the municipality (for instance, through Asian malls) has led to backlash on the part of some members of the long-standing community.

At the same time, in all of the *biracial* municipalities with large Chinese immigrant populations, the immigrant community has developed an extensive network of Chinese-specific institutions. The Chinese community seems to possess a great deal of social capital. Yet as Orr (1999) observes, social capital is not a substitute for economic capital (1999, 185). In Vancouver, Richmond, and Markham the Chinese community possesses high levels of both forms of capital. In Coquitlam, civil society is poorly developed, as immigrants began arriving in large numbers only after Westwood Plateau was developed. Given the strength of social networks in Greater Vancouver, S.U.C.C.E.S.S. has recently stepped in to fill this void in Coquitlam.

In contrast, Surrey is the only biracial municipality in the sample with a predominantly South Asian immigrant community. That community seems to be more divided than Chinese immigrant communities generally are and has not developed ethnospecific South Asian social capital. Furthermore, Surrey's business community does not seem to be pressuring the municipality to adapt its services, even though many of that city's developers are South Asian. At the local level, immigrant inclusion in local governance constitutes a two-stage problem in collective action: first, the immigrant group must be able to mobilize for collective action at the level of civil society; and second, bridges must be created by developing urban regimes. The South Asian community in Surrey has failed to overcome the first-level collective action problem. Even the racialization of the community has not spurred it to mobilize.

Immigrant communities that fail to overcome the first-order collective action problem (i.e., to organize as a community) will find themselves (a) unable to pressure municipalities to respond to their concerns, and (b) unable to participate in policy-productive 'urban regimes.' Furthermore, it is clear that Statistics Canada's category 'South Asian' is too imprecise – specifically, it does not reflect how most South Asian people 'self-identify,' nor does it reflect how they construct their ethnoracial identity. Further research would shed light on the dynamics within this disparate group.

Similarly, the increased complexity of the first-order collective action problem in multiracial municipalities means it is less likely that immigrants will be included in municipal governance in those locales. One can observe the effects of this factor in Mississauga and Brampton, the two suburban multiracial municipalities in the present sample.

One might be tempted to conclude that, owing to the cleavages in its South Asian population, Surrey should be considered a 'multiracial' municipality to reflect this diversity. After all, that city shares the divisions within the immigrant community that are inherent to a multiracial context. However, the way in which the *overall* community *perceives* immigration differs in Surrey from the way in which it is perceived in multiracial municipalities. Backlash against immigration seems to be less likely in heterogeneous, multiracial municipalities – that is, those in which the perception is missing that a single immigrant group is redefining the municipality's cultural norms. It makes a difference how majorities perceive minorities; it also makes a difference how minorities perceive themselves. A municipality with a reactive policy style needs something to react *to* before it can begin developing multiculturalism policies.

There are cleavages within Surrey's immigrant community; at the same time, long-standing residents of that city have reacted to what they see as a large and monolithic group by racializing the community. In other words, social context influences relationships between the long-standing community and the immigrant population even while it influences relations *within* the immigrant population. Hero (1998) contends that 'politics and policies are products of the cooperation, competition and/or conflict between and among dominant and subordinate minority groups, not only of the dominant group within a state' (1998, 10). Therefore we must understand how social context is perceived by *all* members of political communities.

The lack of visible and widespread backlash in the multiracial suburban municipalities does not mean that exclusion from local governance does not matter to immigrant populations. Former Brampton councillor Garnett Manning (2003–6), a member of Brampton's Black community, described Brampton's race relations climate as at a 'boiling point,' noting that members of his community felt excluded from the city's power structures (Manning 2004, interview). Nevertheless, in the absence of political mobilization and community pressure, municipalities – suburban municipalities in particular – tend to resist involving themselves in new policy areas. As former Brampton councillor (and current provincial MPP) Linda Jeffrey put it: 'Councils are paralysed by the thought that they're going to set precedents that they have to continue later on'; put another way, if they do something for one group they will 'have to do that for everybody' (Jeffrey 2004, interview). In sum, multiracial suburban municipalities have not had to manage community backlash, have not been pressured to respond, and contend that the diversity of their populations and the limits on their resources make responding very difficult.

When one removes the influence of uneven community resources from the analysis by removing the two resource-rich urban-core municipalities from the sample, the pattern is straightforward, as evidenced in Table 6.5.

Toronto may be an 'exceptional case' in the sense that it has an exceptional concentration of the country's settlement resources (as well as resources more generally) with which to overcome the difficult collective-action problems that its diversity entails. These resources upset the straightforward patterns that social scientists like to identify. The Toronto case provides the clearest evidence for the need for a complex, resource-based analysis of urban politics and power – factors that urban regime theory highlights. Furthermore, in Toronto we see evidence of the central importance of *leadership* through community and municipal efforts to co-build capacity.

If one removes only Toronto from the sample, the pattern is quite clear. All *biracial* municipalities are either 'responsive' or 'somewhat responsive' and share common forms of political pluralism and institutional development as well as common debates about multiculturalism. All *multiracial* municipalities are 'unresponsive,' share a limited and sometimes competitive form of political pluralism, and lack the initiative to develop governance arrangements.

Why is Toronto an exceptional case? Is it possible that the city has overcome some of the features of ethnic configurations that would normally structure their effects? Differences between Toronto and the other multiracial municipalities, and similarities between Toronto and Vancouver, support an affirmative answer to this question.

Toronto differs from its multiracial counterparts and has more in common with Vancouver in that it is the central city in its city-region. This has many implications. One is that, as an older city, it has benefited from the investment of resources (including settlement resources) from upper levels of government for a longer period of time. In addition, Toronto's ethnoracial minorities have had more *time* to organize and to create bridges than have Mississauga's or Brampton's.

Myer Siemiatycki and his colleagues (2003) have documented the development of interethnic bridges in Toronto through time. The influence of time can also be seen in Vancouver, where large-scale immigration from China resulted in political dynamics similar to those

Table 6.5
Summary of patterns of influence of ethnic configurations in multiculturalism policy making in suburbs

Types of ethnic configurations	Multiracial	Biracial
Visible minorities (as proportion of population)	High	High
Composition of visible minority population	Diverse	Homogeneous
Backlash	No	Yes
Types of political pluralism	Competitive	Limited
Municipal multiculturalism policies	Highly Limited	Limited
Policy styles	Inactive	Reactive
Urban governance relationships to support multiculturalism initiatives	No	Yes
Dominant multiculturalism purposes	Celebrating multiculturalism	Community bridging, manage backlash, avoid segregation/social isolation, and access to services
Municipalities	Mississauga and Brampton (2001)	Markham, Richmond, Surrey, and Coquitlam

in suburban biracial municipalities such as Richmond and Markham. In Vancouver, however, the municipality and civil-society leaders were able to build capacity to manage demographic change over time, which contributed to a greater level of responsiveness than in Richmond or Markham. We also see the influence of time in Coquitlam, which has not had time to develop immigrant settlement and advocacy capacity, because immigration to the city has occurred relatively recently.

Toronto is also exceptional in relation to its multiracial suburban counterparts because its population is so much larger – about 2.5 million people – which means that its three largest visible-minority groups as well as its immigrant population as a whole are very large (see Table 6.1). Rodney Hero's (1998) categories of ethnic configurations measure the proportion of ethnic groups ('Whites,' 'White ethnics,' and ethnoracial 'minorities') in relation to the overall state population. However, he also acknowledges that 'it may be the case that a group's size might also be considered in terms of raw numbers' (1998, 152). Toronto has very large Chinese, South Asian, and Black communities. Each is larger than the entire population of either Richmond or Coquitlam, and the Chinese and South Asian communities are each larger than that population of Markham (Statistics Canada 2007b). Toronto's immigrant population is over one million – that is, its immigrant population is larger than the total population of most Canadian cities.

Finally, the City of Toronto has experienced an exceptional level of institutional upheaval over the past decade (Sancton 2000), including a major amalgamation. This has led to new patterns of political mobilization in the community. For instance, leaders in the anti-amalgamation movement – Citizens for Local Democracy (C4LD) – created bridges with Toronto's visible-minority communities (Siemiatycki et al. 2003). Toronto also suffered disproportionately from budgetary decisions at the federal and provincial levels that led to 'downloading' in the mid-1990s (MacMillan 2006; Good 2007). The social impacts of decisions at the federal and provincial levels led to the development of a strong urban-autonomy movement that is exceptional in Canada. Municipal leaders in many other major cities in Canada support municipal autonomy goals; in Toronto, the movement also has the support of a broad-based group of elites in civil society. Immigrant leaders are included in this alliance and have the support of some of Canada's most powerful business leaders. The impact of neoliberal ideology and the 'politics of restraint' has been more pronounced in Canada's largest city. The important role of intergovernmental decisions – arguably in response to global forces of rescaling – in Toronto's evolution is discussed further in chapter 7.

Toronto is the 'face' of the city-region nationally and globally. Toronto and Vancouver are the central cities of two of Canada's largest city-regions, and their local leaders perceive their municipalities as qualitatively different – as 'global' or 'world' cities. Both cities have linked the attraction, retention, and settlement of immigrants to their capacity to compete for investment in a global economy – a capacity that is supported by stronger levels of civil-society leadership than are found in their surrounding suburbs. The 'selling diversity' paradigm that they have adopted informs a multitude of multiculturalism-related policies (policies that Yasmeen Abu-Laban and Christina Gabriel [2002] have described at the national level). Together, these factors contribute to the 'proactive' approach that both cities have taken to immigrant settlement and multiculturalism policy.

These factors provide a strong case that Toronto has 'overcome' its ethnic configuration; but they also suggest that as a case, Toronto cannot be used to generalize the effects of an ethnic configuration on a municipal society and government. Similarly, the fact that Toronto does not fit the overall pattern should not be seen as a 'falsification' of the social diversity interpretation presented above.

In addition, the divergence between the central city and suburban multiracial municipalities, and the significance of this divergence for the overall value of the social diversity perspective, must be considered in light of strong evidence that in *biracial* municipalities, ethnic configuration has causal effects on local communities and their municipal governments. In Richmond and Markham – two biracial suburban municipalities in two different provinces – the ways in which residents and leaders reacted to immigration, the community debates that arose therefrom, and the ways in which immigrants perceived community reactions, are so strikingly similar that if we were to take one of these municipalities and transplant it into another province or even country, similar community dynamics and responses to multiculturalism might well occur.

As the social diversity interpretation implies, 'the context within which individuals and/or groups are situated is as, if not more, important than the values or ideas that people "bring with them" or "have within"' (Hero 1998, 10). The context is 'transsubjective' or 'transindividual' (ibid.). The strong similarities among biracial municipalities in the sample imply that one could transplant a long-standing resident of a Canadian city into a biracial social context and his or her opinion on immigration and multiculturalism would likely be more similar to those of others in the biracial context than to those of an individual who was situated in another social context (multiracial or homogeneous, for instance). Similarly, one could expect individual immigrants to react correspondingly to the type of racialization that occurs in these locales. The biracial cases in the sample provide especially strong evidence that social context has an impact on political pluralism, on institutional development, and, ultimately, on policy outputs.

In the future, the effects of social context could also be explored at the individual level of analysis, as Hero (1998) does in his work by drawing from existing secondary literature on the influence of race on White attitudes and support for particular issues and public policies. Unfortunately, individual-level data on attitudes towards social change in the eight *municipalities* discussed here are not available. However, Daniel Hiebert (2003) conducted a study of attitudes towards multiculturalism, immigration, and discrimination in five *residential areas* in Greater Vancouver.[4] These residential areas were located in the cities in the Greater Vancouver sample. Hiebert notes a 'curious' finding with respect to the data on discrimination – a finding that supports those discussed here: though immigrants report suffering discrimination more often than do the Canadian born, the pattern is reversed for discrimination in shopping, banking, and dining out (ibid., 33). He does not present his findings by neighbourhood. He does, though, note that feelings of discrimination were more notable in areas such as Richmond, East Vancouver, and Surrey-Delta, where there are many ethnic businesses catering to immigrant and minority clienteles (ibid.). Hiebert's data were collected as part of a larger collaborative project. When the data he and his collaborators collected have been published, it will be interesting to see whether they cast further light (a) on the role played by social context in shaping individual attitudes towards multiculturalism, and (b) from a theoretical perspective, on the value of a social diversity interpretation of local politics. In light of the analysis offered in this book, a comparison of the same data in biracial and multiracial municipalities in Greater Vancouver and the GTA would be very interesting as well. Based on this chapter's theoretical ideas, one might predict that the sense of discrimination among Canadian-born residents is heightened when there is a perceived threat of cultural 'takeover' by a concentrated immigrant minority. One might predict that the issue of concern to the Canadian-born resident would be that many minority businesses in these neighbourhoods cater to a single 'racial' group – an 'Asian' clientele.

A Research Note on the Brampton Case

The 2006 Census indicates that Brampton is now a biracial municipality with a dominant South Asian community. Based on the interpretation offered above, what might one expect of the future politics of multiculturalism in Brampton? The findings discussed in this book suggest that as the South Asian community becomes increasingly concentrated in Brampton, feelings of cultural threat may increase among Canadian-born residents. Therefore, one might expect to see evidence of an emerging community backlash. This could create an incentive for the municipality to intervene by establishing a race relations committee to bridge the immigrant and Canadian-born communities. In other words, we might see the revival of the Brampton Race Relations Action Committee. However, to the extent that Surrey's experience is instructive, Brampton's South Asian community might become isolated and have a more difficult time mobilizing for collective action owing to internal, religion-based cleavages. This could create an incentive for municipal policies that would increase immigrants' access to services and governance. Together these factors, coupled with the fact that the business community has taken an interest in diversity issues, foreshadow a more responsive municipality in the future.

Evidence beyond Canada: American 'Ethnoburbs'

A growing literature in geography provides further evidence to support the theoretical value of a social diversity interpretation of local politics, and of a cross-national research agenda that examines the relationship between immigrant settlement patterns and political processes. The literature on 'ethnoburbs' shows that at least some 'bifurcated' localities in the United States are characterized by similar political dynamics as the 'biracial' Canadian municipalities with concentrations of Chinese residents. The political dynamics that have resulted from demographic change in Richmond and Markham are similar to those characterizing American 'ethnoburbs' – a concept that American geographer Wei Li (1999) has developed to characterize new suburban ethnic clusters of Chinese immigrants.[5]

Li distinguishes the 'ethnoburb' from traditional ethnic ghettos or urban enclaves such as Chinatowns, insofar as actors with economic power deliberately create ethnoburbs, whereas in ethnic ghettos and urban enclaves, 'ethnic people do not have economic power' (Li 1997, 4). The first American ethnoburb emerged in Monterey Park, a suburb of Los Angeles, as a result of large-scale Chinese immigration. The political dynamics that developed in Monterey Park are similar to the dynamics that emerged in Richmond and Markham. For instance, an 'English-only' movement developed, and Chinese immigrant business owners were accused of using Chinese signage to deliberately exclude long-standing residents (ibid.). Changes in the built environment, including the construction of a Buddhist temple, became 'racialized' in Monterey Park (ibid.), just as Asian malls were controversial in Richmond and Markham. In response, the City of Monterey Park initiated a number of multicultural events, including festivals, as well as community round tables that brought together community leaders to share their opinions on issues facing the city (ibid., 19). These community round tables appear to have served the same function as 'ethnic advisory committees' in biracial Canadian suburbs. Furthermore, these responses were similar even though the United States does not have an official policy of multiculturalism.

More recent scholarship has documented the emergence of ethnoburbs in other Pacific Rim countries (Ip 2005; Li 2007). According to Li, the transformation of suburbs in these countries results in 'similar kinds of resistance from longtime local residents,' produces 'racialized incidents,' and often leads to 'similar solutions.' For example, the 'monster homes' controversy is 'a well-known and well-publicized issue in Los Angeles, Silicon Valley, Vancouver, and Auckland' (Li 2007, 14).

In essence, this literature suggests that the social diversity interpretation of local politics can serve as a comparative framework for studying urban governance in high-immigration, multicultural environments. Internationally, what geographers call the ethnoburb appears to be a common type of immigrant settlement, one that results in similar forms of political pluralism that are of interest to political scientists.

The literature on ethnoburbs strengthens rather than undermines the social diversity interpretation. According to Rodney Hero's framework, 'English-only' movements should be more common in ethnoburbs and racialization of the minority group should occur in these locales. However, the question arises: Would these dynamics occur owing to 'bifurcation' (in Hero's typology) or to concentration of a single immigrant community? And to what extent does it matter that many immigrants in ethnoburbs are powerful and deliberately create these communities?

These questions speak to the differences between the way in which Hero theorizes ethnic configurations in the United States and the way in which they are theorized in this study of Canadian communities. Both the ethnoburb literature and the findings discussed in this book suggest that it matters how powerful immigrant communities are. Power influences their ability to contribute to 'social production' and to change the face of local communities in ways that generate a particular reaction from long-standing residents. Together, the findings in this chapter and in the ethnoburb literature point to the potential theoretical fruitfulness of a cross-national social-diversity interpretation of the impact of immigration on the politics of cities.

Concluding Thoughts

To what extent does the social diversity interpretation cast light on the politics of multiculturalism policy development at the local level in Canada? There is convincing evidence that the ethnic configuration of political societies matters. Building on Rodney Hero's work in the United States, this chapter has developed a social diversity framework through which to examine how immigrant settlement patterns have contributed to urban regime building and the politics of multiculturalism at the local level. It has offered two new categories of ethnic configurations – biracial and multiracial – and it has presented convincing evidence that many aspects of the social contexts inherent in these analytical constructs matter to urban regime building and ultimately to multiculturalism policy development.

The ethnic configuration of a community affects the nature of political pluralism. In the biracial cases, we saw that large numbers of a single group appeared to make the immigrant group more threatening. However, this on its own did not result in publicly visible crises in ethnic relations. It was during debates over changes to the built environment that we saw intense intercultural conflict.

Ethnic configurations must be viewed as contextual factors shaping the distribution of resources in local communities. They affect the ways in which civil society develops, and they have an impact on collective-action problems, the resources available in the community to contribute to the management of multiculturalism, and the incentives for the immigrant community to integrate. They also affect how the business community views immigration, as well as its willingness to pool capacity to manage multiculturalism and help municipalities adapt their services.

However, we must also look at intracommunity dynamics to understand the local politics of multiculturalism. In Surrey, for instance, we must look at diversity *within* communities in order to assess whether a group's ability to act collectively is enhanced by geographic concentration. The ethnic configuration of a municipality can also affect the development of a cohesive immigrant business community. We have found that in biracial municipalities with a concentration of Chinese immigrants, the combination of a powerful and well-organized business elite and large numbers of a single group of immigrants can create the conditions for highly visible backlash on the part of long-standing residents.

Furthermore, the ethnic configuration of a municipality affects how difficult it will be for a municipality to respond. In multiracial municipalities a greater investment of time and resources is required to implement multiculturalism policies effectively. Thus, in the absence of backlash and community pressure, in many ways it is no wonder that multiracial suburbs such as Mississauga and Brampton have not responded.

With this in mind, one can appreciate Toronto's exceptionality. Despite the difficulties of building policy capacity in a highly diverse context and the need to settle and integrate more than one million immigrants, Toronto has been relatively responsive and wide-scale immigration has happened relatively smoothly. A broad range of local leaders, including prominent business leaders, have contributed to Toronto's ability to settle immigrants and achieve other long-term multiculturalism objectives. This outcome is both puzzling and interesting for the urban regime scholar. How and why have so many community leaders worked together to manage multiculturalism? What explains the exceptional leadership effort at the local level in Toronto? Parts of the answers to these questions can be found by looking at the external contexts of local governance – that is, at the intergovernmental and (to some extent) global contexts.

7 Multiculturalism and Multilevel Governance: The Role of Structural Factors in Managing Urban Diversity

In their review of the urban regime literature, Karen Mossberger and Gerry Stoker (2001) identify several factors that seem to cause regimes to form and change, including demographic shifts, economic restructuring, federal grant policies, and political mobilization (2001, 811). In chapter 6 we saw that demographic change shapes the urban governance of multiculturalism from 'below,' because the ethnoracial configuration of municipal societies affects the nature of political pluralism as well as patterns of political mobilization at the local level. It also structures the distribution of resources. This chapter explores what Jeffrey Sellers (2002a, 2002b, 2005) calls a 'national infrastructure' – that is, the bundle of ways in which national institutions, policies and cultures structure local politics, policy making, governance, and citizen preferences. In particular, it explores some of the ways in which elements of the intergovernmental system have influenced the local governance of multiculturalism. The notion of 'national infrastructure' brings to light the dynamic relationship between changes in the intergovernmental context and political mobilization at the local level on the one hand and the way in which local developments affect federal and provincial policy decisions on the other. In other words, it stresses the importance of structural factors in urban analysis without negating the influence of local agency.

As this book has pointed out, structural factors are not completely decisive. Furthermore, there are a multitude of structural factors, which result from multiple levels of governments and policies and which intersect in myriad ways that have uneven spatial effects. The concept of 'national infrastructure' captures the multilevel dimensions of decision making and also the idea that local leaders can use structures at multiple levels as supports to achieve particular ends. In this sense, these infrastructures are 'resources' to be used (or not) in local agenda building and implementation.

With respect to crafting multiculturalism policy, though municipalities are a provincial responsibility, federal multiculturalism policies and the normative standard that the federal government has established are important parts of the national infrastructure that one might expect to influence local multiculturalism policy. Yet owing to municipalities' constitutional relationship with provinces, provincial multiculturalism policies matter in a more direct way. Federal and provincial policies furnish concrete policies, which are then emulated at other levels. They also provide resources in local communities through, for example, the funding of immigrant settlement organizations and organizations that serve other multiculturalism-related purposes. One might speak of a 'multiculturalism infrastructure'[1] in Canada that includes the symbolic and material resources furnished by legislation as well as the many government departments and community organizations involved in creating the capacity to manage diversity. For instance, Statistics Canada is an important part of this infrastructure since it collects ethnospecific data as well as data on immigrants. The national 'multiculturalism infrastructure' can also influence the preferences of citizens on the ground. For instance, the consistency of immigrant settlement leaders' preferences for a multicultural model of municipal citizenship can reflect the norms established by the national infrastructure.[2] However, as this book establishes, municipal multiculturalism policy making varies significantly across municipal jurisdictions. Thus, this chapter explores how elements of Canada's national infrastructure influence local governance in a more nuanced way. It does so by examining how a variety of changes in the intergovernmental system have altered the local governance of multiculturalism.

Fiscal federalism is an important gauge of power and an important source of change and flexibility in Canada's federation. By determining the distribution of public financial resources, it structures policy making significantly. The mid-1990s represented a turning point in the evolution of the Canadian federation, for during those years, fiscal relationships among governments were radically restructured. Furthermore, differences in provincial policy decisions in the 1990s in Ontario and British Columbia contributed to different local governance dynamics in those two provinces. Specifically, in Ontario, turbulent provincial–municipal relationships from 1995 onwards injected greater dynamism into urban governance arrangements in municipalities in the GTA relative to those in Greater Vancouver. Decisions by Ontario's Conservative governments (1995–2003)[3] – including a 'local services realignment' or 'disentanglement' exercise and amalgamation – fomented an urban autonomy movement in Toronto. Among the cases in the sample, Toronto experienced the greatest level of municipal stress in the mid to late 1990s. During this turbulent period, B.C.'s multiculturalism infrastructure was more stable and supportive of multiculturalism initiatives and supports to immigrants than Ontario's.

This chapter demonstrates that adjustments to several aspects of the national infrastructure affected Toronto disproportionately, changing the political dynamics of Toronto's regime. More specifically, in response to amalgamation and downloading, local leaders in Toronto increased their efforts to build capacity in several policy areas, including immigrant settlement and integration. Furthermore, immigrant settlement issues made it onto the agenda of the federal and Ontario governments partly because these concerns were a priority of Toronto's powerful urban regime, which began lobbying upper levels of government for a New Deal for Cities. Toronto's urban regime coalition spilled over into the national and regional scales, thus becoming what Julie-Anne Boudreau (2006) calls 'polyscalar.' Local leaders in Toronto became aware that pooling local resources was insufficient to achieve policy goals. They therefore developed national and regional coalitions to pressure upper levels of government to institutionalize new forms of intergovernmental sharing of resources.

The election of Dalton McGuinty's Liberal government in Ontario in 2003 represented an important shift in the provincial–municipal relationship. It followed a dramatic period of municipal reorganization of Toronto's formal governing institutions in the mid to late 1990s that saw 'disentanglement' as well as downloading from upper levels of government. Then in 2003 a 'policy window' in the intergovernmental system opened for Toronto's regime, as political leadership changed simultaneously at the municipal, provincial, and federal levels. The opening of this policy window led to new legislative and political status in Canadian federalism for Canada's largest city. It has also led to a more supportive provincial environment for managing immigration in Toronto.

This analysis must be placed in a context of global economic restructuring. As happened in countries around the world, in the 1980s and 1990s Canadian governments at all levels were influenced by neoliberal ideas and attempted to reduced spending to eliminate budgetary deficits and repay debts. As urbanization progresses internationally, cities have emerged as the central engines of global capitalism. In this environment many urban scholars have noted a rise in the competitiveness of cities. More broadly, scholars argue that there has been a 'rescaling' of the state, with the global economy becoming reterritorialized at the urban scale (Kipfer and Keil 2002; Brenner 2004). Others, including Thomas Courchene (2005a), have described these economic processes as a 'glocalization' of the economy, with economic space becoming simultaneously global and local (urban). These economic processes have in turn contributed to greater competitiveness in cities as well as to new forms of political mobilization.

In Canada, as in many other countries (Uitermark, Rossi, and Houtum 2005), there has also been a rescaling of multiculturalism. The world's migrants have been flowing into a handful of Canadian cities; Toronto and Vancouver are the top two immigrant-receiving city-regions in English-speaking Canada. *How* migrants are incorporated into cities matters greatly to globalization processes (Sassen 1998; Keil 2002, 230). Susan Clarke and Gary Gaile (1998) describe proactive economic-development strategies as part of the new 'work of cities' in a highly competitive global environment. In this new economic context, another important job of municipal governments is to manage multiculturalism. As this book has demonstrated, some local leaders tie this role of cities to economic-development objectives.

This chapter describes broad trends in Canadian fiscal federalism. It also discusses the general nature of provincial–municipal relationships and of provincial multiculturalism infrastructures in the 1990s in Ontario and British Columbia. Both of these factors have had important implications for the local governance of multiculturalism, and their impact has been most apparent in the City of Toronto. The chapter then describes new patterns of political mobilization that developed in Toronto in response to the local implications of the intersection of federal and provincial policy decisions in the mid-1990s. These new forms of mobilization had two interrelated goals: to achieve greater municipal empowerment in the intergovernmental system, and to increase local capacity to address the city's policy challenges, including the challenges of integrating immigrants through local multiculturalism initiatives. This provides part of the explanation of how and why immigrant settlement concerns were included in the goals of Toronto's wide-ranging capacity-building regime. Changes in intergovernmental relationships also contribute to our understanding of why the settlement sector in Toronto supports municipal autonomy initiatives – in other words, why that sector pursues territorial *and* sectoral strategies when advocating on behalf of immigrants.

Like previous ones, this chapter uses urban regime theory as an analytical lens for characterizing and understanding the new patterns of mobilization in Toronto, which have extended beyond the municipal level to include multiple scales. It also describes some recent developments in Canada's intergovernmental system that have grown out of the lobbying efforts of participants in Toronto's regime. This section is meant to illustrate how urban governance arrangements are affected by changes in the intergovernmental system and how local leaders and governance arrangements can bring about changes to the intergovernmental system.

The Changing National Infrastructure: Rescaling the Canadian Federation?

'Rescaling' the state refers to two processes: the territorial reorganization of political authority, and the actions that have been taken by civil-society leaders as part of neoliberal state restructuring since the 1980s. Changes in the spatial dimensions of state authority have been driven by changes in global capitalism that have concentrated capitalism's global infrastructure in specific places. This infrastructure is located in some of the world's largest cities. Globalization has created economic winners and losers so that a hierarchy of cities has emerged. In Canada, high-immigration cities such as Toronto and Vancouver are among the 'winners'; indeed, their status as immigrant-magnet city-regions both reflects and is driven by their national global competitiveness.

The literature on rescaling would have us assume that as cities become the key nodes in the global economy, we will see greater levels of investment in cities by upper levels of government, as well as the emergence of highly competitive urban-governance coalitions. For instance, in *New State Spaces*, Neil Brenner (2004) describes a shift in Europe towards economic-development policies that privilege cities and the rise of new forms of political organization at the metropolitan scale; he refers to these new configurations of state authority as a 'Rescaled Competition State Regime (RCSR).' Rescaling processes have multiple dimensions and implications. The previous chapters described powerful urban regimes in Toronto and Vancouver wherein local leaders tied multiculturalism objectives to growth agendas. One might expect upper levels of government to support these local economic-development agendas. One might also expect strong support for multiculturalism initiatives, which are necessary in order to manage and sustain growth. Indeed, the federal government's own policy discourse links economic growth with diversity (Abu-Laban and Gabriel 2002). Yet there is considerable variation in the extent to which upper levels of government have supported cities and municipalities in their efforts to compete and to manage the integration of large-scale influxes of immigrants.

Thus the literature on rescaling provides a causal explanation for the emergence of *multilevel governance arrangements* – a term used by an interdisciplinary group of scholars to conceptualize these complex relationships and processes. Gary Marks (1993) defines multilevel governance as 'a system of continuous negotiation among nested governments at several territorial tiers – supranational, national, regional, and local – as a broad process of institutional creation and decision reallocation that has pulled some previously centralized functions of the state up to the supranational level and some down to the local/regional level' (Marks 1993, 392, in Young and Leuprecht 2006, 12). According to Julie-Anne Boudreau (2006), rescaling occurs both intentionally and unintentionally (2006, 162); in other words, it is a result of both structural changes and political agency. In particular, Boudreau highlights civil society's important role in the emergence of multilevel, 'rescaled' configurations of political authority. In her work on social mobilization in response to amalgamations in Toronto and Montreal, she uses the term 'polyscalar' to describe new types of coalitions and mobilization strategies that both citizens and leaders in civil society developed at multiple scales in these cities. She observes: 'In both Montreal and Toronto, opponents to mergers and coalitions claiming a general reform of intergovernmental relations in Canada, have developed a series of mobilizing strategies at multiple scales, striking alliances with various levels of government and pitting them against one another.' In her view, 'while rarely directly discussed in intergovernmental relations studies, these types of polyscalar outlooks exploited by civil society actors have an important impact on the kinds of institutional and territorial reorganizations undertaken by state actors, particularly in a context where decision-making processes have been opened by a variety of non-state actors' (ibid.). What is different in her view is that civil-society leaders are not using sector-specific strategies to achieve their ends; rather, they are using territorial strategies and acting at multiple territorial scales at once (ibid., 164). As she explains, 'sectoral strategies of political claims channel efforts into specific policy sectors (housing, language, health, education, etc.) [whereas] jurisdictional and territorial strategies of political claims are attempts by civil society to use one level of government against another or to create a new level of government altogether by asking for a remapping of political and administrative boundaries' (ibid., 166). These strategies are part of a global state of 'territorial flux' created by a 'restructuring-generated crisis' in capitalism (Soja 2000, in ibid., 162). However, municipal and civil-society responses have been strongly shaped by how upper levels of government have responded to global conditions, just as they have shaped the intergovernmental reaction.

Changes in fiscal federalism are a good measure of the intergovernmental system's overall response to global restructuring. Processes of decentralization and fiscal 'downloading' began in the late 1970s in Canada. These processes reached a critical juncture in the 1990s, when major reforms to fiscal transfers were introduced. The most important event in the 1990s with respect to fiscal federalism was Ottawa's decision to combine two major transfers to provinces for social-policy responsibilities – the Canada Assistance Plan (CAP)[4] and Established Programs Financing (EPF)[5] – into a single block grant called the Canada Health and Social Transfer (CHST). With the introduction of the CHST, the federal government eased the conditions on grants and transferred tax points to the provinces; it also dramatically reduced the grant's monetary value.[6] This decision was widely seen as the root cause of a resulting 'fiscal imbalance' in the federation – a situation in which one level of government now had too few revenues to meet its constitutional responsibilities while the other level had more than it needed (Advisory Panel on the Fiscal Imbalance 2006, 12–14). More specifically, the federal decision was seen as a means of 'downloading' fiscal burdens onto provinces. Downloading also had important tri-level implications.

Downloading refers to several manoeuvres on the part of provincial and federal governments. First, upper levels of government can give municipal governments new responsibilities without transferring commensurate resources – what in the United States is commonly referred to as 'unfunded mandates.' A second form of downloading occurs when upper levels of government withdraw unilaterally from a policy field and local governments are left to decide whether to fill the gap in services. A third form occurs when upper levels of government fail to consider the place-specific consequences of their public-policy decisions. Municipalities' de facto role in multiculturalism and immigrant settlement policy in Canada's most important immigrant-receiving urban and suburban municipalities is an important example of this form of downloading.

In federal systems, downloading to municipalities has multiple dimensions. The federal government can decide to download to provinces; the provinces can in turn decide to download onto municipalities. In addition, because of their place-specific consequences, decisions in a variety of policy areas – including multiculturalism and immigrant settlement policy – made at the provincial *and* federal levels may result in unfunded de facto municipal mandates.

In the mid-1990s, federal reductions in transfers to provinces were so dramatic that they led economist Thomas Courchene to argue that the Canadian federation was moving towards a model of 'hourglass federalism' (Courchene 2005a). After introducing the CHST in 1995, Ottawa replaced part of its provincial transfers with direct transfers to citizens[7] and to cities.[8] Of particular interest here, the CHST's implementation in 1995 coincided with Ottawa's decision to create the national Metropolis Project, a research initiative the goal of which was to investigate immigration's national and international impact on cities. As part of this initiative, research centres were established in Toronto and Vancouver (see earlier chapters). The activities of these centres have become important nodes in local-governance arrangements and have contributed to capacity building in immigrant settlement and ethnocultural relations. Given the reductions in federal transfers to provinces for social spending and 'medicare's voracious appetite,' as Ottawa began to fund city initiatives, the provinces 'were forced to starve virtually every other provincial policy area' (ibid., 14). As a consequence, the provinces became irrelevant in many policy areas of vital importance to cities. This in turn created incentives for local leaders to bypass the provinces and to seek direct relations with the federal government.

Courchene contends that the federal government's decisions in this respect were strategic (i.e., intentional) manoeuvres in response to the increased importance of global city-regions in a global knowledge-based economy.[9] This interpretation of the motives underpinning federal decision making in fiscal policy is consistent with what Neil Brenner's (2004) analysis of 'rescaling' in Europe would lead one to expect. Specifically, Brenner describes a shift away from 'spatial Keynesianism' whereby the state redistributes economic activity across space towards a focus on investments in the economic winners – which tend to be a select group of cities. Canada's immigrant-magnet city-regions are clearly within the top economic tier of cities in Canada. As this chapter will show, whatever the federal government's intentions, its actions have contributed to new patterns of political mobilization at different scales and to the use of territorial strategies by local leaders to achieve their desired ends.

However, the provinces (and Ontario in particular) were not simply passive observers that were 'squeezed out' of relevance in the new fiscal arrangements. Provincial decisions in response to these changes varied in Ontario and B.C. This variation has had important implications for municipal governance and for the place of municipalities on the national agenda and within federalism.

The Influence of the Provincial–Municipal Relationship on Urban Multiculturalism Policy Making

Ontario in the 1990s: Municipal Turbulence and Multiculturalism Policy Retrenchment in the Conservative Era

In Ontario, the transition from the New Democratic Party (1990–95) to the Conservative Party (1995–2003) was a time of dramatic change in municipal governance in that province. In 1995, the election of the Conservatives under Mike Harris coincided with the decision by the Liberal government under Jean Chrétien to implement the CHST. The Harris government dramatically reorganized the division of powers between the province and municipalities; it also amalgamated many municipalities in Ontario (including Metro Toronto), in part to prepare them for their new responsibilities; and it reduced services within the province in line with the neoliberal ideology that underpinned the Conservatives' 'Common Sense Revolution.'[10]

Myer Siemiatycki (1998) estimates that as a result of the reorganization of provincial and municipal responsibilities, the new City of Toronto assumed close to $400 million of additional fiscal responsibilities per fiscal year (1998, 5). The City of Toronto approved its operating budget of $7.6 billion for 2006 in March of that year. Of this budget, 36 per cent was devoted to provincially mandated services, yet only 25 per cent of the city's revenues came from provincial grants and subsidies (City of Toronto 2006, 2–3). In his comparative analysis of municipal finance, Melville MacMillan found that downloading to municipalities in the 1990s was primarily an Ontario phenomenon (MacMillan 2006).

The Harris government had a dramatic and more direct effect on the politics of immigrant integration and accommodation in Ontario. Through policy withdrawal, it downloaded responsibility for immigrant integration. The NDP provincial government that preceded the Conservatives had supported proactive policies to include immigrants and ethnoracial minorities in public, social, and economic institutions. During its single term in office the NDP had founded the Ontario Anti-Racism Secretariat and passed the Employment Equity Act (1993). Both were terminated shortly after the Harris government was elected. Frisken and Wallace (2000) summarize the policy change in the multiculturalism/immigrant settlement sector under the Harris government:

> Among the more significant casualties of government cutbacks were Ontario Welcome Houses, of which there were three in Toronto, which provided such settlement services as translation, interpretation, and the publication of information brochures in various languages; a Multilingual Access to Social Assistance Program (MASAP); the Ontario Anti-Racism Secretariat; a Community and Neighbourhood Support Services Program (CNSSP); and the Employment Equity Act. The government also stopped funding Newcomer Language Orientation Classes (NLOC). (Frisken and Wallace 2000, 226)

In addition, the Ontario government replaced the Ontario Settlement and Integration Program (OSIP) with the Newcomer Settlement Program (NSP), reducing its funding dramatically – by almost 50 per cent in 1995 (Simich 2000, 7). It shifted its funding mechanisms from core to project funding and terminated many immigrant settlement programs (ibid.). By withdrawing from this policy field, it indirectly downloaded responsibility for multiculturalism policy and immigrant settlement to the local level. The province left local leaders to choose whether to fill the gap in multiculturalism policy and settlement services; moreover, they were to make this choice in a context of increasing fiscal pressure on already strapped municipal revenues.

Provincial downloading of immigrant settlement and multiculturalism policy has had important consequences at all three levels of government. During the 1990s all of the provinces except Ontario negotiated federal–provincial agreements on immigration. There was thus a significant fiscal gap in Ontario's share of national settlement funding until November 2005, when the province signed an immigration agreement with Ottawa. As the TCSA's manifesto 'Enough Talk' highlighted in 2003, Ontario was receiving 53.2 per cent of Canada's immigrants but only 38 per cent of federal funding for immigrant settlement. In contrast, Quebec received only 15 per cent of Canada's immigrants but 33 per cent of federal funding for immigrant settlement (TCSA 2003, 20). Ontario receives more immigrants than any other province, yet it has been allotted the lowest per capita share for settlement in the country (OCASI 2005, 1). Quebec received $3,806 per immigrant from the federal government for settlement costs, whereas Ontario received only $819 per immigrant (Courchene 2005b, 4). The lack of intergovernmental parity in fiscal transfers in the settlement sector has strongly affected local governance of multiculturalism in the GTA. At the time of the interviews, leaders in the settlement sector on the ground in Toronto often pointed to the disparity between Ontario's share of settlement funds and that of Quebec (Douglas 2003, interview).

The City of Toronto's financial difficulties have been exacerbated by the fact that Toronto receives a disproportionate share of the country's immigrants. In other words, provincial downloading through the redistribution of responsibilities between provincial and local levels has intersected with the place-specific consequences of Canada's national decisions in immigration policy. When upper levels of government cut back on immigrant settlement and other social programs in general, the City of Toronto had to fill the gap. As Peter Clutterbuck and Rob Howarth (2002) put it, the city takes on 'residual responsibilities' in settlement when upper levels of government fail to meet the requirements of successful immigrant settlement (2002, 53). For instance, they note that the city spent approximately '$24 million to provide social assistance to refugees and immigrants whose sponsorships had broken down, and an additional $1.9 million to house refugees in emergency shelfter' (ibid). Furthermore, cutbacks in social services and immigrant settlement programs occurred in a context in which poverty had been racialized. Michael Ornstein's study of both the 1996 and 2001 censuses documents a clear gap between the socio-economic condition of Europeans and non-Europeans in Toronto (Ornstein 2001, 2006). According to Michael Feldman, who was deputy mayor when he was interviewed, the city has a points system for social housing that gives priority to those residents in greatest need. Immigrants tend to have the greatest need in Toronto and are therefore placed at the top of the waiting list. According to him, this creates resentment among long-standing residents, who argue that they have paid taxes all their lives and therefore are more entitled to social benefits than immigrants. In Feldman's view, that is how the city has contributed to a 'those people' syndrome in Toronto (Feldman 2005, interview). Provincial downloading has combined with the place-specific implications of federal decisions in immigration policy to place severe pressure on Toronto's municipal services and budget.

The Harris government also massively restructured Toronto's institutions by amalgamating the former Metro Toronto with its six constituent municipalities – the largest municipal merger in Canadian history.

In sum, the Harris years in the mid to late 1990s were characterized by extraordinary change that strained the municipal system. Downloading to municipalities had been a widespread trend in Canada, one that had placed a great deal of pressure on municipal systems. But as Andrew Sancton (2000) observes: *'Nowhere has the stress been greater than in Ontario,* where the Progressive Conservative government led by Premier Mike Harris has simultaneously forced the creation of Canada's most populous municipality [the new City of Toronto] and drastically reorganized the functional and financial framework for all of the province's municipalities and school boards' (2000, 425; emphasis added). Clearly, between 1995 and 2003, municipalities in Ontario were operating in an extremely volatile provincial environment.

Under amalgamation, the City of Toronto experienced far more stress that other municipal governments in the sample. According to one explanation, the Harris government amalgamated Toronto in order to shift the city's balance of power to the right by flooding council with conservative representatives from the suburbs (Sancton 2003, 13). In other words, the city was targeted for political reasons.

Furthermore, the Harris years left unresolved the issue of regional governance in the GTA. In 1998, around the time of Toronto's amalgamation, the province established a special-purpose body, the Greater Toronto Services Board, to coordinate social, infrastructure, and transportation (including GO Transit, the commuter rail service) policy in the GTA (Siegel 2005, 131). However, the province abolished this body in 2002. Local leaders in Toronto and its outer suburbs were on their own in devising ways to act collectively (ibid.). The lack of a multipurpose regional coordinating body in the GTA constitutes a major institutional gap in the region. In response, forms of 'new regionalism' have developed in the GTA to address gaps in the region's formal governance institutions and in local policy-capacity deficits. These new patterns of political mobilization are part of an ongoing process of rescaling state space in urban Canada.

B.C. in the 1990s: Support for Municipalities and Multiculturalism

There were some similarities in political and policy change in Ontario and B.C. in the 1990s. Generally, though, provincial–municipal relationships in B.C. were comparatively stable and cooperative. Furthermore, the province was consistent in its support of immigrant settlement and other multiculturalism initiatives. B.C. governments did not pursue disentanglement or forced municipal amalgamations. Also, in the late 1990s the trend in municipal legislation in that province was towards greater municipal empowerment.

In B.C., the Municipal Act was amended in 2003 with the passing of the Community Charter. This municipal legislation, touted as the most empowering of its kind in Canada (Tindal and Tindal 2004, 202), applies to three of the four municipalities in the Greater Vancouver sample: Richmond, Surrey, and Coquitlam. It recognizes municipalities as an 'order of government' with concurrent authority with the province in thirteen spheres; it also requires municipal consent to amalgamations (ibid.).

The cooperative nature of provincial–municipal relationships in B.C. builds on a long history of municipal empowerment in that province (Sancton 2002, 272). A separate municipal charter – the Vancouver Charter – which has been in place since 1886, provides the foundation for Vancouver's legislative and fiscal authority. According to Heather Murray (2006), Vancouver 'has had a long history of local government empowerment dating back to its earliest days [that] seems to defy the constitutional limits thesis' (2006, 13, 15). John Lorinc notes B.C.'s 'enduring and far-sighted tradition of provincial forbearance in the affairs of its largest city' (Lorinc 2006, 202).

Community leaders in B.C. agree that downloading of immigrant integration challenges to municipalities has occurred to a certain extent. However, several differences emerged in interviews with leaders in the immigrant settlement sector in Greater Vancouver and the GTA.

In Greater Vancouver, local leaders differ in their perceptions of the shift from the NDP (which governed B.C. from 1996 to 2001) to the Liberals (2001–present) with regard to immigrant settlement. According to Patricia Woroch, Executive Director of the Immigrant Services Society (ISS), both governments made decisions that negatively affected local capacity building in that field (Woroch 2004, interview). Another leader in Vancouver's immigrant settlement sector suggested that the Campbell government (Liberal) has been motivated by an 'ideologically loaded' neoconservative agenda to cut back on services to vulnerable groups, including immigrants (community leader 2004, interview). But the same informant tempered this view by noting that 'to the province's credit,' under Campbell the province continued to provide services to refugees that the federal government does not 'allow.' In other words, the Campbell government has been more flexible with respect to the services it permits settlement agencies to offer refugees than the federal government was when it was the settlement agencies' primary patron.

Settlement leaders seemed to consider the sector to be better off in B.C. than in Ontario. Woroch suggested that the impact of downloading was much less dire in Greater Vancouver than in Ontario during the Conservative years. She noted that settling immigrants in Toronto is more of a 'life-and-death situation' because of the sheer numbers of immigrants arriving annually (Woroch 2004, interview). In other words, whereas the *proportion* of immigrants in relation to the municipal population is similar in the two cities, because Toronto's population is so much larger, so too is the *absolute* number of immigrants.

Another central difference, according to leaders in the settlement sector, is that municipal governments do not play a significant role in B.C.'s immigration and settlement policy. According to them, B.C.'s municipal governments are responding to 'diversity, not immigration' (Welsh 2004, interview). It seems that a more stable relationship with the province has led settlement leaders in B.C. to accept the jurisdictional status quo in immigration and settlement policy to a greater degree than leaders in Toronto.

Academic research also suggests that in B.C. in the 1990s, the provincial environment for immigrant settlement and multiculturalism policy was much more stable and even proactive in addressing the concerns of immigrants and ethnocultural minorities. For instance, David Edgington, Bronwyn Hanna, and colleagues (2001) write that even while the Ontario government was retrenching provincial multiculturalism policies, the B.C. government's policy orientation was 'more committed to multicultural policies and programmes since the early 1990s' (2001, 10). They note that B.C. passed its own Multiculturalism Act in 1993 and began to provide a number of new services to immigrants – for example, it offered settlement councillors and English-language instructors at various language institutions, and it supported community-based programs and heritage-language instructors (ibid.). In B.C., provincial leadership in multiculturalism policy lessened the burden of immigrant integration on municipal governments in Greater Vancouver's principal immigrant-receiving municipalities.

B.C.'s more proactive approach to immigration and settlement is evident in the fact that it negotiated an immigration and settlement agreement with the federal government in 1998, under which it took over Ottawa's traditional role in managing short-term settlement programs. The agreement was renegotiated in 2004. In contrast to Ontario, B.C.'s share of national settlement resources in 2003 exceeded its share of immigrants. B.C. receives about 17 per cent of Canada's immigrants and collects about 20 per cent of Canada's national settlement resources (TCSA 2003, 20).

Also, regional governance institutions have been more stable in B.C. than in Ontario. The district model of regional municipal governance was 'gently imposed' in B.C. in 1965 (Tindal and Tindal 2004, 87). The Greater Vancouver Regional District (GVRD) – the regional district in which Vancouver, Richmond, Surrey, and Coquitlam participate – is a regional coordination body consisting of twenty-one partner municipalities and one electoral district. It delivers essential utility services such as drinking water, sewage treatment, recycling, and garbage disposal. Its mandate includes planning growth and development and protecting air quality and green spaces. Today, regional districts in B.C. (including the GVRD) exist in a 'striking contrast to [forced] municipal consolidations or mergers ... so prevalent in other parts of the country,' including Ontario in the 1990s (Tindal and Tindal 2004, 91).

In sum, the story of the impact of Canada's changing national infrastructure on municipalities in B.C. is one of relative stability compared to municipalities in Ontario. Furthermore, as we saw above, as a result of amalgamation the City of Toronto has experienced more volatility that other municipalities in Ontario.

The Effect of Changing National Infrastructure on the Local Governance of Multiculturalism

Differences in provincial decisions in municipal and multiculturalism policy in the 1990s led to very different governance dynamics in the two cities. In Ontario, the combined effects of downloading in the GTA, municipal restructuring in Toronto, and the Ontario government's failure to provide leadership on several policy issues led to the development ·

of an urban regime in Toronto that is advocating for greater urban empowerment through new fiscal, legislative, and political relationships
between the City of Toronto and upper levels of government.

This movement has been popularly referred to as a 'New Deal' for
the GTA's largest city. The coalition has mobilized to seek new fiscal,
political, and legislative relationships between the city and upper levels of government. Furthermore, multiculturalism goals have become
important to the movement's agenda. An important group within this
coalition – the Toronto City Summit Alliance (TCSA) – has identified
excellence in immigrant settlement as one of Toronto's top five policy
priorities (TCSA 2001).

A 'New Deal for Cities' as a 'Broad Purpose' of Toronto's Regime

The term 'New Deal for Cities' has only recently entered Canadian political discourse. It appeared in a page-one editorial by the former publisher of the *Toronto Star* – John Honderich – published on 12 January
2002. Honderich listed a variety of policy challenges facing the City
of Toronto and then argued that 'nowhere is the [urban] malaise more
evident [in Canada] than in Greater Toronto.' In his view, the central
problem was governance – that Canada's 'antiquated system of government ... leaves cities largely unrepresented and constantly begging
for funds.' He linked Toronto's crisis to a severe fiscal gap in Canadian
federation: 'Torontonians pay out $4 billion more in taxes every year
than Ottawa and Queen's Park put back in.' Given Toronto's situation
in 2002, he expressed 'little wonder there is a growing "charter" movement within the GTA to declare "independence" or seek separate provincial status.' He then declared: 'The *Star* is launching a crusade for a
new deal for cities' (Honderich 2002).

Broadly speaking, the term 'New Deal for Cities' refers to a new status for urban municipalities in Canadian federalism. It refers to a variety of reform proposals that would empower municipal governments
within the intergovernmental system. It has been used to describe new
fiscal, legal, political, and even constitutional relationships between
municipalities and upper levels of government.

According to Heather Murray (2004), conceptualizations of 'urban
autonomy' range from independent city-state status on the one hand
to empowerment through greater tri-level intergovernmental entangle-
ment on the other (2004, 7). Roger Keil and Douglas Young (2003) observed in their study of the politics of municipal autonomy in Toronto:

'We have found no "structured coherence" to this debate but a colorful, yet emerging politics of municipal autonomy' (2003, 95). They found that local leaders perceive 'municipal autonomy' to be the 'solution' to many of the most pressing urban challenges in Toronto: 'For some, [municipal autonomy] meant that greater autonomy might increase business prospects; *for others, it meant that Toronto might be in a better position to deal with the integration and settlement of its large immigrant population*' (ibid., 96; emphasis added).

The New Deal campaign frames the Toronto regime's response to Canada's changing national infrastructure. Local leaders who advocate a New Deal for Cities share the objective of trying to increase the *capacity* of urban governments to address place-specific policy challenges. The inclusion of immigrant settlement policy in this frame has important implications for local capacity building to address multiculturalism in Toronto.

The New Deal for Cities movement in Toronto can be traced to the intersection of several decisions made by upper levels of government in the mid-1990s. The limited literature on this subject suggests that 'the forced amalgamation of Toronto in 1997–1998, coupled with the downloading of social services … has inspired the current charter debate in Toronto' (ibid., 89). Lorinc (2006) offers a similar account of the origins of the urban autonomy movement: 'In Ontario in the late 1990s, the triple whammy of amalgamation, downloading, and laissez-faire planning so alarmed many prominent urbanists that a group, including Jane Jacobs and philanthropist Alan Broadbent, put together a proposal for a "Greater Toronto Charter"' (2006, 204). The timing of these provincial decisions coincided with federal decisions to reduce provincial transfers for social spending. The contours of what Thomas Courchene calls 'hourglass federalism' were emerging by the mid to late 1990s (Courchene 2005a). Changes in fiscal federalism rooted in federal decisions created new incentives for local political mobilization. One could argue that these decisions had been inspired by global economic imperatives and by the global diffusion of neoliberal ideas.

But in Ontario it was provincial decisions that provided the most immediate incentive for political mobilization in Toronto. The Harris government's decision to forcibly amalgamate the constituent municipalities of Toronto inspired a powerful middle-class citizens' movement against the merger. That movement, Citizens for Local Democracy (C4LD), drew from a middle-class reformist movement that had emerged in the 1970s (Boudreau 2006, 42; Keil and Young 2003, 89).

For C4LD, the issue was not simply local democracy; it was also a tax revolt in response to fiscal downloading (Siemiatycki 1998, 5).

At first, C4LD did not seek the support of immigrants and ethnoracial minorities. Originally, it was a mobilization of 'white, British Toronto' (ibid., 5; Horak 1998). However, in response to this gap, a coalition called New Voices of the New City emerged under the leadership of the Council of Agencies Serving South Asians (CASSA). The coalition developed after CASSA made a submission to the province regarding how amalgamation would affect immigrants. In the summer of 1997, local leaders of New Voices of the New City pulled together a coalition of sixty-three immigrant-serving community organizations. Recent immigrant groups dominated this alliance, most of whose members resided outside central Toronto, in three inner suburbs: North York, Scarborough, and Etobicoke. 'A civic alliance of this scale was unprecedented' among Toronto's immigrant communities (Siemiatycki et al. 2003, 440). The co-chair of the alliance noted that 'most of the 63 [participating] groups had never come together voluntarily on any issue' (Fernando 1997, in ibid., 33).

Amalgamation provided an incentive for new immigrant organizations to cooperate. In doing so they inadvertently built bridges linking Toronto's diverse immigrant communities. The coalition facilitated Toronto's efforts to overcome the complex collective-action problems that had long been a feature of its multiracial ethnic configuration. 'Paradoxically, then, the creation of the megacity of Toronto – denounced for undermining local democracy – stimulated unprecedented civic mobilization among immigrant and visible minority communities' (ibid., 441).

Toronto Councillor Shelley Carroll suggested that the political mobilization surrounding amalgamation precipitated a broader change in Metro Toronto's political culture: 'Amalgamation turned suburbanites into activists ... And the citizens actually amalgamated faster than the politicians, because we started banding together with the other cities to protest this thing, accidentally amalgamating ourselves' (Carroll 2004, interview).

C4LD and New Voices of the New City failed to block Toronto's amalgamation. But after amalgamation, C4LD channelled its energies towards new goals, which included secession from the Province of Ontario (Keil and Young 2001). To this end, it entered into coalitions with municipal bureaucrats and politicians, business leaders, academics, the

Federation of Canadian Municipalities, the Toronto Board of Trade, and the Toronto Environmental Alliance (Keil and Young 2003; Boudreau 2006). Some C4LD members even formed a Committee for the Province of Toronto (Boudreau 2006, 170). Local political leaders expressed support for this radical reform option. Mel Lastman, the first mayor of the amalgamated City of Toronto, made the headlines when, at an international meeting in Florida in the fall of 1999, he declared that Toronto should be a province.

Amalgamation's assault on local democracy was a key mobilizing factor for Toronto's urban autonomy movement, which soon turned its attention to reforms implying a lesser degree of autonomy – for example, the establishment of a city charter (ibid.). C4LD's activities spilled over into what would become a 'charter movement,' and, more broadly, a New Deal for Toronto movement.

Immigrant and visible-minority mobilization in response to amalgamation also contributed to a rescaling process in the City of Toronto: 'In the politics of amalgamation in Toronto, immigrant communities were less concerned with preserving the jurisdictional status quo than attempting to assure that an enlarged city government was responsive to their distinct concerns' (Siemiatycki et al. 2003, 441). For instance, Uzma Shakir, a well-known leader in the immigrant settlement sector in Toronto, describes the issue this way:

> One of the reasons I do believe that municipalities must play a role is because people settle in municipalities, they live in cities, they don't live in jurisdictions, they don't define themselves in constitutional, jurisdictional things, they don't care. Immigrants have come here, they have come to Canada, they have chosen Toronto or Mississauga or Markham and that's where they're living their lives and the nearest level of government to them is the municipal government. Ironically, the municipal government is the least resourced as well. So just the demographic pressures alone have to be taken into consideration and we haven't even begun to talk about issues of diversity and racialization and all of that. But even just the massive growth … A city must have the resources to be able to deal with it so that it can continue to build its infrastructure – social as well as physical – its economic base. (Shakir 2003, interview)

Shakir's comments clearly reflect the connections that local leaders in Toronto make among immigration, growth, and economic development. Her comments also reflect the shift that Julie-Anne Boudreau (2006) describes in civil society towards territorial rather than sector-specific strategies.

C4LD mobilized in the absence of an opening in the political opportunity structure at the provincial level (Horak 1998, 21). Yet the prevailing closed and hostile climate did not deter local leaders in Toronto from pursuing greater empowerment for the city after amalgamation. In the absence of political opportunities at the provincial level, local leaders turned their attention to building local capacity and local support for greater municipal autonomy as well as to seeking political opportunities at the federal level. Their strategies became 'polyscalar,' showing little regard for the constitutional/jurisdictional status quo as reflected in the constitutional doctrine that municipalities are 'creatures of provinces' – a doctrine that, as Warren Magnusson (2005) argues, portrays municipal autonomy in an unnecessarily limited way and that forbids federal–municipal relationships.

Mobilizing support for a city charter became one of the most important strategies at the provincial scale. It is always difficult to trace the precise origins of an idea, but some local leaders identify the origins of the city charter idea to a conference held in October 1997. Alan Broadbent had organized the event, called Ideas That Matter, to discuss the work of Jane Jacobs. This event created a great deal of interest in cities. Then in spring 1999, Broadbent convened a group of local elites to discuss the place of cities in Canada and commissioned papers on issues of importance to cities. The meeting was held at the Royal Alexandra Theatre in Toronto – a 'donation'[11] made by Broadbent's friend and well-known Toronto businessman David Mirvish – to develop a Toronto and cities agenda (Broadbent 2003, 1). The outcome of the meeting was the publication of a series of articles in a book titled *Toronto: Considering Self-Government* (2000).

After the meeting, Broadbent invited participants who wanted to continue the discussion into his boardroom. According to Broadbent, about twenty-five people attended. Participants included Jane Jacobs, former mayors (Crombie, Sewell, and Hall), journalists (Michael Valpy, Colin Vaughan, and Richard Gwyn), urban scholars (Patricia McCarney, Meric Gertler, Carl Amrhein, and Enid Slack) a former Ontario deputy minister (Don Stevenson), and a former Toronto councillor (Richard Gilbert). This meeting produced the Greater Toronto Area Charter (2001), modelled on city charters adopted by the European Union and the Federation of Canadian Municipalities. Article Two of this charter lists responsibilities that its drafters believe should be transferred to the region; they include immigrant and refugee settlement (Broadbent Group 2005, 40). As Broadbent recalls: 'It was not very difficult to come up with these powers; they are roughly the powers of a province, in the Canadian context.' In his view, the greater challenge was political – or 'what to do with it' (Broadbent 2003).

The drafters then brought the charter to a committee meeting of GTA mayors and regional chairs. That committee endorsed the charter. The challenge now became a political one. We see a hint of radicalism in Toronto's political culture in Broadbent's recollection of ideas for building political support for urban autonomy: 'Still, while we had been able to put some principles and ideas on the table, nothing much had changed. So we began to wonder what we could do next. Jane [Jacobs] and I had thought from the beginning that ultimately these matters would come down to politics. We had thought about various ways to excite the politics around cities. Colin Vaughan, the late CITY-TV journalist, wanted some dramatic civil disobedience: he kept mentioning the Boston Tea Party. Good television, I suppose, and TV did miss the original' (ibid.).

The solution arrived at was to convene the big-city mayors across Canada to develop a political strategy to influence the federal government. This political strategy was inspired by the advice of Privy Council Office (PCO) staff, who told Jacobs in a meeting that 'the federal government might pay a lot more attention to these [the urban agenda] issues if there seemed to be some political imperative behind them' (ibid.). Thus, the charter's drafters invited the then mayors of Vancouver (Philip Owen), Toronto (Mel Lastman), Montreal (Pierre Bourque), Winnipeg (Glen Murray), and Calgary (Al Duerr) to a meeting in Winnipeg in May 2001 (Broadbent 2008, 10). They called this group the 'C5' or 'Charter 5.'

Another important element of their strategy was to include important leaders in civil society. Each city was to be represented by its mayor and by prominent organizations in civil society representing a variety of sectors, including the social sector, the business sector, and labour. According to Broadbent (2003), 'over time, these representatives have tended to include the representatives of the United Way, as the proxy for the social sector, and the Board of Trade or Chamber of Commerce, as the business proxy, and either heads of regional labour councils or other recognized leaders.' The civil-society participants in the coalition called themselves 'C5 Civil' (ibid.). The C5 Mayors and C5 Civil met for the first time in Winnipeg in May 2001 (ibid.) and then again in

Vancouver in January 2002 and in Montreal in June 2002 (Broadbent 2008, 11). However, after those meetings it would be difficult to bring the mayors and civil society together. Mel Lastman cancelled a meeting that was to be held in Toronto in early 2003 (Broadbent 2003, 3). According to Broadbent, the C5 may have been perceived as a threat by some mayors, because 'its agenda risked their supplicant relations with senior governments [and their] allegiance to the Federation of Canadian Municipalities which has been the traditional vehicle for the city voice' (ibid., 3). C5 Civil met twice in Toronto in 2003 before the short-lived coalition faded (Broadbent 2008).

A full account of the cross-provincial political coalitions that local leaders developed to push the urban agenda onto the federal agenda is beyond the scope of this study. Let it be mentioned, though, that shortly after their initial meeting, a meeting of the C5 Civil, the C5 Mayors, and the Federation of Canadian Municipalities' Big Cities Caucus was held. Paul Martin, who would later become prime minister, was invited to speak (Broadbent 2003).

A publication of The Broadbent Group summarizes the origins of what would become the New Deal for Cities movement: '[Jane] Jacobs, together with businessman and philanthropist Alan Broadbent, initiated a process to bring together five of Canada's largest cities to discuss their mutual needs for greater power and autonomy. The "C5" Mayors began meeting, joined by leaders from the business, labour and civil society from each city, to discuss the unique needs of Canada's largest and most economically vibrant urban regions. These events, together with the sustaining efforts of the Federation of Canadian Municipalities, created the momentum for what has become known as "A New Deal for Cities"' (The Broadbent Group 2005).

Broadbent acknowledges the role played by other agents in promoting ideas of urban autonomy nationally. These others include boards of trade (especially in Calgary and Toronto), the Toronto United Way, the Conference Board of Canada (under Anne Golden), the Winnipeg Branch of the Canadian Union of Public Employees (under Paul Moist), the Canada West Foundation under Roger Gibbins, and the TD Bank (Don Drummond and Derek Burleton worked on the issue), as well as the TCSA under the chairmanship of David Pecaut (Broadbent 2008, 12).

Mayor Lastman had cancelled the proposed C5 meeting in 2003. Even so, under his leadership the City of Toronto began pressing the federal and provincial governments for a New Deal for the City of Toronto. In 2000, Toronto passed a resolution calling for a new relationship with the Province of Ontario. In 2001 the city launched its website to promote urban autonomy – the Canada's Cities campaign – and began strengthening and consolidating its relations with civil society in order to achieve a new relationship with upper levels of government. For instance, in 2002 the city facilitated the development of a powerful element within Toronto's urban empowerment coalition – the TCSA. According to David Crombie, a former Toronto mayor and original summit co-chair, the TCSA emerged as a result of a leadership vacuum at upper levels of government and a confluence of interests and goals between Mayor Lastman and prominent local leaders in civil society. Lastman and several local leaders viewed this summit as an opportunity to take on the province and the federal government; but the coalition also appealed to those who simply wanted to tackle important issues facing the City of Toronto (Crombie 2004, interview). In other words, the coalition appealed to local leaders who wanted to pool local resources to build local capacity as well as to those who wanted to address city concerns through new relationships with upper levels of government. The alliance began in Toronto and has since become a regional coalition.

A central ambiguity in the New Deal for Toronto movement concerns the scale at which increased local autonomy should be granted. For instance, this is a central theme in a document prepared by New Deal advocates titled *Towards a New City of Toronto Act* (Broadbent Group 2005). In *The Limits of Boundaries* (2008), Andrew Sancton uses Toronto's urban autonomy movement as a case study of how the difficulties associated with drawing boundaries of political units undermine the case for city-state status for cities.

In the GTA there is a gap in regional governing institutions.[12] This gap in formal institutional mechanisms at the local level[13] has left room for the development of flexible governance arrangements in the region.

Over time, the urban empowerment coalition in Toronto expanded dramatically. Royson James, a well-known *Toronto Star* columnist on urban issues, noted in an article on 15 June 2005, that Toronto Act Now[14] and the University of Toronto[15] had joined the 'ongoing advocacy [efforts] of the Toronto Board of Trade and the TCSA ... One gets the idea that there is unanimity on the issue.' In his view, of the forty-four city councillors on Toronto Council, 'at least 40 believe in "the cause"' (James 2005). The framework of a New Deal for Cities reflected a broad intersectoral agreement on the solution to many of Toronto's current policy challenges – including immigrant settlement challenges.

The rise of the New Deal for Cities movement in Toronto coincided with the availability of new institutional resources. One unintended consequence of Toronto's amalgamation was that it created a powerful new political unit that could more effectively challenge provincial power. After all, 'with a population of 2.5 million people, Toronto is larger than six provinces; with a budget of $7 billion, Toronto also spends more than those six provinces' (Slack 2005, 1). Furthermore, more citizens directly elect the Mayor of Toronto than any other political leader in Canada. This lends an important political resource to Toronto's mayor – democratic legitimacy.

By increasing the fiscal, territorial, and demographic significance of the new City of Toronto, amalgamation also strengthened governance relationships in the city. Given its size and scope, the new city attracts the attention of powerful organizations in Canada to a greater extent than in the past. Toronto councillor Brian Ashton explains:

> With amalgamation, you created a political unit that had the heft and the size and the issues to establish a new platform. A lot of organizations, associations, that would never have stood on this floor to come and lobby (and I say that in a positive way) council members about issues, suddenly realized 'Oh, my God, we've got this big level of government, we've got a huge purchasing power, it's the media capital of the country,' and certain by-laws that they're capable of passing, even the narrowest of regime responsibilities that we can have, have a significant impact on the rest of the country … So suddenly even national associations are coming back here to say that we've got to have some say in local by-laws. This also makes the local population of stakeholders and interest groups realize that let's come together because we have a megaphone that allows us to advocate our issues on the national scene. So there's a huge political dynamic shift taking place. (Ashton 2004, interview)

The new 'platform' for local organizations that the amalgamated city provided local leaders was coupled with a general retrenchment in provincial government spending and a withdrawal from policy areas related to immigrant settlement and multiculturalism policy. Despite the increasing numbers of immigrants arriving in Toronto, the Harris government was unable to secure a federal–provincial agreement on settlement funding to address the fiscal gap between the numbers of immigrants the province receives and the federal settlement dollars flowing into the province. Ashton describes the lack of leadership from the province as well as the tri-level nature of the political dynamics:

> In a strange way, the province shunned a lot of the responsibilities that should have remained if not gravitated to the provincial level. Particularly when it comes to immigration, I think they were more or less saying that that is a federal issue. Oh, wait a minute, nobody asked them, well, if it's a federal issue, and the feds don't do something, then the city's going to be left as a last resort. Of course, along comes amalgamation, the city gets left as a last resort, you get a huge advocacy opportunity, you get a political paradigm shift starting to happen. So, in a fashion, the province under the Harris government started to move in a direction that made it redundant, unnecessary, merely a banker. (Ashton 2004, interview)

The municipal autonomy debate in Toronto is complex, as are its cross-provincial (or national) dimensions. The urban autonomy movement has a 'multitude of origins' (Keil and Young 2003, 89). What is most important to understand here is that downloading and amalgamation combined to change patterns of mobilization in Toronto. The broad elite consensus among local leaders concerning the 'solution' to what John Honderich described as Toronto's profound 'urban malaise' has been striking. These new forms of political mobilization developed in the context of an antagonistic provincial political opportunity structure. Thus, local leaders' strategies became polyscalar as they turned their efforts to building local and regional alliances and lobbying the federal government. They challenged the institutional and constitutional norms of Canadian federalism. Toronto's regime thus became less concerned with the jurisdictional status quo than with ensuring that the city's public-policy challenges were addressed.

Immigrant settlement concerns have been linked to the New Deal consensus, giving momentum to local capacity building in this area in Toronto. In fact, as early as September 2000, the Maytree Foundation convened a conference to discuss the implications of a Greater Toronto Charter for the immigrant settlement sector. This meeting, styled Forum Towards a Greater Toronto Charter: Implications for Immigrant Settlement, was held at the Metro Central YMCA. The Maytree Foundation has since commissioned papers on how greater autonomy for the city might affect the immigrant settlement sector (See Simich 2000; McIsaac 2003). These papers tend to support a greater role for the city in immigrant settlement. The Toronto Region Immigrant Employment

Council (TRIEC) is the best example of how tying municipal responsiveness to immigrants and ethnocultural minorities to this broader
New Deal coalition has increased the city's power to address some of
the primary concerns of immigrants in Toronto.

Toronto's territorial strategies with respect to immigrant settlement
seem to have influenced Vancouver's approach. In May 2005 (after interviews were conducted in Greater Vancouver) former mayor Larry
Campbell (2002–5) established a working group on immigration in
Vancouver as part of a strategy of the 'Charter 5 (C5)' coalition of cities
to negotiate new relationships with upper levels of government in immigration policy (City of Vancouver 2005, 3). At the time the interviews
were conducted in Greater Vancouver, local leaders tended to define
the issue of municipal responsiveness to immigrants and ethnocultural
minorities as responding to 'diversity, not immigration,' because immigration was a federal and provincial jurisdiction. Framing the issue as
an 'immigration issue' is a territorial strategy to empower municipalities; it is also part of a larger 'movement' to obtain more resources from
upper levels of government. However, unlike in Toronto, in Vancouver
such territorial strategies do not seem to percolate up from 'the ground'
and do not seem to dominate the agenda, since the provincial and federal governments have been relatively responsive to the sector there.

Immigrant Settlement and the New Deal for Cities Movement:
The Emergence of TRIEC

Multiculturalism policies are part of a multifaceted urban agenda within the City of Toronto's urban regime. The TCSA is a key node in the
regime and within its municipal autonomy movement. This alliance
has established several policy priorities, one of which is becoming a
centre of excellence in integrating immigrants.[16] To this end the alliance established the Toronto Region Immigrant Employment Council
(TRIEC) to help deal with one of the most important challenges facing
newcomers – access to employment. Participation in this local initiative is highly intersectoral. TRIEC's membership includes assessment-
service providers, community organizations, employers, foundations,
labour unions, occupational regulatory bodies, and post-secondary
institutions, in addition to representatives of all levels of government –
federal, provincial, and municipal.[17] The Maytree Foundation, Citizenship and Immigration Canada (CIC), Canadian Heritage, and Human

Resources and Skills Development Canada all provide operating funds to TRIEC.

Local policy networks interested in immigrant employment issues have coalesced in this alliance, creating increased capacity in immigrant employment at the city and regional levels. TRIEC has launched a number of its own programs, including a mentorship program whereby immigrants are placed with private-sector and government organizations to gain Canadian experience in their field of expertise. By 2007, TRIEC had placed more than 2,600 mentees in partner organizations; 80 per cent of these people are now employed, with 85 per cent of these employed in their field of choice (TRIEC 2007, 9). TRIEC partners with other organizations to provide resources to both immigrants and employers to facilitate the integration of skilled immigrants into the Toronto workforce. TRIEC is growing significantly. In 2006 it spent just over $1.3 million on its activities. By 2007 this figure was close to $2.3 million (ibid., 21).

Municipal governance arrangements seem to affect the likelihood and nature of cooperative efforts at the regional level. TRIEC was launched in Toronto, which is the only municipality that has been responsive to the concerns and preferences of immigrants and ethnocultural minorities in the GTA sample and whose official motto is 'Diversity Our Strength.' Local leaders from Toronto are overrepresented in TCSA and TRIEC because of Toronto's high level of community capacity – including in immigration and settlement. However, the effort is meant to be regional.

In 2004 the chairs of regional governments in the GTA that have high levels of diversity (Peel and York regions), as well as a representative of one municipality within each region, were asked to participate in TRIEC. Mississauga was the clear choice in Peel, and Markham in York. Tellingly, both regional chairs and Mayor Cousens of Markham accepted the invitation to participate, but Mayor McCallion of Mississauga declined. According to a local leader close to the process, McCallion refused to participate until the federal government reimbursed Peel Region for the costs of immigration incurred by municipalities owing to sponsorship breakdowns (community leader 2004, interview). According to McCallion, she did not participate in TRIEC because its mandate was too limited (McCallion 2004, interview). Mayor Susan Fennel of Brampton accepted the invitation to participate in McCallion's place. TRIEC's 2007 annual report listed Mayor Susan Fennel of Brampton,

Mayor David Miller of Toronto, Bill Fisch, the Regional Chair and CEO of York Region, Emil Kolb, Regional Chair of Peel, and Shirley Hoy, the CAO of the City of Toronto, as the municipal partners (TRIEC 2007, 19).

British Columbia: The Absence of Mobilization for Municipal Autonomy

In B.C. an urban autonomy movement or coalition is absent (Murray 2004, slide 18). As we saw above, some downloading to municipalities has occurred in B.C. but this has not been coupled with a large-scale amalgamation of its oldest city (Vancouver) with the surrounding suburban municipalities. Furthermore, B.C. did not engage in a disentanglement exercise as Ontario had during the Harris years. Municipalities and municipal communities in B.C. did not experience the same level of stress as municipalities in Ontario under the Harris and Eves governments (Sancton 2000; Murray 2004; MacMillan 2006).

Also, municipal regional-governance institutions have been relatively stable in B.C. The GVRD, established in 1965, took steps in 1996 to 'promote multiculturalism in Greater Vancouver' through its Livable Region Strategic Plan (Edgington and Hutton 2002, 10). However, the multiculturalism goals of this regional plan do not seem to have been implemented.

According to Verna Semotuk, a senior planner with the GVRD's Policy and Planning Department, the GVRD does not play a role in multiculturalism and immigration. There are no directions from the GVRD board in these policy fields (Semotuk 2005, interview). Nevertheless, the GVRD board has sometimes raised immigration issues in discussions with upper levels of government (ibid.). Priority areas include increased funding for settlement services, credential recognition, and establishing a mechanism whereby several regional districts could collaborate to disperse immigrants (ibid.). The latter priority is especially interesting. Given the social differences among the twenty-one municipal governments in the GVRD, the policy challenge has been framed as a question of 'dispersal.'

The GVRD does not play an ongoing role in coordinating settlement services or in encouraging multiculturalism policy development at the local level. Vancouver councillor David Cadman, who sat on five GVRD committees during the municipal term before his interview, remarked: 'I can count on one hand the number of times that we've had an immigration theme discussed at the regional level' (Cadman 2004, interview). He offered some reasons for this omission, including the fact that directors[18] of the GVRD tend to feel that immigration is out-side their jurisdiction and do not want to assume the costs of programs that are the responsibility of upper levels of government. As he puts it: 'But I've got to say in all honesty, for many directors there's not a lot of enthusiasm in getting into that area, because it's feeling like, "Well, hang on, we're moving into an area that's really not our jurisdiction and the extent to which we fill that vacuum will mean that we'll be pay-ing for that." And really, that should be the senior levels of government that are doing it and aren't' (ibid.).

Furthermore, owing to their limited resources, municipalities in Greater Vancouver prefer to focus on advocacy surrounding policy areas for which they have a clear mandate (ibid.). Thus the federally focused New Deal for municipalities in Greater Vancouver is about 'getting the federal and provincial governments on board around in-frastructure issues' (ibid.). It seems that the institutions of the GVRD (now Metro Vancouver) might be impeding regional coordination on immigrant-related issues because they have formally removed this is-sue from the regional agenda. This might be because of the diversity of municipal governments that are governed by the district, many of which are not immigrant magnets, unlike the municipalities in our sample.[19] Other policy issues for which the Regional District has a clear mandate take precedence.

But the main reason why new governance arrangements in Greater Vancouver have failed is that the provincial–municipal relationship is a strong. Local leaders can turn to the province for support in many of their capacity-building initiatives. For instance, as a Laurier Institution report describes (and as some interviewees mentioned), the province has launched a program called Employment Access for Skilled Immi-grants (EASI) that is similar to the TRIEC initiative (Laurier Institution 2005, 10). However, this initiative is provincial and does not focus on the Greater Vancouver region specifically.

The Province of British Columbia supports the goals of the City of Vancouver's proactive 'growth machine.' As Vancouver's mayor in the mid-1980s, Mike Harcourt actively cultivated connections with Asia (Mitchell 2004, 57). Provincial politicians began courting investment from Hong Kong in the early 1980s (ibid., 56). When he became premier in 1991, Harcourt returned to Hong Kong to address fears that a more left-leaning NDP government would be unfriendly to investors (ibid., 57). Furthermore, the province strengthened its multiculturalism policy efforts in the 1990s.

The positive relationship between the City of Vancouver and the province is evident in how the position of mayor of Vancouver has become a stepping stone to the premiership. Gordon Campbell, the current premier, was a mayor of Vancouver in the 1990s. In B.C. the positive relationship between the province and municipalities, coupled with provincial support for the city's growth agenda, has meant that local leaders have not mobilized around the issue of municipal autonomy.

Urban Regime 'Spillover': From Urban to Polyscalar Regimes

The new governance arrangements that have emerged in the GTA and the activities of the C5 and C5 Civil are examples of what urban scholar Julie-Anne Boudreau calls 'polyscalar' social mobilization (Boudreau 2006). Changes in the intergovernmental system created incentives for the mobilization of local networks in Toronto and expanded the scope of participation in Toronto's regime. The political mobilization in response to changes in the national infrastructure in the late 1990s was so powerful that it spilled over into regional governance regimes and into what one might call a 'polyscalar regime.' The Toronto regime's coalition-building activities and efforts to lobby upper levels of government produced positive externalities in the region. These efforts have contributed to capacity building in immigrant integration in the region. These political developments provide the context for understanding the dynamic nature of Toronto's regime as well as for policy change in immigrant settlement and multiculturalism policy at the municipal level in Toronto.

'Polyscalar' political coalitions have some of the characteristics of urban regimes in Stone's conception. According to Stone (1989), informal urban regime relationships are driven by two needs: '(1) *institutional scope* (that is, the need to encompass a wide enough scope of institutions to mobilize the resources required to make and implement governing decisions) and (2) *cooperation* (that is, the need to promote enough cooperation and coordination for the diverse participants to reach decisions and sustain action in support of those decisions)' (1989, 9; emphasis added).

These needs arise owing to a municipal government's limited resources and the fragmentation of power in local communities. The polyscalar dimension of Toronto's urban regime addresses the *fragmentation* of the municipal system in Canada as well as the absence of regional institutions in the GTA. The Federation of Canadian Municipalities (FCM) represents Canadian municipalities collectively, but because its membership is so diverse, it does not provide targeted representation for Canada's largest cities. Thus locally based leaders in urban centres have developed cross-provincial coalitions in response to the inability of formal institutions to address their policy concerns. The FCM's Big City Mayors Caucus partly addresses this gap. Indeed, this caucus has been an important advocate for municipal empowerment. Nevertheless, with twenty-two members, it is unable to represent some of the specific needs of Canada's largest centres (Broadbent 2008, 9). Furthermore, the FCM represents only municipal governments. Local leaders in Toronto and in other large Canadian cities have recognized that capacity building for a New Deal requires regime relationships that include civil-society elites. In order to increase municipal policy capacity by pressuring upper levels of government to pool resources more evenly with them, local leaders have expanded political institutions so that they include civil-society organizations. These coalitions are polyscalar insofar as they address gaps in formal institutions at a variety of scales – municipal, regional, cross-provincial, and multilevel.

Furthermore, as with urban regimes, local leaders are building these coalitions specifically to address the policy challenges facing Canada's urban centres – that is, to bring about what Clarence Stone (1989) calls 'enacted change.' Jane Jacobs, Alan Broadbent, and other local leaders in Toronto deliberately created coalitions that included leaders of civil society with the goal of changing the intergovernmental system. Locally based urban-regime relationships that bridge the public and private sectors became an important resource in the efforts of the C5 mayors to pressure upper levels of government to respond to their concerns. The cross-provincial alliance included the C5 Mayors and the C5 Civil.

Urban regimes are also long-lasting. In this regard, the literature is unclear on how long-lasting an urban coalition must be to constitute a 'regime.' In their review of the urban regime literature, Mossberger and Stoker (2001) describe regime relationships as 'relatively stable arrangements that can span a number of administrations' (813) and as a 'longstanding pattern of cooperation rather than a temporary coalition' (829). They also argue that 'on the issue of stability ... short-term collaboration may be described as an emerging regime or a failed regime, depending on the context' (830). Similarly, Christopher Leo (2003) argues that 'the necessary degree of dominance and stability [for a local coalition] to be termed a regime is an empirical one, and a judgment call as well, since there is and probably can be no precise determination of how much dominance and stability is required in order to justify the "regime" label' (2003, 346). The question of stability (and dominance) is therefore subject to interpretation. That said, in order to constitute a regime, the coalition must include the business community, must contribute to the city's capacity to govern, and must include policy agendas that can be traced to the composition of the urban coalition (Mossberger and Stoker 2001, 829). Regional-governance arrangements such as TRIEC and other TCSA initiatives continue in Toronto. However, the C5 Mayors and C5 Civil were short-lived (Broadbent 2008, 11). As Broadbent noted above, this may be because informal alliances compete with an organization that has already been established to serve this purpose – the Big City Mayors Caucus. Existing institutions and organizations can select certain group 'out.'

Local leaders seeking increased urban autonomy for the City of Toronto seem to be employing several political strategies, many of which are related to urban regime building. In fact, building urban regimes at the local level itself constitutes one of the central strategies of the New Deal for Cities movement. The Toronto regime seems to be employing five related strategies:

1 Encouraging municipalities to act like governments rather than as wards of provinces.
2 Building high-powered coalitions of municipal leaders and elites in civil society.
3 Educating and engaging the public in the New Deal debate.
4 Using diverse strategies in efforts to lobby upper levels of government.
5 Addressing unfunded municipal mandates proactively.

Collectively, these strategies reflect the resources and participants in the Toronto regime. The first was inspired in part by a speech that Jane Jacobs made at the first C5 meeting in which she urged the five mayors to break their 'learned dependency' on upper levels of government and begin acting like true government leaders. This strategy involves insisting on a government-to-government relationship between the City of Toronto and upper levels of government (Abrahams 2004, interview). For instance, the City of Toronto used this strategy when it withdrew from the Association of Ontario Municipalities (AMO) during negotiations with the provincial and federal governments over the distribution of the federal Gas Tax Transfer, a new municipal transfer that was introduced by Ottawa during the Martin government.

The second strategy involves creating urban regime relationships and expanding them to include a variety of scales to form polyscalar regimes. The third is possible because of the Toronto regime's diverse and intersectoral participation. For instance, representatives of the Toronto Board of Trade handed out leaflets in subway stations in Toronto that informed residents of the fiscal gap between the taxes Torontonians pay to upper levels of government and the services they receive. Fourth, public education campaigns are important. All of the coalitions described above – including the TCSA – are engaged in such campaigns. The City of Toronto's Canada's Cities Campaign website is also designed to educate the public ('Canada's Cities: Unleash Our Potential').

The fifth strategy involves municipal governments developing local subcoalitions or 'subregimes' to pool capacity to achieve locally significant public policy goals outside their formal mandates. Julia Koschinsky and Todd Swanstrom (2001) have coined the term 'subregime' to describe coalitions of policy subsystems at the city level in housing and community development. However, they do not use the regime literature in the same way as most urban regime theorists. In particular, they do not view urban regimes as unified across issues, preferring to apply Norton Long's concept (1968) of 'ecology of games' when describing urban policy subsystems. Furthermore, they argue that the relationship between a subregime and the overall regime – whether the former is independent of the latter or subordinate to it – is an empirical question (2001, 116). In Toronto, such alliances or subregimes exist in several areas of priority. TRIEC is an important example of a 'subregime' in immigrant employment. Nevertheless, unlike some 'subregimes' that Koschinsky and Swanstrom describe in housing policy, this initiative is strongly integrated with the overall citywide regime. It is a part of a rescaling process that ties immigration and economic development together into a new kind of immigration-driven 'growth machine' (Molotch and Logan 1987) and an urban autonomy movement.

In *A New City Agenda* (2004), John Sewell[20] recommends this strategy to local leaders. His book is a sort of manifesto for the New Deal for Cities agenda, one that recommends steps that cities should take in a number of policy areas, including immigrant settlement. Specifically, he recommends that municipal leaders launch new and innovative programs and policies and ask for money from upper levels of government after the fact. He uses Toronto's innovation in affordable housing policy in 1945, which resulted in the federal National Housing Act (1949), as an example of this strategy. In Sewell's words:

> Cities must adopt a new strategy. They must define very clearly the pro-grams they know they are *capable of delivering* and that have popular support, and then set to work delivering them. The key is to do enough groundwork at the city level so the *public understands the need for programs and supports the city politicians in their push to get authority and finances for them* ... This book advocates that Toronto – and other cities – begin to develop and implement specific programs because just talking generally about the need for money and power is not a strategy. Cities must ask for particular pieces of legislation that allow them to carry out programs they identify as their mandate, and they must be precise about the monies needed. (2004, 91; emphasis added)

Doing the 'groundwork' to establish the conditions for greater urban autonomy involves developing productive urban coalitions. This is precisely the strategy that has been employed in the immigrant settlement sector with the development of TRIEC. Caroline Andrew (2001) also recommends that local leaders develop governance arrangements as a strategy to become more effective and empowered within the intergovernmental system (2001, 108). As she concludes her article, which makes the case for the importance of cities and municipalities: 'We should not ignore the cities, but this will happen only after they demonstrate to us and to the other levels of government that we cannot ignore them' (ibid., 110).

TRIEC: A Regional and Multilevel Subregime in Immigrant Settlement Policy

Urban scholarship in the late 1990s (Leo 1998; Clarke 1999) uncovered regional regimes in American urban areas (Mossberger and Stoker 2001). For instance, Christopher Leo (1998) uncovered a growth containment regime in Portland, Oregon, that was regional in scope. Similarly, TRIEC constitutes a regional subregime that is highly integrated with the City of Toronto's citywide regime. This subregime has multilevel dimensions, given that civil servants at all three levels of government participate in its working groups and the federal government now funds some of its operating costs. TRIEC also differs from the growth containment regime in Portland insofar as its cooperation is not sustained by formal, public institutions at the regional level. Rather, TRIEC developed from the bottom up. Also, it covers the entire GTA, and municipal governments and civil-society leaders participate on a voluntary basis. TRIEC's boundaries are flexible. As such, the informal governance arrangement avoids the difficult task of defining the dynamic city-region's boundaries in a formal way – a central impediment to the urban autonomy project in 'Toronto' in Andrew Sancton's (2008) view.

TRIEC's purpose is to create policy capacity in the area of immigrant integration into the economy through public–private collaboration. It arose out of a need to bring together a diverse set of actors to deal with barriers to immigrant integration into the labour market. Thus, according to urban regime theory (Stone 1989, 6), it arose out of incentives for local leaders to extend the 'institutional scope' of municipal institutions and for 'cooperation' as a result of the fragmentation of interests that affect or have a stake in immigrant employment. This initiative coordinates the resources that must be brought to bear to address the challenge effectively.

The urban regime concept also contributes to our understanding of how TRIEC's informal governance arrangements are maintained. Stone (1989) explains how regimes are developed and maintained by their ability to provide 'selective incentives' to their partners. According to regime theory, there is a systemic bias towards the preferences of the business community, because of uneven access to selective material incentives (which are generally considered most conducive to the maintenance of collective action). Immigrant employment was chosen as the first concrete policy step in the TCSA's goal of achieving excellence in immigrant settlement because it was one on which a broad cross-sector alliance – including the business community – could agree. However, employment is not a central priority only of the business community. As community leader Amanuel Melles observes, employment cuts across many communities and is an issue on which a multicultural population can agree (Melles 2003, interview). Similarly, Debbie Douglas, the executive director of OCASI, mentioned that a broad consensus exists that labour market integration is central to immigrant integration and that this unites TRIEC's diverse participants. Though she recognizes that TRIEC focuses on a particular type of labour market integration (namely, the integration of highly skilled immigrants), given the community consensus on this issue and its importance to successful immigrant settlement, it is important for OCASI to participate in this initiative (Douglas 2003, interview).

More broadly, local leaders in multiple sectors acknowledge that they share a common and interdependent economic fate. The business leaders who participate in TRIEC recognize that the business community has a stake in immigrant incorporation into Toronto's economy. As Dominic D'Alessandro noted in a letter to Prime Minister Paul Martin: 'The Conference Board of Canada calculates that not recognizing immigrants' learning and credentials costs our economy somewhere between $3-billion and $5-billion annually. As a businessman, a private citizen and an immigrant, I see this as a critical issue both for maximizing the economic potential of Canada and for successful nation-building. This is why I am chairing the Toronto Region Immigrant Employment Council' (D'Alessandro 2004).

As urban regime theory implies, the policy preferences of various sectors cannot be assumed. Rather, policy outputs are negotiated within the regime and elites' preferences are shaped by their interactions with other leaders. In Toronto, as in American cities, the systemic bias towards the business community's preferences is strong, but dismissing local politics as only minor variations on growth politics would be misleading. As Stone (1989) observed with respect to the business community in Atlanta: 'Participation in the governing task and the quest for allies ... had an effect on the business elite, broadening its understanding of what constitutes a favorable economic climate' (1989, 195).

In Toronto, regime participants seem to understand the interdependence of economic-growth objectives and multiculturalism policy goals. Local leaders consider the successful integration of immigrants to be one key to a favourable economic climate. Thus, public-education campaigns have become an important strategy in the regime's quest for allies. The importance of politics to urban regime development is clear when one recognizes how many social issues can be framed as economic-development issues. The business case for immigration has made multiculturalism initiatives a priority within Toronto's regime.

As urban regime theory would predict, TRIEC is supported by relationships of the type emphasized in Stone's earlier work. Business supports the council because it would like to see the region and its business community benefit from highly skilled immigrant labour. Immigrant organizations participate because the programs provide immigrants with mentorship opportunities and, ultimately, jobs. The regional regime is also maintained through networks at the municipal level, with Toronto's network playing an especially strong role in this respect.

Clarence Stone's (2001) more recent work draws on the literature dealing with problem definition and issue framing to explain regime decline in Atlanta. He invites urban scholars 'to consider how issue concerns come to be specified as purposes, and how they are *linked*, *enlarged*, and *refined* for action' (2001, 20; emphasis added). Toronto's regional regime in immigrant employment is linked to an *enlarged* coalition fighting for a New Deal for the city. Immigrant integration into Toronto's economy and the continued attraction and retention of immigrants are *linked* to the city's growth objectives. The goal of immigrant integration has been *refined* to focus on immigrant employment, an issue on which there is broad intersectoral and intercommunity consensus. A focus on immigrant employment has facilitated collective action in Toronto's highly diverse, 'multiracial' context.

The New Deal frame also serves a regime maintenance function. Broadly speaking, it serves as a rallying point for local leaders across the GTA. Toronto's regime illustrates the power of the 'gravitational pull' of regime coalitions that Stone (1989) describes in *Regime Politics*:

> As the circle of cooperating allies grows, its effectiveness becomes cumulatively greater. The governing coalition has a kind of gravitational pull; as its own weight increases, its capacity to attract other civic entities increases. As the network of civic cooperation makes its presence felt, others realize that cooperation pays and noncooperation does not. That's what 'go along to get along' means, and it constitutes an effective form of discipline based on the selective-incentive principle. So long as the network of cooperators is large enough in its own right and has no rival network to serve as an alternative, there are significant gains to be made by going along and opportunity costs to be paid for opposition. (1989, 193)

The level of consensus on the goal of achieving a New Deal for Toronto is high, and local leaders have an incentive to support this political project. The broader purpose of the New Deal coalition has contributed to the weight behind calls for new intergovernmental relationships in immigration policy. It has also created an incentive for the immigrant settlement sector to accept a focus on immigrant employment rather than other issues such as affordable housing or poverty – to 'go along to get along.'

Changing the National and Provincial Infrastructures: The Influence of the Toronto Regime

Policy developments in Ontario's municipal system since the Liberals under Dalton McGuinty were elected and at the federal level under former prime minister Paul Martin (2003–6) suggest that regime development at the local level is not necessarily a 'constitutional cul-de-sac,' as David Crombie said it might be (Crombie 2003, interview). Leaders in Toronto's regime have played a significant role in federal and provincial responsiveness to both Toronto's urban agenda and the urban agenda in Canada more generally.

This policy movement at the federal level began in 2003, when Paul Martin's Liberal government (2003–6) created a Cities Secretariat within the Privy Council Office and appointed John Godfrey as Parliamentary Secretary on the New Deal file. The Martin government's major initiatives in 2004 were a 100 per cent rebate for municipalities on the Goods and Services Tax and the appointment of John Godfrey as Minister of State for Infrastructure and Communities. In its 2005 budget the government committed itself to providing municipalities with $5 billion through the Gas Tax Transfer (GTT) over five years (2005 to 2010). The federal government signed gas tax agreements with all provinces in Canada. Toronto was actually included as a partner in the Canada–Ontario agreement.

The politics and policy outputs surrounding the GTT reflect the influence of Toronto's regime. The federal government announced that this money was to be allocated to municipalities – with the provinces as intermediaries – on a per capita basis for municipal projects that encourage environmental sustainability.[21] This way of distributing the funds places large urban centres at a disadvantage.[22] In recognition of the biases of the proposed allocation formula, the federal government decided to transfer an additional $310 million to municipalities, earmarked for municipal transit. This money would be transferred according to a formula preferred by leaders in Toronto and Canada's other major urban centres – the 'ridership formula,' which acknowledges that residents outside central cities benefit from public transit systems within central cities. For instance, residents of Mississauga, Brampton, and Markham benefit from investments in public transit in Toronto. These policy developments are at least partly a result of advocacy on the part of Toronto's regime and the C5.

In Ontario, the politics surrounding the funding formulas for the GTT reflect changes in the Toronto regime's goals, which themselves reflect a new consensus that the city should be treated as an 'order of government' and not as a municipal 'creature.' The City of Toronto withdrew from the Association of Ontario Municipalities (AMO)[23] and insisted on negotiating the transfer on a government-to-government basis. The result was that Toronto became a partner in the federal government's agreement with Ontario (Canada, Ontario, The Association of Ontario Municipalities, The City of Toronto 2005).

In Ontario, the province was not involved in the allocation of the GTT. The AMO manages the distribution of funds and reporting requirements for all municipalities in Ontario except Toronto. The City of Toronto deals directly with the federal government. This development in fiscal relationships – and the accompanying political relationships – is unprecedented in Canada and illustrates the capacity of fiscal federalism to provide flexibility within Canada's constitutionally entrenched division of powers.

The policy effects of Toronto's regime are also evident in recent developments in Ontario's municipal system. In 2003, political leadership changed at all three levels with the election of a new mayor in Toronto, David Miller, who promised to advocate for a New Deal for his city; the election of a Liberal government under Dalton McGuinty in Ontario; and a change in leadership of the Liberal Party at the federal level, when Paul Martin took over as prime minister from Jean Chrétien. Local leaders viewed these political developments as the simultaneous opening of what John Kingdon (1995) calls 'policy windows' at all three levels of government. Philip Abrahams, the City of Toronto's Manager of Intergovernmental Relations, described this new political environment as an 'alignment of the stars' (Abrahams 2003, interview).

According to Kingdon (1995), ideas make it onto governmental agendas when three policy streams intersect: the policy problem stream, the policy solution stream, and the political stream. In Toronto before 2003, leaders in Toronto's urban regime identified many policy 'problems' that needed to be addressed. Their preferred solution to many of these – one of which was immigrant integration – became a New Deal for Toronto. Thus, with two streams tightly 'coupled,' regime entrepreneurs were seeking political opportunities. Changes in political leadership provided these opportunities.

Several important developments have occurred since 2003. In December 2005 the Ontario government introduced Bill 53, the Stronger City of Toronto for a Stronger Ontario Act (hereafter the Stronger City

Act). This bill passed third reading, was given Royal Assent on 12 June 2006, and came into effect in January 2007. This act establishes a more permissive legal framework for establishing by-laws in certain areas; it also delegates increased authority to the city in land-use planning, roads, housing, governance, integrity and accountability, and enforcement (e.g., of fines for contravening municipal by-laws). In addition, the act gives the city new taxation and fiscal authority. For instance, the city can now raise new excise taxes, including liquor and cigarette taxes, and it can now undertake tax increment financing (TIF)[24] to encourage development.

There is some debate over whether the act goes far enough in terms of empowering the City of Toronto because it does not give the City of Toronto authority to raise revenue through taxes that would result in a significant tax yield. Nevertheless, whereas the act did not give the City of Toronto the authority to raise significant new own-source revenues, it is path-breaking insofar as it explicitly recognizes the city's authority to negotiate and enter into agreements with the federal government. This new authority creates a framework for the city to play a policy-making role in areas of particular concern to it.

The act could also have important fiscal consequences. The City of Toronto could negotiate new fiscal transfers from the federal government. Donald Lidstone, a constitutional lawyer and expert in municipal law in Vancouver, describes the Stronger City Act as a 'constitutional milestone [that] will help cities in the rest of Canada in their quest for palpable recognition as an order of government under our constitutional regime' (Lidstone 2005).

The Stronger City Act could have significant implications for Toronto's role in immigrant settlement policy. On 14 December 2005, during a news conference with Ontario's premier and municipal affairs minister after the bill was introduced in the provincial legislature, Mayor David Miller noted that 'for the first time ever, a municipal government – the City of Toronto – will be allowed to negotiate agreements with other governments ... [For example,] as Canada's leading receptor of immigrants, the city will be able to deal directly with the federal government in preparation for the arrival of newcomers to this country' (Miller 2004). The new act recognized in provincial legislation what had already become political practice in Toronto's powerful urban regime. The City of Toronto is now dealing directly with the federal government on the GTT.

Of particular note is the Canada–Ontario Immigration Agreement, which was finalized on 21 November 2005. That agreement increases federal funding of immigrant settlement services in Ontario from about $800 per immigrant to about $3,400.[25] It is the first Canadian immigration agreement to establish a partnership with municipalities.[26] It recognizes the exceptional nature of Toronto[27] as an important immigrant-receiving centre; it also acknowledges the City of Toronto's capacity in immigrant settlement: 'The City of Toronto in particular has developed experience, expertise and community infrastructure to respond sensitively to the social and economic integration needs and potential of immigrants' (Article 5.3.1). Article 5.3.2 commits Canada and Ontario to signing a Memorandum of Understanding (MOU) with the City of Toronto with respect to new intergovernmental relationships in immigration policy. This MOU will 'be consistent with federal, provincial and Toronto commitments to a New Deal for Cities and Communities which involves a seat at the table for municipalities on national issues most important to them' (Article 5.3.3b). This agreement provides the foundation for a New Deal in immigration and settlement policy for the City of Toronto.

Since the signing of the Canada–Ontario Agreement, the province has launched several programs to facilitate immigrants' access to the labour market. These programs reflect TRIEC's priorities. In June 2006, at TRIEC's hireimmigrants.ca seminar – part of that group's 'A World of Experience' week – Queen's Park announced that it would be introducing the Fair Access to Regulated Professions Act that same month. On 12 December 2006 the Fair Access to Regulated Professions Act, 2006, received Royal Assent. This act addresses barriers in thirty-four regulated professions in Ontario, including medicine, accountancy, law, and engineering. In addition, the province has established an internship program for foreign-trained professionals in ministries and Crown agencies – the first provincial program of its kind. (Participants in TRIEC had already launched such mentorship programs at the municipal level and in the private sector.)

On 23 January 2006 a Conservative minority government under Stephen Harper was elected at the federal level without a single elected seat in the urban cores of Canada's three largest cities – Toronto, Vancouver, and Montreal.[28] Harper introduced a 'new' model of federalism – 'open federalism,' which stresses federal respect for provincial jurisdiction. Some proponents of a federal urban agenda fear that the Harper government will ignore the needs of cities, because municipalities are a provincial responsibility. However, this need not be the case. It is possible for the federal government to develop an *urban* agenda without developing relationships with *municipalities* that bypass provinces. It can do so by adopting an 'urban lens' on national policy making, thereby addressing policy areas the consequences of which are primarily urban (Berdahl 2006).

Immigration policy is a good example of a concurrent federal–provincial jurisdiction the consequences of which are mainly urban. At this writing it seems that the Conservative government will continue to address the needs of Canada's immigrant-magnet cities. The Harper government has honoured the Canada–Ontario Immigration Agreement (Canadian Press 2006). The McGuinty and Harper governments seem to have made it a priority to facilitate the integration of immigrants into the economy by addressing barriers to the recognition of foreign credentials. This is an important priority for Toronto's governing regime as well.

Concluding Thoughts

This chapter has demonstrated the important influence of the intergovernmental context on local governance. What Sellers calls 'national infrastructures' affect the dynamics of urban coalitions or 'regimes.' In Toronto, broad changes in fiscal federalism that originated at the federal level intersected with the Ontario Conservative government's decision to disentangle services, download some of the province's fiscal burden onto municipalities, and amalgamate Metro Toronto. The intersection of these changes in the national infrastructure resulted in the mobilization and consolidation of a powerful and wide-ranging network of regime relationships in Toronto around a new policy frame – a New Deal for Toronto. These networks spilled over to multiple scales, including the GTA, cross-provincially, and across levels of government.

Some of the causal factors of regime dynamics that Karen Mossberger and Gerry Stoker (2001) identified in their review of the regime theory literature – including economic restructuring, political mobilization, and changes in federal grant policies – interact in complex ways. Including the concept of national infrastructure in urban regime analyses is a useful way of understanding the complex interdependence of urban governance and the intergovernmental system. Changes in fiscal federalism, combined with a volatile and strained provincial–municipal relationship between the Province of Ontario and the City of Toronto, created incentives for Toronto's regime to focus its attention on the federal government. In the midst of what local leaders perceived as an 'urban crisis' created by the province's exacerbation of urban problems, Toronto's regime partners launched a national campaign for a New Deal for Cities to deal with a more fundamental city problem – the lack of sufficient political, legislative, and fiscal autonomy. The Toronto regime also increased its efforts to build local capacity in areas of particular concern to the city. Furthermore, in the absence of regional institutions, Toronto's leaders took leadership on behalf of the region and began searching for regional allies. This resulted in flexible new regional-governance institutions that incorporated upper levels of government in local capacity-building initiatives, such as TRIEC.

The dynamics of urban regime building in Toronto have important implications for the comparative study of urban regime maintenance and change. This case illustrates the importance of the national infrastructure to local governance. Given the fragmentation of power in urban systems, local leaders have incentives to build public–private coalitions to pool policy capacity. However, the Toronto case demonstrates that imbalances in the distribution of resources exist both in civil society and in the intergovernmental system. Regime theory teaches us that selective financial incentives are especially important to regime maintenance and development. In civil society, the business community possesses a disproportionate share of these important incentives. In the intergovernmental system, upper levels of government possess a greater ability to tax and spend than municipal governments. Therefore, incentives exist to include resource-rich leaders in the public *and* private sectors in urban regimes.

This chapter also illustrates the role of institutional change in regime dynamics. The amalgamation of Metro Toronto had an important effect on patterns of mobilization in that city. Before amalgamation, urban scholars described the city as a progressive 'middle-class regime.'[29] The secondary literature suggests that amalgamation broadened participation in governance. Toronto is the only city in the sample in which a strong urban empowerment coalition emerged, and the only city that was amalgamated. This suggests that amalgamation may have played an important role in urban regime dynamics in Toronto.

Both C4LD and New Voices for a New City mobilized during amalgamation and contributed to a rescaling process in the federation. New Voices for a New City mobilized an unprecedented number of immigrants and immigrant organizations in the core city and the suburbs under one banner. The business community, too, seemed to play a more

274 Municipalities and Multiculturalism

important role in Toronto's governance after amalgamation. Also, the new City of Toronto provided a stronger platform for national organizations, given its size and budget and the mayor's electoral legitimacy.

The importance of downloading, disentanglement, and amalgamation to the mobilization of Toronto's regime around a New Deal with upper levels of government is evident when we compare regime goals in the two most proactive municipalities in the sample – Toronto and Vancouver. A central difference between these two municipalities was that in Toronto, the issue was framed as one of immigration and diversity management, whereas in Vancouver, local leaders were responding to diversity rather than to immigration. In Toronto the issue was framed as an immigration issue because of the Toronto regime's determination to develop new relationships among the three levels of government in immigration policy. The City of Toronto framed its response to its changing ethnoracial demographics as a response to 'immigration' to assert its role in this constitutionally defined area of responsibility.

When we compare Toronto to Markham, Brampton, and Mississauga, we also see the independent importance of local-governance arrangements (including amalgamation) to the way in which local leaders respond to changes in national infrastructure. In Toronto, the scope of the governance regime, combined with the catalyst of amalgamation, led local leaders to challenge upper levels of government in the face of changes in the national infrastructure that were detrimental to the city's well-being.

The Toronto case also reveals the interdependence of local pooling arrangements through urban regimes and capacity building in the intergovernmental system as a whole. Toronto's regime was able to effect change in the intergovernmental system because of its powerful local regime coalition. However, at an even more fundamental level, past decisions of upper levels of government influenced the level of resources that the Toronto regime was able to bring to bear on the intergovernmental system as well as who was included in the governance arrangements. For instance, past funding decisions by upper levels of government in the immigrant settlement and other related sectors concentrated resources in the City of Toronto and influenced local-governance arrangements there. Thus, when the intergovernmental context changed, it provided incentives for the mobilization of the strong civil society in Toronto that upper levels of government had contributed to building. Toronto's regime then successfully lobbied for changes to Canada's national infrastructure. Toronto has become a partner in several intergovernmental agreements and is now governed by a City Charter.

Toronto's ability to respond to immigrants has been enhanced by how the issue has been framed. Local leaders linked immigration and multiculturalism challenges to economic-development issues and prosperity in the city. Because immigrant settlement goals are important priorities in Toronto's local-governance regime, these issues were also an important part of local leaders' calls for a New Deal for Cities. Immigrants' needs and preferences were tied to this powerful regime and national movement, resulting in important new local capacity-building efforts in immigration policy – through the leadership of TRIEC – and the negotiation of an agreement on immigration between Ontario and the federal government that includes municipalities as partners. Toronto is singled out in this agreement because of the lobbying efforts of its regime. The federal and provincial governments now recognize the local capacity that the City of Toronto brings to policy discussions on immigration.

The Toronto case also provides evidence that something more fundamental may be at play. Local leaders would like greater levels of support on the part of upper levels of government. Yet to varying degrees, they also want to exercise greater authority at the local level and want to see this authority decentralized in a formal way. Calls for decentralization of decision making encompass a number of areas, but immigration and settlement policy are always on the list. Toronto's urban autonomy movement and polyscalar forms of political mobilization have been shaped by the incentives provided by the intergovernmental context but can also be situated within broader, ongoing rescaling processes (Boudreau 2006).

The intergovernmental context does not *determine* local policy outputs and urban regime dynamics. Rather, it provides a climate of incentives within which local leaders choose how to respond. Local leaders decide which issues will be included in their priorities, which goals they will pursue, who they will seek as allies in their policy endeavours, and how they will frame policy goals; they also choose strategies for attracting regime participants and maintaining the regime. That said, the intergovernmental context provides an important element in local leaders' context of policy choice.

This chapter and chapter 6 have demonstrated that local-governance arrangements are shaped both from below and from above. In their efforts to build productive public–private coalitions in multiculturalism policy, local leaders are constrained by the ethnic configuration of their municipal population and by the distribution of resources in the inter-governmental system.

Yet within these constraints, local politics matters. The importance of local agency is most evident in Toronto. The city was able to overcome the challenges associated with collective action in a multiracial context because of the presence of exceptional leaders in the public and private sectors. Then, when local leaders realized that local pooling was insufficient to meet their policy goals, they broadened their base of regime support by seeking new allies, launched campaigns to educate the public about Toronto's plight, and began lobbying upper levels of government for a New Deal. These patterns of mobilization did not occur due to an opening in the 'political opportunity structure.' Rather, local leaders mobilized to challenge political opportunity structures that were closed and even hostile to local concerns. The Toronto case demonstrates just how much local agency can matter.

The final chapter summarizes the lessons of this book and discusses what we have learned about the possibility of progressive multiculturalism policy at the local level. What explains municipal responsiveness to immigrants and ethnocultural minorities in the GTA and Greater Vancouver? What theoretical lessons can we draw from this study?

8 Municipal Multiculturalism Policies and the Capacity to Manage Social Change

Canadian municipalities are playing a new and largely unacknowledged role in immigrant settlement and integration. As municipal governments are at the forefront of social change, this book suggests that municipalities in immigrant-magnet city-regions can play an important role in fostering what Mario Polèse and Richard Stren (2000) call 'socially sustainable growth' by steering the development of civil society in the direction of social inclusion and interethnic harmony (2000, 16). Municipalities in these highly diverse city-regions can do so through a variety of local multiculturalism initiatives.

Municipalities can influence the direction of change in civil society in the same way as upper levels of government – that is, by funding community organizations that foster interethnic harmony and encourage interethnic equity. But there are also some actions that only municipalities can take. For instance, only they can serve as public and democratically elected bridges among immigrant groups as well as between immigrants and the long-standing population. They can also lead by example in the community by adapting their own corporations to ensure diversity. Furthermore, because of their ability to collaborate with the local community, municipalities have the potential to be innovative in their responses and to tailor multiculturalism policies to the local context.

The variation in levels of municipal responsiveness documented in this study indicates that not all municipalities actively embrace Canada's countrywide model of official multiculturalism. Indeed, some municipalities may be contributing to *dis*harmony by failing to respond to social change and by fostering a sense of exclusion from local governance among immigrants and ethnocultural minorities. Moreover, since municipal governments are relatively weak, they may not be able to direct the evolution of civil society and adapt their corporate structures as effectively as they might if they had more resources.

Canadian municipalities fall into a threefold typology of municipal responsiveness – 'responsive,' 'somewhat responsive,' and 'unresponsive.' Municipalities vary in the extent to which they are *comprehensive* in their responses to immigrants and ethnocultural minorities, as well as in their *policy styles* – they may be *proactive*, *reactive*, or *inactive* in the multiculturalism policy field.

How does one define responsiveness in an ethnically diverse context? Local leaders of settlement and ethnic organizations perceive the normative framework of Canada's official policy of multiculturalism as 'responsive' to the concerns of immigrants and ethnocultural minorities. They do not consider a laissez-faire public role in ethnocultural relations sufficient, and they expect local public officials to actively address cultural barriers to services and to participation in municipal decision making. In other words, in Canadian cities, immigrants seem to consider the *multicultural citizenship framework* equitable. Municipal multiculturalism policies are resources for immigrants in the integration process.

In the absence of a clear provincial mandate, one might expect variation in municipal approaches to managing diversity; even so, the wide range in responsiveness among the eight cases is somewhat puzzling in light of the constraints on municipal governments' resources imposed by legal frameworks that limit how they can raise revenue. Furthermore, as the lowest level of government in a fragmented system, municipal governments find themselves in a position where they must compete for residents and business investment (Peterson 1981). Neither Ontario nor British Columbia mandates a municipal role in multiculturalism policy, nor do these provinces provide grants to municipalities to accommodate and manage multiculturalism. Thus municipal governments in both provinces are acting without a clear provincial mandate in this area and without additional public resources. They are very much on their own in multiculturalism policy making.

Why do some municipalities nonetheless choose to adapt their services and governance structures to accommodate immigrants and ethnocultural minorities? How do they develop the capacity to respond to such dramatic change in the ethnic composition of their populations? This final chapter begins by summarizing the theoretical lessons of this book. It then proposes a framework for advancing the comparative study of the impact of immigration on the municipal governance of multiculturalism. It concludes by offering lessons for the multiculturalism policy maker.

Towards a Comparative Theory of the Impact of Immigration on City Governance

A multitude of factors influence a municipality's responsiveness to immigrants and ethnocultural minorities. Alan DiGaetano and Elizabeth Strom (2003) suggest an integrated approach to governance that incorporates the three dominant approaches to the study of comparative politics – structure, culture, and rationality. This book, too, proposes an 'integrated approach' – albeit a somewhat differently integrated approach – to the comparative study of multiculturalism policy making at the local level. To understand the complexities of the politics of multiculturalism in Canadian cities, we must combine the insights of urban regime theory, a social diversity perspective, and structural factors, including both institutional perspectives and global rescaling processes. Together, these theoretical ideas incorporate structure, culture, and rationality into urban analysis.

Urban regime theory has been the chief analytical lens through which the complexities of multiculturalism policy making at the local level have been explored. This theory draws one's attention to the important roles played by leadership, relationships among local leaders, and local resources. Though some have questioned the applicability of this theory to Canada, the urban regime concept is amenable to an integrated approach to the study of urban governance. At root, regime theory is a rational choice model of political behaviour in that it views local politics as a problem of collective action. According to regime theorists, the fundamental question in urban politics is how to achieve and sustain cooperation to produce the capacity to develop and implement local agendas. Building on the pioneering work of Marion Orr (1999), we have seen that ethnospecific social capital matters to whether an immigrant group will be included in urban governance arrangements. Moreover, the ethnic configuration of a municipality structures the development of social capital and the intersection of this form of capital with economic capital, besides shaping new political cleavages.

The urban regime concept also incorporates elements of a structural, political economy approach to local power structures through its contention that there is a systematic bias towards including the business community. This bias arises owing to the business community's disproportionate share of material resources in local communities and its ability to offer selective incentives to maintain cooperation. For a full understanding of policy and governance dynamics, we must also place our analyses of the local-level politics of immigration in an intergovernmental context as well as a global one (Leo 1998).

An Urban Regime Framework

In chapters 4 and 5, a framework was developed for looking at the eight cases through an urban regime lens. The factors to which urban regime theory draws one's attention are indeed important to local capacity building in multiculturalism policy. The two most *responsive* municipalities – Toronto and Vancouver – have built lasting regime coalitions that have absorbed multiculturalism policy concerns. *Somewhat responsive* municipalities vary in the extent to which lasting public–private relationships have emerged in response to changes in the ethnocultural demographics of their populations. In the two most responsive of the somewhat responsive municipalities in the sample – Markham and Richmond – socially productive relationships have fostered positive race relations between the largely Chinese immigrant community and the long-standing (largely White) community. Productive coalitions in specific policy arenas have also developed in Surrey and Coquitlam at the departmental level. In Mississauga and Brampton – the *unresponsive* municipalities in the sample – immigrant and ethnocultural minorities do not seem to be represented in the cities' governing arrangements.

A number of factors to which the urban regime concept draws our attention seem to be correlated with municipal responsiveness to immigrants and ethnocultural minorities. First, in responsive municipalities, local political leaders and civil servants acknowledge a municipal role in immigration and settlement even though this role is not mandated provincially. In other words, *political leadership* matters to municipal responsiveness. As Toronto councillor Kyle Rae put it, his city's role in diversity management and in immigration and settlement policy has been 'generated by activist councilors [who] push the envelope because of need' (Rae 2004, interview).

Another factor that influences municipal responsiveness to immigrants and ethnocultural minorities is *how civil society is organized*. A well-organized and well-resourced immigrant settlement sector enhances the possibility for strong leadership in immigrant settlement and other multiculturalism policy goals. For instance, municipal public officials can draw from social networks and from the expertise of the community in policy development in their efforts to engage immigrants and ethnocultural minorities in municipal affairs. Also, a well-organized immigrant community can pressure the municipality to respond and can hold the municipality accountable for its failure to implement policies effectively.[1]

The *organization and orientation of the business community* also matters to municipal responsiveness. In responsive municipalities, the business community acknowledges the importance of immigration to local economic well-being and is willing to pool resources to help the municipal government adapt its services and governance structures. In some cases the immigrant community constitutes either a new business establishment or important developers in the municipality.

Also affecting municipal responsiveness to immigrants and ethnocultural minorities is how multiculturalism policy goals are *framed*. Framing determines who participates in local governance. When immigration is tied to economic-development objectives – as in Toronto and Vancouver – the municipality is more likely to include immigrants and ethnocultural minorities in local governance. In chapter 7 we saw how tying immigrant settlement concerns to the broader New Deal for Cities policy frame led to a greater level of responsiveness to immigrants and ethnocultural minorities in the GTA and also broadened participation in the regime. The importance of framing to municipal responsiveness to immigrants and ethnocultural minorities underscores the significance of both local leadership and political agency. Local media can also play an important role in framing the multiculturalism issue and in mediating local community debates over multiculturalism.

A Social Diversity Interpretation

In chapter 6 we saw that a municipality's ethnoracial configuration contributes to an explanation of the likelihood that a municipality will respond to social change by adapting its services and governance structures to accommodate immigrants and ethnocultural minorities. Bifurcated, biracial municipalities are more likely to be responsive to ethnocultural change than highly heterogeneous, multiracial municipalities. There are several reasons for this. First, the *collective action problem is more easily overcome in bifurcated municipalities*. In addition, a dynamic of community *backlash* followed by a counter-reaction from the immigrant community is more likely to develop in municipalities where there is a large concentration of a single ethnic group. In other words, in biracial municipalities it is more likely that the community will agree that there is a race relations problem. Finally, it is easier for local leaders to respond to a single immigrant group than to a multiplicity of groups.

Nevertheless, one finds that while the ethnic configuration of the municipality matters, so does the *distribution of resources within the municipality and among ethnic groups*. Biracial municipalities in which the ethnocultural minority is Chinese were more responsive than those in which the ethnocultural minority was South Asian. It seems that in municipalities where Chinese immigrants predominate, there is also a powerful Chinese business community that is willing to facilitate municipal responsiveness by donating or pooling its resources.

The ethnic distribution of resources in the municipality also affects how the long-standing community perceives large-scale immigration. In several biracial municipalities with a concentration of Chinese immigrants, we found that the ability of the Chinese business community and of certain wealthy Chinese residents – for instance, in Vancouver's upscale neighbourhood of Kerrisdale – to redefine or challenge the cultural norms of the community or neighbourhood led to resistance to the changes and backlash from some members of the long-standing community.

Also, in the municipalities with large Chinese immigrant populations,· an extensive network of Chinese-specific institutions has developed. The Chinese community seems to possess a great deal of intragroup social capital. In contrast, in Surrey – the biracial municipality in the sample with a large South Asian population – the immigrant community seems to be more divided. Furthermore, Surrey's business community does not seem to be pressuring the municipality to adapt its services.

Why do Chinese immigrant communities seem to have higher levels of social capital than South Asian immigrant communities? Clearly, Statistics Canada's category 'South Asian' is too imprecise. Studies will be need to be conducted to explore whether some immigrant communities have greater levels of social capital than others, and why, and to study the intracommunity dynamics of immigrant communities. Immigrant communities that fail to overcome the first-order collective action problem will not be included in urban regimes.

Backlash against immigration is less likely in heterogeneous municipalities – those in which the perception is missing that a single immigrant group is redefining the municipality's cultural norms. Together, all of the above factors suggest that one can expect action in multiracial municipalities only where political will exists alongside strong leadership.

Urban Regimes, National Infrastructures, and Regime 'Spillover'

We saw in chapter 7 that the intergovernmental context also matters to urban regime dynamics. Its effects, however, are mediated by existing urban-governance arrangements. We can incorporate the intergovernmental system into our understanding of regime dynamics by examining how policy decisions by upper levels of government provide *incentives for mobilization* as well as how those decisions *affect the distribution of resources* at the local level. Furthermore, achieving certain locally important policy goals requires the cooperation of upper levels of government. In that sense, upper levels of government are potential regime partners.

In B.C., a general climate of respect for municipal autonomy, a relative lack of downloading, and the province's willingness to address multiculturalism concerns all meant that a locally based autonomy movement did not emerge in the city-region. The province supports the City of Vancouver's economic-development aspirations and its focus on attracting investment from the Pacific Rim. Indeed, in the 1980s two mayors of the City of Vancouver who supported the local Pacific Rim consensus rose to become premier in the 1990s and early 2000s.[2] The need to develop economic ties with Pacific Rim countries is evident to a broad group of public officials at the provincial and municipal levels as well as to local leaders in civil society.

In Toronto the intergovernmental system has structured the choices of local leaders but has not determined the nature of local governance. In the mid-1990s the provincial government's decision to disentangle services and reduce social spending as well as to amalgamate Metro Toronto drove local regime leaders to reach a consensus on the need for greater autonomy for Toronto. A powerful and extensive network of relationships in that city converged around the concept of a New Deal for the city. The Toronto regime's immigrant settlement goals are tied to this new frame. These networks spilled over to multiple scales, including those of the GTA, cities in other provinces, and higher levels of government. In TRIEC we saw evidence of a regional subregime and subsequently a multilevel one. The results of advocacy efforts of leaders in this powerful subregime were apparent when a new Canada–Ontario Immigration Agreement (2005) was negotiated so as to include Toronto as a partner.

The findings in chapter 7 have important implications for urban regime analysis. Urban regime strategies and dynamics in Toronto point to a central deficiency with the current urban-regime concept: its theoretical focus on the political economy of cities at the expense of the intergovernmental context. For urban regime theorists the central puzzle at the local level is how local leaders are able to achieve the capacity to govern. Local governments in both Canada and the United States face enormous resource constraints, given their junior position in the intergovernmental system. Urban regime theorists point out accurately that local politics matter because, in a fragmented urban system, it is local coalition building that creates the capacity to govern at this level. Nevertheless, as the Toronto case suggests, one cannot take for granted that the desire to build capacity at the local level will be limited to municipal–civil society relationships and that local leaders will be satisfied with the resources available through such governance arrangements. The Toronto case suggests that one cannot take for granted that local leaders will accept the existing distribution of legislative authority and fiscal resources.

Canada's urban scholars have made little use of regime analysis to understand local policy making. The dominant focus has been on the intergovernmental context – on the provincial–local relationship in particular. The highly limited nature of municipal autonomy in Canadian municipal systems would lead one to expect that those municipal leaders who want to develop the capacity to address local challenges would turn to upper levels of government for help instead of developing urban regimes. Furthermore, given the constrained position of municipal governments in the Canadian intergovernmental system, one might deduce that elite leaders in civil society – in the business community in particular – have little incentive to develop ongoing relationships with municipal governments. This intergovernmental reality has led well-known Canadian urban scholar Andrew Sancton (1993) to predict that 'the concept of urban political regimes is unlikely to be of much assistance in analyzing Canadian urban politics because massive provincial influence makes business involvement in such regime politics unnecessary' (1993, 20, in Urbaniak 2003, 11, and 2005, 6).

Since the early 1990s the empirical terrain of local politics in Canada has shifted dramatically. Andrew Sancton (1993) may have been correct in his assessment of the general orientation of local business communities in 1993. The Canadian literature now portrays municipal policy making differently; in doing so it is drawing our attention to the importance of governance arrangements to local capacity building and representation (Andrew 2001; Andrew, Graham, and Philips 2002) and to the multilevel dimensions of local policy making (Leo 1997; Leo 2006; Young and Leuprecht 2006). This book suggests that the urban regime concept adds to our understanding of the relationship between urban governance arrangements and the intergovernmental system in Canada by highlighting the systemic bias of local governance coalitions towards the business community at the municipal level. Multilevel arrangements could alter this bias by substituting public resources for private ones at the municipal level, and by altering the evolution of local civil societies more generally by developing capacity in non-business sectors in local communities. But to the extent that urban and multilevel governance arrangements are developing as a consequence of global economic processes of rescaling that many urban scholars have identified, a political economy perspective of governance has become more valuable. As local leaders perceive a greater need to compete and become more assertive, urban-regime building will become an increasingly common strategy of local-capacity building. Also, upper levels of government may become more willing to support local initiatives by developing a variety of multilevel arrangements. Furthermore, the two processes are related.

This study indicates that a focus on the formal place of municipal institutions within the intergovernmental system misses important ways in which local factors and politics are important. Municipal leaders in Canada do indeed participate in the formation of urban regimes. That the Canadian literature has long focused on the intergovernmental context highlights a serious deficiency in urban regime theory – it fails to address the strong possibility that local leaders will turn to upper levels of government to address their resource needs.

The Toronto case highlights the *interdependence* of the two capacity-building strategies. In Toronto, local leaders built a strong urban regime with broad intersectoral participation not only to pool resources across sectors but also to create the political momentum to extract a greater share of resources from upper levels of government. One might even argue that the participation of civil society and high-profile business and financial institutions – including the TD Bank – has been the single most important factor in Toronto's success at achieving a New Deal with upper levels of government, albeit a limited one (Feldman 2006).

In *A New City Agenda* (2004), John Sewell advocates local innovation and capacity building – what this study calls regime building – as a strategy for demonstrating to upper levels of government the powers a city should have: 'As city government becomes clear about the powers it should have to improve the quality of life for citizens, and as it *takes steps to implement its pursuit of increased authority and effectiveness*, momentum will inevitably develop' (2004, 92; emphasis added). Developing multiculturalism policies and other initiatives to facilitate the integration of immigrants in Toronto without the express authority to do so or the necessary financial resources from the province is one of the best examples of this strategy in practice. The Toronto case demonstrates that when upper levels of government fail to take leadership on important policy questions such as immigrant settlement and multiculturalism policy, and when municipal governments push their limits to fill the gap, community agencies and citizens begin to support a rescaling of statehood to the municipal level, because it is accessible and is considered responsive to their concerns. One of the most striking findings in this study is that *settlement leaders in Toronto support decentralization of responsibility for settlement to the municipal level.*

Business participation in the Toronto regime is especially puzzling in light of Toronto's reputation, among governments in the region, for progressive left-wing politics. The simplest explanation is that local business leaders recognize that 'place matters' and that upper levels of government have not done enough to address the place-specific consequences of their policy decisions. In Toronto the immediate impacts of downloading and disentanglement enabled the New Deal idea to resonate with a broad cross-section of the city's leaders. These measures in tandem broadened the business community's ideas concerning what constitutes a favourable economic climate. In the absence of leadership from upper levels of government, municipal officials and leaders in civil society built urban regime coalitions.

Thus, institutional change can affect urban regime dynamics. Amalgamation had a powerful effect on *patterns of mobilization* in Toronto. It seems to have broadened participation in governance; and as Toronto councillor Shelley Carroll put it, it also seems to have 'turned suburbanites into activists' (Carroll 2004, interview). It also led to an *unprecedented level of cooperation among immigrant groups in the city* under the banner of New Voices for the New City. Toronto is the only city in the sample in which a strong urban empowerment coalition emerged; it is also the only city that was amalgamated. This suggests that amalgamation played an especially important role as a catalyst for ongoing 'rescaling' through political mobilization at the local level.

So it is possible that the changes in the intergovernmental system in Ontario in the 1990s led to the development of the first 'regime' in Toronto after amalgamation. More generally, one might connect the development of urban regimes in Canada to processes of rescaling as the municipal level becomes more important as an arena of growth politics. Vancouver's proactive Pacific Rim initiatives began in 1980 when Mike Harcourt was mayor, and they continue to this day. Furthermore, there is now evidence that, in cooperation with leaders in civil society, municipal leaders in Vancouver have just recently begun to carve out a role in 'immigration policy' instead of limiting the municipality's role to responding to 'diversity.' It seems that local growth coalitions in both cities have become more assertive – a change that could be related to broader global economic processes.

The capacity-building strategies of the leaders in one case – the City of Toronto – illustrate most clearly the *importance of local agency* to local multiculturalism policy making. Vancouver's responsiveness to immigrants and ethnocultural minorities is perhaps more expected than Toronto's in light of the dominant theoretical tenets of the urban politics literature described above. In Vancouver the connection between economic-development objectives and immigration is obvious, given the importance of Chinese immigrant investors and developers to its economy. What is more, the province supports the city's efforts to develop the city as a Pacific gateway. Members of the largely Chinese immigrant community are key players in the city's growth coalition. By actively fostering connections between Vancouver and cities in the Pacific Rim, Vancouver's political leaders are behaving as one would expect in the growth machine literature.

Multiculturalism policy development in Vancouver seems to be at least partly a by-product of the city's economic-development objectives. Local political leaders have decided to foster economic and social linkages with the Pacific Rim, and they consider multiculturalism policies a natural complement to this objective. Predictably, the new community dynamics have been managed within the Pacific Rim consensus among local elites. For instance, ethnocultural tensions relating to cultural preferences in housing have created incentives for local leaders to adopt multiculturalism policies, since those tensions challenge the dominant consensus concerning the desirability of growth – the consensus of the local 'growth machine.' But at the same time, ethnic conflict has helped push the issue of race relations onto the municipal agenda.

Toronto's responsiveness is less easily explained. We know that *resources* in Toronto provide a significant part of the explanation. However, we also saw the power of exceptional *local leaders* and of broad cooperation in the face of a complex collective-action problem. In this way, Toronto is *exceptional* among the cases. Toronto is the only city in the sample with a highly heterogeneous, multiracial ethnic configuration that has been responsive to its immigrant and ethnocultural minority population. Immigrant groups in Toronto have managed to overcome the complex first-order collective-action problem that is inherent in Toronto's ethnoracial configuration as well as in the intersection of its ethnoracial configuration and community resources, even though Toronto's ethnic configuration is much more complex than Mississauga's or Brampton's – the two other multiracial municipalities in the sample.

Toronto's exceptionality emerged again in chapter 7. In response to downloading by upper levels of government and a forced municipal merger, local leaders pulled together the city's networks to challenge upper levels of government. These patterns of mobilization developed in the context of a closed and even hostile provincial political-opportunity structure (Horak 1998). The Toronto case demonstrates just how much local agency can matter. Local leaders resisted changes in the intergovernmental system through regime building. Faced with a hostile province, they went against constitutional convention and lobbied the federal government. Thus, the Toronto case illustrates how resources matter to the ability of local leaders to mount successful resistance.

The strength of local leaders, the resources of those leaders, and the extent to which leaders support the decentralization of responsibility to the City of Toronto are all unique to the city. The city's main newspaper, the *Toronto Star*, is a crusader on behalf of the city. Many Toronto city councillors are activist, notwithstanding their institutional and fiscal constraints. The leadership and capacity in the immigrant settlement sector is unparalleled in Canada. Even the business community – as represented by the Toronto Board of Trade – uses activist strategies on behalf of the city to advocate for a New Deal for Toronto. Leaders of some of Canada's most powerful financial institutions, such as the TD Bank, support a New Deal. Extremely powerful leaders, such as philanthropist and entrepreneur Alan Broadbent, are willing to commit their personal resources to the cause of empowering Toronto. Broadbent, a leader of Toronto's New Deal movement, is also personally committed to the goal of increasing the city's capacity to integrate immigrants in an equitable way. Dominic D'Alessandro, President and CEO of Manulife Financial, another financial powerhouse in Canada, is one of the chairs of TRIEC.

Toronto is also exceptional insofar as it is the only city in the sample in which leaders in the immigrant settlement sector expressed support for a stronger municipal role in immigrant settlement and multiculturalism policy development. Like leaders in other sectors, they support a decentralization of the Canadian federation that would give the City of Toronto more autonomy. Meanwhile, power and 'statehood' have been rescaled to a certain extent to informal networks in civil society – to the city's urban regime.

Toronto provides an example of how political agency limits our ability to generalize in the empirical world. As such, it warrants further attention, which might shed light on the circumstances in which local leaders can overcome constraints – both those in the immediate social context and those imposed by the intergovernmental system. The case could tell us something about the potential for progressive politics at the local level. But in the absence of a strong local (i.e., municipal) state, the arrangements developed in civil society are – as urban regime theory suggests – biased towards the business community. Toronto was able to overcome its constraints in part owing to perceived economic imperatives on the part of the business community and the willingness of powerful business leaders to contribute personal resources to sustain cooperation and contribute to capacity building in immigrant settlement. Immigrant integration is a priority because the economic case was made for this policy goal through the process of regime building.

Furthermore, changes in the global economic system may be pushing local leaders to organize in Toronto. There may be an 'invisible hand' at work – that is, the hand of a changing capitalism that is rescaling statehood. From this perspective, changes in the intergovernmental system threatened Toronto's position in a highly competitive global system of cities. Certainly the literature on rescaling would tie the orientation of local leaders and patterns of political mobilization to global changes in capitalism and a corresponding rescaling of statehood. Indeed, there is evidence that in Toronto something fundamental is at work: local leaders are not simply asking upper levels of government to develop place-sensitive, urban policies. Rather, there seems to be a fundamental desire to decentralize power to the local level.

Local leaders in Toronto perceive the city as the fundamental unit of economic, political, and cultural organization. New governance arrangements have developed at multiple scales – and at 'jumped scales,' in the case of the Charter 5. These types of coalitions are consistent with what Neil Brenner (2004) describes as emerging 'state spaces' in Europe. Though the activities of the Charter 5 were not sustained, a lasting form of 'new regionalism' has developed in the GTA. Some of these developments are what one would expect now that statehood is being 'rescaled' and the metropolitan scale is becoming more important. Julie-Anne Boudreau (2006) has tied these 'polyscalar' forms of political mobilization to global rescaling processes.

Yet it is difficult to draw firm conclusions about globalization's impact on the two city-regions in this book. Globalization has not affected patterns of governance at the city level in a uniform way. Provincial–municipal relationships in B.C. are more stable and historically more respectful of municipal autonomy than those in Ontario. To the extent that globalization is changing patterns of mobilization in Canada's city-regions, its effects are being mediated through past and existing institutional arrangements, both formal and informal. Changes in the intergovernmental context are the proximate structural cause of the differences between the two city-regions.

Thus, we are seeing political mobilization at multiple scales. To a certain extent, we are also seeing a state of territorial flux in the institutionalization of political authority, which is consistent with theories of rescaling. But based on the Canadian evidence, it is difficult to generalize about rescaling processes. Local regimes and the intergovernmental context are mediating the effects of global rescaling.

Local leaders acknowledge that cities are now competing with one another on a global scale. One can identify strong 'growth machines' in the two central cities. However, since growth machines are standard in the United States and Canada, we would need to examine both of these cities through time to see how new these processes are. Local leaders in both Vancouver and Toronto seem to govern for growth, as the growth machine literature would predict. What may be new is the assertiveness of local leaders, their orientation to the global scale, and the emerging consensus that cities are the engines of economic growth in the global context. Also new is the extent to which global processes of immigration are central to growth agendas.

In the absence of government intervention, the degrees of freedom for progressive local policy making may be narrow. Local governance arrangements in support of progressive politics may happen only on the margins. Multiculturalism policies complement growth objectives. What are the implications for the direction of both discourse and action in multiculturalism policy making? It could be that multiculturalism policies will address the concerns of immigrants and ethnocultural minorities only to the extent that they are crucial to maintaining the city's economic competitiveness. However, this book also illustrates the potential of local growth agendas to unite highly diverse populations. We need to look for patterns cross-nationally. How, if at all, are immigration and multiculturalism policy responses contributing to rescaling processes? Are cities competing for immigrants? Are they actively trying to court skilled immigrants? What does this mean for progressive policy making? When it comes to urban governance, which immigrants and ethnocultural minorities are 'in' and which are 'out'? Future research should explore the extent to which immigrants are achieving greater levels of inclusion in urban governance arrangements, because attracting and settling them successfully supports neoliberal growth agendas. We must also know more about the extent to which local governance arrangements support an equitable local multicultural citizenship.

A Cross-National Framework of the Urban Governance of Multiculturalism

These questions all point to the value of developing a cross-national, integrated framework for the urban governance of immigration. Researchers could address the following questions. Has the attraction and retention of immigrants through multiculturalism initiatives become a global strategy in cities' efforts to compete? To what extent have innovative governance arrangements emerged in immigrant settlement to complement the economic-development (i.e., growth) objectives of urban regimes? To what extent do immigrants and ethnocultural minorities benefit from the connection between economic-development goals and successful immigrant settlement? What are the motivations for multiculturalism initiatives, and what types of exchanges do local regime participants make in this area? To what extent do multiculturalism policies at the local level in Canada reflect Canada's national policy context and its commitment to official multiculturalism?

The ways in which some local leaders in Canada tie immigration and successful immigrant settlement to growth objectives are not simply a matter of implementing national policy, since this book identifies considerable variation among local multiculturalism initiatives *within* Canada. Multiculturalism objectives make it onto local agendas through political processes. Thus it is better to view official multiculturalism, along with the norms and ideas that underpin it, as a resource for would-be regime entrepreneurs at the local level. A 'national multiculturalism infrastructure' is part of the 'national infrastructure' that shapes local policy making in Canada. As Irene Bloemraad (2006) found in her comparative study of immigrant integration in Canada and the United States, the Canadian federal government's multiculturalism policies and initiatives confer both material and symbolic benefits to immigrants that are important to successful settlement.

In chapter 6 we saw that the development of urban regimes is shaped by changing patterns of social diversity. Here, too, one can see the potential for a cross-national framework of research. If the ethnic configuration of a municipal unit is significant to its policy outputs, regime development, and form of political pluralism in the ways described above, one should find patterns cross-nationally as well. The degree to which Canadian municipalities vary in their adoption of multiculturalism policies or frameworks suggests that the national policy context is not entirely decisive. The application of Hero's perspective to Canada is, of course, based on this premise. His study's findings add yet more weight to the findings discussed here, which have been based on a limited sample of eight cities. The two studies as well as the 'ethnoburb' literature point to the value of a cross-national, integrated social diversity perspective.

There is theoretical work to be done to develop this framework. Most fundamentally, the categories of ethnic configurations developed in this book differ from Hero's in ways that reflect the available data in Canada, as well as this study's focus on high-immigration centres. Furthermore, historical differences in race relations and patterns of immigration in Canada and the United States have the potential to confound comparisons between the two countries. Nevertheless, in their comparative study of policy making in Canada and the United States, Keith Banting, George Hoberg, and Richard Simeon (1997) argue that patterns of social pluralism in the two countries are converging. According to them, 'new' sources of diversity (feminist and multicultural) represent a point of *societal convergence* between Canada and the United States, in contrast to earlier elements of *societal divergence* as represented by 'language, race, and class' (1997, 399). Ultimately, we will want to know how new sources of social pluralism intersect with these older divisions to shape local political dynamics and governance arrangements.

Hero (1998) suggests that one of the main contributions of the social diversity perspective is that it offers a clearer and more precise explanation of change than the dominant theoretical approaches to the study of state politics in the United States (1998, 10). As immigration continues to change the face of the United States and Canada, we may see more convergence in race relations in the two countries and thus also more opportunities for theoretical cross-fertilization.

To what extent is Hero's typology compatible with the typology of ethnic configurations developed in this book? Using Hero's conceptualization, the two categories – multiracial and biracial – would be subsumed under the category 'bifurcated,' in the sense that both types include high proportions of ethnoracial minorities. What evidence is there to suggest that all of the Canadian municipalities discussed in this book should be considered bifurcated? 'Multiracial' municipalities are characterized by a *limited pluralism with some competition* in suburban municipalities and by a highly *dynamic form of pluralism* in Toronto. As such, they share some features of Hero's 'heterogeneous' political sub-units, which have moderate levels of ethnoracial minorities and high proportions of 'White ethnics' and which are characterized by a 'competitive pluralism.' Thus, though the biracial and multiracial categories focus on 'visible minorities' to the exclusion of 'White ethnics,'[3] one still finds competition among groups (albeit in a limited form in suburban municipalities) and a dynamic form of 'competition' in Toronto.

To a certain extent this finding calls into question Hero's bifurcated category, which groups together all ethnoracial minorities. In other words, Hero's categories do not adequately capture the possibility of competition among ethnoracial minorities.[4] In addition, from a theoretical perspective it is unclear why a combination of what Hero calls 'White ethnics' and ethnoracial minorities would lead to greater competition than a mixture of ethnoracial minorities and what he considers 'Whites.' Together, however, the *largely limited pluralism in the multiracial suburban municipalities* and the *limited pluralism in biracial municipalities* suggest that his hypothesis of the type of pluralism one would expect in bifurcated municipalities is confirmed to some degree.

According to Hero's conceptualization, a bifurcated context 'leads to hierarchical or limited pluralism' owing to the history of race relations in the United States. The form of pluralism that characterizes bifurcated locales is, in his words, 'historically manifested in various legal and political constraints ... Despite major social and political change during the last generation, this condition continues, albeit in modified form' (1998, 16). This inference seems to have been developed with the historical experience of African Americans (and perhaps also Hispanics) in mind, which limits the applicability of this category to Canada. Furthermore, unless we assume that all immigrant racial minorities will experience the same discrimination and hierarchy as an arguably exceptional racial-minority group – African Americans – it is unclear why one would expect limited pluralism also to exhibit hierarchy.[5] From a theoretical perspective, though it seems logical to expect a more limited form of political pluralism in less diverse locales, it is unclear why one should expect a hierarchical pluralism in many of the American locales that Hero would consider bifurcated.

Hero acknowledges that the historical experience of minority groups differs, but he also argues that 'there is enough similarity within groups and enough differences across groups as delineated to support the designations and arguments made' (ibid., 8). He explains that he made the choice to oversimplify ethnic categories for the 'sake of clarity and parsimony' (ibid., 151).

The extent to which hierarchy exists depends on *the power and resources* of the ethnoracial minorities in the community. In addition, the growing literature on 'ethnoburbs' supports the finding of this study that one must incorporate a political economy perspective to understand changing community dynamics as well as the ways in which immigrants' resources structure community reactions and debates (Li 2007). The concentrated settlement of *highly powerful* immigrants capable of changing the cultural face of a locale seems to matter in many ways; for example, it generates a reaction on the part of long-standing residents (i.e., it intensifies feelings of cultural threat), and it affects the immigrants themselves (i.e., they have more power and resources to mobilize and to influence policy making).

There is arguably a greater cultural distance (including language differences) between many immigrant groups than between long-standing residents in the United States and African Americans. Hero notes that the states that have received a large number of Asian and Hispanic immigrants are the bifurcated states that adopted English-only measures in the 1980s and 1990s (Citrin et al. 1990, in ibid., 109).

In the two Canadian 'ethnoburbs' discussed above – Markham and

Richmond – we saw that the reactionary debates about English in Asian malls, which triggered community debate about multiculturalism, ultimately led to greater *responsiveness* on the part of the municipality. One might argue that this is consistent with Hero's finding that though bifurcated and homogeneous states are more likely to adopt official-English measures, bifurcated states generally tend to produce better policy outcomes for ethnoracial minorities than either homogeneous or heterogeneous states.

It is notable that though formal official-English initiatives were not put forward by the long-standing residents, there was conflict over the lack of English-language signage in Asian malls. In addition, except for Toronto, biracial municipalities have been more responsive than multiracial municipalities to ethnocultural diversity. These findings suggest that *ethnic concentration* and the *economic power* of the immigrant community both matter. Absolute and relative numbers are only one type of resource in a community. Economic and social capital matter as well.

A political economy perspective may allow researchers to connect common global processes – migration of human and financial capital – to specific settlements in countries. For instance, the 'ethnoburb' literature connects new forms of suburban settlement to global processes. Such settlements exist in many countries. Thus, in some respects one might expect a convergence in the types of social diversity that countries are facing in light of common global processes. That said, the politics of multiculturalism are affected by historical experiences with 'race relations' as well as by patterns of immigrant settlement. Documented common cross-national experiences with immigration suggest the value of comparison.

This book raises questions with respect to what one might expect of institutional goals and public policies in contexts with varying types of social diversity. Hero suggests that in heterogeneous environments 'there is a need to arbitrate or broker social heterogeneity and complexity,' and that in bifurcated environments, 'government is expected to interfere little with existing stratified conditions, themselves the product of institutions and social relations historically defined in racial/ethnic terms' (ibid., 20). Except in the City of Toronto, local leaders in Canada's heterogeneous *multiracial* municipalities were unresponsive to immigrants and ethnoracial minorities; they also failed to develop informal governance institutions capable of bridging the public–private divide to broker social change. In Canada it was the *biracial*–bifurcated locales that were more likely to intervene to 'broker social heterogeneity.' Vancouver intervened proactively, but has also had to intervene reactively to broker heterogeneity. Richmond and Markham were pressured to intervene in reaction to race relations crises as well as to pressure from socially and economically powerful Chinese immigrant communities.

It is possible that Hero's expectations regarding institutional and policy purposes hold for bifurcated municipalities in which the dominant minority is African American. If so, the hierarchical pluralism that Hero observes would be structured by a historical legacy of stratified social conditions and past institutions. However, these conditions do not seem to apply to either Canadian municipalities or American 'ethnoburbs.'[6] We need to know more about the orientations of municipal governments towards managing and accommodating diversity and how those orientations are related to patterns of social diversity, to the political economy of cities, and to how these two factors intersect.

In this study the importance of the business community's orientation towards multiculturalism objectives and its composition stands out in part because of the importance of the informal arena – and therefore of civil society – to representations of immigrants in governance arrangements and multiculturalism policy development. A glaring puzzle remains in these cases: Why are so few immigrants elected to local councils? This is especially perplexing in the biracial municipalities, where the immigrant community is concentrated. Why hasn't the municipality's ethnic configuration exerted its causal effect through this arena? In Stone's (1989) seminal study, this was the primary arena through which Atlanta's Black community became part of governance there. The ability to control council was an important resource for the Black community, and the White business community needed its support in order to pursue its urban renewal agenda. This is what created the opportunities for cooperation that resulted in Atlanta's biracial regime (ibid.). Perhaps there will be greater levels of responsiveness to immigrants and ethnocultural minorities in Canada once more progress is made in the electoral arena. The democratic process is a resource that immigrant communities can access without being part of the city's economic elite. Even so, as urban regime theory teaches, electoral resources are only one resource among many.

Just as municipal institutions are embedded in other institutional contexts, so are social contexts embedded in other social contexts defined at other scales – municipal, regional, provincial, national, and international. For instance, immigrant settlement patterns are more concentrated in B.C. than in Ontario. Could this be why B.C. has been more consistently responsive to immigrants and ethnocultural minorities? Conversely, is Canada more receptive to immigration because, as a country, it is not biracial (an ethnic configuration that tends to incite backlash at the local level)?

Political theorist Will Kymlicka (2008) has described Canada as something of an exception among countries in its receptiveness to immigrants and ethnocultural minorities. According to him, two factors associated with an unwillingness to accommodate them are the concentration of a single group and an uncontrolled border. These two conditions exist at a smaller scale in biracial municipalities in the sample. As Paul Peterson (1981) emphasizes in *City Limits*, all cities have uncontrolled borders. For him, this is a key reason why one should expect city governments to focus on economic-development policies and to avoid redistribution. In his formulation, cities compete for business investment as well as for residents who will contribute to the city's economic well-being. However, another implication of cities' open borders is that local leaders cannot control immigrant settlement patterns and, ultimately, the pace of the cultural evolution of local communities. As Kymlicka (2008) observes at the country level, backlash has indeed occurred in biracial municipalities in reaction to concentration. Nevertheless, in Canada, the local responses of biracial communities to change seem to be manageable. Kymlicka's argument that Canada's ethnic configuration has contributed to public support for multiculturalism initiatives, coupled with the findings discussed here, suggests that we need to understand how social contexts at different scales are related as well as how government institutions and policies at all levels affect the local governance of immigration. In other words, research attention ought to be paid to how discourses about immigration and multiculturalism as well as policies at other scales are translated to the local level, where immigration and ethnoracial diversity are experienced on a day-to-day basis.

The case of Surrey suggests that intragroup dynamics are also important and that other forms of diversity – in this case *religious diversity* – should be incorporated into a social diversity interpretation of politics. Internal diversity within socially constructed ethnoracial communities may serve as a barrier to community mobilization as well as to the creation of institutions and services in civil society. If majority constructions of race and difference matter, then Surrey ought to be considered a biracial municipality from the perspective of long-standing residents. In other words, the long-standing community may be reacting to large numbers of an ethnoracial group as if that group is cohesive and culturally homogeneous (and thus a potential threat to the municipality's cultural norms). To develop useable categories of social diversity, we would need to understand more about how immigrant communities construct their identities and about how *majority communities* construct the social diversity of their communities in their imaginations.

Cross-national comparisons of the impact of immigration on cities that take into account the intersection of these factors could lead to the development of a powerful framework for predicting policy outcomes based on demographic change. Hero's social diversity interpretation has the benefit of providing a parsimonious explanation of the relationship between the ethnic configuration of all American states and variation in both aggregated and disaggregated measures of policy outcomes, as well as other dependent variables. His theory also has a high level of *generalizability* within the United States. However, in theory building, one must often sacrifice a certain degree of parsimony for accuracy.

If urban scholars are to develop a cross-national research agenda that compares the responsiveness of cities to immigrants and ethnocultural diversity, they must explore the extent to which common categories of political subunits and associated forms of 'political pluralism' can be developed. In this process, we might ask whether other forms of diversity should be taken into account such as *socio-economic* and *religious* diversity. In addition, we must also examine how *patterns of resource distribution* in civil society affect the local governance of immigration and ethnoracial diversity. The social diversity perspective must also incorporate a political economy perspective that takes seriously the role of the business community in urban governance. It may be necessary to sacrifice a degree of *parsimony* in order to extend the theoretical framework cross-nationally. But in return, urban scholars will be rewarded with greater degrees of *generalizability* and *accuracy*.

The social diversity perspective offers the potential to *predict* the development of new political dynamics on the basis of tracking demographic change that results from migration and immigration. The social diversity interpretation is a 'clear' and 'precise' way of theorizing change in a variety of areas of importance to political scientists (Hero 1998, 10). Its theoretical potential is even greater in high-immigration countries in which ethnic configurations are especially dynamic. Moreover, by taking an integrated approach to local governance, we can observe how governments might intervene in managing ethnocultural relations.

To what extent can the social diversity interpretation shed light on the politics of multiculturalism policy development at the local level in Canada? There is convincing evidence that the ethnic configuration of political societies matters. Building on Hero's work, this book has laid the foundation for the development of a social diversity framework through which to examine how immigrant settlement patterns have contributed to urban regime building and the politics of multiculturalism at the local level. It has developed two new categories of ethnic configurations – biracial and multiracial – and has presented evidence that many aspects of the social contexts inherent in these analytical constructs matter to urban regime building and ultimately to multiculturalism policy development.

This book has also proposed an integrated approach to studying the relationship between social diversity and regime building and demonstrated the value of looking at the findings through a regime lens. This lens was something of a microscope in chapters 4 and 5. In chapter 6 the field of view widened to place urban regimes in their social context. In chapter 7 the lens became a telescope for viewing the intergovernmental and even global spheres; that chapter also provided a fuller account of the systemic sources of power to which urban regime theory draws one's attention. This framework has provided a complete picture of the local governance of multiculturalism.

Both large-scale and smaller case studies of political subunits are valuable in theory building. Case studies have the benefit of describing the nature of political pluralism in a more accurate and convincing way; they also allow us to refine categories and explore the causal mechanisms that establish the correlations in larger-scale studies such as Hero's. The comparative case-study method has the benefit of allowing the researcher to observe how causal mechanisms operate through time (by examining sequences) and through space (by comparing cases). Together, comparative methods and large-scale statistical methods could lead to a powerful explanatory framework for understanding one of the most significant policy challenges of our time – the politics of immigration and multiculturalism in urban places.

Making Multiculturalism Work at the Local Level: Lessons for the Policy Maker

Though the multiculturalism policy challenges in the eight cities are similar, they also have place-specific dimensions. The spatial differences in multiculturalism policy challenges mean that all levels of government – including municipal governments – must tailor their policies to the local context. As Neil Bradford has put it succinctly: 'place matters' (Bradford 2002). Because it matters, municipal governments as the governments closest to citizens should be important policy players in multiculturalism policy development at all levels. They should be responsible for adapting their *own* services and governance structures to diversity; indeed, they could offer input on the needs and preferences of their diverse populations that would be valuable to provincial and federal policy makers who are interested in adapting services and governance structures.

Because of the place-specific nature of multiculturalism policy challenges, decentralizing responsibility for elements of multiculturalism policy making to municipal governments – at least in immigrant-magnet cities – may be the most effective way of achieving the goals of the federal Multiculturalism Act (1988). Funding decisions about community-based organizations and immigrant settlement programs could be made municipally, for instance. Throughout the 1990s the responsibility for immigrant settlement was increased in many provinces. Since municipalities are clearly playing a role in the immigrant settlement experience, intentionally or not, the question becomes: Should (and could) municipalities' role in this area be formalized?

At the same time, the variation documented in this study suggests that we should be cautious about how this role is formalized. Clearly, not all local leaders have the same political will to lead in this important policy area. Furthermore, municipalities vary in their capacity to play an effective role in multiculturalism initiatives. To play a more extensive and effective role in managing multiculturalism, municipalities would need additional resources from upper levels of government. Adding multiculturalism initiatives to the services funded by the property tax could fuel a backlash against immigration. Therefore, provincial or federal grants to municipalities would be needed to address the financial implications of a formalized municipal role.

Upper levels of government can continue to play a role in steering the direction of municipal responsiveness to immigrants and ethnocultural minorities by contributing to the development of civil society. For instance, Canadian Heritage and Citizenship and Immigration Canada have played central roles in funding organizations with which municipalities can pool resources to achieve multiculturalism objectives. They have contributed to rescaling processes through initiatives such as the

Metropolis Project, which strengthens local networks and policy capacity. The federal government has been an important player in developing Canada's national 'multiculturalism infrastructure.'

Nevertheless, the distribution of resources is uneven among Canada's city-regions. The bulk of settlement resources are in urban core cities, yet more and more immigrants are settling in suburbs. This unevenness must be addressed. Increased community capacity building in suburban municipalities might well increase municipal responsiveness to immigrants and ethnocultural minorities. From the federal government's perspective, this represents one way to affect municipal governance without interfering with provincial jurisdiction.

This book's findings also suggest that in the long run, multiracial municipalities may need more resources than biracial ones. In multiracial municipalities, because their populations are more diverse, it is more costly to build ethnospecific social capital by funding community organizations. Also, community engagement and bridging is more complex.

Though it might be easier to help immigrant communities build ethnospecific social capital in biracial cities, additional resources would then have to be spent on other initiatives – specifically, ones that address the possible social isolation of immigrants owing to the development of extensive separate institutions in civil society. And, governments might then have to devote resources to initiatives that manage the reaction of long-standing residents to immigrant concentration. A clear policy implication of this study is that multiculturalism policies must also address the concerns of the non-immigrant population.

This book advocates an integrated academic approach to the study of multiculturalism in cities. So as one might expect, it argues that policy responses must be coordinated across levels of government and sectors. Essentially, we must ask the same question Christopher Leo asks in his 2006 article: How can Canada develop policies that are national in scope yet also allow sufficient flexibility for local variation? Leo contends that local communities and municipalities ought to play a larger role in policy making. However, he favours flexible, informal, multilevel governance arrangements over reforms such as city charters that would formalize municipal authority (of likely only a select group of cities).

Flexibility is certainly a virtue; but such arrangements would be subject to unilateral change by not just one (the province) but two upper levels of government. Furthermore, formalizing a municipal role in multiculturalism policy making and immigrant settlement would not preclude the development of creative multilevel arrangements. Indeed, to contribute to the effectiveness of immigrant settlement and diversity management nationally, municipalities in immigrant magnet city-regions would have to be able to exchange information and collaborate with upper levels of government.

It is worth thinking about how a role in multiculturalism initiatives could be formalized without constraining local innovation. Should a broad sphere of jurisdiction in immigrant settlement and other multiculturalism-related initiatives be written into provincial Municipal Acts? Should these responsibilities be incorporated into legislatively tailored city charters in the immigrant-magnet municipalities? In other words, would legislative asymmetry be better? Should formal mechanisms be put in place to coordinate multiculturalism initiatives and to encourage exchanges of best practices at the metropolitan level in fragmented city-regions?

Imagining a strengthened municipal role both in terms of formal delegation of responsibilities and in terms of empowerment within the intergovernmental system also raises this question: How representative are the decision makers such as municipal mayors and other elected officials? As this book has laid out, local councils do not mirror the ethnoracial demographics of their populations. In the interest of supporting the development of more multicultural local democracies, Myer Siemiatycki's (2006) suggestion that provinces should extend the municipal franchise to newcomers ought to be seriously considered. This could be an essential ingredient in strengthening local democracy and in 'managing diversity' in the community. Unrepresentative councils can be disconnected from immigrant communities and unfamiliar with the challenges they face when settling in cities and accessing services. However, this book also points to the importance of a broader conception of representation, since governance also matters, not merely government's formal institutions. How civil societies develop and who is included in the various agencies, boards, and commissions in cities, how chambers of commerce integrate a diverse business community, and how voluntary organizations themselves are governed will shape whose voices are heard in local decision making. Employment equity at the municipal level is also important to governance. The benefits of more equal representation and participation are a question not only of democratic legitimacy but also of effectiveness in managing community change.

If measures to empower municipalities and to strengthen the representativeness of local councils were taken, then empowering immigrant-magnet municipalities within Canadian federalism could itself become a sort of 'multiculturalism policy.' It would strengthen the representation of ethnoracial minorities in the Canadian system of governance as a whole. Conversely, it is worth asking what the repercussions would be if Canada's largest and most diverse municipalities were to retain little power in a situation in which racial minorities were the majorities and concentrated in relatively few cities in Canada. Could strengthening the general place of municipalities within federalism be important to Canada's multiculturalism model of citizenship?

The challenge constitutes what federalism scholar Richard Simeon (2003) describes as the formula needed for a successful federation. One must simultaneously 'build out' by empowering subunits and 'build in' to the overall intergovernmental system. What is clear is that the issue cannot be overlooked. Whether formalized or not, there is no question that municipalities in Canada's immigrant-magnet city-regions play important roles in immigrant settlement and in managing profound changes in their communities. Managing international migration is one of the central governance challenges of the twenty-first century. As the democratic governments closest to Canada's multicultural communities, municipalities play a central part in negotiating multicultural citizenship in Canada.

Postscript

Canada's immigrant-magnet city-regions are highly dynamic social, political, and economic environments. Since the field research was conducted for this book, I have become aware (on an ad hoc basis) of new municipal initiatives in the eight urban and suburban communities. I would like to mention some of these responses here, with the caveat that it is impossible to evaluate these initiatives systematically without conducting further interviews. Furthermore, this list of recent initiatives is by no means exhaustive. All municipalities in the sample seem to have been experimenting with new ways to accommodate immigrants in their populations.

Some of the new initiatives in the least responsive of the municipalities in the sample are especially interesting and warrant further research and policy attention. As many immigrants settle directly in cities and chose to live in suburbs, it will be important to understand how suburban municipalities in immigrant-magnet city-regions develop the capacity to respond to their diverse populations. Civil societies are less developed and resourced than in central cities. In the interest of developing socially sustainable cities, attention ought to be paid to how Canada's most important immigrant suburbs or 'ethnoburbs' can be supported in their efforts to develop the capacity to manage social change.

The City of Surrey has appointed its first Multicultural Advisory Committee, with Councillor Mary Martin as chair. The committee will be composed of community members. It will develop a strategic plan on ethnocultural inclusiveness for the city as well as create a festival to celebrate Surrey's diversity (City of Surrey 2006). This committee could provide citywide leadership on multiculturalism efforts, which in the past have tended to be centred in the Parks, Recreation, and Culture Department. In addition, the committee could be an important means of integrating multiculturalism-related concerns into a citywide governance arrangement. In essence, it could integrate Surrey's 'subregime' into the city's overall governance arrangement.

In 2006, Coquitlam re-established its Multiculturalism Advisory Committee as a separate committee. Recall that this committee was integrated into the Liveable Cities Advisory Committee between 2003 and 2005. The new committee is composed of two council members as well as representatives of the community. Its mandate is to raise awareness about multiculturalism issues, to serve as a place to dialogue on those issues, to address barriers to citizen involvement, and to help implement the city's multiculturalism policy (City of Coquitlam 2006). Since its establishment, the committee seems to have been active. In addition, interestingly, the city seems to be seeking federal aid in its multiculturalism policy-making efforts. Specifically, it has been awarded a grant from Heritage Canada for $150,000 to meet its mandate, which gives it a larger budget than those of other advisory committees discussed in this book, which receive funding only from municipal councils (Coquitlam 2007a, 3).

To put things in perspective, the Richmond Intercultural Advisory Committee operated without a budget for its first two years (2002–3) and then received a budget of $5,000 in 2004 (Sherlock 2004, interview) – a small fraction of the budget of the equivalent committee in Coquitlam. Though the federal government plays an important role in funding community organizations, this development reflects the potential of a more direct federal role in municipal multiculturalism initiatives. The federal government has also named Coquitlam a 'cultural capital' of Canada for its current diversity initiatives and for its plans to undertake new multiculturalism initiatives (Coquitlam Now 2008). Coquitlam also participates on a Provincial Joint Steering Committee for multiculturalism and immigration (City of Coquitlam 2007b). One of Coquitlam's new strategies for building capacity in immigrant settlement appears to focus on fostering relationships of different sorts with upper levels of government.

Even the 'unresponsive' municipalities discussed in this book seem to be making efforts to adapt their services to increase immigrant and ethnocultural-minority access to municipal services. Brampton has launched a pilot project for multilingual telephone services – a simultaneous-interpretation service for residents and the business community.

As the media release acknowledges, fully one-third of residents who contact the city have a first language other than English or French (City of Brampton 2006). And in 2007 the city approved a more comprehensive Multilingual Program that is establishing a policy for translating written communications as well (City of Brampton 2007). It is worth noting that Brampton's seemingly increased level of responsiveness to immigrants and ethnocultural minorities coincides with its shift to what this book calls a biracial ethnic configuration.

Similarly, Mississauga seems to developing governance arrangements to increase immigrants' access to services and to facilitate their economic integration. Mississauga's website now reports that it has been participating in a number of TRIEC initiatives since 2005 (City of Mississauga, 'City of Mississauga Integrates New Canadians into the Workforce'). Furthermore, that website now lists community organizations that can provide translations of information about Mississauga services in eleven languages (City of Mississauga, 'City Hall Languages'). Though this initiative does not appear to involve the dedication of city resources, it suggests that as a corporation, Mississauga is developing ongoing relationships with leaders in the immigrant settlement and related sectors – an important first step towards developing a corporate strategy to increase city access and equity in terms of services and governance. Furthermore, that these arrangements are being advertised on the city's website indicates that Mississauga is moving towards a more multicultural model of citizenship.

Cultural and linguistic diversity has made it more of a challenge for Mississauga and Brampton to respond effectively and equitably than had their immigrant populations been dominated by a single group. Also, the downloading that happened in Ontario beginning especially in the mid-1990s as well as the lack of an immigration agreement in Ontario meant that the province's settlement sector was underfunded. Furthermore, as noted in chapter 4, though many immigrants now settle directly in the 'outer suburbs' such as Mississauga, Brampton, and Markham in the GTA, the spatial pattern of resource distribution is uneven. These structural forces led to Fair Share movements in Peel and York regions, in which Mississauga and Brampton and Markham respectively are located. As suburban immigrant destinations such as these continue to adapt their services and governance structures to immigration, it will be important to ensure that immigrant-serving community organizations in those locales receive the funding they need in order to influence municipal policy making and participate in local governance. The spatial/scalar distribution of resources matters both across levels of government and within city-regions.

This book has discussed differences in how diversity policies have been framed in Toronto and Vancouver. Local leaders in Toronto framed the municipality's role as not only 'diversity management' but also 'immigration and settlement.' Local leaders in Vancouver stressed that the municipality was responding to diversity (and not developing 'immigration' policies, which were viewed as the responsibility of upper levels of government). This book has noted evidence of a convergence in this respect when former Mayor Larry Campbell established a mayor's working group on immigration and settlement in 2005. Since the interviews were conducted, Vancouver appears to have become more assertive in its role in immigration and settlement. Former Vancouver mayor Sam Sullivan (2005–8), on being elected in 2005, re-established the Mayor's Working Group on Immigration in 2006, renaming it the Mayor's Task Force on Immigration (MTFI). The report of the task force acknowledges the municipality's role in immigrant settlement and describes a need to articulate this role to upper levels of government: 'While Federal and Provincial governments are responsible for immigration policy and the funding and delivery of key programs, all three levels of government are actually involved in providing support and services to newcomers. Cities need to articulate their roles and concerns to senior government, and request financial support in providing locally-based integration programs for newcomers' (City of Vancouver 2007, 2). It also stresses the need for consultation with the community and for exchange of best practices with other cities (ibid, 1). The task force membership was multisectoral and included the business community. In addition to the mayor, the task force included leaders of immigrant settlement agencies, an academic, a representative of the Asia Pacific Foundation of Canada, and a representative of the Vancouver Board of Trade. Baldwin Wong, the city's Multicultural Social Planner, was the staff liaison (ibid, 17). The task force represents another example of the city's 'urban regime' in action.

There is also evidence of multisector alliance building and of increased assertiveness of a broad range of local leaders in immigrant-related matters. For instance, one recommendation of the City of Vancouver's Mayor's Task Force on Immigration is to have the 'mayor convene a Summit meeting with key business leaders, employer and sectoral groups to discuss the feasibility of launching a multi-sectoral Immigrant Employment initiative' (ibid., 1). A multisector alliance also appears to have developed in Peel Region, the region in which both Mississauga and Brampton are located. The Peel Newcomer Strategy Group emerged in 2005 (Peel Newcomer Strategy Group website, 'Our History'). These initiatives are reminiscent of the way in which the Toronto City Summit Alliance and its offspring, the Toronto Region Immigrant Employment Council, developed in Toronto.

There is also some new evidence of the impact of global networks on multiculturalism policy making in some of the Canadian municipalities in this sample. For instance, Toronto and Coquitlam (and possibly other municipalities in the sample) have joined an international Coalition of Municipalities Against Racism and Discrimination that UNESCO has pioneered. This initiative is yet another manifestation of polyscalar forms of networking and mobilization and possibility another sign of the ongoing processes of rescaling of political authority. The effectiveness of such initiatives warrants further study, as does their ultimate significance.

Appendix
List of Interviews

Note: All interviews were conducted by Kristin Good and were in-person unless otherwise indicated.

Abrahams, Phillip. Manager, Intergovernmental Relations, City of Toronto, 18 February 2004.

Ahn, Simon. Library Trustee, City of Coquitlam, 17 June 2004.

Ashton, Brian. Councillor, City of Toronto, 13 October 2004.

Augimeri, Maria. Councillor, City of Toronto, 20 September 2004.

Barnes, Linda. Councillor, City of Richmond, 29 April 2004.

Basi, Ravi. Multicultural Outreach Librarian, Newton Library, Surrey Public Library, 20 May 2004.

Bray, Keith. President and CEO, Markham Board of Trade, 12 January 2005.

Brown, Susan. Senior Policy Adviser, Labour Force Development, Economic Development, Culture and Tourism, City of Toronto, 4 December 2003.

Buss, Greg. Chief Librarian, Richmond Public Library, 17 May 2004.

Cadman, David. Councillor, City of Vancouver, 26 April 2004.

Carroll, Shelley. Councillor, City of Toronto, 21 September 2004.

Casipullai, Amy. Policy and Public Education Coordinator, Ontario Council of Agencies Serving Immigrants (OCASI), 26 November 2003.

Cavan, Laurie. Manager of Community and Leisure Services, Parks, Recreation and Culture, City of Surrey, 20 May 2004.

Chatterjee, Alina. Director of Development/Community Engagement, Scadding Court Community Centre, Toronto, 15 December 2003.

Chan, Sherman. Director, MOSAIC, Vancouver, 23 April 2004.

Chaudhry, Naveed. Executive Director, Peel Multicultural Council (PMC), 10 December 2003.

Cheng, Ansar. Director of Settlement, S.U.C.C.E.S.S., 3 May 2004.

Clapman, Ward. Superintendent, Officer in Charge, RCMP, Richmond City Detachment, 27 May 2004.

Crombie, David. CEO, Canadian Urban Institute, Toronto, 4 February 2004.

Crowe, Terry. Manager of Planning, City of Richmond, 29 April 2004.

Dinwoodie, Murray D. General Manager, Planning and Development, City of Surrey, 22 June 2004.

Douglas, Debbie. Executive Director, OCASI, Toronto, 28 November 2003.

Dunn, Sam. Project Coordinator, Best Practices for Working with Homeless Immigrants and Refugees, Access Alliance Multicultural Community Health Centre, Toronto, 3 November 2003.

Feldman, Mike. Deputy Mayor, City of Toronto, 23 September 2004.

Fennel, Susan. Mayor, City of Brampton, 20 September 2004.

Fisch, Bill. Regional Chair and CEO, Regional Municipality of York, 13 April 2004.

Gibson, Grant D. Councillor, City of Brampton, 9 September 2004.

Gill, Charan. Executive Director, PICS, Surrey, 9 February 2005, telephone interview.

Gill, Warren. VP Development, Simon Fraser University, 17 June 2004.

Green, Jim. Councillor, City of Vancouver, 26 April 2004.

Hall, Suzan. Councillor, City of Toronto, 14 January 2004.

Hall, Ric. Superintendent, Officer in Charge, Coquitlam Detachment, RCMP, June 2004.

Hansen, David. RCMP, Richmond City Detachment, 19 May 2004.

Hardy, Bruce. Executive Director, OPTIONs, Surrey, 9 February 2005, telephone interview.

Harrison, Karen. Director of Library Services, Coquitlam, 9 June 2004.

Hewson, Lauren. Committee Clerk, City of Coquitlam, 10 June 2004.

Houlden, Melanie. Deputy Chief Librarian, Library Administration, Surrey Public Library, 20 May 2004.

Huhtala, Kari. Senior Policy Planner, Policy Planning, Urban Development Division, City of Richmond, 18 February 2005, telephone interview.

Iannicca, Nando. Councillor, City of Mississauga, 19 January 2004.

Innes, Rob. Deputy City Clerk, City of Coquitlam, 10 June 2004.

Jamal, Audrey. Executive Director, Canadian Arab Federation (CAF), Toronto, 2 December 2003.

Jeffrey, Linda. MPP Brampton-Centre, February 2004.

Jones, Jim. Regional Councillor, City of Markham, 27 February 2004.

Jones, Warren. City Manager, City of Coquitlam, 10 June 2004.

Keung, Nicolas. Immigration/Diversity Reporter, *Toronto Star*, January 2005.

Kingsbury, Jon. Mayor, City of Coquitlam, 24 June 2004.

Kohli, Rajpal. Adviser, Equal Employment Opportunity Program, City of Vancouver, 28 April 2004.

Lee, Rose. Policy Coordinator, Diversity Management, Strategic and Corporate Policy/Healthy Cities Office, City of Toronto, 17 November 2003.

Leiba, Sheldon. General Manager, Brampton Board of Trade, 27 May 2005, telephone interview.

Louis, Tim. Councillor, City of Vancouver, 11 June 2004.

Magado, Marlene. Chair, Markham Race Relations Committee, Markham, 17 February 2004. Follow-up interview in October 2004.

Manning, Garnett. Councillor, City of Brampton, 5 October 2004.

McCallion, Hazel. Mayor, City of Mississauga, 13 April 2004.

McCallum, Doug. Mayor, City of Surrey, 20 May 2004.

McIsaac, Elizabeth. Program Manager, Maytree Foundation, Toronto, 26 January 2004.

McKitrick, Annie. Executive Director, Surrey Social Futures; School Trustee, Surrey; Member of RIAC, 27 May 2004.

Melles, Amanuel. Executive Director, Family Neighborhood Services, Toronto, 21 January 2004.

Merryweather, Brian. Manager, Human Resources, Human Resources Division, Finance, Technology, and Human Resources, City of Surrey, 22 June 2004.

Mihevc, Joe. Councillor, City of Toronto, 5 December 2003.

Mital, Umendra. City Manager, City of Surrey, 22 June 2004.

Moscoe, Howard. Councillor, City of Toronto, 23 September 2004.

Moore, Elaine. Regional Councillor, City of Brampton, 7 September 2004.

Nuss, Marie. Executive Director, Brampton Neighbourhood Resource Centre, Brampton, 19 February 2004.

Pantalone, Joe. Councillor and Deputy Mayor, City of Toronto, 13 September 2004.

Rae, Kyle. Councillor, City of Toronto, 23 September 2004.

Richmond, Ted. Coordinator, Children's Agenda Program, Laidlaw Foundation, 7 January 2004.

Sales, Jim. Commissioner of Community Services, City of Markham, 2 March 2004.

Sanghera, Balwant. Chair of RIAC, President of Multicultural Concerns Society of Richmond, 4 May 2004.

Schroeder, Scott. Community Coordinator of Diversity Services, City of Richmond, 29 April 2004.

Seepersaud, Andrea. Executive Director, Inter-Cultural Neighbourhood Social Services (ICNSS), Mississauga, 27 November 2004.

Semotuk, Verna. Senior Planner, GVRD, Policy and Planning Department, 16 February 2005, telephone interview.

Shakir, Uzma. Executive Director, Council of Agencies Serving South Asians (CASSA) and President of OCASI, Toronto, 18 December 2003.

Sherlock, Lesley. Social Planner, City of Richmond, 29 April 2004.

Spaxman, Ray. President, Spaxman Consulting Group, May 2004.

Stobie, Charles. Vice-President, Government Relations, Mississauga Board of Trade, 7 January 2005, telephone interview.

Taranu, Alex. Manager, Urban Design and Public Buildings, City of Brampton, 29 July 2004.

Taylor, Margot. Senior Adviser, Employment, Human Resources Division, City of Surrey, 22 June 2004.

Taylor, Susan. Director, Human Services Planning, Planning and Development Services Department, York Region, 23 January 2004.

Thiessen, Peter (Cpl). NCO i/c Communications Media Relations, RCMP, Richmond City Detachment, 19 May 2004.

Townsend, Ted. Manager, Communications and Corporate Programs, City of Richmond, 10 May 2004.

Usman, Khalid. Councillor, City of Markham, 2 March 2004.

Vander Kooy, Magdelena. District Manager, East Region, Toronto Public Library, City of Toronto, 9 December 2003.

Vescera, Mauro. Program Director, Vancouver Foundation, 11 March 2005, telephone interview.

Villeneuve, Judy. City Councillor, City of Surrey, 22 June 2004.

Welsh, Timothy. Program Director, Affiliation of Multicultural Societies and Service Agencies of B.C. (AMSSA), 13 May 2004.

Wong, Baldwin. Multicultural Social Planner, City of Vancouver, 3 May 2004.

Wong, Denzil. Councillor, City of Toronto, 27 September 2004.

Wong, Milton. Chancellor, Simon Fraser University, Vancouver, 12 January 2005, telephone interview.

Woodman, Lesley Ann. Executive Director, Surrey-Delta Immigrant Services Society, Surrey, 24 June 2004.

Woodsworth, Ellen. City Councillor, City of Vancouver, 26 May 2004.

Woroch, Patricia. Executive Director, Immigrant Services Society of British Columbia, 21 June 2004.

Anonymous Participants

Board Members of an immigrant-serving organization, Mississauga, 24 November 2003.

Four Mississauga civil servants, City of Mississauga, 27 November 2003.

Toronto civil servant, Toronto Public Health, 9 December 2003.

Executive director of an immigrant-serving organization, York Region, 16 December 2003.

Markham civil servant, Human Resources, City of Markham, 2 March 2004.

Municipal civil servant, Regional Municipality of Peel, 9 March 2004.

B.C. civil servant, MCAWS, Government of British Columbia, 1 March 2005, telephone interview.

Notes

1: The Municipal Role in 'Managing' Multiculturalism

1 Some scholars and practitioners distinguish the 'multicultural' model of citizenship from the traditional American 'melting pot' model of integration, in which the onus is on immigrants to adapt to the receiving culture. However, empirical research suggests that the differences between the Canadian and American approaches to accommodating ethnocultural differences are much more nuanced (see Hero 1998, 2007; Hero and Preuhs 2006; Banting et al. 2006).

2 This word is in quotation marks to acknowledge the socially constructed nature of 'race.' The data concerning the 'racial' composition of the Canadian population are based on the Canadian-made concept of 'visible minorities,' which has a racial basis. Federal policies and Statistics Canada have adopted the 1986 Employment Equity Act's definition of 'visible minorities': 'persons, other than Aboriginal people, who are non-Caucasian in race or non-white in colour.' Data on Canada's 'visible minority' population are collected in order to support the implementation of Canada's official multiculturalism.

3 According to Statistics Canada, '[a] census metropolitan area (CMA) … is formed by one or more adjacent municipalities centred on a large urban area (known as the urban core). A CMA must have a total population of at least 100,000, of which 50,000 or more must live in the urban core … To be included in the CMA … other adjacent municipalities must have a high degree of integration with the central urban area, as measured by commuting flows derived from census place of work data' (Statistics Canada n.d.a.).

4 This term is synonymous with the Vancouver CMA and the territory

covered by Metro Vancouver (the former Greater Vancouver Regional District). Recently, the GVRD board (which governs Metro Vancouver) changed its name to Metro Vancouver 'to achieve greater recognition for who [they] are and what [they] do and to give [their] board greater ability to influence at the local, national and international levels' (Metro Vancouver, 'Frequently Asked Questions'). Metro Vancouver is a political decision-making body and corporate entity under which three other corporate entities operate: the Greater Vancouver Regional District, the Greater Vancouver Water District, and the Greater Vancouver Sewerage and Drainage District. Metro Vancouver also owns the Metro Vancouver Housing Corporation (ibid.). The decision-making body is still legally called the GVRD. This book uses both Greater Vancouver and the Vancouver CMA to refer to the geographical city-region. Since it is more straightforward, the former is used unless the book refers to data that Statistics Canada collected, in which case it uses Statistics Canada's concept of CMA. It uses the term GVRD to refer to the corporate entity that continues to exist but has been renamed Metro Vancouver, since it reflects the language of the interviewees and of the secondary literature at the time of the interviews and research.

2: Linking Urban Regime Theory, Social Diversity, and Local Multiculturalism Policies

1 Mossberger and Stoker (2001) make a similar point with respect to shifting academic attention to the broader concept of 'policy networks' rather than regimes. In their view, 'the cost of moving to a higher level of abstraction is to embrace a concept that says even less about how or why coordination may occur' (2001, 821).
2 Elazar (1966, 1970) identifies three political cultures within states – 'moralistic,' 'individualistic,' and 'traditionalistic' – to explain differences in state politics and policies. Hero's theoretical framework complements Elazar's insofar as what he calls 'homogeneous' states tend to be 'moralistic,' heterogeneous states tend to be 'individualistic,' and 'bifurcated' states tend to be 'traditionalistic' (Hero 1998, 9).
3 These data were collected from municipal websites in June 2004 and based on the interviews conducted for this book.
4 Historically, municipal legislation has been highly *restrictive*, permitting municipalities to exercise only those powers for which they can identify express authority in provincial legislation. The two central legal concepts in the current debate about the degree of autonomy delegated to munici-

pal governments by provinces – *natural person powers* and *spheres of jurisdiction* – are explained by Tindal and Tindal in the most recent edition of their *Local Government in Canada* (2009, 180, Box 6.4).

5 As the City Solicitor at the City of Toronto explains, a municipal charter 'codifies the laws applicable to the particular city and contains powers and responsibilities not given to other municipalities in the province' (City Solicitor, City of Toronto 2000, 3). City charters recognize the distinctiveness of urban centres and are a form of asymmetrical provincial-municipal relationship.

6 Donald Lidstone's comment is posted on the City of Toronto's website under 'Comments on the City of Toronto Act.'

7 Like Canadian scholars, within the American context some urban-regime theorists argue that other levels of government influence and participate in urban regimes (Jones and Bachelor 1993; Burns 2002). Like provincial leaders, state political officials participate in local governance arrangements in American cities (Burns 2002).

8 A caveat is in order here: some municipalities with significantly lower immigration rates than the cases discussed here have begun to develop multiculturalism policies in their efforts to attract and retain immigrants.

3: A Comparative Overview of Municipal Multiculturalism Policies

1 Robert Putnam (1993) uses these evaluative criteria in his study of the institutional performance of regional institutions in Italy (1993, 65).

2 The three main settlement programs have been the Immigrant Settlement and Adaptation Program (ISAP), the Host Program, and the Language Instruction for Newcomers Program (LINC).

3 The book focuses on policy *outputs* rather than policy *outcomes* in measuring municipal responsiveness for the same reason as Putnam did: 'social outcomes are influenced by many factors besides governments' (ibid., 66). It is difficult to establish a direct causal relationship between a particular policy and its impact or outcome. In addition, even if one could isolate the causal effect of a policy, there might be a 'time lag' before one is able to observe the effect of the policy. The potential outcomes of many policies that are important to immigrants and ethnocultural minorities are difficult to measure, and the specific goals of policies (and therefore also definitions of outcomes) can change over time. In addition, the potential outcomes of policies are numerous and might have an impact at many levels in society (individual, institutional, community, etc.). The issue of 'who decides' what constitutes a valid measurement of a policy outcome is also an important

question, especially in multiculturalism policy. Detractors of multicultur-alism policies sometimes cite the difficulties of measuring their societal impact (according to their personal ideas of what constitutes a valid 'policy outcome') as a justification for not expending resources on such policies. Because of these difficulties, the analysis focuses on policy outputs – on the practices, initiatives, and written policies of municipal governments. In addition, the book evaluates the implementation of multiculturalism poli-cies with the help of interviews conducted with leaders in the immigrant settlement sector and leaders of ethnocultural minority organizations.

4 Where possible, interviews were conducted with civil servants in police services, public-health departments, library-service agencies, parks and recreation-services departments, and planning departments. Also, data on the responsiveness of other departments were collected on a more ad hoc basis. The goal was to ascertain the level of activity of a range of municipal departments and agencies.

5 This categorization builds on Marcia Wallace and Frances Frisken's (2000) typology of possible policy responses to immigration and ethnocultural diversity. As with their typology, the policy categories described here over-lap somewhat.

6 Their typology, in turn, builds on Ellen Tate and Louise Quesnel's (1995) categories of 'proactive' and 'reactive' policy styles.

7 See Appendix for a list of people interviewed for this study.

8 While this manuscript was being written, the City of Toronto's website was checked several times. A Diversity Advocate had not yet been ap-pointed. Then on 18 August 2008, the website indicated that Joe Mihevc had taken the position.

9 This is a measure developed by Statistics Canada. The measure constitutes 'a well-defined methodology which identities those who are substantially worse off than the average' (Fellegi 1997). Though anti-poverty groups use it as a measure of poverty, Statistics Canada researchers emphasize that poverty is a relative concept whose definition varies by society and that the agency does not consider it a measure of poverty (ibid.).

10 The RIAC comprises a councillor who serves as a liaison to council, sixteen council-appointed voting members (including six citizens), four represent-atives of the Richmond Community Services Advisory Council, two youth representatives, and representatives from School District 38, the Royal Canadian Mounted Police, Richmond Health Services, and the Ministry of Children and Family Development.

11 The way in which police services are administered varies across munici-palities. The City of Toronto and the City of Vancouver have independent

police forces. Outside Toronto, in the GTA, police services are a regional responsibility. Thus, Peel Region administers the police services of Mississauga and Brampton, and York Region administers Markham's police services. In Greater Vancouver, suburban municipalities can choose between creating an independent police force or contracting police services to the federal RCMP. Richmond, Surrey, and Coquitlam have all pursued the latter option. Under this arrangement, the RCMP detachment is bound by federal rules but is also contractually obligated to the municipality. Under the contract, municipalities fund police services and in this way shape RCMP detachments in significant ways. RCMP detachments must be responsive to the concerns of municipal officials, who otherwise might opt for an independent police force. At the same time, municipalities that contract their police services out to the RCMP are constrained in ways that municipalities with independent police forces are not. For instance, municipalities with their own forces can decide to hire officers from ethnoracial-minority communities; in contrast, the federal government decides who will be assigned to the detachment. Thus, to diversify RCMP staff, RCMP superintendents (i.e., the leaders of RCMP detachments) must show creative leadership and commitment.

12 The federal RCMP has mounted a nationwide effort to recruit visible minorities to its training centre in Regina ('RCMP No Longer Colour Blind' 2003, 1). This initiative was motivated in part by the RCMP's philosophical shift towards 'community policing,' according to which the focus of policing moves from enforcement towards building relationships of trust between communities and the police.

13 It was unclear whether the drive-by shootings to which this interviewee was referring were acts of interracial violence.

14 The Surrey-Delta Immigrant Services Society has been renamed DiverseCity community resources society since the interviews were conducted in the region in 2004.

15 The full name of this organization is OPTIONS: Services to Communities Society. Though it appears to be an acronym, it is not.

16 It is instructive that this community leader referred to the City of Surrey as 'we.' It sounds as if he is an 'insider' in Surrey's governance arrangements, while other organizations such as SDISS are 'outsiders.'

17 In general, the interviews reveal that lone visible-minority representatives on councils are often highly knowledgeable about the concerns of immigrants and visible minorities. Also, several non–visible-minority councillors observed that when visible minorities are elected to council, they often serve as bridges between ethnocultural minorities and the council.

18 MPP Linda Jeffrey also mentioned that the city has been criticized for not hiring members of the Sikh community.

19 To use a minor example of how decision makers' assumptions can make some groups feel included or excluded in city events, the city's choice of a rock 'n' roll band for its New Year's Eve celebration appealed much more to 'White' residents than to Blacks and South Asians. Also, Councillor Manning mentioned what he called a 'cookie cutter' photo of exclusively White people that was used for the cover of Brampton's *Recreation Guide*. Apparently, some citizens were so angry about this photo that they called the city 'screaming' (Manning 2004, interview). In his view, all city commissioners should be required to attend community events to learn about Brampton's diverse communities so that they can bring this knowledge to the city.

20 The Town of Markham also participates in the Toronto Region Immigrant Employment Council (TRIEC), a regional coalition in the Greater Toronto Area (GTA) that was created to address barriers to immigrants' integration into the economy. The Town of Markham also mentors immigrants through TRIEC's 'Career Bridge' program, which places immigrants in participating city bureaucracies and in private-sector jobs to help them gain Canadian experience.

21 Hero (1998) found that American 'Official English' policies were most common in two types of political units – homogeneous and bifurcated (1998, 108). Hérouxville falls into the former category.

4: Determinants of Multiculturalism Policies in the Greater Toronto Area

1 Geographer Michael Doucet (2001) found that Toronto is indeed one of the most diverse cities in the world but that the UN did not in fact make such a declaration.

2 Dillon's rule refers to a decision made by Judge John F. Dillon in 1868 in *Merriam vs. Moody's Executors*: 'A municipal corporation possesses and can exercise the following powers and no others; first, those granted in express words; second, those necessarily implied or necessarily incident to the power expressly granted; third, those absolutely essential to the declared objects and purposes of the corporation – not simply convenient but indispensable; and fourth, any fair doubt as to the existence of a power is resolved by the courts against the corporation' (Tindal and Tindal 2004, 196).

3 'Home rule' provisions, which permit local governments to act in any area that is not explicitly prohibited by state legislation, are common in the western states of the United States (ibid., 197–8).

4 The term 'access and equity' was the dominant way of describing the multiculturalism policies of the City of Toronto and Metropolitan Toronto before amalgamation. Since amalgamation the policy discourse has shifted towards 'managing diversity,' as reflected in the name of the city's primary institutional support for its multiculturalism policies – the Diversity Management and Community Engagement Unit.

5 On 31 October 2008 the government of Ontario announced that it would progressively upload the cost of social services from municipalities to the province. The process will be complete by 2018 (Government of Ontario 2008).

6 Bramptonians elect five city councillors and five regional councillors (who sit on Peel Regional Council) to represent them at the municipal level. Elaine Moore is currently a regional councillor but has also served as a city councillor (for three years) and as a Peel District School Board Trustee (for eleven years). In Mississauga, city councillors sit on both the local city council and Peel Regional Council. The mayors of both Brampton and Mississauga sit on both the local and regional councils.

7 Linda Jeffrey mentioned Brampton's Emergency Preparedness Plan as an important exception to this rule.

8 Lower-tier municipalities in the two-tiered structures in the GTA offer many services of potential importance to the immigrant settlement process – for instance, recreation services and library services.

9 In American 'strong mayor' systems, mayors exercise powers similar to those held by the president at the national level, such as the power to appoint their own administration and to exercise a veto (Banfield and Wilson 1963, 80).

10 Municipal councils vary somewhat in structure across the country; one result is that mayors have different degrees of power. Some municipalities have 'executive committees' chaired by the mayor, which concentrate power to a certain extent. However, in the absence of strong political parties, the decisions of the executive are subject to an 'undisciplined' council. Few Canadian cities have political parties at the local level, and where they do exist, the parties are not as strong as at the provincial and federal levels. Former Montreal mayor Jean Drapeau's (1960–86) Civic Party is an exception in this respect. For an overview of municipal governing structures in Canada, see Tindal and Tindal, *Local Government in Canada* (2009), ch. 8.

11 The Town of Milton posted figures taken from *Novae Res Urbis* – GTA Edition, 18 and 25 July, to show where it stands relative to other municipalities in the GTA. The municipalities with the lowest residential property-tax

rates in the GTA in 2008 were Toronto, Milton, Caledon, and Mississauga (Town of Milton website).

12 As David Crombie put it, Mel Lastman was not a 'tenter' (by which he meant that Lastman did not bring people together in cooperative efforts) (Crombie 2004, interview).

13 Toronto's council is four times the size of Mississauga's. There are eleven council members in Mississauga (including the mayor); in Toronto there are forty-five (including the mayor).

14 Though Toronto does not have a party system, there are informal divisions between 'left' and 'right' as well as numerous other cleavages on council.

15 Grantmakers Concerned with Immigrants and Refugees provides resources to private foundations that are trying to effect change in areas of importance to immigrants and refugees. See GCIR, 'About GCIR.'

16 Dominic D'Alessandro, President and CEO of Manulife Financial, and Diane Bean, Senior Vice-President of Corporate Human Resources at Manulife Financial, co-chair TRIEC.

17 People for Education is a charitable organization of parents who work to preserve a fully funded public-education system in Ontario.

18 Citizens for Local Democracy, popularly known as 'C4LD,' was a coalition that developed to protest the Conservative government's decision to amalgamate Metro Toronto and its constituent municipalities.

19 This group of residents was not formally organized, but acted through social networks and individually.

20 At the city level, the link between diversity and economic development has been influenced by the writings of Richard Florida. Florida (2002) argues that a city's economic fortunes are tied to its ability to attract the ethnically and sexually diverse 'creative class.' For example, he links a city's level of tolerance of gays and of ethnic minorities to its ability to thrive in a global economy. In Toronto's economic-development office, Florida's best-selling book, *The Rise of the Creative Class* (2002), is on staff bookshelves (Brown 2003, interview); it has become something of a 'Bible' for them.

21 Pal's (1995) study focuses on the power dynamics between civil society and the federal government – a level of government with significantly more resources than municipal governments.

5: Determinants of Multiculturalism Policies in Greater Vancouver

1 The Downtown Eastside is a high-needs neighbourhood in Vancouver with high rates of poverty, drug addiction, and crime.

2 Safe injection sites for severe cases of heroin addiction were established in

Vancouver as part of a project called the North American Opiate Media-
tions Initiative (NAOMI). See http://www.city.vancouver.bc.ca/fourpil-
lars/newsletter/Mar04/NAOMI.htm.

3 Canada's 38th general election was held on 28 June 2004. Judy Villeneuve
was interviewed on 22 June 2004, six days before that election. At the time
of the interview cited here, local leaders were anticipating movement on
the federal government's 'New Deal for Cities and Communities' agenda
should a Liberal government be elected.

4 In Greater Vancouver, councils are elected through an at-large system.
Therefore, city councillors do not necessarily represent all neighbourhoods
in a municipality. In fact, the entire council could be composed of councillors who live in the same neighbourhood.

5 Kingsbury mentioned Japanese people. However, according to the 2001
Census, there are 850 residents out of a total of 112,890 in Coquitlam who
identify as Japanese (Statistics Canada 2002).

6 The 2001 Census recorded 112,890 residents in Coquitlam. Yet in 2002 only
57,222 people were eligible to vote in Coquitlam's election. Data concerning ineligible residents were not collected; still, one might hypothesize
that many were foreign-born residents. Also, of the 57,222 eligible voters, a
mere 15,969 cast ballots – a turnout rate of 27.7 percent of residents eligible
to vote. Thus only 14.1 percent of the population determined the election
results (City of Coquitlam, 'Official Results ...').

7 Daniel Chiu received 5,723 votes in the 2002 municipal election. The eight
councillors who were successful received between 6,163 and 8,732 votes.
Chiu was tenth on the list (ibid.).

8 The two councillors who were elected for the first time in 2002 were Fin
Donnelly and Barry Lynch.

9 Since the interviews were conducted, the party system has changed. A new
party, Vision Vancouver, has emerged from 'COPE Classic' supporters.
The NPA elected six members in the 2005 election along with its candidate
for mayor (Sam Sullivan). Vision Vancouver elected four candidates, and
COPE elected one member. Then in 2008, led by the Vision Vancouver
mayoral candidate (current Mayor Gregor Robertson), a coalition of Vision
Vancouver, COPE, and the Vancouver Green Party was victorious. The
City of Vancouver's responsiveness to multiculturalism continues as parties change and new electoral coalitions emerge on council.

10 Harcourt would later become an NDP Premier of British Columbia
(1991–6). He was named Prime Minister Martin's special adviser on cities
in December 2003. In this role he travelled across the country to consult
with Canadians on the state of Canada's cities. His research produced a

report titled *From Restless Communities to Resilient Places* (External Advisory Committee 2006).

11 In other words, this idea was diffused from the City of Toronto to the City of Vancouver through the C5 Forum, a coalition of mayors and civil-society leaders from five cities – Vancouver, Calgary, Winnipeg, Toronto, and Montreal – that lobbied the federal government for more resources for cities. This forum is discussed further in chapter 8.

12 *Directory: B.C. Multicultural, Anti-Racism, Immigrant, and Community Service Organizations* – a document published by the B.C. government which lists many of the most prominent immigrant-settlement organizations in Greater Vancouver – lists many more in Vancouver than elsewhere in the city-region.

13 The S.U.C.C.E.S.S. website now indicates that government funding constitutes 71 per cent of its budget (accessed 13 May 2009). The figure cited in the text was on the website during the research phase of this project (2003–5).

14 These funds are now administered by the province under the Agreement for Canada–British Columbia Cooperation on Immigration 2004.

15 The Vancouver Foundation's mission includes but is broader than simply addressing challenges related to ethnocultural diversity. For more information, see Vancouver Foundation website, 'About Us.'

16 This fact was reported in an article in 2004. However, the article does not specify which year *Time* voted Fung one of Canada's most powerful individuals.

17 The 'long-standing community' is primarily White and of European background.

18 Since the interviews were conducted, MOSAIC has been listed as a member of AMSSA. AMSSA's website was accessed on 25 July 2008. When the website was accessed on 17 May 2009, MOSAIC was no longer listed as a member (AMSSA, 'AMSSA Membership').

19 OCASI represents the settlement sector in Ontario. However, it is located in Toronto and appears to adopt strategies that reflect Toronto's more contentious political culture.

20 The University of British Columbia, Simon Fraser University, and the University of Victoria participate in this research alliance in British Columbia. One of the primary goals of the alliance is to foster the development of action-oriented research through partnerships between government and community organizations.

21 In *Crossing the Neoliberal Line* (2004), Katharyne Mitchell describes these controversies in detail, arguing that they reflect the neoliberal transforma-

tions of states that result when global migratory processes disrupt existing forms of liberal ideology (2004, 3).

22 Vancouver is an exception in this respect. In its municipal charter it lists social planning as a municipal responsibility.

23 The authors cite an interview with Kari Huhtala, who was also interviewed for this study.

24 Along with the cases in this study, Burnaby is one of Canada's most significant immigrant-receiving suburban municipalities. In 2006 its population was 200,855 and its foreign-born and visible-minority populations represented 50.6 and 55.4 percent of the population respectively (Statistics Canada 2007b).

25 The term 'Asian' is somewhat misleading. In Greater Vancouver, local people tend to refer to Chinese organizations and cultural amenities as 'Asian' and to 'South Asian' organizations and cultural amenities as 'Indian,' 'East Indian,' or 'Indo-Canadian' (Villeneuve 2004, interview).

26 There is a great deal of academic debate concerning the characteristics of 'global cities,' 'word-class cities,' and 'world cities.' See Caroline Andrew and Patrick Smith (1999) for an overview of this debate among Canadian urban scholars. Few would place Vancouver in the category of 'global city' as defined by the comparative literature. Following Saskia Sassen's *The Global City* (2001), the term generally refers to the top tier in the international hierarchy of cities – that is, the cities (including New York, London, and Tokyo) that control the global economy.

27 The present research did not uncover evidence of a direct relationship between VanCity and the City of Vancouver. VanCity has ongoing relationships with immigrant-settlement agencies, which in turn have lasting relationships with the city (and with Baldwin Wong, the city's multicultural social planner, in particular).

28 Crowe distinguished between 'facilitating' and 'leading.' However, facilitating is also a form of leadership. In fact, urban-regime theory notes the cooperative dimension of leadership. Urban-regime theory implies 'co-leadership.'

29 In reality, this would have been beyond the scope of municipal authority.

30 This concept is new in Richmond. It was developed in Quebec as a normative alternative to the concept of multiculturalism. The terms 'multiculturalism' and 'interculturalism' mean different things to different people, but according to some, the latter term emphasizes cultural integration to a greater extent than the former.

31 According to the 2006 Census, 57 per cent of Surrey's immigrant population does not speak English at home. Punjabi is by far the most common

non-English language in Surrey, with almost 43,000 Surrey residents speaking this language at home. It is followed by Chinese languages (just over 11,000 residents), Korean (just over 5,000), Hindi (just over 5,000), and Tagalog (just under 5,000) (British Columbia 2008).

32 The municipal legislation that now governs Coquitlam is the Community Charter (2003).This legislation lists 'fostering the economic, social and environmental well-being of its [a municipality's] community' as one of four municipal purposes (Community Charter, SBC 2003, c. 26, Part II, Division I, 7(d)). http://www.bclaws.ca/Recon/document/freeside/-%20 C%20-/Community%20Charter%20%20SBC%202003%20%20c.%2026/00_ Act/03026_02.xml#section7

33 This does not mean that local leaders do not recognize the importance of positive intercultural relations to creating a climate conducive to business prosperity and growth.

6: The Relationship between Urban Regimes, Types of Social Diversity, and Multiculturalism Policies

1 Hero deduces the three forms of political pluralism from the literature on state politics and from his theoretical framework. However, he does not describe the political dynamics within states in any detail to illustrate the nature of these forms of pluralism in practice.

2 The term 'race' is used in the categories, because they were developed on the basis of Statistics Canada's 'visible minority' category, which emphasizes colour and 'race,' defining visible minorities as 'non white in colour and non Caucasian in race.' However, many categories do not constitute what is commonly considered 'racial' categories. For instance, the categories 'Chinese' and 'South Asian' are arguably national and geographical constructions, not 'racial' ones.

3 However, multiracial municipalities share a common feature with Hero's (1998) heterogeneous configuration as well – the presence of a moderate number of 'white ethnics.'

4 These areas are Vancouver's eastside (including Strathcona, Grandview–Woodland, and South Main Street), Kerrisdale–Oakridge–Shaughnessy, Richmond, an area that includes parts of Delta and northwest Surrey, and an area in the Tri-Cities (Coquitlam, Port Coquitlam, Port Moody) (Hiebert 2003, 8–9).

5 David Edgington, Michael Goldberg, and Thomas Hutton (2003) also make this observation with respect to Richmond.

7: Multiculturalism and Multilevel Governance: The Role of Structural Factors in Managing Urban Diversity

1 Karim Karim (2008) refers to Canada's 'legislative and bureaucratic infrastructure' to support pluralism in a recent paper produced for the Global Centre for Pluralism's inaugural round table.
2 As Sellers (2002b) explains: 'An infrastructure may impose not only specific or direct effects on the conditions that elites and activists most immediately involved in governance face but diffuse or indirect effects through influences on preferences of political constituencies, consumers, and firms' (2002b, 623).
3 Mike Harris led the Conservative government from 1995 until April 2002, when Ernie Eves replaced him as leader. Eves was defeated by the Liberals under Dalton McGuinty in 2003. This chapter focuses on the Harris era, because many of the decisions that most affected urban-regime dynamics in Toronto were made during Harris's tenure as premier.
4 The Canada Assistance Plan was a shared-cost program between the federal and provincial governments to provide social services. This program was launched in 1966.
5 The Established Programs Financing grant was a block grant under which the federal government transferred money to the provinces to fund post-secondary education and health. This program was launched in 1977.
6 The CHST reduced funding for social services, post-secondary education, and health from $18.3 billion in 1995–6 to $12.5 billion in 1997–8 (Courchene 2005b, 4).
7 For example, the federal government introduced the Millennium Scholarship Program and the Child Tax Benefit.
8 Examples include the GST exemption, the federal gas-tax transfer (GTT), and homelessness grants under the Supporting Communities Partnership Initiative (SCPI).
9 In his view, in order to adjust to the new, knowledge-based economy paradigm, 'Ottawa transferred aspects of the old-paradigm of nation building (forestry, mining, energy etc.) to provinces, presumably in part to make room on the federal policy plate for new-paradigm policies and programs,' many of which imply new fiscal relationships with Canada's largest city-regions (Courchene 2005a, 13–14).
10 The Conservative party used this political slogan to describe its platform during the 1995 election. The 'revolution' involved a variety of neoliberal-inspired reforms, including budgetary reforms, dramatic cuts to social programs, downloading to cities, and reductions in income taxes.

11 An example of how local civil-society leaders pooled resources to develop the capacity to pressure upper levels of government to give Toronto a new status within Canadian federalism.

12 In this context, 'regional governing institutions' refer to corporate institutions for governing the entire metropolitan area or the Greater Toronto Area, and not to the regional municipalities that constitute the second tier of suburban municipalities in the Greater Toronto Area, such as Peel Region.

13 The province has since taken a leadership role in land-use planning policy.

14 Toronto Act Now is a 'new coalition of social advocacy and environmental groups [that] entered the fray ... to ensure the voice of ordinary people is at least heard' (James 2005).

15 Dr Patricia McCarney, one of the local leaders who participated in the drafting of the Greater Toronto Area Charter (2001), is the Director of the Global Cities Program at the University of Toronto's Munk Centre for International Studies.

16 Others include crafting a new fiscal deal for cities, improving Toronto's physical infrastructure, reviving tourism in Toronto, creating a world-class research alliance, investing in people (through early childhood education, public education, and post-secondary education), strengthening the social and community infrastructure, and supporting the arts and cultural industries. See Toronto City Summit Alliance, 'Enough Talk: An Action Plan for the Toronto Region.' http://www.torontoalliance.ca/docs/TCSA_report.pdf

17 See TRIEC, 'About Us,' for a list of participants.

18 Regional Districts in British Columbia are governed by a board of directors 'comprising councillors appointed by and from the councils of incorporated municipalities within its boundaries and representatives elected from the population of the unorganized areas' (Tindal and Tindal 2004, 87). To account for differences in the size of constituent municipalities, a system of weighted voting exists with respect to budgetary decisions and when decisions are being made that will only affect a particular area of the district (ibid.). Regional districts do not levy their own taxes, but bill municipal governments for the services they provide their members. In the case of unincorporated municipalities, they bill the province (ibid., 88).

19 Murray's hypothesis that the GVRD might impede the development of a strong urban-autonomy movement owing to the fact that it brings together a diverse group of competing interests supports this interpretation (Murray 2004, slide 20).

20 John Sewell is a former Toronto mayor, a journalist, and a city activist.

21 Eligible projects included infrastructure projects in water, waste water,

solid-waste management, community energy, capacity building, and transit; and – in communities with populations of less than 500,000 – roads and bridges, presumably because in smaller communities basic infrastructure is less developed.

22 For instance, the population of Mississauga is similar to that of Winnipeg. However, because Mississauga is a suburban municipality that borders Toronto, its needs are very different from Winnipeg's. Winnipeg is the main urban centre in Manitoba and is much older. Its infrastructure is also much older. Furthermore, Mississauga's location in the GTA means that residents of Mississauga benefit from Toronto's infrastructure, including its public-transit system. Thus, the City of Toronto's portion of the GTT will benefit residents of the entire region who work in or visit Toronto. In the Greater Toronto Area, municipalities that border Toronto can 'free ride' on the city's infrastructure investments.

23 The AMO 'is a non-profit organization representing almost all of Ontario's 445 municipal governments and provides a variety of services and products to members and non-members' (AMO 2008). Its equivalent organization at the countrywide level is the Federation of Canadian Municipalities (FCM).

24 'Tax increment financing (TIF) is an economic development tool that municipalities can use to stimulate private investment and development in targeted areas by capturing the increased tax revenue generated by the private development itself and using the tax revenues to pay for public improvements and infrastructure necessary to enable development' (Bond n.d., 1).

25 See the Ministry of Citizenship and Immigration, Government of Ontario Fact Sheet, on the Canada–Ontario Immigration Agreement on the Ministry's website.

26 Annex F of the agreement deals with 'Partnerships with Municipalities.' The Annex recognizes that 'Canada and Ontario share a mutual interest in fostering partnerships and the participation of municipal governments and community and private sector stakeholders in immigration' (1.1). Priorities for tri-level partnerships include the following: information sharing and consultation (4.1), the attraction and retention of immigrants (4.2), and immigrant settlement and integration (4.3). The agreement will be implemented with the assistance of a Municipal Immigration Committee (5.2). According to the terms of the agreement, this new administrative structure is 'consistent with federal, provincial and AMO commitment to a New Deal for Cities and Communities which involves a seat at the table for municipalities on national issues most important to them' (Canada–Ontario Immigration Agreement, 2005).

27 Article 5.3 of Annex F acknowledges that 'in the past five years, up to 50% of all immigrants to Canada have arrived annually in the Toronto census metropolitan area alone and that this creates particular challenges in terms of maintaining services to all residents of this area while ensuring the efficient integration of newcomers into the community' (5.3.1) (ibid.).

28 Former Conservative cabinet minister David Emerson was elected in 2006 in the riding of Vancouver-Kingsway as a Liberal and crossed the floor after the election.

29 See for instance Horak (1998).

8: Municipal Multiculturalism Policies and the Capacity to Manage Social Change

1 Irene Bloemraad (2006) argues that funding for immigrant-settlement organizations is an important part of the explanation for Canada's greater level of success in immigrant-naturalization rates and levels of political incorporation relative to the United States.

2 Mike Harcourt was Mayor of Vancouver between 1980 and 1986 and Premier of British Columbia from 1991 to 1996. The current premier, Gordon Campbell, was Mayor of Vancouver from 1986 to 1993 and has been Premier of B.C. since 2001.

3 'White ethnics' were not included in the categorization, though interestingly, they tend to be more numerous in multiracial municipalities.

4 Hero (1998) nevertheless acknowledges: 'There is, of course, extensive inter- and intra-group complexity, and there also may be interminority political competition' (1998, 11).

5 Hero does not define what he means by hierarchical pluralism. However, it appears to mean that racial minorities have a say but an unequal one in relation to Whites. In his other work, Hero (1992) has developed the concept of 'two-tiered pluralism' to express a similar idea.

6 This is not to say that race-based inequalities do not exist in Canada. Rather, the question needs to be examined empirically. The only ethnoracial 'group' in Canada that approximates the African-American experience is Aboriginal peoples.

References

Abu-Laban, Yasmeen. 2008. 'Pluralism as Process: The Role of Liberal Democratic Institutions.' Unpublished paper presented at the inaugural round
table of the Global Centre for Pluralism, Ottawa, 13 May.
– 1997. 'Ethnic Politics in a Globalizing Metropolis: The Case of Vancouver.'
In *Politics of the City: A Canadian Perspective*, ed. Timothy L. Thomas. Scarborough: Nelson. 77–96.
Abu-Laban, Yasmeen, and Christina Gabriel. 2002. *Selling Diversity: Immigration, Multiculturalism, Employment Equity, and Globalization.* Peterborough:
Broadview.
Access Alliance Multicultural Community Health Centre. 2003 (March).
'Best Practices for Working with Homeless Immigrants and Refugees.' To-
ronto. http://atwork.settlement.org/sys/atwork_library_detail.asp?doc_
id=1003145
Advisory Panel on the Fiscal Imbalance. 2006. 'Reconciling the Irreconcilable:
Addressing Canada's Fiscal Imbalance.' Report submitted to the Council
of the Federation, 31 March 2006. http://www.councilofthefederation.ca/
pdfs/Report_Fiscalim_Mar3106.pdf
Ail, Josh, Dawn Dobson-Borsoi, and Rob Eley. n.d. 'Closing the Cultural Gap:
The City of Surrey.' Report commissioned by the City of Surrey. Burnaby:
B.C. Institute of Technology.
AMO (Association of Municipalities of Ontario). 'A Guide to AMO Member
Benefits and Services.' http://www.amo.on.ca/AM/Template.
cfm?Section=About_AMO&Template=/CM/ContentDisplay.cfm&
ContentID=152512
AMSSA. 'AMSSA Membership.' http://www.amssa.org/members/index.htm
Andrew, Caroline. 2001. 'The Shame of (Ignoring) the Cities.' *Journal of Cana-
dian Studies* 35, no. 4: 100–10.

Andrew, Caroline, Katherine A. Graham, and Susan D. Philips, eds. 2002. *Urban Affairs: Back on the Policy Agenda*. Montreal and Kingston: McGill–Queen's University Press.

Andrew, Caroline, and Patrick Smith. 1999. 'World-Class Cities: Can or Should Canada Play?' In *World-Class Cities: Can Canada Play?* ed. Caroline Andrew, Pat Armstrong, and André Lapierre. Ottawa: University of Ottawa Press. 5–25.

Bailey, Robert W. 1999. *Gay Politics, Urban Politics: Identity and Economics in the Urban Setting*. New York: Columbia University Press.

Banfield, Edward C., and James Q. Wilson. 1963. *City Politics*. Cambridge, MA: Harvard University Press.

Banting, Keith, George Hoberg, and Richard Simeon, eds. 1997. *Degrees of Freedom: Canada and the United States in a Changing World*. Montreal and Kingston: McGill–Queen's University Press.

Banting, Keith, Richard Johnston, Will Kymlicka, and Stuart Soroka. 2006. 'Do Multiculturalism Policies Erode the Welfare State? An Empirical Analysis.' In *Multiculturalism and the Welfare State: Recognition and Redistribution in Contemporary Democracies*, ed. Keith Banting and Will Kymlicka. New York: Oxford University Press. 49–91.

Basran, Gurcharn S., and B. Singh Bolaria. 2003. *The Sikhs in Canada: Migration, Race, Class, and Gender*. New Dehli: Oxford University Press.

Belgrave, Roger. 1995. 'Bell Supporters Come Out in Force.' *Markham Economist and Sun*, 30 August.

Bell, Carole. 1995. Letter to the Editor. *Markham Economist and Sun*, 16 August.

Berdahl, Loleen. 2006. 'How the Harper Government Can Court Canada's Big Cities.' *Calgary Herald*, 26 February.

Bloemraad, Irene. 2006. *Becoming a Citizen: Incorporating Immigrants and Refugees in the United States and Canada*. Berkeley: University of California Press.

Bond, Kenneth W. n.d. 'Tax Increment Financing – Can You? Should You?' Squire Sanders Legal Counsel Worldwide. http://www.nysedc.org/memcenter/TIF%20Paper.pdf

Boudreau, Julie-Anne. 2006. 'Intergovernmental Relations and Polyscalar Social Mobilization: The Cases of Montreal and Toronto.' In *Canada: The State of the Federation 2004*, ed. Robert Young and Christian Leuprecht. Montreal and Kingston: McGill-Queen's University Press. 161–80.

Bradford, Neil. 2002. 'Why Cities Matter: Policy Research Perspectives for Canada.' Canadian Policy Research Networks (CPRN) Discussion Paper no. F23, June. http://www.cprn.org/doc.cfm?doc=168&l=en

Brampton Board of Trade. http://www.bramptonbot.com

– 'Mandate of Multiculturalism Committee.' http://www.bramptonbot.com/committees.htm

Brenner, Neil. 2004. *New State Spaces: Urban Governance and the Rescaling of Statehood*. Oxford: Oxford University Press.

Bridson-Boyczuk, Karen. 2004. 'Business Leaders Singing City's Praises: Business Leaders Still Bullish about City.' *Mississauga News,* 27 November.

Broadbent, Alan. 2008. *Urban Nation: Why We Need to Give Power Back to the Cities to Make Canada Strong.* Toronto: HarperCollins.

– 2003. 'New Structures/New Connections.' Speech to Conference on Municipal–Federal–Provincial Relations. Queen's University, Institute of Intergovernmental Relations, 9–10 May, Kingston. http://www.queensu.ca/iigr/conf/Arch/03/03-2/Broadbent.pdf

– 2001. 'The Philanthropic Contract: Mutual Benefit for the Public Good.' Ottawa: Caledon Institute of Social Policy, June. http://www.scribd.com/doc/8177190/Alan-Broadbent-The-Philanthropic-Contract-2001

Broadbent Group. 2005. *Towards a New City of Toronto Act.* Toronto: Zephyr.

Browning, Rufus P., Dale R. Marshall, and David H. Tabb. 1984. *Protest Is Not Enough: The Struggle of Blacks and Hispanics for Equality in the United States.* Berkeley: University of California Press.

Burns, Peter. 2002. 'The Intergovernmental Regime and Public Policy in Hartford, Connecticut.' *Journal of Urban Affairs* 24, no. 1: 55–73.

Cairns, Alan C. 1985. 'The Embedded State: State-Society Relations in Canada.' In *State and Society: Canada in Comparative Perspective,* ed. Keith Banting. Toronto: University of Toronto Press, in cooperation with the Royal Commission on the Economic Union and Development Prospects for Canada and the Canadian Government Publications Centre. Ottawa: Supply Services Canada. 53–86.

'Canada's Cities: Unleash Our Potential.' http://www.canadascities.ca/index.htm

Canada-Ontario Immigration Agreement. 2005. 'Annex F,' Citizenship and Immigration, http://www.cic.gc.ca/EnGLIsh/department/laws-policy/agreements/ontario/ont-2005-annex-f.asp

Canada, Ontario, Association of Municipalities of Ontario, and City of Toronto. 2005. Agreement for the Transfer of Federal Gas Tax Revenues under the New Deal for Cities and Communities. 17 July. http://www.infc.gc.ca/altformats/pdf/gtf-fte-on-eng.pdf

Canadian Press. 2006. 'Queen's Park Welcomes Immigration Funding from Feds,' *Toronto Star,* 15 December. http://www.thestar.com/article/153151

Carabram. http://www.carabram.org

Carens, Joseph H. 2000. *Culture, Citizenship, and Community: A Contextual Exploration of Justice as Evenhandedness.* Oxford: Oxford University Press.

Carassauga. http://www.carassauga.mantis.biz

CERIS. 'Governance Board and Directors.' http://ceris.metropolis.net/frameset_e.html

Chin, Joe. 2008. '"Forget about Being Debt-Free": Hazel.' *Mississauga News*, 12 June. http://www.mississauga.com/article/15194

Chong, Dennis. 1991. *Collective Action and the Civil Rights Movement*. Chicago: University of Chicago Press.

CIC (Citizenship and Immigration Canada). 2002. *Facts and Figures 2002: Immigration Overview*. http://www.cic.gc.ca/english/pub/facts2002/immigration/immigration_4.html

Citrin, Jack, Beth Reingold, and Donald P. Green. 1990. 'The "Official English" Movement and the Symbolic Politics of Language in the United States.' *Western Political Quarterly* 43, no. 3: 535–60.

City of Brampton. 2007. 'City of Brampton Approves Multilingual Program.' Media release 07–006, 17 January 2007. http://www.brampton.ca/media-releases/07-006.pdf

– 2006. 'Brampton Launches Pilot Project for Multilingual Telephone Services.' Media release 06-017, 27 January 2006. http://www.city.brampton.on.ca/media-releases/06-017.tml

City of Coquitlam. 2007a. 'Multiculturalism Advisory Committee.' Minutes – Regular Committee Meeting, 6 November 2007. http://www.coquitlam.ca/NR/rdonlyres/99B3D5CD-D1AD-474C-A2AF-CD77724D0013/76366/CITYDOCS616297v1RC_COTW_feb252008_59911.PDF

– 2007b. 'To: Acting City Manager. From: Manager Corporate Planning. Subject: Participation on Provincial Joint Steering Committee on Multiculturalism. For: Committee of the Whole.' 4 October. File 01-0620-01/000/2007-1.

– 2006. 'Multiculturalism Advisory Committee – Terms of Reference.' Policy and Procedure Manual, ch. 5. November. File 01-0540-00/01-002/1, Doc. 457607 vol. 1.

– 2003. 'Liveable Communities Advisory Committee.' Policy and Procedure Manual, 3 November, rev. 19 January 2004, File 01-0540-20/536/2003-1, Doc 213113.

– 2002. 'Official Results of the 2002 Local Government Election.' http://www.coquitlam.ca/City+Hall/City+Government/Election/_Official+Results+of+the+2002+Local+Government+Election.htm

City of Mississauga. 'City Hall – Languages.' http://www.mississauga.ca/portal/cityhall/languages

– 'City of Mississauga Integrates New Canadians Into the Workforce.' http://www.mississauga.ca/portal/cityhall/pressreleases?pdf

City of Richmond. 2002. 'Proposed Richmond Intercultural Advisory Committee.' Report to General Purposes Committee. File 4055-01. 7 February.

- 1996. 'Advisory Committee on Intercultural Relations – Minutes.' 18 April 1996.
- 1994a. 'Memorandum re: Report on Multiculturalism.' File 0100-E6. 7 January.
- 1994b. 'Report to Committee of the Whole re: Ethnic Relations.' File 0100-E6. 15 August.

City of Surrey. 2006. News release: 'Mayor Dianne Watts appoints Coun. Mary Martin as Surrey's first Multicultural Advisory Committee Chair.' 5 December. http://www.surrey.ca/Whats+New/News+Releases/Old+-+2006/December/Mayor+Dianne+Watts+appoints+Coun.+Marvin+Hunt+Chair+of+Intergovernmental+Advisory+Committee.htm

- 1997. 'Task Force Report on Intercultural Inclusivity: Reaching Out in Surrey.' Parks and Recreation Department. January.

City of Toronto. 'Diversity Advocate.' http://www.toronto.ca/diversity/advocate.htm

- 2006. Backgrounder: '2006 City Operating Budget of $7.6 Approved by Council.' 30 March. http://www.toronto.ca/budget2006/pdf/2006operatingbackgrounder_march30_final.pdf
- 2004. 'Review of the Implementation of Recommendations of the Final Report of the Task Force on Community Access and Equity.' Clause embodied in Report no. 3 of the Audit Committee, as adopted by the Council of the City of Toronto at its meeting on 18–20 May 2004.
- 2001. 'Immigration and Settlement Policy Framework.' Clause embodied in Report no. 4 of the Community Services Committee, as adopted by the Council of the City of Toronto at its meeting held on 30 May–1 June 2001.

City of Vancouver. 'Multiculturalism and Diversity: Role of Social Planning in Multiculturalism and Diversity,' http://vancouver.ca/commsvcs/socialplanning/initiatives/multicult/civicpolicy.htm

- n.d. 'Building Inclusive Community: Diversity Policy and Practice in the City of Vancouver.'
- 2007. 'Report of the Mayor's Task Force on Immigration,' November. http://vancouver.ca/commsvcs/socialplanning/initiatives/multicult/PDF/0711_MTFI_report.pdf
- 2005. 'Administrative Report.' Mayor's Working Group on Immigration in consultation with Director of Social Planning. http://vancouver.ca/ctyclerk/cclerk/20051004/documents/rr1.pdf
- 1999. 'Administrative Report'. RTS No. 943, CC File No. 1304.
- 1997. 'Equal Employment Opportunity Program: Progress Report 1986–1996.' May.

City Solicitor, City of Toronto. 2000. 'Powers of Canadian Cities – The Legal Framework.' June (updated October 2001). http://www.canadascities.ca

Clarke, Susan E. 1999. 'Regional and Transnational Regimes: Multi-Level Governance Processes in North America.' Paper presented at the annual meeting of the American Political Science Association, September, Atlanta.

Clarke, Susan E., and Gary L. Gaile. 1998. *The Work of Cities*. Minneapolis: University of Minnesota Press.

Clutterbuck, Peter, and Rob Howarth. 2002. 'Toronto's Quiet Crisis: The Case for Social and Community Infrastructure Investment.' Research Paper no. 198, University of Toronto, November. http://www.urbancentre.utoronto.ca/pdfs/curp/Clutterbuck_198_Toronto.pdf

Coquitlam Now. 2008. 'It's Official – Coquitlam Is a Cultural Capital of Canada,' http://www2.canada.com/coquitlamnow/news/story.html?id=dd6644c0-8034-410d-9696-c5124ef195a1&k=63027

Courchene, Tom. 2007. 'Global Futures for Canada's Global Cities.' Montreal: Institute for Research on Public Policy. *Policy Matters* 8, no. 2 (June). http://www.irpp.org/wp/archive/wp2005-03.pdf

– 2005a. 'City State and the State of Cities: Political-Economy and Fiscal Federalism Dimensions.' Montreal: Institute for Research on Public Policy. http://www.irpp.org/wp/archive/wp2005-03.pdf

– 2005b. 'Vertical and Horizontal Fiscal Imbalances: An Ontario Perspective.' Background notes for a presentation to the Standing Committee on Finance, House of Commons, 4 May.

Dahl, Robert A. 1961. *Who Governs? Democracy and Power in an American City*. New Haven: Yale University Press.

D'Alessandro, Dominic. 2004. 'Capitalize on Immigrants' Promise.' *Globe and Mail*, 15 September.

Dewing, Michael, and Marc Leman. 2006. 'Canadian Multiculturalism.' Library of Parliament, p. 23. http://www.parl.gc.ca/information/library/PRBpubs/936-e.htm

DiGaetano, Alan, and Elizabeth Strom. 2003. 'Comparative Urban Governance: An Integrated Approach.' *Urban Affairs Review* 38, no. 3: 356–93.

Diverse City. 'The Greater Toronto Leadership Project.' http://www.diversecitytoronto.ca

Doucet, Michael. 2001. 'The Anatomy of an Urban Legend: Toronto's Multicultural Reputation.' CERIS working paper no. 16. April. http://ceris.metropolis.net/Virtual%20Library/WKPP%20List/WKPP2001/CWP16_Doucet_final.pdf

– 1999. 'Toronto in Transition: Demographic Change in the Late Twentieth Century.' CERIS working paper no. 6. May. http://ceris.metropolis.net/research-policy/wkpp_list.htm

Edgington, David W., Michael A. Goldberg, and Thomas Hutton. 2003. 'The
Hong Kong Chinese in Vancouver.' Research on Immigration and Integration
in the Metropolis (RIIM), Vancouver Centre of Excellence, working paper
series no. 03–12. http://mbc.metropolis.net/research/working/2003.html

Edgington, David W., Bronwyn Hanna, Thomas Hutton, and Susan Thomp-
son. 2001. 'Urban Governance, Multiculturalism, and Citizenship in Sydney
and Vancouver.' Research on Immigration and Integration in the Metropolis
(RIIM), Vancouver Centre of Excellence, working paper series no. 01–05.
http://mbc.metropolis.net/research/working/2001.html

Edgington, David W., and Thomas A. Hutton. 2002. 'Multiculturalism and Local Government in Greater Vancouver.' Research on Immigration and Integration in the Metropolis (RIIM), Vancouver Centre of Excellence, working
paper series no. 02–06. http://mbc.metropolis.net/research/working/2002.
html

Elkin, Stephen. 1987. *City and Regime in the American Republic*. Chicago: University of Chicago Press.

Fainstein, Norman I., and Susan S. Fainstein. 1986. *Restructuring the City*. New
York: Longman.

FCCM (Federation of Chinese Canadians in Markham). http://www.fccm.ca/
index2.html

Feldman, Lionel. 2006. 'Urban Policy Making: Substance, Process Strategy in
the Quest for a New Deal for Toronto.' Speech delivered at the Local and
Urban Politics section (CPSA) dinner at annual meeting of the Canadian
Political Science Association, 3 June, Toronto.

Fellegi, Ivan P. 1997. 'On Poverty and Low Income.' Statistics Canada.

Ferman, Barbara. 2002. 'Broadening the Franchise: Charter Reform and Neigh-
borhood Representation in Los Angeles.' Prepared for the John Randolph
Haynes and Dora Haynes Foundation Conference on Reform, L.A. Style:
The Theory and Practice of Urban Governance at Century's Turn. Univer-
sity of Southern California School of Policy, Planning, and Development,
Los Angeles, 19–20 September 2002.

– 1996. *Challenging the Growth Machine: Neighborhood Politics in Chicago and
Pittsburgh*. Lawrence: University Press of Kansas.

Florida, Richard. 2002. *The Rise of the Creative Class*. New York: Basic.

Francis, Diane. 2001. 'Cities Fight for Fair Refugee Policy.' *National Post*, 15
May.

Frisken, Frances, and Marcia Wallace. 2003. 'Governing the Multicultural City-
Region.' *Canadian Public Administration* 46, no. 2: 153–77.

– 2000. 'The Response of the Municipal Public Service Sector to the Challenge
of Immigrant Settlement.' Rev. May 2002. http://www.settlement.org/
downloads/Municipal_Sector.pdf

Funders' Network on Racism and Poverty. http://www.rapnet.ca

Garber, Judith A., and David L. Imbroscio. 1996. 'The Myth of the North American City Reconsidered: Local Constitutional Regimes in Canada and the United States.' *Urban Affairs Review* 31, no. 5: 595–624.

GCIM (Global Commission on International Migration). 2005. 'Migration in an Interconnected World: New Directions for Action.' 88. http://www.gcim.org/attachements/gcim-complete-report-2005.pdf

GCIR (Grantmakers Concerned with Immigrants and Refugees). 'About GCIR.' http://www.gcir.org/about

Gherson, Giles. 2005. 'Push Pedal to Metal on New Deal Campaign.' *Toronto Star*, 5 February, A2.

Gillespie, Kerry. 2004. 'A Star Recruit to Fight for Cities: Honderich Hired as Mayor's Envoy – He'll Champion Urban "New Deal."' *Toronto Star*, 27 May, B1.

Goldberg, Michael A, and John Mercer. 1986. *The Myth of the North American City: Continentalism Challenged*. Vancouver: UBC Press.

Good, Kristin. 2007. 'Urban Regime Building as a Strategy of Intergovernmental Reform: The Case of Toronto's Role in Immigrant Settlement.' Paper presented at the Canadian Political Science Association Annual Conference, Saskatoon, May 30–June 1.

– 2006. 'Multicultural Democracy in the City: Explaining Municipal Responsiveness to Immigrants and Ethnocultural Minorities.' PhD diss., Department of Political Science, University of Toronto.

– 2005. 'Patterns of Politics in Canada's Immigrant-Receiving Cities and Suburbs: How Settlement Patterns Shape the Municipal Role in Multiculturalism Policy.' *Policy Studies* 26, nos. 3 and 4: 261–89.

– 2004. 'Explaining Municipal Responsiveness to Immigration: An Urban Regime Analysis of Toronto and Mississauga.' Centre for Urban and Community Studies, Research Paper no. 199, December 2004.

Government of British Columbia. February 2008. '2006 Census Fact Sheet: Surrey.' Welcome BC: Multiculturalism and Immigration Branch, February. http://www.llbc.leg.bc.ca/public/PubDocs/bcdocs/440579/surrey2006.pdf

Government of Canada. 2003. *Multiculturalism: Respect, Equality, Diversity: Program Guidelines*. July. Ottawa: Canadian Heritage.

Government of Canada. External Advisory Committee on Cities and Communities. 2006. Final Report: *From Restless Communities to Resilient Places: Building a Stronger Future for All Canadians*. http://www.civicgovernance.ca/files/uploads/munities_to_resilient_places_Mike_Harcourt_0.pdf

Government of Ontario. 2008. 'Fact Sheet: Uploading Ontario Works.' http://

www.news.ontario.ca/mah/en/2008/10/fact-sheet-uploading-ontario-works.html

Graham, Katherine A., Susan D. Philips, and Allan M. Maslove. 1998. *Urban Governance in Canada: Representation, Resources, and Restructuring*. Toronto: Harcourt Canada.

GVRD (Greater Vancouver Regional District), Policy and Planning Department. 2003. '2001 Census Bulletin no. 6 – Immigration.' February.

Hansen, Darah. 2003. 'RCMP No Longer Colour Blind.' *Richmond News*, 22 November, pp. 1, 3.

Harding, Alan. 1995. 'Elite Theory and Growth Machines.' In *Theories of Urban Politics*, ed. David Judge, Gerry Stoker, and Harold Wolman. Thousand Oaks: Sage. 35–53.

Hiebert, Daniel. 2003. 'Are Immigrants Welcome? Introducing the Vancouver Community Studies Survey.' RIIM working paper no. 03-06. March. http://mbc.metropolis.net/Virtual%20Library/2003/wp03-06.pdf

Hero, Rodney E. 2007. *Racial Diversity and Social Capital: Equality and Community in America*. New York: Cambridge University Press.

– 2003. 'Multiple Theoretical Traditions in American Politics and Racial Policy Inequality.' *Political Research Quarterly* 56, no. 4 (December): 401–8.

– 1998. *Faces of Inequality*. New York: Oxford University Press.

– 1992. *Latinos and the U.S. Political System: Two-Tiered Pluralism*. Philadelphia: Temple University Press.

Hero, Rodney E., and Robert R. Preuhs. 2006. 'Multiculturalism and Welfare Policies in the U.S.A.: A State-Level Comparative Analysis.' In *Multiculturalism and the Welfare State: Recognition and Redistribution in Contemporary Democracies*, ed. Keith Banting and Will Kymlicka. New York: Oxford University Press. 121–51.

Honderich, John. 2002. 'Wanted: A New Deal for Canada's Cities.' *Toronto Star*, 12 January, A1.

Horak, Martin. 1998. 'The Power of Local Identity: C4LD and the Anti-Amalgamation Mobilization in Toronto.' Centre for Urban and Community Studies, Research Paper no. 195.

Horan, Cynthia. 2002. 'Racializing Regime Politics: Innovations in Regime Theory.' *Journal of Urban Affairs* 24, no. 1: 19–33.

Huhtala, Kari. 2004. 'Richmond – A City of Cultural Fusion and Change.' Information leaflet, 17 February.

Hunter, Floyd. 1953. *Community Power Structure: A Study of Decision Makers*. Chapel Hill: University of North Carolina Press.

Hurst, Lynda. 2005. 'How the Doctrine of "Frenchness" Failed.' *Toronto Star*, 10 November, A6.

Hutton, Thomas. 1998. 'The Transformation of Canada's Pacific Metropolis: A Study of Vancouver.' Montreal: Institute for Research on Public Policy.

Imbroscio, David L. 1997. *Reconstructing City Politics: Alternative Economic Development Regimes*. Thousand Oaks: Sage.

Inglis, Christine. 1996. 'Multiculturalism: New Policy Responses to Diversity.' MOST Policy Papers no. 4. Paris: UNESCO, http://www.unesco.org/most/pp4.htm#practice

IOM (International Organization for Migration). 'Regional and County Figures.' http://www.iom.int/jahia/Jahia/pid/255

Ip, David. 2005. 'Contesting Chinatown: Place-Making and the Emergence of "Ethnoburbia" in Brisbane, Australia.' *GeoJournal* 64, no. 1: 63–74.

James, Royson. 2005. 'New Deal Gathers Steam: Miller Pleads with Councillors to Mobilize Constituents – City, Province to Hold Public Meetings on Issues Next Week.' *Toronto Star*, 15 June, B1.

Jones, Brian D., and Lynn W. Bachelor. 1993. *The Sustaining Hand: Community Leadership and Corporate Power*, 2nd rev. ed. Lawrence: University Press of Kansas.

Judge, David. 1995. 'Pluralism.' In *Theories of Urban Politics*, ed. David Judge, Gerry Stoker, and Harold Wolman. Thousand Oaks: Sage. 13–34.

Karim, Karim H. 2008. 'Recognizing Difference: How Has Multiculturalism Actually Worked?' Unpublished paper presented at the inaugural round table of the Global Centre for Pluralism, Ottawa, 13 May.

Karyo Communications. 2000. 'Intercultural Marketing Plan.' Surrey Parks, Recreation, and Culture, City of Surrey, 1 November.

Keil, Roger, and Douglas Young. 2003. 'A Charter for the People? A Research Note on the Debate about Municipal Autonomy in Toronto.' *Urban Affairs Review* 39, no. 1: 87–102.

Kingdon, John. 1995. *Agendas, Alternatives, and Public Policies*. New York: Longman.

Kipfer, Stefan, and Roger Keil. 2002. 'Toronto Inc? Planning the Competitive City in the New Toronto.' *Antipode* (March): 227–64.

Kolb, Emil. 2004. Letter to the Honourable Judy Sgro, Office of the Chair, Regional Municipality of Peel, 19 August.

Koschinsky, Julia, and Todd Swanstrom. 2001. 'Confronting Policy Fragmentation: A Political Approach to the Role of Housing Nonprofits.' *Policy Studies Review* 18, no. 4: 111–27.

Krivel, Peter. 1995. 'Councillor Sparks "Racism" Protest.' *Toronto Star*, 21 August, A6.

Kymlicka, Will. 2008. 'Canadian Pluralism in Comparative Perspective.' Unpublished paper presented at the inaugural round table of the Global Centre for Pluralism, Ottawa, 13 May.

- 2003. 'Being Canadian.' *Government and Opposition* 38, no. 3: 357–85.
- 1998. *Finding Our Way: Rethinking Ethnocultural Relations in Canada.* Toronto: Oxford University Press.
- 1995. *Multicultural Citizenship.* Toronto: Oxford University Press.

Lauria, Mickey, ed. 1997. *Reconstructing Urban Regime Theory: Regulating Urban Politics in a Global Economy.* Thousand Oaks: Sage.

Laurier Institution. 2005. 'Diversity 2010: Leveraging the 2010 Olympic and Paralympic Games to Brand and Make Greater Vancouver a Truly Multicultural Community.' Reference WD 2351, 31 March 2005. http://www.thelaurier.ca/pdf/diversity_2010.pdf

Leo, Christopher. 2006. 'Deep Federalism: Respecting Community Difference in National Policy.' *Canadian Journal of Political Science* 39, no. 3: 481–506.
- 2003. 'Are There Urban Regimes in Canada? Comment on Timothy Cobban's "The Political Economy of Urban Development: Downtown Revitalization in London, Ontario, 1993–2002."' *Canadian Journal of Urban Research* 12, no. 2: 344–8.
- 1998. 'Regional Growth Management Regime: The Case of Portland, Oregon.' *Journal of Urban Affairs* 20: 363–94.
- 1997. 'City Politics in an Era of Globalization.' In *Reconstructing Urban Regime Theory: Regulating Urban Politics in a Global Economy,* ed. Mickey Lauria. Thousand Oaks: Sage.

Levi, Margaret. 1996. 'Social Capital and Unsocial Capital: A Review Essay of Robert Putnam's *Making Democracy Work.*' *Politics and Society* 24 (March): 45–55.

Ley, David. 2007. 'Multiculturalism: A Canadian Defence.' Research on Immigration and Integration in the Metropolis, Vancouver Centre of Excellence, working paper no. 07–04. http://mbc.metropolis.net/Virtual%20Library/2007/WP07-04.pdf

Ley, David, Daniel Hiebert, and Geraldine Pratt. 1992. 'Time to Grow Up? From Urban Village to World City, 1966–91.' In *Vancouver and its Region,* ed. Graeme Wynn and Timothy Oke. Vancouver: UBC Press, 234–66.

Ley, David, Peter Murphy, Kris Olds, and Bill Randolph. 2001. 'Immigration and Housing in Gateway Cities: The Cases of Sydney and Vancouver.' RIIM, Vancouver Centre of Excellence, working paper no. 01–03. http://mbc.metropolis.net/Virtual%20Library/2001/wp0103.pdf

Li, Wei. 2007. 'Introduction: Asian Immigration and Community in the Pacific Rim.' In *From Urban Enclave to Ethnic Suburb: New Asian Communities in Pacific Rim Countries,* ed. Wei Li. Honolulu: University of Hawaii Press. 1–22.
- 1999. 'Building Ethnoburbia: The Emergence and Manifestation of the Chinese Ethnoburb in Los Angeles' San Gabriel Valley.' *Journal of Asian American Studies* 2, no. 1: 1–28.

– 1997. 'Ethnoburb versus Chinatown: Two Types of Urban Ethnic Communities in Los Angeles.' *Cybergeo: European Journal of Geography* (online). http://www.cybergeo.eu/index1018.html

Lichbach, Mark Irving, and Alan S. Zuckerman, eds. 1997. *Comparative Politics: Rationality, Culture, and Structure.* Cambridge: Cambridge University Press.

Lidstone, Donald. 2005. 'Comments on the City of Toronto Act.' http://www.toronto.ca/mayor_miller/torontoact_comments

Lijphart, Arend. 1975. 'The Comparable-Cases Strategy in Comparative Research.' *Comparative Political Studies* 8, no. 2: 158–77.

Lim, April, Lucia Lo, Myer Siemiatycki, and Michael Doucet. 2005. 'Newcomer Services in the Greater Toronto Area: An Exploration of the Range and Funding Sources of Settlement Services.' CERIS working paper no. 35, January. http://ceris.metropolis.net/Virtual%20Library/WKPP%20List/WKPP2005/CWP35_Lim-Lo-Siemiatycki_Final.pdf

Link, Michael W., and Robert W. Oldendick. 1996. 'Social Construction and White Attitudes toward Equal Opportunity and Multiculturalism.' *Journal of Politics* 55, no. 1: 191–206.

Lipsky, Michael M. 1976. 'Toward a Theory of Street-Level Bureaucracy.' In *Theoretical Perspectives on Urban Politics,* ed. Willis D. Hawley and Michael Lipsky. Englewood Cliffs: Prentice-Hall. 196–213.

Lo, Lucia, Lu Wang, Shuguang Wang, and Yinhuan Yuan. 2007. 'Immigrant Settlement Services in the Toronto CMA: A GIS-Assisted Analysis of Supply and Demand.' CERIS working paper no. 59, July. http://ceris.metropolis.net/Virtual%20Library/WKPP%20List/WKPP2007/CWP59.pdf

Logan, John R., and Harvey L. Molotch. 1987. *Urban Fortunes: The Political Economy of Place.* Berkeley: University of California Press.

Long, Norton E. 1968. 'The Local Community as an Ecology of Games.' In *The Search for Community Power,* ed. Willis D. Wawley and Frederick M. Wirt. Englewood Cliffs: Prentice-Hall.

Lorinc, John. 2006. *The New City: How the Crisis in Canada's Urban Centres Is Reshaping the Nation.* Toronto: Penguin.

MacMillan, Melville. 2006. 'Municipal Relations with the Federal and Provincial Governments: A Fiscal Perspective.' In *Canada: The State of the Federation 2004,* ed. Robert Young and Christian Leuprecht. Montreal and Kingston: McGill–Queen's University Press.

Magnusson, Warren. 2005. 'Are Municipalities Creatures of the Provinces?' *Journal of Canadian* Studies 39, no. 2: 5–29.

– 1985. 'The Local State in Canada: Theoretical Perspectives.' *Canadian Public Administration* 28, no. 4: 575–99.

Markham Board of Trade. 1995. Media release. 29 August.

Mascoll, Philip, and Jim Rankin. 2005. 'Racial Profiling Exists.' *Toronto Star,* 31 March, A1, A20.

Mayor's Advisory Committee. 1996. 'Working Together Towards Better Understanding and Harmony in the Town of Markham.' June.

Maytree Foundation. 2004. 'Annual Report.' Toronto. http://maytree.com/ PDF_Files/AnnualReport2004.pdf

McIsaac, Elizabeth. 2003. 'Nation Building through Cities: A New Deal for Immigrant Settlement in Canada.' Ottawa: Caledon Institute of Social Policy. http://epe.lac-bac.gc.ca/100/200/300/caledon_institute/nation_building/ 553820436.pdf

McRoberts, Kenneth. 1997. *Misconceiving Canada: The Struggle for National Unity.* Toronto: Oxford University Press.

Metropolis. http://canada.metropolis.net/index_e.html

Metro Vancouver. 'Frequently Asked Questions': Facts and Figures. http:// www.metrovancouver.org/about/Pages/faqs.aspx

Miller, David. 2004. 'Mayor's Remarks at the News Conference with the Premier and the Minister of Municipal Affairs and Housing at the Introduction of the New City of Toronto Act.' http://www.toronto.ca/mayor_miller/ speeches/cta_remarks.htm

Ministry of Citizenship and Immigration, Government of Ontario. 'Canada and Ontario sign historic immigration agreement.' http://www.news.ontario.ca/archive/en/2005/11/21/c768397cd-27996-tpl.html

Mississauga News. http://www.mississauga.com

Mitchell, Katharyne. 2004. *Crossing the Neoliberal Line: Pacific Rim Migration and the Metropolis.* Philadelphia: Temple University Press.

Molotch, Harvey. 1976. 'The City as a Growth Machine.' *American Journal of Sociology* 82, no. 2: 309–30.

Mossberger, Karen, and Gerry Stoker. 2001. 'The Evolution of Urban Regime Theory: The Challenge of Conceptualization.' *Urban Affairs Review* 36, no. 6: 810–35.

Murray, Heather. 2006. 'Rethinking Intergovernmental Relations in Canada? An Analysis of City–Provincial Relations in Winnipeg and Vancouver.' Paper prepared for the annual conference of the Canadian Political Science Association, York University, Toronto, 1 June. http://www.cpsa-acsp.ca/ papers-2006/Murray-Heather.pdf

– 2004. 'The Urban Autonomy Debate in Canada: The Rhetoric, the Rationale, and the Reality.' Presentation prepared for the Local Government Institute and School of Public Administration Seminar Series, University of Victoria, 22 October. http://publicadmin.uvic.ca/cpss/lgi/pdfs/murray_oct22_ presentation.pdf

Nevitte, Neil. 1996. *The Decline of Deference: Canadian Value Change in Cross-National Perspective.* Mississauga: Broadview.

Olds, Kris. 2001. *Globalization and Urban Change: Capital, Culture, and Pacific Rim Megaprojects.* Oxford: Oxford University Press.

Olson, Mancur. 1965. *The Logic of Collective Action.* Cambridge, MA: Harvard University Press.

Ornstein, Michael. 2006. 'Ethno-Racial Groups in Toronto: A Demographic and Socio-Economic Profile 1971–2001' (Ornstein Report update). Institute for Social Research, York University, January. http://www.isr.yorku.ca/download/Ornstein--Ethno-Racial_Groups_in_Toronto_1971-2001.pdf

– 2000. 'Ethno-Racial Inequality in the City of Toronto: An Analysis of the 1996 Census' (Ornstein Report). Prepared for the Access and Equity Unit Strategic and Corporate Policy Division, Chief Administrator's Office, City of Toronto, May. http://www.toronto.ca/diversity/pdf/ornstein_fullreport.pdf Ornstein. 2000.

Orr, Marion. 1999. *Black Social Capital: The Politics of School Reform in Baltimore, 1986–1998.* Lawrence: University Press of Kansas.

Orr, Marion, and Valerie C. Johnson. 2008. *Power in the City: Clarence Stone and the Politics of Inequality.* Lawrence: University Press of Kansas.

Orr, Marion, and Gerry Stoker. 1994. 'Urban Regimes and Leadership in Detroit.' *Urban Affairs Quarterly* 30, no. 1: 48–73.

Owens, Michael. 2001. 'Pulpits and Policy: The Politics of Black Church-Based Community Development in New York City, 1980–2000.' PhD diss., State University of New York, Albany.

Pal, Leslie. 1995. *Interests of State: The Politics of Language, Multiculturalism, and Feminism in Canada.* Montreal and Kingston: McGill–Queen's University Press.

Peel Newcomer Strategy Group. 'Our History.' http://peelnewcomer.org/index.php?option=com_content&task=view&id=16&Itemid=167

Peterson, Paul E. 1981. *City Limits.* Chicago: University of Chicago Press.

Pierre, Jon. 2005. 'Comparative Urban Governance: Uncovering Complex Causalities.' *Urban Affairs Review* 40, no. 4: 446–62.

Pierson, Paul. 1993. 'When Effect Becomes Cause: Policy Feedback and Political Change.' *World Politics* 45 (July): 595–28.

Poirier, Christian. 2006. 'Ethnocultural Diversity, Democracy, and Intergovernmental Relations in Canadian Cities.' In *Canada: The State of the Federation 2004,* ed. Robert Young and Christian Leuprecht. Montreal and Kingston: McGill–Queen's University Press.

Polèse, Mario, and Richard Stren. 2000. 'Understanding the New Sociocultural Dynamics of Cities: Comparative Urban Policy in a Global Context.' In *The*

Social Sustainability of Cities: Diversity and the Management of Change, ed. Mario Polèse and Richard Stren. Toronto: University of Toronto Press. 3–38.

Przeworski, Adam, and Henry Teune. 1970. *The Logic of Comparative Social Inquiry*. New York: John Wiley.

Putnam, Robert. 2007. 'E Pluribus Unum: Diversity and Community in the 21st Century.' 2006 Johan Skytte Prize Lecture. *Scandinavian Political Studies* 30, no. 2: 137–74.

– 1993. *Making Democracy Work: Civic Traditions in Modern Italy*. Princeton: Princeton University Press.

Pynn, Larry. 1997. 'Richmond's Asian Malls Want to Attract All Races.' *Vancouver Sun*, 6 December, B1.

Queen, Lisa. 1995. 'York's Cultural Segregation Increases Threat of Conflict.' *The Era-Banner*, 25 June.

'RCMP No Longer Colour Blind' [editorial]. 2003. *Richmond News*, 22 November.

RIAC (Richmond Intercultural Advisory Committee). 2004. '2004–2010 Richmond Intercultural Strategic Plan and Work Program.' Prepared with the support of Larry Axelrod, PhD, Project Consultant, The Neutral Zone Coaching and Consulting Services, and the City of Richmond. January. http://www.richmond.ca/__shared/assets/2004_-_2010_Richmond_Intercultural_Strategic_Plan_and_Work_Program9791.pdf

Rowe, Mary W. 2000. *Toronto: Considering Self-Government*. Toronto: Ginger.

Sancton, Andrew. 2008. The *Limits of Boundaries: Why City-Regions Cannot Be Self-Governing*. Montreal and Kingston: McGill-Queen's University Press.

– 2006. 'Why Municipal Amalgamations? Halifax, Toronto, Montreal.' In *Canada: The State of the Federation 2004*, ed. Robert Young and Christian Leuprecht. Montreal and Kingston: McGill–Queen's University Press. 119–37.

– 2002. 'Municipalities, Cities, and Globalization: Implications for Canadian Federalism.' In *Canadian Federalism: Performance, Effectiveness, and Legitimacy*, ed. Herman Bakvis and Grace Skogstad. Toronto: Oxford University Press. 261–77.

– 2000. 'The Municipal Role in the Governance of Canadian Cities.' In *Canadian Cities in Transition*, 2nd ed., ed. Trudi Bunting and Pierre Filion. Toronto: Oxford University Press. 425–42.

– 1994. 'Mayors as Political Leaders.' In *Leaders and Leadership in Canada*, ed. Maureen Mancuson, Richard Price, and Ronald Wayenberg. Toronto: Oxford University Press. 174–89.

Sandercock, Leonie. 1998. *Towards Cosmopolis: Planning for Multicultural Cities*. Chichester: Wiley.

Sartori, Giovanni. 1970. 'Concept Misformation in Comparative Politics.' *American Political Science Review* 64, no. 2: 1033–53.

Sassen, Saskia. 2001. *The Global City: New York, London, and Tokyo.* 2nd ed. Princeton: Princeton University Press.

–   1998. 'Whose City Is It? Globalization and the Formation of New Claims.' In *Globalization and Its Discontents: Essays of the New Mobility of People and Money*, ed. Saskia Sassen. New York: New Press. xix–xxxvi.

Sellers, Jeffrey M. 2005. 'Re-placing the Nation: An Agenda for Comparative Urban Politics.' *Urban Affairs Review* 40, no. 4: 419–45.

–   2002a. *Governing from Below: Urban Regions and the Global Economy.* Cambridge: Cambridge University Press.

–   2002b. 'The Nation-State and Urban Governance: Toward a Multilevel Analysis. *Urban Affairs Review* 37, no. 5: 611–41.

Sewell, John. 2004. *A New City Agenda.* Toronto: Zephyr.

Siegel, David. 2005. 'Municipal Reform in Ontario: Revolutionary Evolution.' In *Municipal Reform in Canada: Reconfiguration, Re-empowerment, and Rebalancing*, ed. Joseph Garcea and Edward LeSage. Toronto: Oxford University Press. 127–48.

Siemiatycki, Myer. 2006. 'The Municipal Franchise and Social Inclusion in Toronto: Policy and Practice.' Inclusive Cities Canada.

–   1998. 'Immigration and Urban Politics in Toronto.' Paper presented to the Third International Metropolis Conference, Israel, 29 November–3 December. http://www.international.metropolis.net/events/israel/papers/Siemiatycki.html

Siemiatycki, Myer. 2006. 'The Municipal Franchise and Social Inclusion in Toronto: Policy and Practice: Executive Summary.' Inclusive Cities Canada and the Community Social Planning Council of Toronto (CSPC), October. http://www.cdhalton.ca/pdf/icc/ICC_Municipal_Franchise_and_Social_Inclusion_in_Toronto.pdf

Siemiatycki, Myer, Tim Rees, Roxana Ng, and Khan Rahi. 2003. 'Integrating Community Diversity in Toronto: On Whose Terms?' In *The World Is a City*, ed. Paul Anisef and Michael Lamphier. Toronto: University of Toronto Press. 371–456.

Simeon, Richard. 2003. 'Federalism and Decentralization in Canada.' Paper presented at the 2nd International Conference on Decentralization. http://www.forumfed.org

Simich, Laura. 2000. *Towards a Greater Toronto Charter: Implications for Immigrant Settlement.* For the Maytree Foundation, Toronto: Zephyr.

Slack, Enid. 2005. 'Easing the Fiscal Restraints: New Revenue Tools in the City of Toronto Act.' Munk Centre for International Studies, University of Toronto, 21 February. http://ideas.repec.org/p/ttp/itpwps/0507.html

Smith, Patrick. 1992. 'The Making of a Global City: Fifty Years of Constituent

Diplomacy – the Case of Vancouver.' *Canadian Journal of Urban Research* 1, no. 1: 90–112.

Smith, Patrick, and Kennedy Stewart. 2006. 'Local Whole-of-Government Policymaking in Vancouver: Beavers, Cats, and the Mushy Middle Thesis.' In *Canada: The State of the Federation 2004*, ed. Robert Young and Christian Leuprecht. Montreal and Kingston: McGill–Queen's University Press. 251–72.

Statistics Canada. 2008a. *Canada's Ethnocultural Mosaic, 2006 Census.* Cat. no. 97-562-X. Ottawa: Minister of Industry, April. http://www12.statcan.ca/english/census06/analysis/ethnicorigin/pdf/97-562-XIE2006001.pdf

– 2008b. '2006 Census: Ethnic Origins, Visible Minorities, Place of Work and Mode of Transportation.' *The Daily*, 2 April, cat no. 11-001-XIE, Ottawa: Minister of Industry. http://www.statcan.gc.ca/daily-quotidien/080402/dq080402-eng.pdf

– 2007a. '2006 Census: Immigration, Citizenship, Language, Mobility, and Migration.' *The Daily*, 4 December, cat. no. 11-001-XIE, Ottawa: Minister of Industry. http://www.statcan.gc.ca/daily-quotidien/071204/dq071204-eng.pdf

– 2007b. '2006 Community Profiles.' 2006 Census, 13 March, cat. no. 92-591-XWE. Ottawa: Minister of Industry. http://www12.statcan.ca/english/census06/data/profiles/community/Index.cfm?Lang=E

– 2007c. Immigration in Canada: A Portrait of the Foreign-born Population, 2006 Census, cat, no. 97-557-XIE, December. Ottawa: Minister of Industry. http://www12.statcan.gc.ca/english/census06/analysis/immcit/pdf/97-557-XIE2006001.pdf

– 2005. 'Study: Canada's Visible Minority Population in 2017.' *The Daily*, 22 March cat. no. 11-001-XIE, Ottawa: Minister of Industry. 6–7. http://www.statcan.gc.ca/daily-quotidien/050322/dq050322b-eng.htm

– 2004. 'Study: Immigrants in Canada's Urban Centres.' *The Daily*, 18 August, cat. no. 11-001-XIE. Ottawa: Minister of Industry. http://www.statcan.gc.ca/daily-quotidien/040818/dq040818-eng.pdf

– 2003. *2001 Census: Analysis Series. Canada's Ethnocultural Portrait: The Changing Mosaic.* Cat. no. 96F0030XIE2001008, 23 January. Ottawa: Minister of Industry. http://www12.statcan.gc.ca/english/census01/products/analytic/companion/etoimm/pdf/96F0030XIE2001008.pdf

– 2002. 'Community profiles: 2001 Census.' 27 June. Cat. no. 93F0053XIE. http://www12.statcan.ca/english/Profil01/CP01/Index.cfm?Lang=E

– n.d.a. 'Census metropolitan area (CMA) and census agglomeration (CA),' in Census Dictionary, website: http://www12.statcan.ca/english/census06/reference/dictionary/geo009.cfm

- n.d.b. 'Selected Religions by Immigrant Status and Period of Immigration, 2001 Counts, for Census Subdivisions (Municipalities) with 5,000-plus Population – 20% Sample.' http://www12.statcan.ca/english/census01/products/highlight/religion/Page.cfm?Lang=E&Geo=CSD&Code=5915004 &View=3b&Table=1&StartRec=1&Sort=2&B1=5915004&B2=Counts

Stoker, Gerry. 1998. 'Governance as Theory: Five Propositions.' *International Social Science Journal* 50, no. 155: 17–28.

Stoker, Gerry, and Karen Mossberger. 1994. 'Urban Regime Theory in Comparative Perspective.' *Environment and Planning C, Government and Policy* 12: 195–212.

Stone, Clarence. 2008. 'Urban Regimes and the Capacity to Govern: A Political Economy Approach.' In *Power in the City: Clarence Stone and the Politics of Inequality*, ed. Marion Orr and Valerie C. Johnson. Lawrence: University Press of Kansas. 76–107.

- 2005. 'Looking Back to Look Forward: Reflections on Urban Regime Analysis.' *Urban Affairs Review* 40, no. 3: 309–41.

- 2001. 'The Atlanta Experience Re-examined: The Link between Agenda and Regime Change.' *International Journal of Urban and Regional Research* 25, no. 1: 20–34.

- 1989. *Regime Politics: Governing Atlanta 1946–1988*. Lawrence: University Press of Kansas.

Stone, Clarence, Jeffrey R. Henig, Bryan D. Jones, and Carol Pierannunzi. 2001. *Building Civic Capacity: The Politics of Reforming Urban Schools*. Lawrence: University Press of Kansas.

Stone, Clarence N., Robert K. Whelan, and William J. Murin. 1986. *Urban Policy Politics in a Bureaucratic Age*. Englewood Cliffs: Prentice-Hall.

S.U.C.C.E.S.S. 'Donations.' http://www.successbc.ca/eng/component/option,com_wrapper/Itemid,127

Tate, Ellen, and Louise Quesnel. 1995. 'Accessibility of Municipal Services for Ethnocultural Populations in Toronto and Montreal.' *Canadian Public Administration* 38, no. 3: 325–51.

TCSA (Toronto City Summit Alliance). 2003. 'Enough Talk: An Action Plan for the Toronto Region.' April. http://www.torontoalliance.ca/docs/TCSA_report.pdf

- 'Emerging Leaders Network.' http://www.torontoalliance.ca/tcsa_initiatives/eln

Tindal, C. Richard, and Susan Nobes Tindal. 2009. *Local Government in Canada*, 7th ed. Toronto: Nelson.

Tindal, C. Richard, and Susan Nobes Tindal. 2004. *Local Government in Canada*, 6th ed. Toronto: Nelson.

Town of Markham. 2005. 'Markham Race Relations Committee.' http://www.markham.ca/Markham/Departments/Council/StdCmte/MRRC.htm
– 2002. 'Report to Finance and Administration re: Multilingual Interpretive Services.' 4 November.
Town of Milton. 2008. 'Milton GTA Tax Comparison.' http://www.milton.ca/ecodev/TAX_COMPARISON.pdf
TRIEC (Toronto Region Immigrant Employment Council). 'About Us – Council Members.' http://www.triec.ca/about/TRIEC/council
– 2007. 'Strength in Collaboration.' Annual Review. http://www.triec.ca/files/47/original/TRIEC_2007_AnnualReview.pdf
Uitermark, Justus, Ugo Russi, and Henk Van Houtum. 2005. 'Reinventing Multiculturalism: Urban Citizenship and the Negotiation of Ethnic Diversity in Amsterdam.' *International Journal of Urban and Regional Research* 29, no. 3: 622–40.
Urbaniak, Tom. 2005. 'Beyond Regime Theory: Mayoral Leadership, Suburban Development, and the Politics of Mississauga, Ontario.' PhD diss., University of Western Ontario.
– 2003. 'Regime Theory and the Politics of Mississauga, 1960–1976.' Paper presented at the annual Canadian Political Science Association Meeting, Halifax.
Vancouver Foundation. 'About Us.' http://www.vancouverfoundation.bc.ca/about/index.htm
Verma, Sonia. 2002. 'Newspaper a Fearless Crusader: Star Has a Storied History of Taking Up a Good Cause.' *Toronto Star*, 2 November, A1.
Walker, Jack L. 1983. 'The Origins and Maintenance of Interest Groups in America.' *American Political Science Review* 77 (June): 390–406.
Wallace, Marcia, and Frances Frisken. 2000. 'City-Suburban Differences in Government Responses to Immigration in the Greater Toronto Area.' Centre for Urban and Community Studies, University of Toronto, research paper no. 197.
White, Stephen. 1992a. 'Brampton Aims to Eliminate Racism.' *Toronto Star*, 17 September, BR4.
– 1992b. 'Multicultural Agencies to Cut Duplication.' *Toronto Star*, 17 September, BR4.
Young, Mary Lynn. 2004. 'Ethnic Media Blooms in Wake of Tsunamis.' workopolis.com, 30 December.
Young, Robert, and Christian Leuprecht, eds. 2006. *Canada: The State of the Federation 2004*. Montreal and Kingston: McGill–Queen's University Press.

Index

316n1; on regime change, 26; on regime relationships, 261; on regimes, 231; on regime theory, 45–6

Stone, Clarence: on business community, 266; on business interests, 219; on civic capacity, 117; on enacted change, 261; on local councils, 296; on regime coalitions, 267; on regime decline, 267; on regime development, 265; on relationships, 260; on small wins, 185; and Toronto, 127–8; on urban regime theory, 17–20, 22–7, 32, 35–6, 44, 177–8

Stren, Richard, 12, 277

Strom, Elizabeth, 39–40, 279

Stronger City of Toronto for a Stronger Ontario Act (Bill 53), 269–70

structure and structuring, 24–5, 128

subregimes. *See* urban regime theory

Sullivan, Sam, 307, 323n9

Surrey: backlash in, 77; as biracial municipality, 202, 207; business community in, 75, 78, 161–2, 187, 220, 282; city departments in, 76–7, 146, 187–8; civil service in, 154; community capacity in, 156, 188; community dynamics of, 208; community leaders in, 75–8, 162, 169–70, 208, 211, 319n16; employment equity in, 75; and ethnic configuration, 220–1; financial limitations in, 146–7; and governance arrangements, 210–11; and intragroup dynamics, 297–8; language distribution in, 326n32; media in, 164; multiculturalism in, 193, 304–5; multilingual services in, 78; political culture in, 151, 169–72; race and racism in, 319n13; responsiveness of, 75–9; role of, 145–6; South Asians in, 220–1; Surrey-Delta Immigrant Services Society (SDISS), 77–8, 162, 172, 187; *Surrey Leader,* 164; urban regime theory in, 186–8

Swanstrom, Todd, 263

Tabb, David H., 34, 52, 54

Task Force on Access and Equity, 58

Tate, Ellen, 318n5

Tator, Carol, 59

taxation, 269–70

tax increment financing, 270, 329n24

Teune, Henry, 43–4

Tindal, Richard, 95, 105, 317n4

Tindal, Susan Nobes, 95, 105, 317n4

Toronto: access and equity in, 58–9, 63–4, 96–8, 125–6, 321n4; amalgamation of, 242, 247–50, 254, 273–4, 286–7; biracial municipalities in, 203t; Board of Trade, 119; business community in, 110–13, 126–7, 131–2, 215, 219, 266, 274, 286–9; Canada-Ontario Immigration Agreement, 270–1, 330n27; capacity in, 108–10, 219, 222, 233, 257, 260–2; city charter, 250–1; city departments, 64; community leaders in, 58–63, 65, 94, 107, 111, 119–20, 127, 130–1; core policies of, 58; Diversity Management and Community Engagement Unit (DMU), 58, 113–14, 126; and downloading, 239, 241; ethnic diversity in, 92–3, 322n20; as exceptional case, 222, 224–5, 288–9; Gas Tax Transfer (GTT), 268–9, 329n22; and governance arrangements, 215, 242, 253, 328n12; Greater Toronto Services Board, 242; Immigration and Settlement Policy Framework, 60–1; influence of, 256, 268–72, 325n28; language use in, 52, 64; and multiculturalism, 139–42; multilingual services in, 59; as multiracial municipality, 201t, 212, 214; municipal civil services, 113–14; and national infrastructure changes, 233; number of immigrants, 244; policy capacity of, 125–9; political culture in, 98, 118–20, 129–31; property taxes in, 105, 321–2n11; race and racism in, 62–4; regime of, 260–4, 273, 283–90; responsiveness of, 57–65, 87, 93–4, 96; selling diversity framework, 126; social housing, 241; Stronger City Act, 269–70; structure of council, 107, 127, 322n13–14; *Toronto: Considering Self-Government,* 250; Toronto Act Now, 253, 328n14; Toronto City Summit Alliance (TCSA), 111, 130, 215, 240–1, 253, 256, 328n16; *Toronto Star,* 114–15, 130; *Towards a New City of Toronto Act,* 253; University of Toronto, 253, 328n15; and urban regime theory, 124–32. *See also* Lastman, Mel; Miller, David; munici-

Studies in Comparative Political Economy and Public Policy